Management Information Systems

Course:
Business Driven Technology for K201 and K204

Coordinator: Amy Kinser

Indiana University–Kelley School of Business
Operations and Decision Technologies

McGraw-Hill/Irwin

A Division of The McGraw·Hill Companies

McGraw–Hill Primis

ISBN–10: 0–39–091777–X
ISBN–13: 978–0–39–091777–5

Text:

Business Driven Technology, Third Edition
Baltzan–Phillips–Haag

This book was printed on recycled paper.

Management Information Systems

http://www.primisonline.com

111   MGISGEN   ISBN-10: 0-39-091777-X   ISBN-13: 978-0-39-091777-5

Management Information Systems

Contents

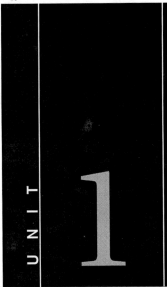

Achieving Business Success

CORE UNITS

Unit 1: Achieving Business Success

Unit 2: Exploring Business Intelligence

Unit 3: Streamlining Business Operations

Unit 4: Building Innovation

Unit 5: Transforming Organizations

BUSINESS PLUG-INS

B1. >>Business Basics

B2. >>Business Process

B3. >>Hardware and Software

B4. >>Enterprise Architectures

B5. >>Networks and Telecommunications

B6. >>Information Security

B7. >>Ethics

B8. Supply Chain Management

B9. Customer Relationship Management

B10. Enterprise Resource Planning

B11. E-Business

B12. Emerging Trends and Technologies

B13. Strategic Outsourcing

B14. Systems Development

B15. Project Management

TECHNOLOGY PLUG-INS

T1. >>Personal Productivity Using IT

T2. >>Basic Skills Using Excel

T3. Problem Solving Using Excel

T4. Decision Making Using Excel

T5. Designing Database Applications

T6. Basic Skills Using Access

T7. Problem Solving Using Access

T8. Decision Making Using Access

T9. Designing Web Pages

T10. Creating Web Pages Using HTML

T11. Creating Web Pages Using Dreamweaver

T12. Creating Gantt Charts with Excel and Microsoft Project

UNIT ONE OPENING CASE

Apple—Merging Technology, Business, and Entertainment

Apple Computer Inc., back from near oblivion, is setting the pace in the digital world with innovation and creativity that has been missing from the company for the past 20 years. The introduction of the iPod, a brilliant merger of technology, business, and entertainment, catapulted Apple back into the mainstream.

Capitalizing on New Trends

In 2000, Steve Jobs was fixated on developing video editing software for the Macintosh. But then he realized millions of people were using computers and CD burners to make audio CDs and to download digital songs called MP3s from illegal online services like Napster. Jobs was worried that he was looking in the wrong direction and had missed the MP3 bandwagon.

Jobs moved fast. He began by purchasing SoundStep from Jeff Robbin, a 28-year-old software engineer and former Apple employee. SoundStep was developing software that simplified the importing and compression of MP3 songs. Robbin and a couple of other programmers began writing code from scratch and developed the first version of iTunes for the Mac in less than four months. This powerful and ingenious database could quickly sort tens of thousands of songs in a multitude of ways and find particular tracks in nanoseconds.

Jobs next challenged the team to make iTunes portable. He envisioned a Walkman-like player that could hold thousands of songs and be taken anywhere. The idea was to modify iTunes and build a tiny new system for what was basically a miniature computer, along with a user interface that could sort and navigate music files with the same sophistication as iTunes on the Mac. The iPod was born nine months later.

Jobs noticed that one last key element was missing, an online store for buying downloadable songs. Such a store would need an e-business infrastructure that could automatically deliver songs and track billing and payments for conceivably millions of purchases. In the spring of 2003, 18 months after the launch of the iPod, Apple's iTunes Music Store opened for business. The company's goal was to sell 1 million songs in the first six months. It hit this goal in six days.

4

Baltzan–Phillips–Haag:
Business Driven
Technology, Third Edition

I. Achieving Business
Success

Introduction

© The McGraw–Hill
Companies, 2009

Capitalizing on the iPod

With millions of iPods in the hands of consumers, other companies are noticing the trend and finding ways to capitalize on the product. John Lin created a prototype of a remote control for the iPod. Lin took his prototype to *Macworld* where he found success. A few months later, Lin's company had Apple's blessing and a commitment for shelf space in its retail stores. "This is how Apple supports the iPod economy," Lin said.

In the iPod-dominated market, hundreds of companies have been inspired to develop more than 500 accessories—everything from rechargers for the car to $1,500 Fendi bags. Eric Tong, vice president at Belkin, a cable and peripheral manufacturer, believes that 75 percent of all iPod owners purchase at least one accessory—meaning that 30 million accessories have been sold. With most of the products priced between $10 and $200, that puts the iPod economy well over $300 million and perhaps as high as $6 billion. Popular iPod accessories include:

- Altec Lansing Technologies—iPod speakers and recharger dock ($150).
- Belkin—TuneCast mobile FM transmitter ($40).
- Etymotic Research—high-end earphones ($150).
- Griffin Technology—iTrip FM transmitter ($35).
- Kate Spade—Geneva faux-croc mini iPod holder ($55).
- Apple—socks set in six colors, green, purple, blue, orange, pink, and gray ($29).
- Apple—digital camera connector ($29).

Capitalizing on the Future

The latest iPod packs music, audiobooks, podcasts, photos, video, contacts, calendars, games, clocks, and locks in a design up to 45 percent slimmer than the original iPod. It also boasts stamina (up to 20 hours of battery life), generous capacity (30GB or 60GB of storage), a great personality (intuitive, customizable menus), and a touch of genius (the Apple Click Wheel). The latest features include:

- **Videos**—Choose from over 2,000 music videos at the iTunes Music Store or purchase ad-free episodes of a favorite ABC or Disney television show and watch them on the go.
- **Podcasts**—The iTunes Podcast Directory features thousands of free podcasts, or radio-style shows, including favorites from such big names as ABC News, Adam Curry, ESPN, KCRW, and WGBH.
- **Audiobooks**—The digital shelves of the iTunes Music Store are stocked with more than 11,000 audiobooks, including such exclusives as the entire Harry Potter series.
- **Photos**—With storage for up to 25,000 photos, iPod users can view photo slide shows—complete with music—on an iPod or on a TV via the optional video cable.

Capitalizing on the iPhone

The Apple iPhone is a revolutionary new mobile phone that allows customers to make a call by simply touching a name or number in an address book, a favorites list, or a call log. It also automatically syncs all contacts from a PC, Mac, or Internet

Baltzan–Phillips–Haag:
Business Driven
Technology, Third Edition

I. Achieving Business
Success

Introduction

© The McGraw–Hill
Companies, 2009

5

services, and it allows customers to select voice-mail messages in any order—just like e-mail. Customers can easily construct a favorites list for frequently made calls and can quickly merge calls to create conference calls.

The iPhone's most impressive feature is a rich e-mail client. With its advanced Safari browser, one of the most advanced Web browsers to be offered on a portable device, iPhone lets customers see Web pages the way they were designed to be seen, then easily zoom in by simply tapping on the multi-touch display with a finger. Safari also includes built-in Google and Yahoo! search capabilities. The iPhone can multitask, allowing customers to read a Web page while downloading e-mail in the background over wireless networks. Expect the iPhone accessory business to be as powerful and vast as the iPod accessory business. A few of the new iPhone accessories include:

- iPhone Bluetooth headset—$149.
- iPhone doc—$49.
- iPhone stereo headset—$29.
- Apple Doc Connector to USB—$29.

iPod's Impact on the Music Business

In the digital era, the unbundling of CDs through the purchase of individual tracks lets consumers pay far less to get a few of their favorite songs rather than buying an entire album. Many analysts predicted that the iPod's success coupled with the consumer's ability to choose individual song downloads would lead to increased revenues for music businesses. However, the industry is seeing individual downloads cannibalizing album profits and failing to attract new music sales. "I've still never bought a download," said Eneka Iriondo-Coysh, a 21-year-old graphic-design student in London who has owned a 10,000 song-capacity iPod for more than two years. "I do it all from my CDs," mostly hip-hop and soul.

The global music industry has been under siege for years amid declining sales. Record companies suffer from piracy, including billions of dollars in lost revenue due to bootlegged CDs. At the same time, music faces new competition for consumer time and money from video games, DVDs, and mobile phones. At traditional record stores, DVDs and games are taking an increasing amount of shelf space, squeezing out CDs. The music download numbers suggest that the iPod's iconic success is not translating into new music sales the way the evolution from vinyl albums to cassettes and then CDs did. For many users, the portable devices are just another way of stocking and listening to music, not an incentive to buy new music.

iPod Security Leaks

Nike and Apple partnered to create a unique iPod accessory, the Nike iPod SportKit. The Kit consists of two components—a wireless *sensor* that fits into Nike + Air Zoom Moire sneakers and a small white *receiver* that plugs in to an iPod Nano—that communicate using wireless radio protocols. The University of Washington's Department of Science and Engineering recently discovered that customers who use the kit while exercising are subject to an invasion of privacy by becoming a surveillance target. Researchers revealed that security flaws in the new radio-frequency ID-powered device make it easy for tech-savvy stalkers, thieves, and corporations to track every movement an unsuspecting SportKit customer makes. With a simple surveillance tool, a malicious individual could track SportKit owners while they are working out, as well as when they are casually walking around town, a parking lot, or a college campus. With just a few hundred dollars and a little know-how, someone could even plot a SportKit customer's running routes on a Google map without the runner's knowledge. The tracked individuals do not even need to have their iPods with them, just the RFID device.[1]

Introduction

Information is everywhere. Most organizations value information as a strategic asset. Consider Apple and its iPod, iPod accessories, and iTunes Music Store. Apple's success depends heavily on information about its customers, suppliers, markets, and operations for each of these product lines. For example, Apple must be able to predict the number of people who will purchase an iPod to help estimate iPod accessory and iTunes sales within the next year. Estimating too many buyers will lead Apple to produce an excess of inventory; estimating too few buyers will potentially mean lost sales due to lack of product (resulting in even more lost revenues).

Understanding the direct impact information has on an organization's bottom line is crucial to running a successful business. This text focuses on information, business, technology, and the integrated set of activities used to run most organizations. Many of these activities are the hallmarks of business today—supply chain management, customer relationship management, enterprise resource planning, outsourcing, integration, e-business, and others. The five core units of this text cover these important activities in detail. Each unit is divided into chapters that provide individual learning outcomes and case studies. In addition to the five core units, there are technology and business "plug-ins" (see Figure Unit 1.1) that further explore topics presented in the five core units. "Plug-in pointers" provided at the end of each chapter identify the relevant plug-ins.

The chapters in Unit 1 are:

- **Chapter One**—Business Driven Technology.
- **Chapter Two**—Identifying Competitive Advantages.
- **Chapter Three**—Strategic Initiatives for Implementing Competitive Advantages.
- **Chapter Four**—Measuring the Success of Strategic Initiatives.
- **Chapter Five**—Organizational Structures That Support Strategic Initiatives.

Opportunities for Knowledge Workers

FIGURE UNIT 1.1

The Format and Approach of This Text

Business Plug-Ins	CORE UNITS	Technology Plug-Ins
B1. Business Basics		T1. Personal Productivity Using IT
B2. Business Process	Unit 1: Achieving Business Success	T2. Basic Skills Using Excel
B3. Hardware and Software		T3. Problem Solving Using Excel
B4. Enterprise Architectures		T4. Decision Making Using Excel
B5. Networks and Telecommunications	Unit 2: Exploring Business Intelligence	T5. Designing Database Applications
B6. Information Security		
B7. Ethics		T6. Basic Skills Using Access
B8. Supply Chain Management	Unit 3: Streamlining Business Operations	T7. Problem Solving Using Access
B9. Customer Relationship Management		T8. Decision Making Using Access
B10. Enterprise Resource Planning	Unit 4: Building Innovation	T9. Designing Web Pages
B11. E-Business		T10. Creating Web Pages Using HTML
B12. Emerging Trends and Technologies	Unit 5: Transforming Organizations	T11. Creating Web Pages Using Dreamweaver
B13. Strategic Outsourcing		
B14. Systems Development		T12. Creating Gantt Charts with Excel and Microsoft Project
B15. Project Management		

Business Driven Technology

LEARNING OUTCOMES

1.1. Compare management information systems (MIS) and information technology (IT).

1.2. Describe the relationships among people, information technology, and information.

1.3. Identify four different departments in a typical business and explain how technology helps them to work together.

1.4. Compare the four different types of organizational information cultures and decide which culture applies to your school.

Information Technology's Role in Business

Students frequently ask, "Why do we need to study information technology?" The answer is simple: Information technology is everywhere in business. Understanding information technology provides great insight to anyone learning about business.

FIGURE 1.1

Technology in *BusinessWeek* and *Fortune*

It is easy to demonstrate information technology's role in business by reviewing a copy of popular business magazines such as *BusinessWeek, Fortune,* or *Fast Company.* Placing a marker (such as a Post-it Note) on each page that contains a technology-related article or advertisement indicates that information technology is everywhere in business (see Figure 1.1). These are *business* magazines, not *technology* magazines, yet they are filled with technology. Students who understand technology have an advantage in business, and gaining a detailed understanding of information technology is important to all students regardless of their area of expertise.

The magazine articles typically discuss such topics as databases, customer relationship management, Web services, supply chain management, security, ethics, business intelligence, and so on. They also focus on companies such as Siebel, Oracle, Microsoft, and IBM. This text explores these topics in detail, along with reviewing the associated business opportunities and challenges.

INFORMATION TECHNOLOGY'S IMPACT ON BUSINESS OPERATIONS

Figure 1.2 highlights the business functions receiving the greatest benefit from information technology, along with the common business goals associated with information technology projects according to *CIO* magazine.[2]

Achieving the results outlined in Figure 1.2, such as reducing costs, improving productivity, and generating growth, is not easy. Implementing a new accounting system or marketing plan is not likely to generate long-term growth or reduce costs across an entire organization. Businesses must undertake enterprisewide initiatives to achieve broad general business goals such as reducing costs. Information technology plays a critical role in deploying such initiatives by facilitating communication and increasing business intelligence. For example instant messaging and WiMax allow people across an organization to communicate in new and innovative ways.[3]

Understanding information technology begins with gaining an understanding of how businesses function and IT's role in creating efficiencies and effectiveness across the organization. Typical businesses operate by functional areas (often called functional silos). Each functional area undertakes a specific core business function (see Figure 1.3).[4]

Functional areas are anything but independent in a business. In fact, functional areas are *interdependent* (see Figure 1.4 on page 11). Sales must rely on information from operations to understand inventory, place orders, calculate transportation costs, and gain insight into product availability based on production schedules. For an organization to succeed, every department or functional area must work together sharing common information and not be a "silo." Information technology can enable departments to more efficiently and effectively perform their business operations.

Any individual anticipating a successful career in business whether it is in accounting, finance, human resources, or operation management must understand the basics of information technology.

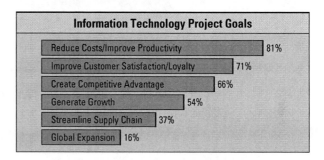

FIGURE 1.2

Business Benefits and Information Technology Project Goals

Information Technology Basics

Information technology (IT) is a field concerned with the use of technology in managing and processing information. Today, the term *information technology* has ballooned to encompass many aspects of computing and technology, and the term is more recognizable than ever. The information technology umbrella can be quite large, covering many fields that deal with the use of electronic computers and computer software to convert, store, protect, process, transmit, and retrieve information securely. Information technology can be an important enabler of business success and innovation. This is not to say that IT *equals* business success and innovation or that IT *represents* business success and innovation. Information technology is most useful when it leverages the talents of people. Information technology in and of itself is not useful unless the right people know how to use and manage it effectively.

Management information systems is a business function just as marketing, finance, operations, and human resources are business functions. Formally defined, *management information systems (MIS)* is a general name for the business function and academic discipline covering the application of people, technologies, and procedures—collectively called information systems—to solve business problems.[5]

FIGURE 1.3

Departmental Structure of a Typical Organization

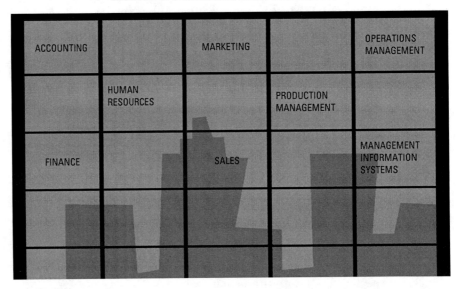

COMMON DEPARTMENTS IN AN ORGANIZATION

- **Accounting** provides quantitative information about the finances of the business including recording, measuring, and describing financial information.

- **Finance** deals with the strategic financial issues associated with increasing the value of the business, while observing applicable laws and social responsibilities.

- **Human resources (HR)** includes the policies, plans, and procedures for the effective management of employees (human resources).

- **Sales** is the function of selling a good or service and focuses on increasing customer sales, which increases company revenues.

- **Marketing** is the process associated with promoting the sale of goods or services. The marketing department supports the sales department by creating promotions that help sell the company's products.

- **Operations management** (also called **production management**) includes the methods, tasks, and techniques organizations use to produce goods and services. Transportation (also called logistics) is part of operations management.

- **Management information systems (MIS)** is a general name for the business function and academic discipline covering the application of people, technologies, and procedures—collectively called information systems—to solve business problems.

Information Technology

When beginning to learn about management information systems it is important to understand the following:

- Data, information, and business intelligence.
- IT resources.
- IT cultures.

DATA, INFORMATION, AND BUSINESS INTELLIGENCE

It is important to distinguish between data, information, and business intelligence. **Data** are raw facts that describe the characteristics of an event. Characteristics for a sales event could include the date, item number, item description, quantity ordered, customer name, and shipping details. **Information** is data converted into a meaningful and useful context. Information from sales events could include

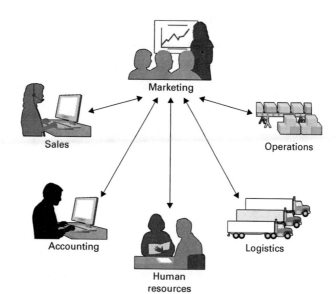

FIGURE 1.4

Marketing Working with Other Organizational Departments

Functional organization—Each functional area has its own systems and communicates with every other functional area (diagram displays Marketing communicating with all other functional areas in the organization).

best-selling item, worst-selling item, best customer, and worst customer. **Business intelligence** refers to applications and technologies that are used to gather, provide access to, and analyze data and information to support decision-making efforts. Business intelligence helps companies gain a more comprehensive knowledge of the factors affecting their business, such as metrics on sales, production, and internal operations, which help companies make better business decisions (see Figures 1.5, 1.6, 1.7).

IT RESOURCES

The plans and goals of the IT department must align with the plans and goals of the organization. Information technology can enable an organization to increase efficiency in manufacturing, retain key customers, seek out new sources of supply, and introduce effective financial management.

It is not always easy for managers to make the right choices when using IT to support (and often drive) business initiatives. Most managers understand their business initiatives well, but are often at a loss when it comes to knowing how to use

FIGURE 1.5

Data in an Excel Spreadsheet

OrderDate	ProductName	Quantity	Unit Price	Total Sales	Unit Cost	Total Cost	Profit	Customer	SalesRep
04-Jan-10	Mozzarella cheese	41	24	984	18	738	246	The Station	Debbie Fernande
04-Jan-10	Romaine lettuce	90	15	1,350	14	1,260	90	The Station	Roberta Cross
05-Jan-10	Red onions	27	12	324	8	216	108	Bert's Bistro	Loraine Schultz
06-Jan-10	Romaine lettuce	67	15	1,005	14	938	67	Smoke House	Roberta Cross
07-Jan-10	Black olives	79	12	948	6	474	474	Flagstaff House	Loraine Schultz
07-Jan-10	Romaine lettuce	46	15	690	14	644	46	Two Bits	Loraine Schultz
07-Jan-10	Romaine lettuce	52	15	780	14	728	52	Pierce Arrow	Roberta Cross
08-Jan-10	Red onions	39	12	468	8	312	156	Mamm'a Pasta Palace	Loraine Schultz
09-Jan-10	Romaine lettuce	66	15	990	14	924	66	The Dandelion	Loraine Schultz
10-Jan-10	Romaine lettuce	58	15	870	14	812	58	Carmens	Loraine Schultz
10-Jan-10	Pineapple	40	33	1,320	28	1,120	200	The Station	Loraine Schultz

Rows of data in an Excel spreadsheet.

FIGURE 1.6

Data Turned into Information

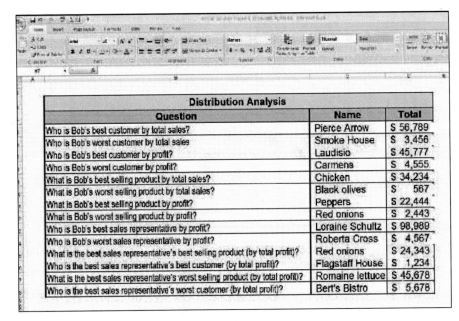

OrderDate	Product Name	Quantity	Unit Price	Total Sales	Unit Cost	Total Cost	Profit	Customer	SalesRep
15-Feb-10	Chicken	41	36	1,476	25	1,025	451	Smoke House	Roberta Cross
19-Feb-10	Chicken	50	36	1,800	25	1,250	550	Smoke House	Roberta Cross
03-Mar-10	Chicken	64	36	2,304	25	1,600	704	Pierce Arrow	Roberta Cross
12-Apr-10	Chicken	2	36	72	25	50	22	Laudisio	Roberta Cross
08-Jul-10	Chicken	94	36	3,384	25	2,350	1,034	Pierce Arrow	Roberta Cross
20-Nov-10	Chicken	15	36	540	25	375	165	Two Bitts	Roberta Cross
28-Nov-10	Chicken	6	36	216	25	150	66	Laudisio	Roberta Cross
30-Nov-10	Chicken	51	36	1,836	25	1,275	561	Pierce Arrow	Roberta Cross

Data features, such as Autofilter, turn data into information. This view shows all of Roberta Cross's chicken sales.

FIGURE 1.7

Information Turned into Business Intelligence

Distribution Analysis		
Question	**Name**	**Total**
Who is Bob's best customer by total sales?	Pierce Arrow	$ 56,789
Who is Bob's worst customer by total sales	Smoke House	$ 3,456
Who is Bob's best customer by profit?	Laudisio	$ 45,777
Who is Bob's worst customer by profit?	Carmens	$ 4,555
What is Bob's best selling product by total sales?	Chicken	$ 34,234
What is Bob's worst selling product by total sales?	Black olives	$ 567
What is Bob's best selling product by profit?	Peppers	$ 22,444
What is Bob's worst selling product by profit?	Red onions	$ 2,443
Who is Bob's best sales representative by profit?	Loraine Schultz	$ 98,989
Who is Bob's worst sales representative by profit?	Roberta Cross	$ 4,567
What is the best sales representative's best selling product (by total profit)?	Red onions	$ 24,343
Who is the best sales representative's best customer (by total profit)?	Flagstaff House	$ 1,234
What is the best sales representative's worst selling product (by total profit)?	Romaine lettuce	$ 45,678
Who is the best sales representative's worst customer (by total profit)?	Bert's Bistro	$ 5,678

Advanced analytical tools, such as Pivot Tables, uncover business intelligence in the data. For example, best customer, worst customer, and best sales representative's best selling product.

and manage IT effectively in support of those initiatives. Managers who understand what IT is, and what IT can and cannot do, are in the best position for success.

Putting It All Together

In essence,

- *People* use
- *information technology* to work with
- *information* (see Figure 1.8).

Those three key resources—people, information, and information technology (in that order of priority)—are inextricably linked. If one fails, they all fail. Most important, if one fails, then chances are the business will fail.

IT CULTURES

An organization's culture plays a large role in determining how successfully it will share information. Culture will influence the way people use information (their information behavior) and will reflect the importance that company leaders attribute to the use of information in achieving success or avoiding failure. Four common information-sharing cultures exist in organizations today: information-functional, information-sharing, information-inquiring, and information-discovery (see Figure 1.9).[6]

An organization's IT culture can directly affect its ability to compete in the global market. If an organization operates with an information-functional culture it will have a great degree of difficulty operating. Getting products to market quickly and creating a view of its end-to-end (or entire) business from sales to billing will be a challenge. If an organization operates with an information-discovery culture it will be able to get products to market quickly and easily see a 360-degree view of its entire organization. Employees will be able to use this view to better understand the market and create new products that offer a competitive advantage.

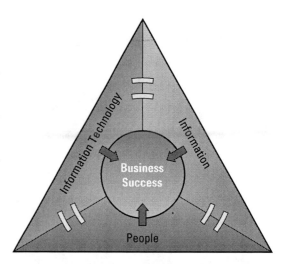

FIGURE 1.8

The Relationship among People, Information, and Information Technology

FIGURE 1.9

Different Information Cultures found in Organizations

Organizational Information Cultures	
Information-Functional Culture	Employees use information as a means of exercising influence or power over others. For example, a manager in sales refuses to share information with marketing. This causes marketing to need the sales manager's input each time a new sales strategy is developed.
Information-Sharing Culture	Employees across departments trust each other to use information (especially about problems and failures) to improve performance.
Information-Inquiring Culture	Employees across departments search for information to better understand the future and align themselves with current trends and new directions.
Information-Discovery Culture	Employees across departments are open to new insights about crises and radical changes and seek ways to create competitive advantages.

OPENING CASE STUDY QUESTIONS

1. Explain how Apple achieved business success through the use of information, information technology, and people.

2. Describe the types of information employees at an Apple store require and compare it to the types of information the executives at Apple's corporate headquarters require. Are there any links between these two types of information?

3. Identify the type of information culture that would have the greatest negative impact on Apple's operations.

Chapter One Case: The World is Flat—Thomas Friedman

In his book, *The World is Flat,* Thomas Friedman describes the unplanned cascade of technological and social shifts that effectively leveled the economic world, and "accidentally made Beijing, Bangalore, and Bethesda next-door neighbors." Chances are good that Bhavya in Bangalore will read your next X-ray, or as Friedman learned firsthand, "Grandma Betty in her bathrobe" will make your JetBlue plane reservation from her Salt Lake City home.

Friedman believes this is Globalization 3.0. "In Globalization 1.0, which began around 1492, the world went from size large to size medium. In Globalization 2.0, the era that introduced us to multinational companies, it went from size medium to size small. And then around 2000 came Globalization 3.0, in which the world went from being small to tiny. There is a difference between being able to make long-distance phone calls cheaper on the Internet and walking around Riyadh with a PDA where you can have all of Google in your pocket. It is a difference in degree that's so enormous it becomes a difference in kind," Friedman states. Figure 1.10 displays Friedman's list of "flatteners."

Friedman says these flatteners converged around the year 2000 and "created a flat world: a global, Web-enabled platform for multiple forms of sharing knowledge and work, irrespective of time, distance, geography, and increasingly, language." At the very moment this platform emerged, three huge economies materialized—those of India, China, and the former Soviet Union—"and 3 billion people who were out of the game, walked onto the playing field." A final convergence may determine the fate of the United States in this chapter of globalization. A "political perfect storm," as Friedman describes it—the dot-com bust, the attacks of 9/11, and the Enron scandal—"distract us completely as a country." Just when we need to face the fact of globalization and the need to compete in a new world, "we're looking totally elsewhere."

Friedman believes that the next great breakthrough in bioscience could come from a 5-year-old who downloads the human genome in Egypt. Bill Gates's view is similar: "Twenty years ago, would you rather have been a B-student in Poughkeepsie or a genius in Shanghai?

FIGURE 1.10

Thomas Friedman's 10 Forces That Flattened the World

1. Fall of the Berlin Wall	The events of November 9, 1989, tilted the worldwide balance of power toward democracies and free markets.
2. Netscape IPO	The August 9, 1995, offering sparked massive investment in fiber-optic cables.
3. Work flow software	The rise of applications from PayPal to VPNs enabled faster, closer coordination among far-flung employees.
4. Open-sourcing	Self-organizing communities, such as Linux, launched a collaborative revolution.
5. Outsourcing	Migrating business functions to India saved money *and* a Third World economy.
6. Offshoring	Contract manufacturing elevated China to economic prominence.
7. Supply-chaining	Robust networks of suppliers, retailers, and customers increased business efficiency.
8. Insourcing	Logistics giants took control of customer supply chains, helping mom-and-pop shops go global.
9. Informing	Power searching allowed everyone to use the Internet as a "personal supply chain of knowledge."
10. Wireless	Wireless technologies pumped up collaboration, making it mobile and personal.

Twenty years ago you'd rather be a B-student in Poughkeepsie. Today, it is not even close. You'd much prefer to be the genius in Shanghai because you can now export your talents anywhere in the world."[7]

Questions

1. Do you agree or disagree with Friedman's assessment that the world is flat? Be sure to justify your answer.
2. What are the potential impacts of a flat world for a student performing a job search?
3. What can students do to prepare themselves for competing in a flat world?
4. Identify a current flattener not mentioned on Friedman's list.

<< BUSINESS PLUG-IN POINTERS

Review the **Business Plug-In B1 "Business Basics"** for an introduction to business fundamentals beginning with the three most common business structures—(1) sole proprietorship, (2) partnership, (3) corporation—and then focusing on the internal operations of a corporation, including accounting, finance, human resources, sales, marketing, operations/production, and management information systems.

Review the **Business Plug-In B2 "Business Process."** This plug-in dives deeper into the world of business by reviewing business processes, continuous process improvement, business process reengineering, and business process modeling. There are a number of sample business process models diagramming such processes as order entry, online bill payment, e-business processes, and process improvement.

Review the **Business Plug-In B3 "Hardware and Software"** to cover the two basic categories of information technology. Information technology can be composed of the Internet, a personal computer, a cell phone that can access the Web, a personal digital assistant, or presentation software. All of these technologies help to perform specific information processing tasks. This plug-in covers the basics including terminology, business uses, and common characteristics.

Review the **Business Plug-In B4 "Enterprise Architectures,"** which includes the plans for how an organization will build, deploy, use, and share its data, processes, and IT assets. To support the volume and complexity of today's user and application requirements, information technology needs to take a fresh approach to enterprise architectures by constructing smarter, more flexible environments that protect it from system failures and crashes. A solid enterprise architecture can decrease costs, increase

BUSINESS PLUG-IN POINTERS >>

standardization, promote reuse of IT assets, and speed development of new systems. The end result is that the right enterprise architecture can make IT cheaper, strategic, and more responsive.

Review the Business Plug-In B5 "Networks and Telecommunications" for a detailed look at telecommunication systems and networks. Businesses around the world are moving to network infrastructure solutions that allow greater choice in how they go to market; the solutions have a global reach. These alternatives include wireless, voice-over Internet protocol (VoIP), and radio-frequency identification (RFID). This plug-in takes a detailed look at key telecommunication, network, and wireless technologies that are integrating businesses around the world.

TECHNOLOGY PLUG-IN POINTER >>

Review the Technology Plug-In T1 "Personal Productivity Using IT" for a walk-through on how to take advantage of your computer's many features, including data management, antivirus software, zip files, backup solutions, e-mail etiquette, PC performance, and spam control.

CHAPTER 2 — Identifying Competitive Advantages

Identifying Competitive Advantages

To survive and thrive, an organization must create a competitive advantage. A *competitive advantage* is a product or service that an organization's customers place a greater value on than similar offerings from a competitor. Unfortunately, competitive advantages are typically temporary because competitors often seek ways to duplicate the competitive advantage. In turn, organizations must develop a strategy based on a new competitive advantage.

When an organization is the first to market with a competitive advantage, it gains a first-mover advantage. The *first-mover advantage* occurs when an organization can significantly impact its market share by being first to market with a competitive advantage. FedEx created a first-mover advantage several years ago when it developed its customer self-service software allowing people and organizations to request a package pick-up, print mailing slips, and track packages online. Other parcel delivery services quickly followed with their own versions of the software. Today, customer self-service on the Internet is a standard for doing business in the parcel delivery industry.

As organizations develop their competitive advantages, they must pay close attention to their competition through environmental scanning. *Environmental scanning* is the acquisition and analysis of events and trends in the environment external to an organization. Information technology has the opportunity to play an important role in environmental scanning. For example, Frito-Lay, a premier provider of snack foods such as Cracker Jacks and Cheetos, does not just send its representatives into grocery stores to stock shelves—they carry handheld computers and record the product offerings, inventory, and even product locations of competitors. Frito-Lay uses this information to gain business intelligence on everything from how well competing products are selling to the strategic placement of its own products.

Organizations use three common tools to analyze and develop competitive advantages: (1) the Five Forces Model, (2) the three generic strategies, and (3) value chains.

Panera Bread

The Five Forces Model—Evaluating Business Segments

Organizations frequently face a decision as to whether to enter a new industry or industry segment. Michael Porter's Five Forces Model is a useful tool to aid in this

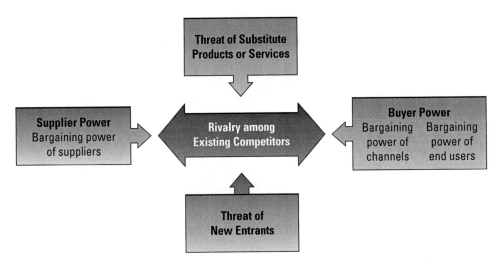

FIGURE 2.1

Porter's Five Forces Model

Competitive Advantage

challenging decision. The **Five Forces Model** helps determine the relative attractiveness of an industry and includes the following five forces (see Figure 2.1):

1. Buyer power.
2. Supplier power.
3. Threat of substitute products or services.
4. Threat of new entrants.
5. Rivalry among existing competitors.

The following introduction to each force provides detailed examples of how information technology can develop a competitive advantage.

BUYER POWER

Buyer power in the Five Forces Model is high when buyers have many choices of whom to buy from and low when their choices are few. To reduce buyer power (and create a competitive advantage), an organization must make it more attractive for customers to buy from it than from its competition. One of the best IT-based examples is the loyalty programs that many organizations offer. ***Loyalty programs*** reward customers based on the amount of business they do with a particular organization. The travel industry is famous for its loyalty programs such as frequent-flyer programs for airlines and frequent-stayer programs for hotels.

Keeping track of the activities and accounts of many thousands or millions of customers covered by loyalty programs is not practical without large-scale IT systems. Loyalty programs are a good example of using IT to reduce buyer power. Because of the rewards (e.g., free airline tickets, upgrades, or hotel stays) travelers receive, they are more likely to be loyal to or give most of their business to a single organization.

opposites

SUPPLIER POWER

Supplier power in the Five Forces Model is high when buyers have few choices of whom to buy from and low when their choices are many. Supplier power is the converse of buyer power: A supplier organization in a market will want buyer power to be low. A ***supply chain*** consists of all parties involved, directly or indirectly, in the procurement of a product or raw material. In a typical supply chain, an organization will probably be both a supplier (to customers) and a customer (of other supplier organizations) (see Figure 2.2).

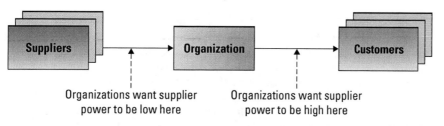

FIGURE 2.2

An Organization within the Supply Chain

As a buyer, the organization can create a competitive advantage by locating alternative supply sources. IT-enabled business-to-business (B2B) marketplaces can help. A *business-to-business (B2B) marketplace* is an Internet-based service that brings together many buyers and sellers. One important variation of the B2B marketplace is a private exchange. A *private exchange* is a B2B marketplace in which a single buyer posts its needs and then opens the bidding to any supplier who would care to bid. Bidding is typically carried out through a reverse auction. A *reverse auction* is an auction format in which increasingly lower bids are solicited from organizations willing to supply the desired product or service at an increasingly lower price. As the bids get lower and lower, more and more suppliers drop out of the auction. Ultimately, the organization with the lowest bid wins. Internet-based reverse auctions are an excellent example of the way that information technology can reduce supplier power for an organization and create a competitive advantage.

THREAT OF SUBSTITUTE PRODUCTS OR SERVICES

The *threat of substitute products or services* in the Five Forces Model is high when there are many alternatives to a product or service and low when there are few alternatives from which to choose. Ideally, an organization would like to be in a market in which there are few substitutes for the products or services it offers. Of course, that is seldom possible in any market today, but an organization can still create a competitive advantage by using switching costs. *Switching costs* are costs that can make customers reluctant to switch to another product or service.

A switching cost need not have an associated *monetary* cost. Amazon.com offers an example. As customers purchase products at Amazon.com over time, Amazon begins to develop a unique profile of their shopping and purchasing habits. When a customer visits Amazon.com repeatedly, Amazon can begin to offer products tailored to that particular customer based on the customers' profile. If the customer decides to shop elsewhere, there is an associated switching cost because the new site will not have the profile of the customer's past purchases. In this way Amazon.com has reduced the threat of substitute products or services by tailoring customer offerings and creating a "cost" to the consumer to switch to another online retailer.

(cancellation fees)
(customization)

THREAT OF NEW ENTRANTS

The *threat of new entrants* in the Five Forces Model is high when it is easy for new competitors to enter a market and low when there are significant entry barriers to entering a market. An *entry barrier* is a product or service feature that customers have come to expect from organizations in a particular industry and must be offered by an entering organization to compete and survive. For example, a new bank must offer its customers an array of IT-enabled services, including ATM use, online bill paying, and account monitoring. These are significant barriers to entering the banking market. At one time, the first bank to offer such services gained a valuable first-mover advantage, but only temporarily, as other banking competitors developed their own IT systems.

RIVALRY AMONG EXISTING COMPETITORS

Rivalry among existing competitors in the Five Forces Model is high when competition is fierce in a market and low when competition is more complacent. Although competition is always more intense in some industries than in others, the overall trend is toward increased competition in almost every industry.

The retail grocery industry is intensively competitive. While Kroger, Safeway, and Albertson's in the United States compete in many different ways, essentially they try to beat or match the competition on price. Most of them have loyalty programs that give shoppers special discounts. Customers get lower prices while the store gathers valuable information on buying habits to craft pricing strategies. In the future, expect to see grocery stores using wireless technologies to track customer movement throughout the store and match it to products purchased to determine purchasing sequences. Such a system will be IT-based and a huge competitive advantage to the first store to implement it.

Since margins are quite low in the grocery retail market, grocers build efficiencies into their supply chains, connecting with their suppliers in IT-enabled information partnerships such as the one between Wal-Mart and its suppliers. Communicating with suppliers over telecommunications networks rather than using paper-based systems makes the procurement process faster, cheaper, and more accurate. That equates to lower prices for customers and increased rivalry among existing competitors.

The Three Generic Strategies—Creating a Business Focus

Once the relative attractiveness of an industry is determined and an organization decides to enter that market, it must formulate a strategy for entering the new market. An organization can follow Porter's three generic strategies when entering a new market: (1) broad cost leadership, (2) broad differentiation, or (3) a focused strategy. Broad strategies reach a large market segment, while focused strategies target a niche market. A focused strategy concentrates on either cost leadership or differentiation. Trying to be all things to all people, however, is a recipe for disaster, since it is difficult to project a consistent image to the entire marketplace. Porter suggests that an organization is wise to adopt only one of the three generic strategies. (See Figure 2.3.)

FIGURE 2.3

Porter's Three Generic Strategies

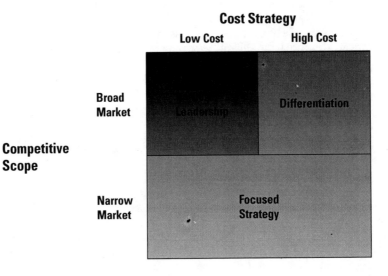

FIGURE 2.4

Three Generic Strategies in the Auto Industry

To illustrate the use of the three generic strategies, consider Figure 2.4. The matrix shown demonstrates the relationships among strategies (cost leadership versus differentiation) and market segmentation (broad versus focused).

- **Hyundai** is following a broad cost leadership strategy. Hyundai offers low-cost vehicles, in each particular model stratification, that appeal to a large audience.

- **Audi** is pursuing a broad differentiation strategy with its Quattro models available at several price points. Audi's differentiation is safety, and it prices its various Quattro models (higher than Hyundai) to reach a large, stratified audience.

- **Kia** has a more focused cost leadership strategy. Kia mainly offers low-cost vehicles in the lower levels of model stratification.

- **Hummer** offers the most focused differentiation strategy of any in the industry (including Mercedes-Benz).

Value Chain Analysis—Targeting Business Processes

Once an organization enters a new market using one of Porter's three generic strategies, it must understand, accept, and successfully execute its business strategy. Every aspect of the organization contributes to the success (or failure) of the chosen strategy. The business processes of the organization and the value chain they create play an integral role in strategy execution. Figure 2.5 combines Porter's Five Forces and his three generic strategies creating business strategies for each segment.[8]

VALUE CREATION

A *business process* is a standardized set of activities that accomplish a specific task, such as processing a customer's order. To evaluate the effectiveness of its business processes, an organization can use Michael Porter's value chain approach. An organization creates value by performing a series of activities that Porter identified as the value chain. The *value chain* approach views an organization as a series of

Generic Strategies			
Industry Force	**Cost Leadership**	**Differentiation**	**Focused**
Entry Barriers	Ability to cut price in retaliation deters potential entrants.	Customer loyalty can discourage potential entrants.	Focusing develops core competencies that can act as an entry barrier.
Buyer Power	Ability to offer lower price to powerful buyers.	Large buyers have less power to negotiate because of few close alternatives.	Large buyers have less power to negotiate because of few alternatives.
Supplier Power	Better insulated from powerful suppliers.	Better able to pass on supplier price increases to customers.	Suppliers have power because of low volumes, but a differentiation-focused firm is better able to pass on supplier price increases.
Threat of Substitutes	Can use low price to defend against substitutes.	Customers become attached to differentiating attributes, reducing threat of substitutes.	Specialized products and core competency protect against substitutes.
Rivalry	Better able to compete on price.	Brand loyalty to keep customers from rivals.	Rivals cannot meet differentiation-focused customer needs.

FIGURE 2.5

Generic Strategies and Industry Forces

processes, each of which adds value to the product or service for each customer. To create a competitive advantage, the value chain must enable the organization to provide unique value to its customers. In addition to the firm's own value-creating activities, the firm operates in a value system of vertical activities including those of upstream suppliers and downstream channel members. To achieve a competitive advantage, the firm must perform one or more value-creating activities in a way that creates more overall value than do competitors. Added value is created through lower costs or superior benefits to the consumer (differentiation).

Organizations can add value by offering lower prices or by competing in a distinctive way. Examining the organization as a value chain (actually numerous distinct but inseparable value chains) leads to the identification of the important activities that add value for customers and then finding IT systems that support those activities. Figure 2.6 depicts a value chain. Primary value activities, shown at the bottom of the graph, acquire raw materials and manufacture, deliver, market,

FIGURE 2.6

A Graphical Depiction of a Value Chain

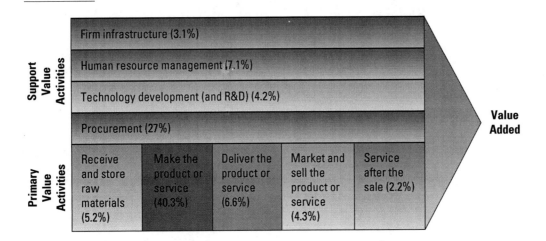

sell, and provide after-sales services. Support value activities, along the top of the graph, such as firm infrastructure, human resource management, technology development, and procurement, support the primary value activities.

The goal here is to survey the customers and ask them the extent to which they believe each activity adds value to the product or service. This generates a quantifiable metric, displayed in percentages in Figure 2.6, for how each activity adds value (or reduces value). The competitive advantage decision then is to (1) target high value-adding activities to further enhance their value, (2) target low value-adding activities to increase their value, or (3) perform some combination of the two.

Organizations should attempt to use information technology to add value to both primary and support value activities. One example of a primary value activity facilitated by IT is the development of a marketing campaign management system that could target marketing campaigns more efficiently, thereby reducing marketing costs. The system would also help the organization better pinpoint target market needs, thereby increasing sales. One example of a support value activity facilitated by IT is the development of a human resources system that could more efficiently reward employees based on performance. The system could also identify employees who are at risk of leaving their jobs, allowing the organization to find additional challenges or opportunities that would help retain these employees and thus reduce turnover costs.

Value chain analysis is a highly useful tool in that it provides hard and fast numbers for evaluating the activities that add value to products and services. An organization can find additional value by analyzing and constructing its value chain in terms of Porters' Five Forces (see Figure 2.7). For example, if an organization wants to decrease its buyers' or customers' power it can construct its value chain activity of "service after the sale" by offering high levels of quality customer service. This will increase the switching costs for its customers, thereby decreasing their power.

Strategy

FIGURE 2.7

The Value Chain and Porter's Five Forces

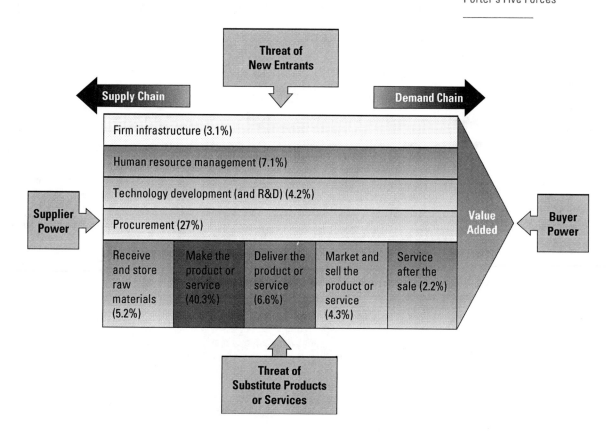

Analyzing and constructing its support value activities can help an organization decrease the threat of new entrants. Analyzing and constructing its primary value activities can help an organization decrease the threat of substitute products or services.

A company can implement its selected strategy by means of programs, budgets, and procedures. Implementation involves organization of the firm's resources and motivation of the employees to achieve objectives. How the company implements its chosen strategy can have a significant impact on its success. In a large company, the personnel implementing the strategy are usually different from those formulating the strategy. For this reason, proper communication of the strategy is critical. Failure can result if the strategy is misunderstood or if lower-level managers resist its implementation because they do not understand the process for selecting the particular strategy.

An organization must continually adapt to its competitive environment, which can cause its business strategy to change. To remain successful, an organization should use Porter's Five Forces, the three generic strategies, and value chain analysis to adopt new business strategies.

OPENING CASE STUDY QUESTIONS

1. How can Apple use environmental scanning to gain business intelligence?
2. Using Porter's Five Forces Model, analyze Apple's buyer power and supplier power.
3. Which of the three generic strategies is Apple following?
4. Which of Porter's Five Forces did Apple address through the introduction of the iPhone?

Chapter Two Case: Say "Charge It" with Your Cell Phone

Wireless operators, credit card companies, and retailers are working on a technology that allows customers to purchase items by using their cell phones. For example, a customer could purchase a can of soda by dialing a telephone number on the dispensing machine and have the charge for the soda show up on the customer's cell phone bill. Working prototypes are currently in use in South Korea, Japan, and Europe.

The ability to charge items to a cell phone has significant business potential because, unlike in the United States, credit cards are not nearly as popular in other countries. In Japan and China, for example, people are much more likely to have a cell phone than a credit card.

Japanese consumers use credit cards for only 5.6 percent of their personal spending compared with 33 percent of U.S. consumer spending.

The payoff for credit card companies and cell phone operators from this technology could be enormous. By associating a credit card with a cell phone, banks and credit card companies hope to persuade consumers to buy products, such as soda, with their cell phones instead of pocket change. Of course, they will reap transaction fees for each transaction. Mobile phone operators see the technology as a way to increase traffic on their networks as well as to position cell phones as an even more useful and, thus, essential device for consumers. Retailers envision easier transactions also leading to more sales.

MasterCard International and Nokia are currently testing a cell phone credit card for the U.S. market. The phones have a special chip programmed with the user's credit card information and a radio-frequency transmitting circuit. Consumers can simply tap their phone on a special device at a checkout counter equipped with a receiving device that costs the retailer about $80. Betsy Foran-Owens, vice president for Product Services at MasterCard International, commented that with this technology, "You don't even have to get off your phone to pay. You can just tap this thing down at the register." She also noted, "If you're not going to carry cash around, what are you going to carry? Your mobile phone."

The only players who might not look favorably on the technology are the traditional telephone companies, who must certainly view the technology as just one more threat to their traditional telephone business.[9]

Questions

1. Do you view this technology as a potential threat to traditional telephone companies? If so, what counterstrategies could traditional telephone companies adopt to prepare for this technology?

2. Using Porter's Five Forces describe the barriers to entry for this new technology.

3. Which of Porter's three generic strategies is this new technology following?

4. Describe the value chain of the business of using cell phones as a payment method.

5. What types of regulatory issues might occur due to this type of technology?

6. How could Apple's iPhone use this technology to gain a competitive advantage?

Strategic Initiatives for Implementing Competitive Advantages

3.1. List and describe the four basic components of supply chain management.

3.2. Explain customer relationship management systems and how they can help organizations understand their customers.

3.3. Summarize the importance of enterprise resource planning systems.

3.4. Identify how an organization can use business process reengineering to improve its business.

Strategic Initiatives

Trek, a leader in bicycle products and accessories, gained more than 30 percent of the worldwide market by streamlining operations through the implementation of several IT systems. According to Jeff Stang, director of IT and operational accounting, the most significant improvement realized from the new systems was the ability to obtain key management information to drive business decisions in line with the company's strategic goals. Other system results included a highly successful Web site developed for the 1,400 Trek dealers where they could enter orders directly, check stock availability, and view accounts receivable and credit summaries. Tonja Green, Trek channel manager for North America, stated, "We wanted to give our dealers an easier and quicker way to enter their orders and get information. Every week the number of Web orders increases by 25 to 30 percent due to the new system."[10]

This chapter introduces high-profile strategic initiatives that an organization can undertake to help it gain competitive advantages and business efficiencies—supply chain management, customer relationship management, business process reengineering, and enterprise resource planning. Each of these strategic initiatives is covered in detail throughout this text. This chapter provides a brief introduction only.

Supply Chain Management

Rocketboom

To understand a supply chain, consider a customer purchasing a Trek bike from a dealer. On one end, the supply chain has the customer placing an order for the bike with the dealer. The dealer purchases the bike from the manufacturer, Trek. Trek purchases raw materials such as packaging material, metal, and accessories from many different suppliers to make the bike. The supply chain for Trek encompasses every activity and party involved in the process of fulfilling the order from the customer for the new bike.

Supply chain management (SCM) involves the management of information flows between and among stages in a supply chain to maximize total supply chain effectiveness and profitability. The four basic components of supply chain management are:

1. **Supply chain strategy**—the strategy for managing all the resources required to meet customer demand for all products and services.

2. **Supply chain partners**—the partners chosen to deliver finished products, raw materials, and services including pricing, delivery, and payment processes along with partner relationship monitoring metrics.

3. **Supply chain operation**—the schedule for production activities including testing, packaging, and preparation for delivery. Measurements for this component include productivity and quality.

4. **Supply chain logistics**—the product delivery processes and elements including orders, warehouses, carriers, defective product returns, and invoicing.

Dozens of steps are required to achieve and carry out each of the above components. SCM software can enable an organization to generate efficiencies within these steps by automating and improving the information flows throughout and among the different supply chain components.

Wal-Mart and Procter & Gamble (P&G) implemented a tremendously successful SCM system. The system linked Wal-Mart's distribution centers directly to P&G's manufacturing centers. Every time a Wal-Mart customer purchases a P&G product, the system sends a message directly to the factory alerting P&G to restock the product. The system also sends an automatic alert to P&G whenever a product is running low at one of Wal-Mart's distribution centers. This real-time information allows P&G to efficiently make and deliver products to Wal-Mart without having to maintain large inventories in its warehouses. The system also generates invoices and receives payments automatically. The SCM system saves time, reduces inventory, and decreases order-processing costs for P&G. P&G passes on these savings to Wal-Mart in the form of discounted prices.[11]

Figure 3.1 diagrams the stages of the SCM system for a customer purchasing a product from Wal-Mart. The diagram demonstrates how the supply chain is dynamic and involves the constant flow of information between the different parties. For example, the customer generates order information by purchasing a product from Wal-Mart. Wal-Mart supplies the order information to its warehouse or distributor. The warehouse or distributor transfers the order information to the manufacturer, who provides pricing and availability information to the store and replenishes the product to the store. Payment funds among the various partners are transferred electronically.[12]

Effective and efficient supply chain management systems can enable an organization to:

■ Decrease the power of its buyers.

■ Increase its own supplier power.

■ Increase switching costs to reduce the threat of substitute products or services.

Supply Chain

FIGURE 3.1

Supply Chain for a Product Purchased from Wal-Mart

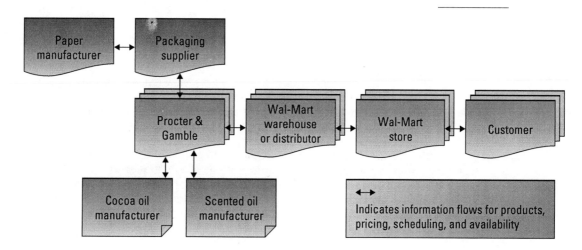

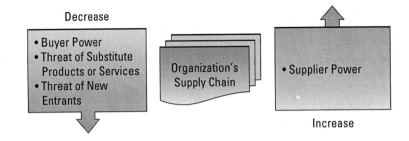

FIGURE 3.2

Effective and Efficient Supply Chain Management's Effect on Porter's Five Forces

- Create entry barriers thereby reducing the threat of new entrants.
- Increase efficiencies while seeking a competitive advantage through cost leadership (see Figure 3.2).

Customer Relationship Management

Today, most competitors are simply a mouse-click away. This intense marketplace has forced organizations to switch from being sales focused to being customer focused.

Charles Schwab recouped the cost of a multimillion-dollar customer relationship management system in less than two years. The system, developed by Siebel, allows the brokerage firm to trace each interaction with a customer or prospective customer and then provide services (retirement planning, for instance) to each customer's needs and interests. The system gives Schwab a better and more complete view of its customers, which it can use to determine which customers are serious investors and which ones are not. Automated deposits from paychecks, for example, are a sign of a serious investor, while stagnant balances signal a nonserious investor. Once Schwab is able to make this determination, the firm allocates its resources accordingly, saving money by not investing time or resources in subsidizing nonserious investors.[13]

Customer relationship management (CRM) involves managing all aspects of a customer's relationship with an organization to increase customer loyalty and retention and an organization's profitability. CRM allows an organization to gain insights into customers' shopping and buying behaviors in order to develop and implement enterprisewide strategies. Kaiser Permanente undertook a CRM strategy to improve and prolong the lives of diabetics. After compiling CRM information on 84,000 of its diabetic patients among its 2.4 million northern California members, Kaiser determined that only 15 to 20 percent of its diabetic patients were getting their eyes checked routinely. (Diabetes is the leading cause of blindness.) As a result, Kaiser is now enforcing more rigorous eye-screening programs for diabetics and creating support groups for obesity and stress (two more factors that make diabetes even worse). This CRM-based "preventive medicine" approach is saving Kaiser considerable sums of money and saving the eyesight of diabetic patients.[14]

Figure 3.3 provides an overview of a typical CRM system. Customers contact an organization through various means including call centers, Web access, e-mail, faxes, and direct sales. A single customer may access an organization multiple times through many different channels. The CRM system tracks every communication between the customer and the organization and provides access to CRM information within different systems from accounting to order fulfillment. Understanding all customer communications allows the organization to communicate effectively with each customer. It gives the organization a detailed understanding of each customer's products and services record regardless of the customer's preferred communication channel. For example, a customer service representative

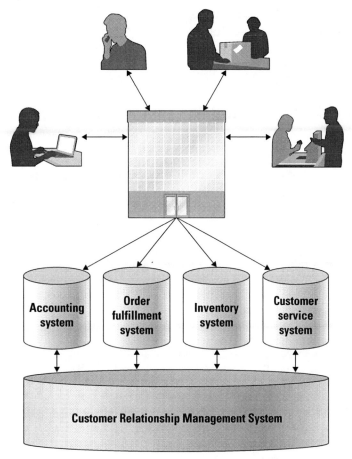

FIGURE 3.3

CRM Overview

Accounting system

Order fulfillment system

Inventory system

Customer service system

Customer Relationship Management System

◄─► Customer information flows are represented by arrows.

can easily view detailed account information and history through a CRM system when providing information to a customer such as expected delivery dates, complementary product information, and customer payment and billing information.

CRM STRATEGY

Eddie Bauer ships 110 million catalogs a year, maintains two Web sites, and has over 600 retail stores. The company collects information through customer transactions and analyzes the information to determine the best way to market to each individual customer. Eddie Bauer discovered that customers who shop across all three of its distribution channels—catalogs, Web sites, and stores—spend up to five times more than customers who shop through only one channel.

Michael Boyd, director of CRM at Eddie Bauer, stated, "Our experience tells us that CRM is in no way, shape, or form a software application. Fundamentally, it is a business strategy to try to optimize profitability, revenue, and satisfaction at an individual customer level. Everything in an organization, every single process, every single application, is a tool that can be used to serve the CRM goal."[15]

It is important to realize that CRM is not just technology, but also a strategy that an organization must embrace on an enterprise level. Although there are many technical components of CRM, it is actually a process and business goal simply enhanced by technology. Implementing a CRM system can help an organization

30 Baltzan–Phillips–Haag:
Business Driven
Technology, Third Edition

I. Achieving Business
Success

3. Strategic Initiatives for
Implementing Competitive
Advantages

© The McGraw–Hill
Companies, 2009

identify customers and design specific marketing campaigns tailored to each customer, thereby increasing customer spending. A CRM system also allows an organization to treat customers as individuals, gaining important insights into their buying preferences and behaviors and leading to increased sales, greater profitability, and higher rates of customer loyalty.

Business Process Reengineering

A *business process* is a standardized set of activities that accomplish a specific task, such as processing a customer's order. *Business process reengineering (BPR)* is the analysis and redesign of workflow within and between enterprises. The concept of BPR traces its origins to management theories developed as early as the 19th century. The purpose of BPR is to make all business process the best-in-class. Frederick Taylor suggested in the 1880s that managers could discover the best processes for performing work and reengineer the processes to optimize productivity. BPR echoes the classical belief that there is one best way to conduct tasks. In Taylor's time, technology did not allow large companies to design processes in a cross-functional or cross-departmental manner. Specialization was the state-of-the-art method to improve efficiency given the technology of the time.[16]

BPR reached its heyday in the early 1990s when Michael Hammer and James Champy published their best-selling book, *Reengineering the Corporation*. The authors promoted the idea that radical redesign and reorganization of an enterprise (wiping the slate clean) sometimes was necessary to lower costs and increase quality of service and that information technology was the key enabler for that radical change. Hammer and Champy believed that the workflow design in most large corporations was based on invalid assumptions about technology, people, and organizational goals. They suggested seven principles of reengineering to streamline the work process and thereby achieve significant improvement in quality, time management, and cost (see Figure 3.4).[17]

FINDING OPPORTUNITY USING BPR

Companies frequently strive to improve their business processes by performing tasks faster, cheaper, and better. Figure 3.5 displays different ways to travel the same road. A company could improve the way that it travels the road by moving from foot to horse and then from horse to car. However, true BPR would look at taking a different path. A company could forget about traveling on the same old road and use an airplane to get to its final destination. Companies often follow the same indirect path for doing business, not realizing there might be a different, faster, and more direct way of doing business.[18]

Creating value for the customer is the leading factor for instituting BPR, and information technology often plays an important enabling role. Radical and

Business
Process

FIGURE 3.4

Seven Principles of
Business Process
Reengineering

Seven Principles of Business Process Reengineering	
1	Organize around outcomes, not tasks.
2	Identify all the organization's processes and prioritize them in order of redesign urgency.
3	Integrate information processing work into the real work that produces the information.
4	Treat geographically dispersed resources as though they were centralized.
5	Link parallel activities in the workflow instead of just integrating their results.
6	Put the decision point where the work is performed, and build control into the process.
7	Capture information once and at the source.

fundamentally new business processes enabled Progressive Insurance to slash the claims settlement from 31 days to four hours. Typically, car insurance companies follow this standard claims resolution process: The customer gets into an accident, has the car towed, and finds a ride home. The customer then calls the insurance company to begin the claims process, which usually takes over a month (see Figure 3.6).[19]

Progressive Insurance improved service to its customers by offering a mobile claims process. When a customer has a car accident he or she calls in the claim on the spot. The Progressive claims adjustor comes to the accident and performs a mobile claims process, surveying the scene and taking digital photographs. The adjustor then offers the customer on-site payment, towing services, and a ride home (see Figure 3.6).[20]

A true BPR effort does more for a company than simply improve it by performing a process better, faster, and cheaper. Progressive Insurance's BPR effort redefined best practices for its entire industry. Figure 3.7 displays the different types of change an organization can achieve, along with the magnitude of change and the potential business benefit.[21]

FIGURE 3.5

Better, Faster, Cheaper or BPR

PITFALLS OF BPR

One hazard of BPR is that the company becomes so wrapped up in fighting its own demons that it fails to keep up with its competitors in offering new products or services. While American Express tackled a comprehensive reengineering of its credit card business, MasterCard and Visa introduced a new product—the corporate procurement card. American Express lagged a full year behind before offering its customers the same service.[22]

Enterprise Resource Planning

Today's business leaders need significant amounts of information to be readily accessible with real-time views into their businesses so that decisions can be made when they need to be, without the added time of tracking data and generating reports. **Enterprise resource planning (ERP)** integrates all departments and functions throughout an organization into a single IT system (or integrated set of IT systems) so that employees can make decisions by viewing enterprisewide information on all business operations.

Many organizations fail to maintain consistency across business operations. If a single department, such as sales, decides to implement a new system without

FIGURE 3.6

Auto Insurance Claims Processes

Company A: Claims Resolution Process
Progressive Insurance: Claims Resolution Process

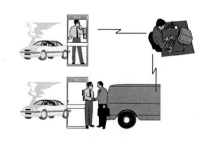

Resolution Cycle Time: 3–8 weeks

Resolution Cycle Time: 30 min–3 hours

FIGURE 3.7

The Benefits and Magnitude of Change

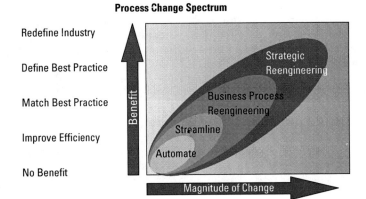

Process Change Spectrum

considering the other departments, inconsistencies can occur throughout the company. Not all systems are built to talk to each other and share data, and if sales suddenly implements a new system that marketing and accounting cannot use or is inconsistent in the way it handles information, the company's operations become siloed. Figure 3.8 displays sample data from a sales database, and Figure 3.9 displays samples from an accounting database. Notice the differences in data formats, numbers, and identifiers. Correlating this data would be difficult, and the inconsistencies would cause numerous reporting errors from an enterprisewide perspective.

Los Angeles is a city of 3.5 million, with 44,000 city employees, and a budget of $4 billion. Yet a few years ago each department conducted its own purchasing. That meant 2,000 people in 600 city buildings and 60 warehouses were ordering material. Some 120,000 purchase orders (POs) and 50,000 checks per year went to more than 7,000 vendors. Inefficiency was rampant.

"There was a lack of financial responsibility in the old system, and people could run up unauthorized expenditures," said Bob Jensen, the city's ERP project manager. Each department maintained its own inventories on different systems. Expense-item

FIGURE 3.8

Sales Information Sample

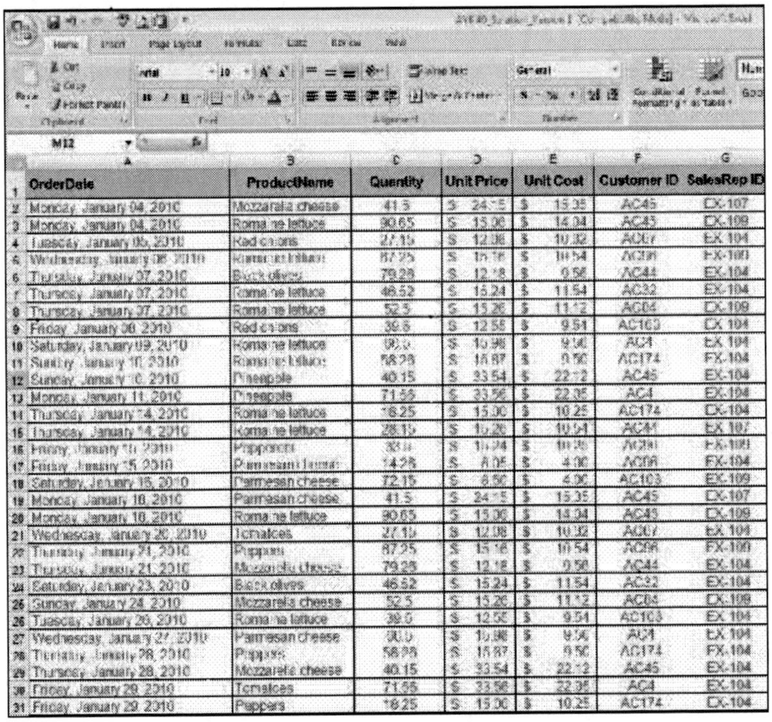

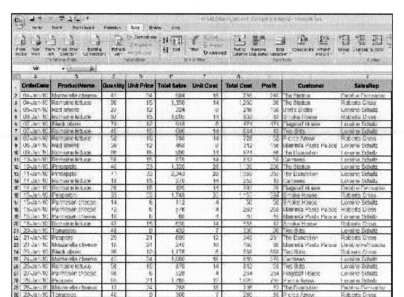

FIGURE 3.9

Accounting Information Sample

mismatches piled up. One department purchased one way, others preferred a different approach. Mainframe-based systems were isolated. The city chose an ERP system as part of a $22 million project to integrate purchasing and financial reporting across the entire city. The project resulted in cutting the check processing staff in half, processing POs faster than ever, reducing the number of workers in warehousing by 40 positions, decreasing inventories from $50 million to $15 million, and providing a single point of contact for each vendor. In addition, $5 million a year has been saved in contract consolidation.[23]

Figure 3.10 shows how an ERP system takes data from across the enterprise, consolidates and correlates the data, and generates enterprisewide organizational reports. Original ERP implementations promised to capture all information onto one true "enterprise" system, with the ability to touch all the business processes within the organization. Unfortunately, ERP solutions have fallen short of these promises, and typical implementations have penetrated only 15 to 20 percent of

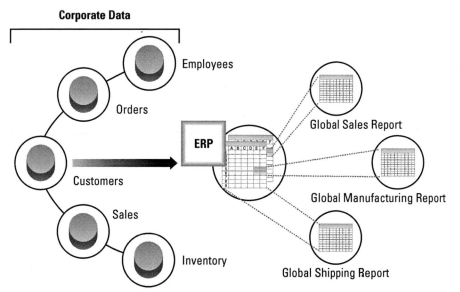

FIGURE 3.10

Enterprise Resource Planning System

the organization. The issue ERP intends to solve is that knowledge within a majority of organizations currently resides in silos that are maintained by a select few, without the ability to be shared across the organization, causing inconsistency across business operations.[24]

OPENING CASE STUDY QUESTIONS

1. Evaluate how Apple can gain business intelligence through the implementation of a customer relationship management system.

2. Create an argument against the following statement: "Apple should not invest any resources to build a supply chain management system."

3. Why would a company like Apple invest in BPR?

Chapter Three Case: Consolidating Touchpoints for Saab

Saab Cars USA imports more than 37,000 Saab sedans, convertibles, and wagons annually and distributes the cars to 220 U.S. dealerships. Saab competes in the premium automotive market, and its primary rivals attract customers through aggressive marketing campaigns, reduced prices, and inexpensive financing. Saab decided that the answer to beating its competition was not to spend capital on additional advertising, but to invest in Siebel Automotive, a customer relationship management system.

Until recently, the company communicated with its customers through three primary channels: (1) dealer network, (2) customer assistance center, (3) lead management center. Traditionally, each channel maintained its own customer database, and this splintered approach to managing customer information caused numerous problems for the company. For example, a prospective customer might receive a direct-mail piece from Saab one week, then an e-mail with an unrelated offer from a third-party marketing vendor the next week. The local dealer might not know of either activity, and therefore might deliver an ineffective pitch when the customer visited the showroom that weekend. Al Fontova, direct marketing manager with Saab Cars USA, stated he had over 3 million customer records and 55 files at three different vendors. Analyzing this information in aggregate was complicated, inefficient, and costly.

Saab required a solution that would provide a consolidated customer view from all three touchpoints. In 2002, Saab implemented the Siebel CRM solution, which provides Saab's call center employees with a 360-degree view of each customer, including prior service-related questions and all the marketing communications they have received. Known internally as "TouchPoint," the Siebel application provides Saab's dealers with a powerful Web-based solution for coordinating sales and marketing activities. These tracking capabilities enable Saab to measure the sales results of specific leads, recommend more efficient selling techniques, and target its leads more precisely in the future. Using Siebel Automotive, Saab received the following benefits:

- Direct marketing costs decreased by 5 percent.
- Lead follow-up increased from 38 percent to 50 percent.
- Customer satisfaction increased from 69 percent to 75 percent.
- Saab gained a single view of its customers across multiple channels.[25]

Questions

1. Explain how implementing a CRM system enabled Saab to gain a competitive advantage.
2. Estimate the potential impact to Saab's business if it had not implemented a CRM system.
3. What additional benefits could Saab receive from implementing a supply chain management system?
4. Create a model of Saab's potential supply chain.
5. How is Saab's CRM implementation going to influence its SCM practices?

TECHNOLOGY PLUG-IN POINTER

Review the **Technology Plug-In T2 "Basic Skills Using Excel"** for an introduction to Excel including workbooks, worksheets, cells, data, menus, formats, formulas, charts, graphs, and more.

CHAPTER 4

Measuring the Success of Strategic Initiatives

LEARNING OUTCOMES

4.1. Compare efficiency IT metrics and effectiveness IT metrics.

4.2. List and describe five common types of efficiency IT metrics.

4.3. List and describe four types of effectiveness IT metrics.

4.4. Explain customer metrics and their importance to an organization.

Online Job
Search
Industry

Measuring Information Technology's Success

IT has become an important part of organizations' strategy, competitive advantage, and profitability. There is management pressure to build systems faster, better, and at minimum cost. The return on investment that an organization can achieve from the money it spends on IT has come under increased scrutiny from senior business executives and directors. Consequently, IT now has to operate like other parts of the organization, being aware of its performance and its contribution to the organization's success and opportunities for improvement. So what is it that managers need to know about measuring the success of information technology?

The first thing managers need to understand about IT success is that it is incredibly difficult to measure. Determining the return on investment (ROI) of new computer equipment is difficult. For example, what is the ROI of a fire extinguisher? If the fire extinguisher is never used, the return on the investment is low. If the extinguisher puts out a fire that could destroy the entire building, then its ROI is high. This is similar to IT systems. If a company implements a $5,000 firewall to virus attacks on the computer systems and it never stops a virus, the company lost $5,000. If the firewall stops viruses that could have cost the company millions of dollars, then the ROI of that firewall is significantly greater than $5,000. A few questions banking executives recently raised regarding their IT systems include:

- Is the internal IT operation performing satisfactorily?
- Should I outsource some or all of the IT operations?
- How is my outsourcer performing?
- What are the risk factors to consider in an IT project?
- What questions should be asked to ensure an IT project proposal is realistic?
- What are the characteristics of a healthy project?
- Which factors are most critical to monitor to ensure the project remains on track?

Peter Drucker, a famous management guru, once stated that if you cannot measure it, you cannot manage it. Managers need to ask themselves how they are going to manage IT projects if they cannot find a way to measure the projects.[26]

IT professionals know how to install and maintain information systems. Business professionals know how to run a successful business. But how does a company decide if an information system helps make a business successful?

The answer lies in the metrics. Designing metrics requires an expertise that neither IT nor business professionals usually possess. Metrics are about neither technology nor business strategy. The questions that arise in metrics design are almost philosophical: How do you define success? How do you apply quantifiable measures to business processes, especially qualitative ones like customer service? What kind of information best reflects progress, or the lack of it?

Key performance indicators (KPIs) are the measures that are tied to business drivers. Metrics are the detailed measures that feed those KPIs. Performance metrics fall into a nebulous area of business intelligence that is neither technology- nor business-centered, but this area requires input from both IT and business professionals to find success. Cisco Systems implemented a cross-departmental council to create metrics for improving business process operations. The council developed metrics to evaluate the efficiency of Cisco's online order processing and discovered that due to errors, more than 70 percent of online orders required manual input and were unable to be automatically routed to manufacturing. By changing the process and adding new information systems, within six months the company doubled the percentage of orders that went directly to manufacturing.[27]

Effective Business

Efficiency and Effectiveness

Organizations spend enormous sums of money on IT to compete in today's fast-paced business environment. Some organizations spend up to 50 percent of their total capital expenditures on IT. To justify these expenditures, an organization must measure the payoff of these investments, their impact on business performance, and the overall business value gained.

Efficiency and effectiveness metrics are two primary types of IT metrics. *Efficiency IT metrics* measure the performance of the IT system itself including throughput, speed, and availability. *Effectiveness IT metrics* measure the impact IT has on business processes and activities including customer satisfaction, conversion rates, and sell-through increases. Peter Drucker offers a helpful distinction between efficiency and effectiveness. Drucker states that managers "Do things right" and/or "Do the right things." Doing things right addresses efficiency—getting the most from each resource. Doing the right things addresses effectiveness—setting the right goals and objectives and ensuring they are accomplished.[28]

Effectiveness focuses on how well an organization is achieving its goals and objectives, while efficiency focuses on the extent to which an organization is using its resources in an optimal way. The two—efficiency and effectiveness—are definitely interrelated. However, success in one area does not necessarily imply success in the other.

Benchmarking—Baseline Metrics

Regardless of what is measured, how it is measured, and whether it is for the sake of efficiency or effectiveness, there must be *benchmarks,* or baseline values the system seeks to attain. *Benchmarking* is a process of continuously measuring system results, comparing those results to optimal system performance (benchmark values), and identifying steps and procedures to improve system performance.

Consider e-government worldwide as an illustration of benchmarking efficiency IT metrics and effectiveness IT metrics (see survey results in Figure 4.1). From an

Efficiency	Effectiveness
1. United States (3.11)	1. Canada
2. Australia (2.60)	2. Singapore
3. New Zealand (2.59)	3. United States
4. Singapore (2.58)	4. Denmark
5. Norway (2.55)	5. Australia
6. Canada (2.52)	6. Finland
7. United Kingdom (2.52)	7. Hong Kong
8. Netherlands (2.51)	8. United Kingdom
9. Denmark (2.47)	9. Germany
10. Germany (2.46)	10. Ireland

FIGURE 4.1

Comparing Efficiency IT and Effectiveness IT Metrics for E-Government Initiatives

effectiveness point of view, Canada ranks number one in terms of e-government satisfaction of its citizens. (The United States ranks third.) The survey, sponsored by Accenture, also included such attributes as CRM practices, customer-service vision, approaches to offering e-government services through multiple-service delivery channels, and initiatives for identifying services for individual citizen segments. These are all benchmarks at which Canada's government excels.[23]

In contrast, the *United Nations Division for Public Economics and Public Administration* ranks Canada sixth in terms of efficiency IT metrics. (It ranked the United States first.) This particular ranking based purely on efficiency IT metrics includes benchmarks such as the number of computers per 100 citizens, the number of Internet hosts per 10,000 citizens, the percentage of the citizen population online, and several other factors. Therefore, while Canada lags behind in IT efficiency, it is the premier e-government provider in terms of effectiveness.[29]

Governments hoping to increase their e-government presence would benchmark themselves against these sorts of efficiency and effectiveness metrics. There is a high degree of correlation between e-government efficiency and effectiveness, although it is not absolute.

The Interrelationships of Efficiency and Effectiveness IT Metrics

Efficiency IT metrics focus on the technology itself. Figure 4.2 highlights the most common types of efficiency IT metrics.

While these efficiency metrics are important to monitor, they do not always guarantee effectiveness. Effectiveness IT metrics are determined according to an organization's goals, strategies, and objectives. Here, it becomes important to consider the strategy an organization is using, such as a broad cost leadership strategy (Wal-Mart, for example), as well as specific goals and objectives such as increasing new customers by 10 percent or reducing new-product development cycle times to six months. Broad, general effectiveness metrics are outlined in Figure 4.3.

In the private sector, eBay constantly benchmarks its information technology efficiency and effectiveness. Maintaining constant Web site availability and optimal throughput performance is critical to eBay's success.[30] Jupiter Media Metrix ranked

FIGURE 4.2

Common Types of Efficiency IT Metrics

Efficiency IT Metrics	
Throughput	The amount of information that can travel through a system at any point.
Transaction speed	The amount of time a system takes to perform a transaction.
System availability	The number of hours a system is available for users.
Information accuracy	The extent to which a system generates the correct results when executing the same transaction numerous times.
Web traffic	Includes a host of benchmarks such as the number of page views, the number of unique visitors, and the average time spent viewing a Web page.
Response time	The time it takes to respond to user interactions such as a mouse click.

Effectiveness IT Metrics	
Usability	The ease with which people perform transactions and/or find information. A popular usability metric on the Internet is degrees of freedom, which measures the number of clicks required to find desired information.
Customer satisfaction	Measured by such benchmarks as satisfaction surveys, percentage of existing customers retained, and increases in revenue dollars per customer.
Conversion rates	The number of customers an organization "touches" for the first time and persuades to purchase its products or services. This is a popular metric for evaluating the effectiveness of banner, pop-up, and pop-under ads on the Internet.
Financial	Such as return on investment (the earning power of an organization's assets), cost-benefit analysis (the comparison of projected revenues and costs including development, maintenance, fixed, and variable), and break-even analysis (the point at which constant revenues equal ongoing costs).

FIGURE 4.3

Common Types of Effectiveness IT Metrics

eBay as the Web site with the highest visitor volume (efficiency) for the fourth year in a row, with an 80 percent growth from the previous year. The eBay site averaged 8 million unique visitors during each week of the holiday season that year with daily peaks exceeding 12 million visitors. To ensure constant availability and reliability of its systems, eBay implemented ProactiveNet, a performance measurement and management-tracking tool. The tool allows eBay to monitor its environment against baseline benchmarks, which helps the eBay team keep tight control of its systems. The new system has resulted in improved system availability with a 150 percent increase in productivity as measured by system uptime.[31]

Be sure to consider the issue of security while determining efficiency and effectiveness IT metrics. When an organization offers its customers the ability to purchase products over the Internet it must implement the appropriate security—such as encryption and Secure Sockets Layers (SSLs; denoted by the lock symbol in the lower right corner of a browser window and/or the "s" in https). It is actually inefficient for an organization to implement security measures for Internet-based transactions as compared to processing nonsecure transactions. However, an organization will probably have a difficult time attracting new customers and increasing Web-based revenue if it does not implement the necessary security measures. Purely from an efficiency IT metric point of view, security generates some inefficiency. From an organization's business strategy point of view, however, security should lead to increases in effectiveness metrics.

Figure 4.4 depicts the interrelationships between efficiency and effectiveness. Ideally, an organization should operate in the upper right-hand corner of the graph, realizing both significant increases in efficiency and effectiveness. However, operating in the upper left-hand corner (minimal effectiveness with increased efficiency) or the lower right-hand corner (significant effectiveness with minimal efficiency) may be in line with an organization's particular strategies. In general, operating in the lower left-hand corner (minimal efficiency and minimal effectiveness) is not ideal for the operation of any organization.

FIGURE 4.4

The Interrelationships between Efficiency and Effectiveness

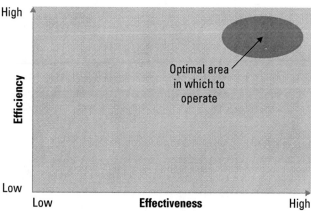

Optimal area in which to operate

Metrics for Strategic Initiatives

What is a metric? A metric is nothing more than a standard measure to assess performance in a particular area. Metrics are at the heart of a good, customer-focused management system and any program directed at continuous improvement. A focus on customers and performance standards shows up in the form of metrics that assess the ability to meet customers' needs and business objectives.

Business leaders want to monitor key metrics in real-time to actively track the health of their business. Most business professionals are familiar with financial metrics. Different financial ratios are used to evaluate a company's performance. Companies can gain additional insight into their performance by comparing financial ratios against other companies in their industry. A few of the more common financial ratios include:

- Internal rate of return (IRR)—the rate at which the net present value of an investment equals zero.
- Return on investment (ROI)—indicates the earning power of a project and is measured by dividing the benefits of a project by the investment.
- Payback method —number of years to recoup the cost of an initiative based on projected annual net cash flow.
- Break-even analysis—determines the volume of business required to make a profit at the current prices charged for the products or services. For example, if a promotional mailing costs $1,000 and each item generates $50 in revenue, the company must generate 20 sales to break even and cover the cost of the mailing. The break-even point is the point at which revenues equal costs. The point is located by performing a break-even analysis. All sales over the break-even point produce profits; any drop in sales below that point will produce losses (see Figure 4.5).

Most managers are familiar with financial metrics but unfamiliar with information system metrics. The following metrics will help managers measure and manage their strategic initiatives:

- Web site metrics.
- Supply chain management (SCM) metrics.
- Customer relationship management (CRM) metrics.
- Business process reengineering (BPR) metrics.
- Enterprise resource planning (ERP) metrics.

FIGURE 4.5

Break-Even Analysis

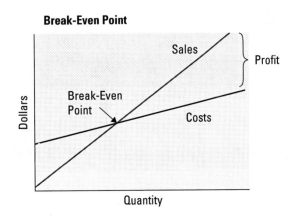

WEB SITE METRICS

Most companies measure the traffic on a Web site as the primary determinant of the Web site's success. However, heavy Web site traffic does not necessarily indicate large sales. Many organizations with lots of Web site traffic have minimal sales. A company can use Web traffic analysis or Web analytics to determine the revenue generated, the number of new customers acquired, any reductions in customer service calls, and so on. The Yankee Group reports that 66 percent of companies determine Web site success solely by measuring the amount of traffic. New customer acquisition ranked second on the list at 34 percent, and revenue generation ranked third at 23 percent. Figure 4.6 displays a few metrics managers should be familiar with to help measure Web site success along

Web Site Metrics

- **Abandoned registrations:** Number of visitors who start the process of completing a registration page and then abandon the activity.

- **Abandoned shopping carts:** Number of visitors who create a shopping cart and start shopping and then abandon the activity before paying for the merchandise.

- **Click-through:** Count of the number of people who visit a site, click on an ad, and are taken to the site of the advertiser.

- **Conversion rate:** Percentage of potential customers who visit a site and actually buy something.

- **Cost-per-thousand (CPM):** Sales dollars generated per dollar of advertising. This is commonly used to make the case for spending money to appear on a search engine.

- **Page exposures:** Average number of page exposures to an individual visitor.

- **Total hits:** Number of visits to a Web site, many of which may be by the same visitor.

- **Unique visitors:** Number of unique visitors to a site in a given time. This is commonly used by Nielsen/Net ratings to rank the most popular Web sites.

FIGURE 4.6

Web Site Metrics

Metrics

Supply Chain Management Metrics

- **Back order:** An unfilled customer order. A back order is demand (immediate or past due) against an item whose current stock level is insufficient to satisfy demand.

- **Customer order promised cycle time:** The anticipated or agreed upon cycle time of a purchase order. It is a gap between the purchase order creation date and the requested delivery date.

- **Customer order actual cycle time:** The average time it takes to actually fill a customer's purchase order. This measure can be viewed on an order or an order line level.

- **Inventory replenishment cycle time:** Measure of the manufacturing cycle time plus the time included to deploy the product to the appropriate distribution center.

- **Inventory turns (inventory turnover):** The number of times that a company's inventory cycles or turns over per year. It is one of the most commonly used supply chain metrics.

FIGURE 4.7

Supply Chain Management Metrics

with an organization's strategic initiatives. A Web-centric metric is a measure of the success of Web and e-business initiatives. Of the hundreds of Web-centric metrics available, some are general to almost any Web or e-business initiative and others are dependent on the particular initiative.[32]

SUPPLY CHAIN MANAGEMENT (SCM) METRICS

Supply chain management metrics can help an organization understand how it's operating over a given time period. Supply chain measurements can cover many areas including procurement, production, distribution, warehousing, inventory, transportation, and customer service. However, a good performance in one part of the supply chain is not sufficient. A supply chain is only as strong as its weakest link. The solution is to measure all key areas of the supply chain. Figure 4.7 displays common supply chain management metrics.[33]

CUSTOMER RELATIONSHIP MANAGEMENT (CRM) METRICS

Wondering what CRM metrics to track and monitor using reporting and real-time performance dashboards? Best practice is no more than seven (plus or minus two) metrics out of the hundreds possible should be used at any given management level. Figure 4.8 displays common CRM metrics tracked by organizations.

FIGURE 4.8

CRM Metrics

Sales Metrics	Service Metrics	Marketing Metrics
■ Number of prospective customers	■ Cases closed same day	■ Number of marketing campaigns
■ Number of new customers	■ Number of cases handled by agent	■ New customer retention rates
■ Number of retained customers	■ Number of service calls	■ Number of responses by marketing campaign
■ Number of open leads	■ Average number of service requests by type	■ Number of purchases by marketing campaign
■ Number of sales calls	■ Average time to resolution	■ Revenue generated by marketing campaign
■ Number of sales calls per lead	■ Average number of service calls per day	■ Cost per interaction by marketing campaign
■ Amount of new revenue	■ Percentage compliance with service-level agreement	■ Number of new customers acquired by marketing campaign
■ Amount of recurring revenue	■ Percentage of service renewals	■ Customer retention rate
■ Number of proposals given	■ Customer satisfaction level	■ Number of new leads by product

BUSINESS PROCESS REENGINEERING (BPR) AND ENTERPRISE RESOURCE PLANNING (ERP) METRICS

Business process reengineering and enterprise resource planning are large, organizationwide initiatives. Measuring these types of strategic initiatives is extremely difficult. One of the best methods is the balanced scorecard. This approach to strategic management was developed in the early 1990s by Drs. Robert Kaplan of the Harvard Business School and David Norton. Addressing some of the weaknesses and vagueness of previous measurement techniques, the balanced scorecard approach provides a clear prescription as to what companies should measure in order to balance the financial perspective.[34]

The *balanced scorecard* is a management system, in addition to a measurement system, that enables organizations to clarify their vision and strategy and translate them into action. It provides feedback around both the internal business processes and external outcomes in order to continuously improve strategic performance and results. When fully deployed, the balanced scorecard transforms strategic planning from an academic exercise into the nerve center of an enterprise. Kaplan and Norton describe the innovation of the balanced scorecard as follows:

> The balanced scorecard retains traditional financial measures. But financial measures tell the story of past events, an adequate story for industrial age companies for which investments in long-term capabilities and customer relationships were not critical for success. These financial measures are inadequate, however, for guiding and evaluating the journey that information age companies must make to create future value through investment in customers, suppliers, employees, processes, technology, and innovation.[35]

The balanced scorecard views the organization from four perspectives, and users should develop metrics, collect data, and analyze their business relative to each of these perspectives:

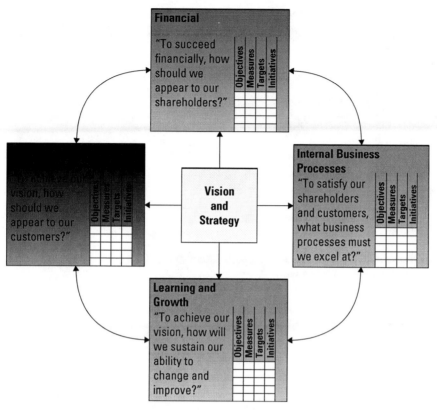

FIGURE 4.9

The Four Primary Perspectives of the Balanced Scorecard

- The learning and growth perspective.
- The internal business process perspective.
- The customer perspective.
- The financial perspective (see Figure 4.9).[36]

Recall that companies cannot manage what they cannot measure. Therefore, metrics must be developed based on the priorities of the strategic plan, which provides the key business drivers and criteria for metrics that managers most desire to watch. Processes are then designed to collect information relevant to these metrics and reduce it to numerical form for storage, display, and analysis. Decision makers examine the outcomes of various measured processes and strategies and track the results to guide the company and provide feedback. The value of metrics is in their ability to provide a factual basis for defining:

- Strategic feedback to show the present status of the organization from many perspectives for decision makers.
- Diagnostic feedback into various processes to guide improvements on a continuous basis.
- Trends in performance over time as the metrics are tracked.
- Feedback around the measurement methods themselves and which metrics should be tracked.
- Quantitative inputs to forecasting methods and models for decision support systems.[37]

One warning regarding metrics—do not go crazy. The trick is to find a few key metrics to track that provide significant insight. Remember to tie metrics to other financial and business objectives in the firm. The key is to get good insight without becoming a slave to metrics. The rule of thumb is to develop seven key metrics, plus or minus two.[38]

OPENING CASE STUDY QUESTIONS

1. Formulate a strategy describing how Apple can use efficiency IT metrics to improve its business.

2. Formulate a strategy describing how Apple can use effectiveness IT metrics to improve its business.

3. List three CRM metrics Apple should track, along with the reasons these metrics will add value to Apple's business strategy.

4. List three SCM metrics Apple should track, along with the reasons these metrics will add value to Apple's business strategy.

5. How can Apple use the balanced scorecard to make its business more efficient?

Chapter Four Case: How Do You Value Friendster?

Jonathan Abrams is keeping quiet about how he is going to generate revenue from his Web site, Friendster, which specializes in social networking. Abrams is a 33-year-old Canadian software developer whose experiences include being laid off by Netscape and then moving from one start-up to another. In 2002, Abrams was unemployed, not doing well financially, and certainly not looking to start another business, when he developed the idea for Friendster. He quickly coded a working prototype and watched in amazement as his Web site took off.

The buzz around social networking start-ups has been on the rise. A number of high-end venture capital (VC) firms, including Sequoia and Mayfield, have invested more than $40 million into social networking start-ups such as LinkedIn, Spoke, and Tribe Networks. Friendster received over $13 million in venture capital from Kleiner, Perkins, Caufield, Byers, and Benchmark Capital, which reportedly valued the company at $53 million—a startling figure for a company that had yet to generate even a single dime in revenue.

A year after making its public debut, Friendster was one of the largest social networking Web sites, attracting over 5 million users and receiving more than 50,000 page views per day. The question is how do efficiency metrics, such as Web traffic and page views, turn into cash flow? Everyone is wondering how Friendster is going to begin generating revenue.

The majority of Abrams's competitors make their money by extracting fees from their subscribers. Friendster is going to continue to let its subscribers meet for free but plans to charge them for premium services such as the ability to customize their profile page. The company also has plans to extend beyond social networking to an array of value-added services such as friend-based job referrals and classmate searches. Abrams is also looking into using his high-traffic Web site to tap into the growing Internet advertising market.

Abrams does not appear concerned about generating revenue or about potential competition. He states, "Match.com has been around eight years, has 12 million users, and has spent many millions of dollars on advertising to get them. We're a year old, we've spent zero dollars on advertising, and in a year or less, we'll be bigger than them—it's a given."

The future of Friendster is uncertain. Google offered to buy Friendster for $30 million even though there are signs, both statistical and anecdotal, that Friendster's popularity may have peaked.[39]

Questions

1. How could you use efficiency IT metrics to help place a value on Friendster?

2. How could you use effectiveness IT metrics to help place a value on Friendster?

3. Explain how a venture capital company can value Friendster at $53 million when the company has yet to generate any revenue.

4. Explain why Google would be interested in buying Friendster for $30 million when the company has yet to generate any revenue.

5. Google purchased You Tube for $1.65 billion. Do you think this was a smart investment? Why or why not?

CHAPTER 5

Organizational Structures That Support Strategic Initiatives

Organizational Structures

Employees across the organization must work closely together to develop strategic initiatives that create competitive advantages. Understanding the basic structure of a typical IT department including titles, roles, and responsibilities will help an organization build a cohesive enterprisewide team.

IT Roles and Responsibilities

Raven Biotechnologies

Information technology is a relatively new functional area, having been around formally in most organizations only for about 40 years. Job titles, roles, and responsibilities often differ dramatically from organization to organization. Nonetheless, clear trends are developing toward elevating some IT positions within an organization to the strategic level.

Most organizations maintain positions such as chief executive officer (CEO), chief financial officer (CFO), and chief operations officer (COO) at the strategic level. Recently there are more IT-related strategic positions such as chief information officer (CIO), chief technology officer (CTO), chief security officer (CSO), chief privacy officer (CPO), and chief knowledge officer (CKO).

J. Greg Hanson is proud to be the first CIO of the U.S. Senate. Contrary to some perceptions, the technology found in the Senate is quite good, according to Hanson. Hanson's responsibilities include creating the Senate's technology vision, leading the IT department, and deploying the IT infrastructure. Hanson must work with everyone from the 137 network administrators to the senators themselves to ensure that everything is operating smoothly. Hanson is excited to be the first CIO of the U.S. Senate and proud of the sense of honor and responsibility that comes with the job.[40]

The **chief information officer (CIO)** is responsible for (1) overseeing all uses of information technology and (2) ensuring the strategic alignment of IT with business goals and objectives. The CIO often reports directly to the CEO. (See Figure 5.1 for the average CIO compensation.) CIOs must possess a solid and detailed understanding of every aspect of an organization coupled with tremendous insight into the capability of IT. Broad functions of a CIO include:

1. *Manager*—ensure the delivery of all IT projects, on time and within budget.
2. *Leader*—ensure the strategic vision of IT is in line with the strategic vision of the organization.

3. *Communicator*—advocate and communicate the IT strategy by building and maintaining strong executive relationships.[41]

Although CIO is considered a position within IT, CIOs must be concerned with more than just IT. According to a recent survey (see Figure 5.2), most CIOs ranked "enhancing customer satisfaction" ahead of their concerns for any specific aspect of IT. CIOs with the broad business view that customer satisfaction is more crucial and critical than specific aspects of IT should be applauded.[42]

The *chief technology officer (CTO)* is responsible for ensuring the throughput, speed, accuracy, availability, and reliability of an organization's information technology. CTOs are similar to CIOs, except that CIOs take on the additional responsibility for effectiveness of ensuring that IT is aligned with the organization's strategic initiatives. CTOs have direct responsibility for ensuring the *efficiency* of IT systems throughout the organization. Most CTOs possess well-rounded knowledge of all aspects of IT, including hardware, software, and telecommunications.

The *chief security officer (CSO)* is responsible for ensuring the security of IT systems and developing strategies and IT safeguards against attacks from hackers and viruses. The role of a CSO has been elevated in recent years because of the number of attacks from hackers and viruses. Most CSOs possess detailed knowledge of networks and telecommunications because hackers and viruses usually find their way into IT systems through networked computers.

The *chief privacy officer (CPO)* is responsible for ensuring the ethical and legal use of information within an organization. CPOs are the newest senior executive position in IT. Recently, 150 of the Fortune 500 companies added the CPO position to their list of senior executives. Many CPOs are lawyers by training, enabling them to understand the often complex legal issues surrounding the use of information.[43]

The *chief knowledge officer (CKO)* is responsible for collecting, maintaining, and distributing the organization's knowledge. The CKO designs programs and systems that make it easy for people to reuse knowledge. These systems create repositories of organizational documents, methodologies, tools, and practices, and they establish methods for filtering the information. The CKO must continuously encourage employee contributions to keep the systems up-to-date. The CKO can contribute directly to the organization's bottom line by reducing the learning curve for new employees or employees taking on new roles.

Danny Shaw was the first CKO at Children's Hospital in Boston. His initial task was to unite information from disparate systems to enable analysis of both the efficiency and effectiveness of the hospital's care. Shaw started by building a series of small, integrated information systems that quickly demonstrated value. He then gradually built on those successes, creating a knowledge-enabled organization one layer at a time. Shaw's information systems have enabled administrative and clinical operational analyses.[44]

All the above IT positions and responsibilities are critical to an organization's success. While many organizations may not have a different individual for each of these positions, they must have leaders taking responsibility for all these areas of concern. The individuals responsible for enterprisewide IT and IT-related issues must provide guidance and support to the organization's employees. Figure 5.3 displays the personal skills pivotal for success in an executive IT role.

Industry	Average CIO Compensation
Wholesale/Retail/Distribution	$243,304
Finance	$210,547
Insurance	$197,697
Manufacturing	$190,250
Medical/Dental/Health Care	$171,032
Government	$118,359
Education	$ 93,750

FIGURE 5.1

Average CIO Compensation by Industry

FIGURE 5.2

What Concerns CIOs the Most?

Percentage	CIO's Concerns
94%	Enhancing customer satisfaction
92	Security
89	Technology evaluation
87	Budgeting
83	Staffing
66	ROI analysis
64	Building new applications
45	Outsourcing hosting

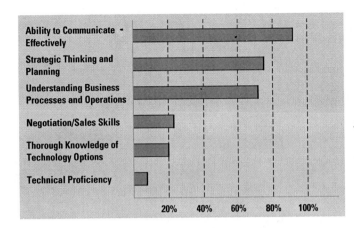

FIGURE 5.3

Skills Pivotal for Success in Executive IT Roles

The Gap between Business Personnel and IT Personnel

One of the greatest challenges today is effective communication between business personnel and IT personnel. Business personnel possess expertise in functional areas such as marketing, accounting, sales, and so forth. IT personnel have the technological expertise. Unfortunately, a communications gap often exists between the two. Business personnel have their own vocabularies based on their experience and expertise. IT personnel have their own vocabularies consisting of acronyms and technical terms. Effective communication between business and IT personnel should be a two-way street with each side making the effort to better understand the other (including through written and oral communication).

IMPROVING COMMUNICATIONS

Business personnel must seek to increase their understanding of IT. Although they do not need to know every technical detail, it will benefit their careers to understand what they can and cannot accomplish using IT. Business managers and leaders should read business-oriented IT magazines, such as *InformationWeek* and *CIO*, to increase their IT knowledge.

At the same time, an organization must develop strategies for integrating its IT personnel into the various business functions. Too often, IT personnel are left out of strategy meetings because of the belief they do not understand the business so they will not add any value. That is a dangerous position to take. IT personnel must understand the business if the organization is going to determine which technologies can benefit (or hurt) the business. With a little effort to communicate, IT personnel, by providing information on the functionality available in CRM systems, might add tremendous value to a meeting about how to improve customer service. Working together, business and IT personnel have the potential to create customer-service competitive advantages.

It is the responsibility of the CIO to ensure effective communications between business and IT personnel. While the CIO assumes the responsibility on an enterprisewide level, it is also each employee's responsibility to communicate effectively on a personal level.

Organizational Fundamentals—Ethics and Security

Ethics and security are two fundamental building blocks that organizations must base their businesses on. Such events as the Enron and Martha Stewart scandals along with 9/11 have shed new light on the meaning of ethics and security. When the behavior of a few individuals can destroy billion-dollar organizations because of a lapse in ethics or security, the value of highly ethical and highly secure organizations should be evident. Review the Ethics and Security plug-ins to gain a detailed understanding of these topics. Due to the importance of these topics, they will be readdressed throughout this text.

ETHICS

Ian Clarke, the inventor of a file-swapping service called Freenet, decided to leave the United States for the United Kingdom, where copyright laws are more lenient. Wayne Rosso, the inventor of a file-sharing service called Grokster, left the United States for Spain, again saying goodbye to tough U.S. copyright protections. File sharing encourages a legal network of shared thinking that can improve drug research, software development, and flow of information. The United States copyright laws, designed decades before the Internet was invented, make file sharing and many other Internet technologies illegal.[45]

The ethical issues surrounding copyright infringement and intellectual property rights are consuming the e-business world. Advances in technology make it easier and easier for people to copy everything from music to pictures. Technology poses new challenges for our *ethics*—the principles and standards that guide our behavior toward other people. Review Figure 5.4 for an overview of concepts, terms, and ethical issues stemming from advances in technology.

In today's electronic world, privacy has become a major ethical issue. *Privacy* is the right to be left alone when you want to be, to have control over your own personal possessions, and to not be observed without your consent. Some of the most problematic decisions organizations face lie in the murky and turbulent waters of privacy. The burden comes from the knowledge that each time employees make a decision regarding issues of privacy, the outcome could sink the company some day.

The Securities and Exchange Commission (SEC) began inquiries into Enron's accounting practices on October 22, 2001. David Duncan, the Arthur Andersen partner in charge of Enron, instructed his team to begin destroying paper and electronic Enron-related records on October 23, 2001. Kimberly Latham, a subordinate to Duncan, sent instructions on October 24, 2001, to her entire team to follow Duncan's orders and even compiled a list of computer files to delete. Arthur Andersen blames Duncan for destroying thousands of Enron-related documents. Duncan blames the Arthur Andersen attorney, Nancy Temple, for sending him a memo instructing him to destroy files. Temple blames Arthur Andersen's document deletion policies.[46]

Regardless of who is to blame, the bigger issue is that the destruction of files after a federal investigation has begun is both unethical and illegal. A direct corporate order to destroy information currently under federal investigation poses a dilemma for any professional. Comply, and you participate in potentially criminal activities; refuse, and you might find yourself looking for a new job.[47]

Privacy is one of the biggest ethical issues facing organizations today. Trust between companies, customers, partners, and suppliers is the support structure of the e-business world. One of the main ingredients in trust is privacy. Widespread fear about privacy continues to be one of the biggest barriers to the growth of e-business. People are concerned their privacy will be violated as a consequence of interactions on the Web. Unless an organization can effectively address this issue of privacy, its customers, partners, and suppliers may lose trust in the organization, which hurts its business. Figure 5.5 displays the results from a *CIO* survey as to how privacy issues reduce trust for e-business.[48]

Ethics

Privacy

Intellectual property	Intangible creative work that is embodied in physical form.
Copyright	The legal protection afforded an expression of an idea, such as a song, video game, and some types of proprietary documents.
Fair use doctrine	In certain situations, it is legal to use copyrighted material.
Pirated software	The unauthorized use, duplication, distribution, or sale of copyrighted software.
Counterfeit software	Software that is manufactured to look like the real thing and sold as such.

FIGURE 5.4

Issues Affected by Technology Advances

FIGURE 5.5

Primary Reasons Privacy Issues Reduce Trust for E-Business

1. Loss of personal privacy is a top concern for Americans in the 21st century.
2. Among Internet users, 37 percent would be "a lot" more inclined to purchase a product on a Web site that had a privacy policy.
3. Privacy/security is the number one factor that would convert Internet researchers into Internet buyers.

SECURITY

State Farm Bank

Smoking is not just bad for a person's health; it seems that it is also bad for company security, according to a new study. With companies banning smoking inside their offices, smokers are forced outside—usually to specific smoking areas in the back of the building. The doors leading out to them are a major security hole, according to a study undertaken by NTA Monitor Ltd., a U.K.-based Internet security tester.

NTA's tester was able to easily get inside a corporate building through a back door that was left open so smokers could easily and quickly get out and then back in, according to the company. Once inside, the tester asked an employee to take him to a meeting room, claiming that the IT department had sent him. Even without a pass, he reportedly gained access unchallenged and was then able to connect his laptop to the company's network.[49]

Organizational information is intellectual capital. Just as organizations protect their assets—keeping their money in an insured bank or providing a safe working environment for employees—they must also protect their intellectual capital. An organization's intellectual capital includes everything from its patents to its transactional and analytical information. With security breaches on the rise and computer hackers everywhere, an organization must put in place strong security measures to survive.

The Health Insurance Portability and Accountability Act (HIPAA) protects the privacy and security of personal health records and has the potential to impact every business in the United States.[50] HIPAA affects all companies that use electronic data interchange (EDI) to communicate personal health records. HIPAA requires health care organizations to develop, implement, and maintain appropriate security measures when sending electronic health information. Most important, these organizations must document and keep current records detailing how they are performing security measures for all transmissions of health information. On April 21, 2005, security rules for HIPAA became enforceable by law.[51]

According to recent Gartner polls, less than 10 percent of all health care organizations have begun to implement the security policies and procedures required by HIPAA. The Health Information Management Society estimates that 70 percent of all health care providers failed to meet the April 2005 deadline for privacy rule compliance. Health care organizations need to start taking HIPAA regulations seriously since noncompliance can result in substantial fines and even imprisonment.[52]

Beyond the health care industry, all businesses must understand the importance of information security, even if it is not enforceable by law. *Information security* is a broad term encompassing the protection of information from accidental or intentional misuse by persons inside or outside an organization. With current advances in technologies and business strategies such as CRM, organizations are able to determine valuable information—such as who are the top 20 percent of their customers who produce 80 percent of their revenues. Most organizations view this type of information as valuable intellectual capital, and they are implementing security measures to prevent the information from walking out the door or falling into the wrong hands.

Security

Adding to the complexity of information security is the fact that organizations must enable employees, customers, and partners to access all sorts of information electronically to be successful. Doing business electronically automatically creates tremendous information security risks for organizations. There are many technical aspects of security, but the biggest information security issue is not technical, but human. Most information security breaches result from people misusing

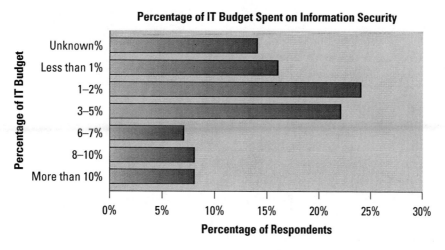

FIGURE 5.6

Organizational Spending on Information Security

an organization's information either intentionally or inadvertently. For example, many individuals freely give up their passwords or leave them on sticky notes next to their computers, leaving the door wide open to intruders.

Figure 5.6 displays the typical size of an organization's information security budget relative to the organization's overall IT budget from the CSI/FBI 2004 Computer Crime and Security Survey. Forty-six percent of respondents indicated that their organization spent between 1 and 5 percent of the total IT budget on security. Only 16 percent indicated that their organization spent less than 1 percent of the IT budget on security.[53]

Figure 5.7 displays the spending per employee on computer security broken down by both public and private industries. The highest average computer security investment per employee was found in the transportation industry.[54]

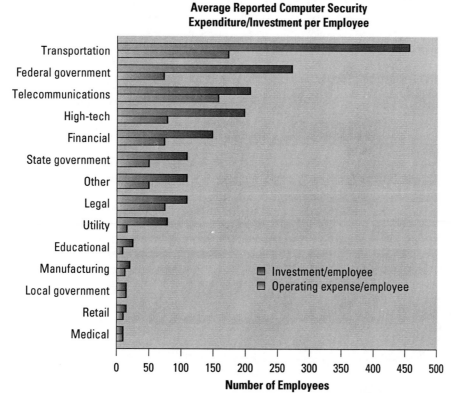

FIGURE 5.7

Computer Security Expenditures/Investments by Industry

Security is perhaps the most fundamental and critical of all the technologies/ disciplines an organization must have squarely in place to execute its business strategy. Without solid security processes and procedures, none of the other technologies can develop business advantages.

OPENING CASE STUDY QUESTIONS

1. Predict what might have happened to Apple if its top executives had not supported investments in IT.

2. Explain why it would be unethical for Apple to allow its customers to download free music from iTunes.

3. Evaluate the effects on Apple's business if it failed to secure its customer information and all of it was accidentally posted to an anonymous Web site.

4. Explain why Apple should have a CIO, CTO, CPO, CSO, and CKO.

5. Describe how the Nike+iPod SportKit caused security issues for the company. Do you think Nike or Apple acted unethically when they developed the SportKit? Why or why not?

Chapter Five Case: Executive Dilemmas in the Information Age

The vast array of business initiatives from supply chain management, customer relationship management, business process reengineering, and enterprise resource planning makes it clear that information technology has evolved beyond the role of mere infrastructure to the support of business strategy. Today, in more and more industries, IT is a business strategy and is quickly becoming a survival issue.

Board and executive team agendas are increasingly peppered with, or even hijacked by, a growing range of IT issues from compliance to ethics and security. In most companies today, computers are key business tools. They generate, process, and store the majority of critical business information. Executives must understand how IT can affect a business by successfully addressing a wide range of needs—from large electronic discovery projects to the online review of document collections by geographically dispersed teams. A few examples of executive IT issues follow.

Stolen Proprietary Information

A computer company investigated to determine if an executive who accepted a job with a competitor stole proprietary information. The hard drive from the executive's laptop and desktop machine were forensically imaged. The analysis established that the night before the executive left, he downloaded all of the company's process specifications and distributor agreements, which he then zipped and e-mailed to the competitor. Additionally, reconstruction of deleted files located e-mails between the executive and the competitor discussing his intent to provide the proprietary information if he was offered additional options in the new company.

Sexual Harassment

A woman employed by a large defense contractor accused her supervisor of sexual harassment. The woman was fired from her job for poor performance and subsequently sued her ex-boss and the former employer.

A computer company was retained by the plaintiff's attorneys to investigate allegations of the former supervisor's harassing behavior. After making a forensic image backup of the ex-boss's hard drive, the forensic company was able to recover deleted electronic messages that showed the ex-boss had a history of propositioning women under his supervision for "special favors." A situation that might have been mired in a "he said/she said" controversy was quickly resolved; the woman got her job back, and the real culprit was terminated.

Stolen Trade Secrets

The board of directors of a technical research company demoted the company's founder and CEO. The executive, disgruntled because of his demotion, was later terminated. It was subsequently determined that the executive had planned to quit about the same time he was fired and establish a competitive company. Upon his termination, the executive took home two computers; he returned them to the company four days later, along with another company computer that he had previously used at home. Suspicious that critical information had been taken, the company's attorneys sent the computers to a computer forensic company for examination.

After making a forensic image backup of the hard drives, the forensic analysis identified a file directory that had been deleted during the aforementioned four-day period that had the same name as the competing company the executive had established. A specific search of the deleted files in this directory identified the executive's "to do list" file. This file indicated the executive planned to copy the company's database (valued at $100 million) for his personal use. Another item specified the executive was to "learn how to destroy evidence on a computer."

The computer forensic company's examination also proved that the executive had been communicating with other competing companies to establish alliances, in violation of the executive's nondisclosure agreement with the company. It was also shown that numerous key company files were located on removable computer storage media that had not been turned over by the executive to the company.[55]

Questions

1. Explain why understanding technology, especially in the areas of security and ethics, is important for a CEO. How do a CEO's actions affect the organizational culture?
2. Identify why executives in nontechnological industries need to worry about technology and its potential business ramifications.
3. Describe why continuously learning about technology allows an executive to better analyze threats and opportunities.
4. Identify three things that a CTO, CPO, or CSO could do to prevent the above issues.

<< BUSINESS PLUG-IN POINTERS

Review the Business Plug-In B6 "Information Security" for an overview of security issues and features including information security policies and plans, hackers, viruses, public key encryption, digital certificates, digital signatures, firewalls, and authentication, authorization, and detection and response technologies.

Review the Business Plug-In B7 "Ethics" for an overview of privacy laws, ethical computer use policy, Internet use policy, information privacy policy, acceptable use policy, e-mail privacy policy, anti-spam policy, monitoring technologies, and monitoring policies.

✳ UNIT SUMMARY

Understanding and working with technology have become an integral part of life in the 21st century. Most students take courses in various disciplines in their educational careers, such as in marketing, operations management, management, finance, accounting, and information technology, each of which is designed to provide insight into the tasks of each functional area. In the business world, these are all intertwined and inextricably linked.

Information technology can be an important enabler of business success and innovation and is most useful when it leverages the talents of people. Technology in and of itself is not useful unless the right people know how to use and manage it effectively.

Organizations use information technology to capture, process, organize, distribute, and massage information. Information technology enables an organization to:

- Integrate all functional areas and the tasks they perform.
- Gain an enterprisewide view of its operations.
- Efficiently and effectively utilize resources.
- Realize tremendous market and industry growth by gaining insight into the market at large (through environmental scanning) and insight into internal operations.

✳ KEY TERMS

Balanced scorcard, 42
Benchmark, 37
Benchmarking, 37
Business intelligence, 11
Business process, 21, 30
Business process
  reengineering (BPR), 30
Business-to-business (B2B)
  marketplace, 19
Buyer power, 18
Chief information officer
  (CIO), 46
Chief knowledge officer
  (CKO), 47
Chief privacy officer (CPO), 47
Chief security officer
  (CSO), 47
Chief technology officer
  (CTO), 47
Competitive advantage, 17
Copyright, 49
Counterfeit software, 49

Customer relationship
  management (CRM), 28
Data, 10
Effectiveness IT metrics, 37
Efficiency IT metrics, 37
Enterprise resource planning
  (ERP), 31
Entry barrier, 19
Environmental scanning, 17
Ethics, 49
Fair use doctrine, 49
First-mover advantage, 17
Five Forces Model, 18
Information, 10
Information accuracy, 38
Information security, 50
Information technology
  (IT), 9
Intellectual property, 49
Key performance indicator
  (KPI), 37
Loyalty program, 18

Management information
  systems (MIS), 9
Pirated software, 49
Privacy, 49
Private exchange, 19
Response time, 38
Reverse auction, 19
Rivalry among existing
  competitors, 20
Supplier power, 18
Supply chain, 18
Supply chain management
  (SCM), 26
System availability, 38
Switching cost, 19
Threat of new entrants, 19
Threat of substitute products or
  services, 19
Throughput, 38
Transaction speed, 38
Value chain, 21
Web traffic, 38

Baltzan–Phillips–Haag:
Business Driven
Technology, Third Edition

I. Achieving Business
Success

Unit Summary

© The McGraw–Hill
Companies, 2009

55

★ UNIT CLOSING CASE ONE

How Levi's Jeans Got into Wal-Mart

People around the world recognize Levi's as an American icon, the cool jeans worn by movie stars James Dean and Marilyn Monroe. However, the company failed to keep up with the fast-changing tastes of American teenagers. In particular, it missed the trend to baggy jeans that caught hold in the mid-1990s. Sales plummeted from $7.1 billion in 1996 to $4.1 billion in 2003, and Levi Strauss & Co.'s U.S. market share dropped from 18.7 percent in 1997 to 12 percent in 2003, a huge decline in both dollars and market share.

Analyzing and Responding to What Happened

Competition hit Levi Strauss on both the high and low ends. Fashion-conscious buyers were drawn to high-priced brands like Blue Cult, Juicy, and Seven, which had more fashion ca-chet than Levi's. On the low end, parents were buying Wrangler and Lee jeans for their kids because on average they cost about $10 less than Levi's Red Tab brand. Wrangler and Lee were also the brands they found at discount retailers such as Wal-Mart, Target, and T. J. Maxx. David Bergen, Levi's chief information officer (CIO), described the company as "getting squeezed," and "caught in the jaws of death."

CEO Philip A. Marineau came to Levi Strauss from PepsiCo in 1999, a year after he helped PepsiCo surpass Coca-Cola in sales for the first time. Marineau recruited Bergen in 2000 from Carstation.com. Marineau quickly realized that turning Levi's around would entail manufacturing, marketing, and distributing jeans that customers demanded, particularly customers at the low end where the mass market was located.

Bergen was eager to join Marineau's team because of his background in clothing, retailing, and manufacturing with companies such as The Gap and Esprit de Corps in the 1980s. He knew that Marineau's plan to anticipate customer wants would require up-to-date IT applications such as data warehousing, data mining, and customer relationship management (CRM) systems. He also knew that selling to mass market retailers would require upgrades to Levi's supply chain management (SCM) systems, and he understood that globalization would necessitate standardized enterprise resource planning (ERP) systems. Overall, it was a challenge any ambitious CIO would covet. After all, designing and installing IT systems that drive and achieve key business initiatives is what it is all about.

Joining Wal-Mart

Wal-Mart was a pioneer in supply chain management systems, having learned early on that driving costs out of the supply chain would let the company offer products to customers at the lowest possible prices, while at the same time assuring that products the customers demanded were always on the stores shelves. Becoming one of Wal-Mart's 30,000 suppliers is not easy. Wal-Mart insists that its suppliers do business using up-to-date IT systems to manage the supply chain—not just the supply chain between Wal-Mart and its suppliers, but the supply chains between the suppliers and their suppliers as well. Wal-Mart has strict supply chain management system requirements that its business partners must meet.

Wal-Mart's requirements presented Levi Strauss with a serious hurdle to overcome because its supply chain management systems were in bad shape. Executives did not even have access to key information required to track where Levi products were moving in the supply chain. For example, they did not know how many pairs of jeans were in the factory awaiting shipment, how many were somewhere en route, or how many had just been unloaded at a customer's warehouse. According to Greg Hammann, Levi's U.S. chief customer officer, "Our supply chain could not deliver the services Wal-Mart expected."

Bergen created a cross-functional team of key managers from IT, finance, and sales to transform Levi's systems to meet Wal-Mart's requirements. Their recommendations included network upgrades, modifications to ordering and logistics applications, and data warehouse improvements. Although Bergen realized that about half the changes required to accommodate the state-of-the-art demands of Wal-Mart would be a waste of resources because these systems were being replaced by a new SAP enterprise software system over the next five years, the company could not wait for the SAP installation if it wanted Wal-Mart's business now, so it decided to move forward with the changes.

Levi's successful transformation of its supply chain management system allowed the company to partner with Wal-Mart. The company introduced at Wal-Mart its new signature line, which sells for around $23 and has fewer details in the finish than Levi's other lines; no trademark pocket stitching or red tab, for example. Wal-Mart wants big-name brands to lure more affluent customers into its stores, while still maintaining the low price points all Wal-Mart customers have come to expect. Wal-Mart Senior Vice President Lois Mikita notes that Wal-Mart "continues to tailor its selection to meet the needs of customers from a cross section of income levels and lifestyles." She also states she is impressed with the level of detail Levi's has put into its systems transformation efforts to "make the execution of this new launch 100 percent."

Achieving Business Success Through IT

Bergen's changes were a success and the percentage of products delivered on time quickly rose from 65 percent to 95 percent primarily because of the updated supply chain management system. Levi's total sales were also up in the third and fourth quarters of 2003, for the first time since 1996. In 2003, Levi's appeared on NPD Fashionworld's top 10 list of brands preferred by young women, ending an absence of several years. Marshall Cohen, a senior industry analyst at NPD Groups Fashionworld, a research group that tracks apparel and footwear market trends, noted that Levi's "hadn't been close to that for a while. Teens hadn't gravitated toward Levi's in years. That was incredible. A lot of that has to do with having the right style in the right place at the right time." The improved systems, Cohen noted, also helped the company get the right sizes to the right stores.

Another highly successful IT system implemented by Levi Strauss is a digital dashboard that executives can display on their PC screens. The dashboard lets an executive see the status of a product as it moves from the factory floor to distribution centers to retail stores. For example, the dashboard can display how Levi's 501 jeans are selling at an individual Kohl's store compared to forecasted sales. "When I first got here, I didn't see anything," Hammann says. "Now I can drill down to the product level."

The digital dashboard alerts executives to trends that under the previous systems would have taken weeks to detect. For example, in 2002 Levi Strauss started to ship Dockers Stain Defender pants. Expected sales for the pants were around 2 million pairs. The digital dashboard quickly notified key executives that the trousers were selling around 2.5 million pairs.

This information enabled them to adjust production upward in time to ship more pants, meet the increased demand, and avoid lost sales. The company also uses the systems to control supply during key seasonal sales periods such as back-to-school and Christmas.

"If I look overconfident, I'm not," says Bergen. "I'm very nervous about this change. When we trip, we have to stand up real quick and get back on the horse, as they say." As if to reinforce Bergen's point, Gib Carey, a supply chain analyst at Bain, notes, "The place where companies do fail is when they aren't bringing anything new to Wal-Mart. Wal-Mart is constantly looking at 'How can I get the same product I am selling today at a lower price somewhere else?' "[56]

Questions

1. Explain how Levi Strauss & Co. achieved business success through the use of information, information technology, and people.

2. Using Porter's Five Forces Model, analyze Levi Strauss's buyer power and supplier power. Which of Porter's Five Forces did Levi Strauss address through the implementation of its updated supply chain management system?

3. Which of the three generic strategies is the company following?

4. Evaluate how Levi Strauss can gain business intelligence through the implementation of a customer relationship management system.

5. How can Levi Strauss use efficiency IT metrics and effectiveness IT metrics to improve its business?

6. David Bergen, Levi Strauss CIO, put together a cross-functional team of key managers from IT, finance, and sales to transform the company's systems to meet Wal-Mart's requirements. Analyze the relationships between these three business areas and determine why Bergen chose them to be a part of his cross-functional team.

7. Predict what might happen to Wal-Mart's business if it failed to secure its partner's information and all sales information for all products was accidentally posted to an anonymous Web site.

✳ UNIT CLOSING CASE TWO

Business 2.0: Bad Business Decisions

Business 2.0 magazine looked at the top 100 bad business decisions of all time including bungled layoffs, customer-service snafus, executive follies, and other madness. Five of the top 10 bad business decisions of all time were made because business personnel did not understand information technology; these five are highlighted below. Perhaps one good reason to pay attention in this course is so that you will not end-up on Business 2.0's bad business decisions![57]

Bad Business Decision 3 of 10: Starbucks

Winner: Dumbest Moment—Marketing

Starbucks directs baristas in the Southeastern United States to e-mail a coupon for a free iced coffee to friends and family members. But e-mail knows no geographic boundaries and, worse, can be printed repeatedly.

After the e-mail spreads to every corner of the country and is reproduced en masse, Starbucks yanks the offer, leading disgruntled customer Kelly Coakley to file a $114 million class-action lawsuit.

Bad Business Decision 4 of 10: Radioshack

Winner: Dumbest Moment—Human Resources

From: RadioShack
To: RadioShack employees
Subject: Your former job

RadioShack fires 400 staffers via e-mail. Affected employees receive a message that reads, "The work force reduction notification is currently in progress. Unfortunately your position is one that has been eliminated."

Bad Business Decision 7 of 10: AOL

Winner: Dumbest Moment—Data Security

In an "attempt to reach out to the academic community with new research tools," AOL releases the search queries of 657,000 users.

Though AOL insists that the information contains no personally identifiable data, *The New York Times* and other news outlets promptly identify a number of specific users, including searcher No. 4417749, soon-to-be-ex-AOL-subscriber Thelma Arnold of Lilburn, Georgia, whose queries include "women's underwear" and "dog that urinates on everything."

The gaffe leads to the resignation of AOL's chief technology officer and a half-billion-dollar class-action lawsuit.

Bad Business Decision 8 of 10: UCLA

Winner: Dumbest Moment—E-Commerce

On the morning of April 3, 2006, Amazon.com sends an e-mail headed "UCLA Wins!" to virtually everyone to whom it has ever sold a sports-related item, attempting to hawk a cap celebrating the Bruins' stirring victory in college basketball's championship game.

Just one problem: The game isn't scheduled to be played until later that night. When it is, UCLA is trounced by Florida, 73–57.

Bad Business Decision 9 of 10: Bank of America

Winner: Dumbest Moment—Outsourcing

After Bank of America announces plans to outsource 100 tech support jobs from the San Francisco Bay Area to India, the American workers are told that they must train their own replacements in order to receive their severance payments.

Here are a few other bad ones that did not make the top 10, but are worth mentioning.

Bad Business Decision: McDonald's

Guess the translator took the phrase "viral marketing" a bit too literally. McDonald's runs a promotional contest in Japan in which it gives away 10,000 Mickey D's-branded MP3 players.

The gadgets come preloaded with 10 songs—and, in some cases, a version of the QQPass family of Trojan horse viruses, which, when uploaded to a PC, seek to capture passwords, user names, and other data and then forward them to hackers.

Bad Business Decision: General Motors

Then again, viral marketing can be messed up in English too. As part of a cross promotion with the NBCTV show *The Apprentice*, GM launches a contest to promote its Chevy Tahoe SUV. At Chevyapprentice.com, viewers are given video and music clips with which to create their own 30-second commercials.

Among the new Tahoe ads that soon proliferate across the Web are ones with taglines like "Yesterday's technology today" and "Global warming isn't a pretty SUV ad—it's a frightening reality."

Bad Business Decision: New York Times Company

We were wondering how Billy the paperboy could afford that gold-plated Huffy. News carriers and retailers in Worcester, Massachusetts, get an unexpected bonus with their usual shipment of the *Telegram & Gazette:* the credit and debit card numbers of 240,000 subscribers to the paper and its sister publication, the *Boston Globe,* both owned by the New York Times Co.

The security breach is the result of a recycling program in which paper from the *Telegram & Gazette*'s business office is reused to wrap bundles of newspapers.

Bad Business Decision: Sony

PC-B-Q. Defects in batteries made by Sony for portable computing cause a handful of notebooks to burst into spectacularly photogenic flames.

The end result is the biggest computer-related recall ever, as Dell replaces the batteries in more than 4 million laptops. In short order, Apple (1.8 million), Lenovo/IBM (500,000), and others do the same.[58]

QUESTION

1. Explain why understanding information technology and management information systems can help you achieve business success—or more importantly, help you avoid business disasters—regardless of your major.

✳ MAKING BUSINESS DECISIONS

1. **Competitive Analysis**

   Cheryl O'Connell is the owner of a small, high-end retailer of women's clothing called Excelus. Excelus's business has been successful for many years, largely because of Cheryl's ability to anticipate the needs and wants of her loyal customer base and provide them with personalized service. Cheryl does not see any value in IT and does not want to invest any capital in something that will not directly affect her bottom line. Develop a proposal describing the potential IT-enabled competitive opportunities or threats Cheryl might be missing by not embracing IT. Be sure to include a Porter's Five Forces analysis and discuss which one of the three generic strategies Cheryl should pursue.

2. **Using Efficiency and Effectiveness Metrics**

   You are the CEO of a 500-bed acute care general hospital. Your internal IT department is responsible for running applications that support both administrative functions (e.g., patient accounting) as well as medical applications (e.g., medical records). You need assurance that your IT department is a high quality operation in comparison to similar hospitals. What metrics should you ask your CIO to provide you to give the assurance you seek? Provide the reasoning behind each suggested metric. Also, determine how the interrelationship between efficiency metrics and effectiveness metrics can drive your business's success.

3. Building Business Relationships

Synergistics Inc. is a start-up company that specializes in helping businesses build successful internal relationships. You have recently been promoted to senior manager of the Business and IT Relationship area. Sales for your new department have dwindled over the last two years for a variety of reasons including the burst of the technological stock bubble, recent economic conditions, and a poorly communicated business strategy. Your first task on the job is to prepare a report detailing the following:

- Fundamental reasons for the gap between the IT and business sides.
- Strategies you can take to convince your customers that this is an area that is critical to the success of their business.
- Strategies your customers can follow to ensure that synergies exist between the two sides.

4. Acting Ethically

Assume you are an IT manager and one of your projects is failing. You were against the project from the start; however, the project had powerful sponsorship from all of the top executives. You know that you are doomed and that the project is doomed. The reasons for the failure are numerous including the initial budget was drastically understated, the technology is evolving and not stable, the architecture was never scaled for growth, and your resources do not have the necessary development skills for the new technology. One of your team leads has come to you with a plan to sabotage the project that would put the project out of its misery without assigning any blame to the individuals on the project. Create a document detailing how you would handle this situation.

5. Determining IT Organizational Structures

You are the chief executive officer for a start-up telecommunications company. The company currently has 50 employees and plans to ramp up to 3,000 by the end of the year. Your first task is to determine how you are going to model your organization. You decide to address the IT department's organizational structure first. You need to consider if you want to have a CIO, CPO, CSO, CTO, and CKO, and if so, what their reporting structure will look like and why. You also need to determine the different roles and responsibilities for each executive position. Once you have compiled this information, put together a presentation describing your IT department's organizational structure.

6. Comparing CRM Vendors

As a team, search the Internet for at least one recent and authoritative article that compares or ranks customer relationship management systems. Select two packages from the list and compare their functions and features as described in the article(s) you found as well as on each company's Web site. Find references in the literature where companies that are using each package have reported their experiences, both good and bad. Draw on any other comparisons you can find. Prepare a presentation for delivery in class on the strengths and weaknesses of each package, which one you favor, and why.

7. Applying the Three Generic Strategies

The unit discussed examples of companies that pursue differentiated strategies so that they are not forced into positions where they must compete solely on the basis of price.

Pick an industry and have your team members find and compare two companies, one that is competing on the basis of price and another that has chosen to pursue a differentiated strategy enabled by the creative use of IT. Some industries you may want to consider are clothing retailers, grocery stores, airlines, and personal computers. Prepare a presentation for the class on the ways that IT is being used to help the differentiating company compete against the low-cost provider. Before you begin, spend some class time to make sure each team selects a different industry if at all possible.

8. The Five Forces Model

Your team is working for a small investment company that specializes in technology investments. A new company, Geyser, has just released an operating system that plans to compete with Microsoft's operating systems. Your company has a significant amount of capital invested in Microsoft. Your boss, Jan Savage, has asked you to compile a Porter's Five Forces analysis for Microsoft to ensure that your company's Microsoft investment is not at risk.

✳ APPLY YOUR KNOWLEDGE

1. Capitalizing on Your Career

Business leaders need to be involved in information technology—any computer-based tool that people use to work with information and support the information and information-processing needs of an organization—for the following (primary) reasons:

- The sheer magnitude of the dollars spent on IT must be managed to ensure business value.
- Research has consistently shown that when business leaders are involved in information technology, it enables a number of business initiatives, such as gaining a competitive advantage, streamlining business processes, and even transforming entire organizations.
- Research has consistently shown that when business leaders are not involved in IT, systems fail, revenue is lost, and even entire companies can fail as a result of poorly managed IT.

One of the biggest challenges facing organizations is, "How do we get general business leaders involved in IT?" Research has shown that involvement is highly correlated with personal experience with IT and IT education, including university classes and IT executive seminars. Once general business leaders understand IT through experience and education, they are more likely to be involved in IT, and more likely to lead their organizations in achieving business success through IT.

Project Focus

1. Search the Internet to find examples of the types of technologies that are currently used in the field or industry that you plan to pursue. For example, if you are planning on a career in accounting or finance, you should become familiar with financial systems such as Oracle Financials. If you are planning a career in logistics or distribution, you should research supply chain management systems. If you are planning a career in marketing, you should research customer relationship management systems, blogs, and e-marketing.

2. IT is described as an enabler/facilitator of competitive advantage, organizational effectiveness, and organizational efficiency. As a competitive tool, IT can differentiate an organization's products, services, and prices from its competitors by improving product quality, shortening product development or delivery time, creating new IT-based products and

services, and improving customer service before, during, and after a transaction. Search the Internet and find several examples of companies in the industry where you plan to work that have achieved a competitive advantage through IT.

3. Create a simple report of your findings; include a brief overview of the type of technologies you found and how organizations are using them to achieve a competitive advantage.

2. Achieving Alignment

Most companies would like to be in the market-leading position of JetBlue, Dell, or Wal-Mart, all of which have used information technology to secure their respective spots in the marketplace. These companies have a relentless goal of keeping the cost of technology down by combining the best of IT and business leadership.

It takes more than a simple handshake between groups to start on the journey toward financial gains; it requires operational discipline and a linkage between business and technology units. Only recently have companies not on the "path for profits" followed the lead of their successful counterparts, requiring more operational discipline from their IT groups as well as more IT participation from their business units. Bridging this gap is one of the greatest breakthroughs a company can make.

Companies that master the art of finely tuned, cost-effective IT management will have a major advantage. Their success will force their competitors to also master the art or fail miserably. This phenomenon has already occurred in the retail and wholesale distribution markets, which have had to react to Wal-Mart's IT mastery, as one example. Other industries will follow. This trend will change not only the face of IT, but also the future of corporate America.

As world markets continue to grow, the potential gains are greater than ever. However, so are the potential losses. The future belongs to those who are perceptive enough to grasp the significance of IT and resourceful enough to synchronize business management and information technology.

Project Focus

1. Use any resource to answer the question, "Why is business-IT alignment so difficult?" Use the following questions to begin your analysis:
   a. How do companies prioritize the demands of various business units as they relate to IT?
   b. What are some of the greatest IT challenges for the coming year?
   c. What drives IT decisions?
   d. Who or what is the moving force behind IT decisions?
   e. What types of efficiency metrics and effectiveness metrics might these companies use to measure the impact of IT?
   f. How can a company use financial metrics to monitor and measure IT investments?
   g. What are some of the issues with using financial metrics to evaluate IT?

3. Market Dissection

To illustrate the use of the three generic strategies, consider Figure AYK.1. The matrix shown demonstrates the relationships among strategies (cost leadership versus differentiation) and market segmentation (broad versus focused).

- Hyundai is following a broad cost leadership strategy. Hyundai offers low-cost vehicles, in each particular model stratification, that appeal to a large audience.
- Audi is pursuing a broad differentiation strategy with its Quattro models available at several price points. Audi's differentiation is safety and it prices its various Quattro models (higher than Hyundai) to reach a large, stratified audience.

| | Cost Leadership strategy | Differentiation strategy |

Broad market

Focused market

FIGURE AYK.1

Porter's Three Generic Strategies

- Kia has a more focused cost leadership strategy. Kia mainly offers low-cost vehicles in the lower levels of model stratification.
- Hummer offers the most focused differentiation strategy of any in the industry (including Mercedes-Benz).

Project Focus Focus

Create a similar graph displaying each strategy for a product of your choice. The strategy must include an example of the product in each of the following markets: (1) cost leadership, broad market, (2) differentiation, broad market, (3) cost leadership, focused market, and (4) differentiation, focused market. Potential products include:

- Cereal
- Dog food
- Soft drinks
- Computers
- Shampoo
- Snack foods
- Jeans
- Sneakers
- Sandals
- Mountain bikes
- TV shows
- Movies

4. Grading Security

Making The Grade is a nonprofit organization that helps students learn how to achieve better grades in school. The organization has 40 offices in 25 states and more than 2,000 employees. The company wants to build a Web site to offer its services online. Making The Grade's online services will provide parents seven key pieces of advice for communicating with their children to help them achieve academic success. The Web site will offer information on how to maintain open lines of communication, set goals, organize academics, regularly track progress, identify trouble spots, get to know their child's teacher, and celebrate their children's successes.

Project Focus

You and your team work for the director of information security. Your team's assignment is to develop a document discussing the importance of creating information security polices and an information security plan. Be sure to include the following:

- The importance of educating employees on information security.
- A few samples of employee information security policies specifically for Making The Grade.
- Other major areas the information security plan should address.
- Signs the company should look for to determine if the Web site is being hacked.
- The major types of attacks the company should expect to experience.

5. Eyes Everywhere

The movie *Minority Report* chronicled a futuristic world where people are uniquely identifiable by their eyes. A scan of each person's eyes gives or denies them access to rooms, computers, and anything else with restrictions. The movie portrayed a black market in new eyeballs to help people hide from the authorities. (Why did they not just change the database entry instead? That would have been much easier, but a lot less dramatic.)

The idea of using a biological signature is entirely plausible since biometrics is currently being widely used and is expected to gain wider acceptance in the near future because forging documents has become much easier with the advances in computer graphics programs and color printers. The next time you get a new passport, it may incorporate a chip that has your biometric information encoded on it. Office of Special Investigations agents with fake documents found that it was relatively easy to enter the United States from Canada, Mexico, and Jamaica, by land, sea, and air.

The task of policing the borders is daunting. Some 500 million foreigners enter the country every year and go through identity checkpoints. More than 13 million permanent-resident and border-crossing cards have been issued by the U.S. government. Also, citizens of 27 countries do not need visas to enter this country. They are expected to have passports that comply with U.S. specifications that will also be readable at the border.

In the post-9/11 atmosphere of tightened security, unrestricted border crossing is not acceptable. The Department of Homeland Security is charged with securing the nation's borders, and as part of this plan, new entry/exit procedures were instituted at the beginning of 2003. An integrated system, using biometrics, will be used to identify foreign visitors to the United States and reduce the likelihood of terrorists entering the country.

Early in 2003, after 6 million biometric border-crossing cards had been issued, a pilot test conducted at the Canadian border detected more than 250 imposters. The testing started with two biometric identifiers: photographs for facial recognition and fingerprint scans. As people enter and leave the country, their actual fingerprints and facial features are compared to the data on the biometric chip in the passport.[59]

Project Focus

In a group, discuss the following:

1. How do you feel about having your fingerprints, facial features, and perhaps more of your biometric features encoded in documents like your passport? Explain your answer.
2. Would you feel the same way about having biometric information on your driver's license as on your passport? Why or why not?

3. Is it reasonable to have different biometric identification requirements for visitors from different nations? Explain your answer. What would you recommend as criteria for deciding which countries fall into what categories?

4. The checkpoints U.S. citizens pass through upon returning to the country vary greatly in the depth of the checks and the time spent. The simplest involves simply walking past the border guards who may or may not ask you your citizenship. The other end of the spectrum requires that you put up with long waits in airports where you have to line up with hundreds of other passengers while each person is questioned and must produce a passport to be scanned. Would you welcome biometric information on passports if it would speed the process, or do you think that the disadvantages of the reduction in privacy, caused by biometric information, outweigh the advantages of better security and faster border processing? Explain your answer.

6. Setting Boundaries

Even the most ethical people sometimes face difficult choices. Acting ethically means behaving in a principled fashion and treating other people with respect and dignity. It is simple to say, but not so simple to do since some situations are complex or ambiguous. The important role of ethics in our lives has long been recognized. As far back as 44 B.C., Cicero said that ethics are indispensable to anyone who wants to have a good career. Having said that, Cicero, along with some of the greatest minds over the centuries, struggled with what the rules of ethics should be.

Our ethics are rooted in our history, culture, and religion, and our sense of ethics may shift over time. The electronic age brings with it a new dimension in the ethics debate—the amount of personal information that we can collect and store, and the speed with which we can access and process that information.[60]

Project Focus

In a group, discuss how you would react to the following situations:

1. A senior marketing manager informs you that one of her employees is looking for another job and she wants you to give her access to look through her e-mail.
2. A vice president of sales informs you that he has made a deal to provide customer information to a strategic partner, and he wants you to burn all of the customer information onto a DVD.
3. You are asked to monitor your employee's e-mail to discover if he is sexually harassing another employee.
4. You are asked to install a video surveillance system in your office to watch if employees are taking office supplies home with them.
5. You are looking on the shared network drive and discover that your boss's entire hard drive has been copied to the network for everyone to view. What do you do?
6. You have been accidentally copied on an e-mail from the CEO, which details who will be the targets of the next round of layoffs. What would you do?

7. Porter's Five Forces

Porter's Five Forces Model is an easy framework to understand market forces. Break into groups and choose two products from the list below to perform a Porter's Five Forces analysis.

- Laptop computer and desktop computer.
- PDA and laptop computer.
- iPod and Walkman.
- DVD player and VCR player.
- Digital camera and Polaroid camera.

- Cell phone and Blackberry PDA.
- Coca-Cola plastic bottle and Coca-Cola glass bottle.
- GPS device and a road atlas.
- Roller skates and Rollerblades.
- Digital books and printed books.
- Digital paper and paper.

8. Measuring Efficiency and Effectiveness

In a group, create a plan to measure the efficiency and effectiveness of this course and recommendations on how you could improve the course to make it more efficient and more effective. You must determine ways to benchmark current efficiency and effectiveness and ways to continuously monitor and measure against the benchmarks to determine if the course is becoming more or less efficient and effective (class quizzes and exams are the most obvious benchmarks). Be sure your plan addresses the following:

- Design of the classroom.
- Room temperature.
- Lighting and electronic capabilities of the classroom.
- Technology available in the classroom.
- Length of class.
- E-mail and instant messaging.
- Students' attendance.
- Students' preparation.
- Students' arrival time.
- Quizzes and exams (frequency, length, grades).

9. Discovering Reengineering Opportunities

In an effort to increase efficiency, your college has hired you to analyze its current business processes for registering for classes. Analyze the current business processes from paying tuition to registering for classes and determine which steps in the process are:

- Broken
- Redundant
- Antiquated

Be sure to define how you would reengineer the processes for efficiency.

10. Reorganizing an Organization

The AAA Management Company specializes in the management of rental properties and generates over $20 million in revenues each year and has more than 2,000 employees throughout the United States, Canada, and Mexico. The company has just hired a new CEO, David Paul. David is planning to reorganize the company so that it operates more efficiently and effectively. Next is the new organizational structure that he plans to present to the board of directors on Monday. Break into groups and explain the advantages and disadvantages of such a reporting structure. Reorganize the reporting structure in the way that will be most beneficial to the operations of the company, being sure to justify the new structure.

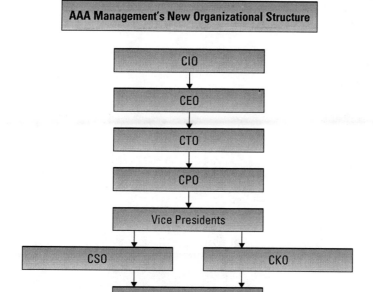

AAA Management's New Organizational Structure

CIO → CEO → CTO → CPO → Vice Presidents → CSO / CKO → Managers → Analysts

11. Contemplating Sharing

Bram Cohen is the creator of one of the most successful peer-to-peer (P2P) programs ever developed, BitTorrent. BitTorrent allows users to quickly upload and download enormous amounts of data, including files that are hundreds or thousands of times bigger than a single MP3. BitTorrent's program is faster and more efficient than traditional P2P networking.

Cohen showed his code to the world at a hacker conference, as a free, open source project aimed at computer users who need a cheap way to swap software online. But the real audience turns out to be TV and movie fanatics. It takes hours to download a ripped episode of *Alias* or *Monk* off Kazaa, but BitTorrent can do it in minutes. As a result, more than 20 million people have downloaded the BitTorrent application. If any one of them misses a favorite TV show, no worries. Surely, someone has posted it as a "torrent." As for movies, if you can find it at Blockbuster, you can probably find it online somewhere—and use BitTorrent to download it. "Give and ye shall receive" became Cohen's motto, which he printed on T-shirts and sold to supporters.[61]

Project Focus

There is much debate surrounding the ethics of peer-to-peer networking. Do you believe BitTorrent is ethical or unethical? Justify your answer.

UNIT

2

Exploring Business Intelligence

CORE UNITS

Unit 1: Achieving Business Success

Unit 2: Exploring Business Intelligence

Unit 3: Streamlining Business Operations

Unit 4: Building Innovation

Unit 5: Transforming Organizations

BUSINESS PLUG-INS

B1. Business Basics

B2. Business Process

B3. Hardware and Software

B4. Enterprise Architectures

B5. Networks and Telecommunications

B6. Information Security

B7. Ethics

B8. Supply Chain Management

B9. Customer Relationship Management

B10. Enterprise Resource Planning

B11. E-Business

B12. Emerging Trends and Technologies

B13. Strategic Outsourcing

B14. Systems Development

B15. Project Management

TECHNOLOGY PLUG-INS

T1. Personal Productivity Using IT

T2. Basic Skills Using Excel

T3. >>Problem Solving Using Excel

T4. Decision Making Using Excel

T5. >>Designing Database Applications

T6. >>Basic Skills Using Access

T7. >>Problem Solving Using Access

T8. Decision Making Using Access

T9. Designing Web Pages

T10. Creating Web Pages Using HTML

T11. Creating Web Pages Using Dreamweaver

T12. Creating Gantt Charts with Excel and Microsoft Project

UNIT TWO OPENING CASE

It Takes a Village to Write an Encyclopedia

The concept of gathering all the world's knowledge in a single place goes back to the ancient Library of Alexandria, but the modern concept of a general-purpose, widely distributed, printed encyclopedia dates from shortly before the 18th century. The Internet has expanded on the concept with the development of Wikipedia. Founded by Jimmy Wales, Wikipedia is a project to produce a free content encyclopedia that can have thousands of contributors and be edited by anyone, and it now contains millions of articles and pages worldwide. Wikipedia ranks among the top 15 online destinations worldwide.

A wiki is a type of Web site connected to a database that allows users to easily add and edit content and is especially suited for collaborative writing. The name is based on the Hawaiian term *wiki,* meaning quick, fast, or to hasten. In essence, wiki is a simplification of the process of creating Web pages combined with a database that records each individual change, so that at any time, a page can be reverted to any of its previous states. A wiki system may also provide tools that allow users to easily monitor the constantly changing state of the wiki and discuss the issues that emerge in trying to achieve a general consensus about wiki content.

Wikipedia Tightens the Reins

Wikipedia is exploding with information. The site originally allowed unrestricted access so that people could contribute without registering. As with any database management system, governance is a key issue. Without governance, there is no control over how information is published and maintained.

When you research Wikipedia, you find stories about how competing companies are removing and editing each other's entries in Wikipedia to gain market share. The *Washington Post* reported that Capitol Hill is playing "WikiPolitics" by editing representatives' and senators' biographies and speeches. Wikipedia had to temporarily block certain Capitol Hill Web addresses from altering entries.

Wikipedia recently began tightening its rules for submitting entries following the disclosure that it ran a piece falsely implicating a man in the Kennedy assassinations.

John Seigenthaler Sr., who was Robert Kennedy's administrative assistant in the early 1960s, wrote an article revealing that Wikipedia had run a biography claiming Seigenthaler had been suspected in the assassinations of the former attorney general and his brother, President John F. Kennedy. Wikipedia now requires users to register before they can create and edit articles.

Wikipedia has grown into a storehouse of pieces on topics ranging from medieval art to nanotechnology. The volume of content is possible because the site relies on volunteers, including many experts in their fields, to submit entries and edit previously submitted articles. The Web site hopes that the registration requirement will limit the number of stories being created. "What we're hopeful to see is that by slowing that down to 1,500 a day from several thousand, the people who are monitoring this will have more ability to improve the quality," Wales said. "In many cases the types of things we see going on are impulse vandalism."

The Future of Wiki

Can the wisdom of crowds trump the genius of Google? Wales believes that it not only can, but it will. Wales plans to launch a new search engine called Wikiasari, and hopes that it could someday overtake Google as the Web search leader.

Like Wikipedia, Wikiasari will rely on the support of a volunteer community of users. The idea is that Web surfers and programmers will be able to bring their collective intelligence to bear, to fine-tune search results and make the experience more effective for everyone. "If you search in Google, a lot of the results are very, very good and a lot of the results are very, very bad," Wales says. What that shows, Wales says, is that mathematical formulas alone do not produce consistently relevant results. "Human intelligence is still a very important part of the process," he says.

People can contribute to Wikiasari in one of two ways. The first is by enabling ordinary computer users to rerank search results. When a user performs a search on Wikiasari, the engine will return results based on a formula akin to Google's Page-Rank system, which determines relevance by counting the number of times other Web pages link to a specific page, among other things. Unlike Google, however, users will then be able to reorder the results based on which links they find most useful by selecting an edit function. Wikiasari's servers will then store the new results along with the original query. When the same query is made in the future, Wikiasari will return the results in the order saved by most users.

Potential Web users with programming knowledge have a second way to contribute. Wikiasari's technology is based on Apache's open-source Web search software Lucene and Nutch, and Wales plans to unveil all the company's computer code to the outside world. This kind of open-source development is in sharp contrast to the approach of the leading search engines, which do not release their search ranking formulas. Yet Wales contends that his open approach will ultimately prevail, because anyone any place in the world can weigh in with tweaks to Wikiasari's code to help return more relevant results.

A Fly in the Wiki

Wikipedia will fail in four years, crushed under the weight of an automated assault by marketers and others seeking online traffic. So says law professor Eric Goldman, who predicts Wikipedia's downfall. Goldman, a professor at the Santa Clara University School of Law, argues that Wikipedia will see increasingly vigorous efforts to subvert its editorial process, much as Digg.com has seen. As marketers become more determined and turn to automated tools to alter Wikipedia entries to generate online traffic, Goldman predicts Wikipedians will burn out trying to keep entries clean.

"Thus, Wikipedia will enter a death spiral where the rate of junkiness will increase rapidly until the site becomes a wasteland," Goldman writes. "Alternatively, to prevent this death spiral, Wikipedia will change its core open-access architecture, increasing the database's vitality by changing its mission somewhat."

As precedent, Goldman cites the fate of the Open Directory Project, a user-edited Web directory, which he says "is now effectively worthless." "I love Wikipedia," Goldman concludes. "I use it every day. Based on the stats from my Google personalized search, Wikipedia is the Number one site I click on from Google search results. So I'm not rooting for it to fail. But the very architecture of Wikipedia contains the seeds of its own destruction. Without fame or fortune, I don't think Wikipedia's incentive system is sustainable."[1]

Introduction

Information is powerful. Information is useful in telling an organization how its current operations are performing and estimating and strategizing how future operations might perform. New perspectives open up when people have the right information and know how to use it. The ability to understand, digest, analyze, and filter information is a key to success for any professional in any industry. Unit Two demonstrates the value an organization can uncover and create by learning how to manage, access, analyze, and protect organizational information. The chapters in Unit Two are:

- **Chapter Six**—Valuing Organizational Information.
- **Chapter Seven**—Storing Organizational Information—Databases.
- **Chapter Eight**—Accessing Organizational Information—Data Warehouse.

CHAPTER 6

Valuing Organizational Information

LEARNING OUTCOMES

6.1. Describe the broad levels, formats, and granularities of information.

6.2. Differentiate between transactional and analytical information.

6.3. List, describe, and provide an example of each of the five characteristics of high quality information.

6.4. Assess the impact of low quality information on an organization and the benefits of high quality information on an organization.

Organizational Information

Google recently reported a 200 percent increase in sales of its new Enterprise Search Appliance tool. Companies use the tool within an enterprise information portal (EIP) to search corporate information for answers to customer questions and to fulfill sales orders. Hundreds of Google's customers are already using the tool—Xerox, Hitachi Data Systems, Nextel Communications, Procter & Gamble, Discovery Communications, Cisco Systems, Boeing. The ability to search, analyze, and comprehend information is vital for any organization's success. The incredible 200 percent growth in sales of Google's Search Appliance tool is a strong indicator that organizations are coveting technologies that help organize and provide access to information.[2]

Information is everywhere in an organization. When addressing a significant business issue, employees must be able to obtain and analyze all the relevant information so they can make the best decision possible. Organizational information comes at different levels and in different formats and "granularities." *Information granularity* refers to the extent of detail within the information (fine and detailed or coarse and abstract). Employees must be able to correlate the different levels, formats, and granularities of information when making decisions. For example, if employees are using a supply chain management system to make decisions, they might find that their suppliers send information in different formats and granularity at different levels. One supplier might send detailed information in a spreadsheet, another supplier might send summary information in a Word document, and still another might send aggregate information from a database. Employees will need to compare these different types of information for what they commonly reveal to make strategic SCM decisions. Figure 6.1 displays types of information found in organizations.

Successfully collecting, compiling, sorting, and finally analyzing information from multiple levels, in varied formats, exhibiting different granularity can provide tremendous insight into how an organization is performing. Taking a hard look at organizational information can yield exciting and unexpected results such as potential new markets, new ways of reaching customers, and even new ways of doing business.

Digital Domain

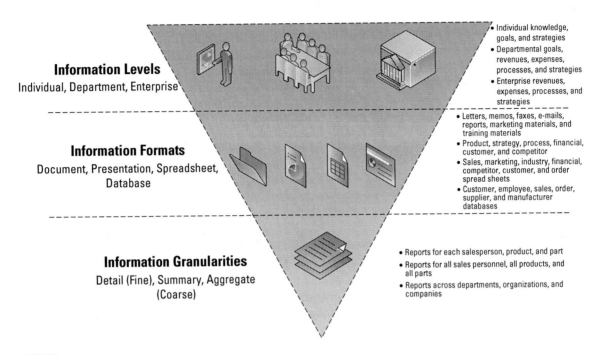

Information Levels
Individual, Department, Enterprise

- Individual knowledge, goals, and strategies
- Departmental goals, revenues, expenses, processes, and strategies
- Enterprise revenues, expenses, processes, and strategies

Information Formats
Document, Presentation, Spreadsheet, Database

- Letters, memos, faxes, e-mails, reports, marketing materials, and training materials
- Product, strategy, process, financial, customer, and competitor
- Sales, marketing, industry, financial, competitor, customer, and order spread sheets
- Customer, employee, sales, order, supplier, and manufacturer databases

Information Granularities
Detail (Fine), Summary, Aggregate (Coarse)

- Reports for each salesperson, product, and part
- Reports for all sales personnel, all products, and all parts
- Reports across departments, organizations, and companies

FIGURE 6.1

Levels, Formats, and Granularities of Organizational Information

Samsung Electronics took a detailed look at over 10,000 reports from its resellers to identify "lost deals" or orders lost to competitors. The analysis yielded the enlightening result that 80 percent of lost sales occurred in a single business unit, the health care industry. Furthermore, Samsung was able to identify that 40 percent of its lost sales in the health care industry were going to one particular competitor. Before performing the analysis, Samsung was heading into its market blind. Armed with this valuable information, Samsung is changing its selling strategy in the health care industry by implementing a new strategy to work more closely with hardware vendors to win back lost sales.[3]

Not all companies are successful at managing information. Staples, the office-supplies superstore, opened its first store in 1986 with state-of-the-art technology. The company experienced rapid growth and soon found itself overwhelmed with the resulting volumes of information. The state-of-the-art technology quickly became obsolete, and the company was unable to obtain any insight into its massive volumes of information. A simple query such as identifying the customers who purchased a computer, but not software or peripherals, took hours. Some queries required several days to complete and by the time the managers received answers to their queries it was too late for action.[4]

After understanding the different levels, formats, and granularities of information, it is important to look at a few additional characteristics that help determine the value of information. These characteristics are type (transactional and analytical), timeliness, and quality.

Information

The Value of Transactional and Analytical Information

Transactional information encompasses all of the information contained within a single business process or unit of work, and its primary purpose is to support the performing of daily operational tasks. Examples of transactional information are withdrawing cash from an ATM, making an airline reservation, or purchasing stocks. Organizations capture and store transactional information in databases, and they use it when performing operational tasks and repetitive decisions such as analyzing daily sales reports and production schedules to determine how much inventory to carry.

Analytical information encompasses all organizational information, and its primary purpose is to support the performing of managerial analysis tasks. Analytical information includes transactional information along with other information such as market and industry information. Examples of analytical information are trends, sales, product statistics, and future growth projections. Analytical information is used when making important ad hoc decisions such as whether the organization should build a new manufacturing plant or hire additional sales personnel. Figure 6.2 displays different types of transactional and analytical information.

The Value of Timely Information

The need for timely information can change for each business decision. Some decisions require weekly or monthly information while other decisions require daily information. Timeliness is an aspect of information that depends on the situation. In some industries, information that is a few days or weeks old can be relevant while in other industries information that is a few minutes old can be almost worthless. Some organizations, such as 911 centers, stock traders, and banks, require consolidated, up-to-the-second information, 24 hours a day, seven days a week. Other organizations, such as insurance and construction companies, require only daily or even weekly information.

Real-time information means immediate, up-to-date information. *Real-time systems* provide real-time information in response to query requests. Many organizations use real-time systems to exploit key corporate transactional information. In a survey of 700 IT executives by Evans Data Corp., 48 percent of respondents said they were already analyzing information in or near real-time, and another 25 percent reported plans to add real-time systems.[5]

The growing demand for real-time information stems from organizations' need to make faster and more effective decisions, keep smaller inventories, operate more efficiently, and track performance more carefully. But timeliness is relative. Organizations need fresh, timely information to make good decisions. Information also needs to be timely in the sense that it meets employees' needs—but no more. If employees can absorb information only on an hourly or daily basis, there is no need to gather real-time information in smaller increments. For example, MBIA Insurance Corp. uses overnight updates to feed its real-time systems. Employees use

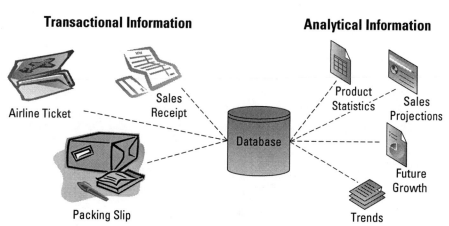

Transactional Information   **Analytical Information**

Airline Ticket

Sales Receipt

Packing Slip

Database

Product Statistics

Sales Projections

Future Growth

Trends

FIGURE 6.2

Transactional versus Analytical Information

this information to make daily risk decisions for mortgages, insurance policies, and other services. The company found that overnight updates were sufficient, as long as users could gain immediate access to the information they needed to make business decisions during the day.[6]

Most people request real-time information without understanding one of the biggest pitfalls associated with real-time information—continual change. Imagine the following scenario: Three managers meet at the end of the day to discuss a business problem. Each manager has gathered information at different times during the day to create a picture of the situation. Each manager's picture may be different because of this time discrepancy. Their views on the business problem may not match since the information they are basing their analysis on is continually changing. This approach may not speed up decision making, and may actually slow it down.

The timeliness of the information required must be evaluated for each business decision. Organizations do not want to find themselves using real-time information to make a bad decision faster.

The Value of Quality Information

Westpac Financial Services (WFS), one of the four major banks in Australia, serves millions of customers from its many core systems, each with its own database. The databases maintain information and provide users with easy access to the stored information. Unfortunately, the company failed to develop information-capturing standards, which led to inconsistent organizational information. For example, one system had a field to capture e-mail addresses while another system did not. Duplicate customer information among the different systems was another major issue, and the company continually found itself sending conflicting or competing messages to customers from different operations of the bank. A customer could also have multiple accounts within the company, one representing a life insurance policy and one representing a credit card. WFS had no way to identify that the two different customer accounts were for the same customer.

WFS had to solve its information quality problems immediately if it was to remain competitive. The company purchased NADIS (Name & Address Data Integrity Software), a software solution that filters customer information, highlighting missing, inaccurate, and redundant information. Customer service ratings are on the rise for WFS now that the company can operate its business with a single and comprehensive view of each one of its customers.[7]

Business decisions are only as good as the quality of the information used to make the decisions. Figure 6.3 reviews five characteristics common to high quality information: accuracy, completeness, consistency, uniqueness, and timeliness. Figure 6.4 highlights several issues with low quality information including:

1. The first issue is *missing* information. The customer's first name is missing. (See #1 in Figure 6.4.)

FIGURE 6.3

Five Common Characteristics of High Quality Information

Accuracy	Are all the values correct? For example, is the name spelled correctly? Is the dollar amount recorded properly?
Completeness	Are any of the values missing? For example, is the address complete including street, city, state, and zip code?
Consistency	Is aggregate or summary information in agreement with detailed information? For example, do all total fields equal the true total of the individual fields?
Uniqueness	Is each transaction, entity, and event represented only once in the information? For example, are there any duplicate customers?
Timeliness	Is the information current with respect to the business requirements? For example, is information updated weekly, daily, or hourly?

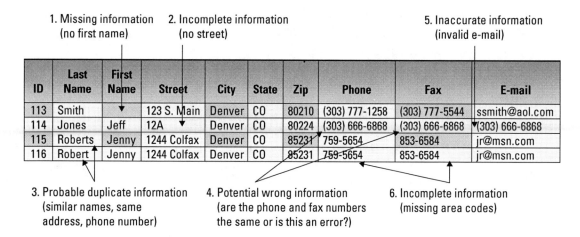

FIGURE 6.4

Low Quality Information Example

2. The second issue is *incomplete* information since the street address contains only a number and not a street name.

3. The third issue is a probable *duplication* of information since the only slight difference between the two customers is the spelling of the last name. Similar street addresses and phone numbers make this likely.

4. The fourth issue is potential *wrong* information because the customer's phone and fax numbers are the same. Some customers might have the same number for phone and fax line, but the fact that the customer also has this number in the e-mail address field is suspicious.

5. The fifth issue is definitely an example of *inaccurate* information since a phone number is located in the e-mail address field.

6. The sixth issue is *incomplete* information since there is not a valid area code for the phone and fax numbers.

Recognizing how low quality information issues occur will allow organizations to begin to correct them. The four primary sources of low quality information are:

1. Online customers intentionally enter inaccurate information to protect their privacy.

2. Different systems have different information entry standards and formats.

3. Call center operators enter abbreviated or erroneous information by accident or to save time.

4. Third-party and external information contains inconsistencies, inaccuracies, and errors.[8]

Addressing the above sources of information inaccuracies will significantly improve the quality of organizational information and the value that can be extracted from the information.

UNDERSTANDING THE COSTS OF POOR INFORMATION

Using the wrong information can lead to making the wrong decision. Making the wrong decision can cost time, money, and even reputations. Every business decision is only as good as the information used to make the decision. Bad information can cause serious business ramifications such as:

■ Inability to accurately track customers, which directly affects strategic initiatives such as CRM and SCM.

■ Difficulty identifying the organization's most valuable customers.

- Inability to identify selling opportunities and wasted revenue from marketing to nonexisting customers and nondeliverable mail.
- Difficulty tracking revenue because of inaccurate invoices.
- Inability to build strong relationships with customers—which increases buyer power.

UNDERSTANDING THE BENEFITS OF GOOD INFORMATION

High quality information can significantly improve the chances of making a good decision and directly increase an organization's bottom line. Lillian Vernon Corp., a catalog company, used Web analytics to discover that men preferred to shop at Lillian Vernon's Web site instead of looking through its paper catalog. Based on this information, the company began placing male products more prominently on its Web site and soon realized a 15 percent growth in sales to men.[9]

Another company discovered that Phoenix, Arizona, is not a good place to sell golf clubs, even with its high number of golf courses. An analysis revealed that typical golfers in Phoenix are either tourists or conventioneers. These golfers usually bring their clubs with them while visiting Phoenix. The analysis further revealed that two of the best places to sell golf clubs in the United States are Rochester, New York, and Detroit, Michigan.[10]

There are numerous examples of companies that have used their high quality information to make solid strategic business decisions. High quality information does not automatically guarantee that every decision made is going to be a good one, since people ultimately make decisions. But such information ensures that the basis of the decisions is accurate. The success of the organization depends on appreciating and leveraging the true value of timely and high quality information.

OPENING CASE STUDY QUESTIONS

1. Determine if an entry in Wikipedia is an example of transactional information or analytical information.

2. Describe the impact to Wikipedia if the information contained in its database is of low quality.

3. Review the five common characteristics of high quality information and rank them in order of importance to Wikipedia.

4. Explain how Wikipedia is resolving the issue of poor information.

Chapter Six Case: Fishing for Quality

The Alaska Department of Fish and Game requires high quality information to manage the state's natural resources, specifically to increase fishing yields, while ensuring the future of many species. Using fish counts, the department makes daily decisions as to which districts will be open or closed to commercial fishing. If the department receives poor information from fish counts, then either too many fish escape or too many are caught. Allowing too many salmon to swim upstream could deprive fishermen of their livelihoods. Allowing too many to be caught before they swim upstream to spawn could diminish fish populations—yielding devastating effects for years to come.

Because of the incredible size of Alaskan fisheries, the Commercial Fisheries Division's decisions have global impact. Its information is relied upon by individual fishermen who want to know the best places to fish, by corporations around the world that need information on which to base business strategies for seafood processing and marketing, by researchers, and by legislators. With so much at stake, the Division of Commercial Fisheries set out to improve the quality of its information by implementing a system that can gather the information from remote parts of the state and analyze it quickly to determine the daily outcomes.

Originally, the department captured information in spreadsheets that were e-mailed from station to station before being entered into the system. There was no central information set to work from, and more often than not, the information was low quality. Decisions were based on inaccurate and, because of delays in posting, untimely information.

With the implementation of an Oracle database, the department significantly improved the quality and timeliness of its information. Each time a commercial fishing boat within Alaska's jurisdiction unloads at a processing plant, the catch is weighed and details of the catch, such as species caught, weight, and quantity, are recorded on a fish ticket. This information is entered into the new system. To gather fish escapement information from remote areas, field workers positioned in towers scan rivers to visibly count fish. This information is radioed in the next morning.

Information from fish processed the previous day is keyed in by 10:00 a.m., and one hour later, the managers and fisheries across the state have all the information they require to make accurate decisions. They then announce on the radio and on their Web site, which receives more than 3,000 hits on an average day, whether or not fishermen can fish that day.

Fisheries are now managed with timely, centralized, and accurate information. Web pages summarize daily catches for certain areas, like Bristol Bay, whose annual sockeye salmon season, which lasts only a few weeks, is closely monitored by fish processors worldwide. With the enormous quantities of fish caught, salmon fisheries worldwide adjust their production levels based on the results of the annual Bristol Bay sockeye salmon season. This is just one reason producing fast, quality information is critical to managing Alaska's natural resources.[11]

Questions

1. Describe the difference between transactional and analytical information and determine which type the Alaska Department of Fish and Game is using to make decisions.

2. Explain the importance of quality information for the Alaska Department of Fish and Game.

3. Review the five common characteristics of high quality information and rank them in order of importance for the Alaska Department of Fish and Game.

4. Do the managers at the Alaska Department of Fish and Game have all the information they require to make an accurate decision? Explain the statement "it is never possible to have all of the information required to make the best decision possible."

CHAPTER **7**

Storing Organizational Information—Databases

LEARNING OUTCOMES

7.1. Define the fundamental concepts of the relational database model.

7.2. Evaluate the advantages of the relational database model.

7.3. Compare relational integrity constraints and business-critical integrity constraints.

7.4. Describe the benefits of a data-driven Web site.

7.5. Describe the two primary methods for integrating information across multiple databases.

Storing Organizational Information

Organizational information is stored in a database. Applications and programs, such as supply chain management systems, and customer relationship management systems, access the data in the database so the program can consult it to answer queries. The records retrieved in answer to questions become information that can be used to make decisions. The computer program used to manage and query a database is known as a database management system (DBMS). The properties and design of database systems are included in the study of information science.

The central concept of a database is that of a collection of records, or pieces of information. Typically, a given database has a structural description of the type of facts held in that database: This description is known as a schema. The schema describes the objects that are represented in the database and the relationships among them. There are a number of different ways of organizing a schema, that is, of modeling the database structure: These are known as database models (or data models). The most commonly used model today is the relational model, which represents all information in the form of multiple related tables each consisting of rows and columns. This model represents relationships by the use of values common to more than one table. Other models, such as the hierarchical model, and the network model, use a more explicit representation of relationships.

Many professionals consider a collection of data to constitute a database only if it has certain properties; for example, if the data are managed to ensure integrity and quality, if it allows shared access by a community of users, if it has a schema, or if it supports a query language. However, there is no definition of these properties that is universally agreed upon. [12]

Relational Database Fundamentals

There are many different models for organizing information in a database, including the hierarchical database, network database, and the most prevalent—the relational database model. Broadly defined, a *database* maintains information about various types of objects (inventory), events (transactions), people (employees), and places (warehouses). In a **hierarchical database model,** information is organized into a tree-like structure that allows repeating information using parent/child relationships in such a way that it cannot have too many relationships. Hierarchical structures were widely used in the first mainframe database management systems. However, owing to their restrictions, hierarchical structures often cannot be used to relate to structures that exist in the real world. The **network database model** is a flexible way of representing objects and their relationships. Where the hierarchical model structures data as a tree of records, with each record having one parent record and many children, the network model allows each record to have multiple parent and child records, forming a lattice structure. The **relational database model** is a type of database that stores information in the form of logically related two-dimensional tables. This text focuses on the relational database model.

Database

Consider how the Coca-Cola Bottling Company of Egypt (TCCBCE) implemented an inventory-tracking database to improve order accuracy by 27 percent, decrease order response time by 66 percent, and increase sales by 20 percent. With over 7,400 employees, TCCBCE owns and operates 11 bottling plants and 29 sales and distribution centers, making it one of the largest companies in Egypt.

Traditionally, the company sent distribution trucks to each customer's premises to take orders and deliver stock. Many problems were associated with this process including numerous information entry errors, which caused order-fulfillment time to take an average of three days. To remedy the situation, Coca-Cola decided to create presales teams equipped with handheld devices to visit customers and take orders electronically. On returning to the office, the teams synchronized orders with the company's inventory-tracking database to ensure automated processing and rapid dispatch of accurate orders to customers.[13]

ENTITIES AND ATTRIBUTES

Figure 7.1 illustrates the primary concepts of the relational database model—entities, entity classes, attributes, keys, and relationships. An **entity** in the relational database model is a person, place, thing, transaction, or event about which information is stored. A table in the relational database model is a collection of similar entities. The tables of interest in Figure 7.1 are *CUSTOMER, ORDER, ORDER LINE, PRODUCT,* and *DISTRIBUTOR.* Notice that each entity class (the collection of similar entities) is stored in a different two-dimensional table. **Attributes,** also called fields or columns, are characteristics or properties of an entity class. In Figure 7.1 the attributes for *CUSTOMER* include *Customer ID, Customer Name, Contact Name,* and *Phone.* Attributes for *PRODUCT* include *Product ID, Product Description,* and *Price.* Each specific entity in an entity class (e.g., Dave's Sub Shop in the *CUSTOMER* table) occupies one row in its respective table. The columns in the table contain the attributes.

KEYS AND RELATIONSHIPS

To manage and organize various entity classes within the relational database model, developers must identify primary keys and foreign keys and use them to create logical relationships. A **primary key** is a field (or group of fields) that uniquely identifies a given entity in a table. In *CUSTOMER,* the *Customer ID* uniquely identifies each entity (customer) in the table and is the primary key. Primary keys are important because they provide a way of distinguishing each entity in a table.

A **foreign key** in the relational database model is a primary key of one table that appears as an attribute in another table and acts to provide a logical relationship between the two tables. Consider Hawkins Shipping, one of the distributors appearing in the *DISTRIBUTOR* table. Its primary key, *Distributor ID,* is DEN8001. Notice that *Distributor ID* also appears as an attribute in the ORDER table. This establishes the fact that Hawkins Shipping (*Distributor ID* DEN8001) was responsible

FIGURE 7.1

Potential Relational
Database for Coca-Cola
Bottling Company of Egypt
(TCCBCE)

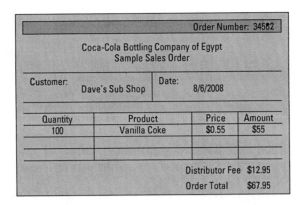

Order Number: 34562

Coca-Cola Bottling Company of Egypt
Sample Sales Order

| Customer: Dave's Sub Shop | Date: 8/6/2008 |

Quantity	Product	Price	Amount
100	Vanilla Coke	$0.55	$55

| | Distributor Fee | $12.95 |
| | Order Total | $67.95 |

CUSTOMER

Customer ID	Customer Name	Contact Name	Phone
23	Dave's Sub Shop	David Logan	(555)333-4545
43	Pizza Palace	Debbie Fernandez	(555)345-5432
765	T's Fun Zone	Tom Repicci	(555)565-6655

ORDER

Order ID	Order Date	Customer ID	Distributor ID	Distributor Fee	Total Due
34561	7/4/2008	23	DEN8001	$22.00	$145.75
34562	8/6/2008	23	DEN8001	$12.95	$67.95
34563	6/5/2008	765	NY9001	$29.50	$249.50

ORDER LINE

Order ID	Line Item	Product ID	Quantity
34561	1	12345AA	75
34561	2	12346BB	50
34561	3	12347CC	100
34562	1	12349EE	100
34563	1	12345AA	100
34563	2	12346BB	100
34563	3	12347CC	50
34563	4	12348DD	50
34563	5	12349EE	100

DISTRIBUTOR

Distributor ID	Distributor Name
DEN8001	Hawkins Shipping
CHI3001	ABC Trucking
NY9001	Van Distributors

PRODUCT

Product ID	Product Description	Price
12345AA	Coca-Cola	$0.55
12346BB	Diet Coke	$0.55
12347CC	Sprite	$0.55
12348DD	Diet Sprite	$0.55
12349EE	Vanilla Coke	$0.55

for delivering orders 34561 and 34562 to the appropriate customer(s). Therefore, *Distributor ID* in the *ORDER* table creates a logical relationship (who shipped what order) between *ORDER* and *DISTRIBUTOR*.

Relational Database Advantages

From a business perspective, database information offers many advantages, including:

- Increased flexibility.
- Increased scalability and performance.
- Reduced information redundancy.
- Increased information integrity (quality).
- Increased information security.

INCREASED FLEXIBILITY

Databases tend to mirror business structures, and a good database can handle changes quickly and easily, just as any good business needs to be able to handle changes quickly and easily. Equally important, databases provide flexibility in allowing each user to access the information in whatever way best suits his or her needs. The distinction between logical and physical views is important in understanding flexible database user views. The *physical view* of information deals with the physical storage of information on a storage device such as a hard disk. The *logical view* of information focuses on how users logically access information to meet their particular business needs. This separation of logical and physical views is what allows each user to access database information differently. That is, while a database has only one physical view, it can easily support multiple logical views. In the previous database illustration, for example, users could perform a query to determine which distributors delivered shipments to Pizza Palace last week. At the same time, another person could perform some sort of statistical analysis to determine the frequency at which Sprite and Diet Coke appear on the same order. These represent two very different logical views, but both views use the same physical view.

Consider another example—a mail-order business. One user might want a CRM report presented in alphabetical format, in which case last name should appear before first name. Another user, working with a catalog mailing system, would want customer names appearing as first name and then last name. Both are easily achievable, but different logical views of the same physical information.

INCREASED SCALABILITY AND PERFORMANCE

The official Web site of The American Family Immigration History Center, www .ellisisland.org, generated over 2.5 billion hits in its first year of operation. The site offers easy access to immigration information about people who entered America through the Port of New York and Ellis Island between 1892 and 1924. The database contains over 25 million passenger names correlated to 3.5 million images of ships' manifests.[14]

Only a database could "scale" to handle the massive volumes of information and the large numbers of users required for the successful launch of the Ellis Island Web site. *Scalability* refers to how well a system can adapt to increased demands. *Performance* measures how quickly a system performs a certain process or transaction. Some organizations must be able to support hundreds or thousands of online users including employees, partners, customers, and suppliers, who all want to access and share information. Databases today scale to exceptional levels, allowing all types of users and programs to perform information-processing and information-searching tasks.

REDUCED INFORMATION REDUNDANCY

Redundancy is the duplication of information, or storing the same information in multiple places. Redundant information occurs because organizations frequently capture and store the same information in multiple locations. The primary problem with redundant information is that it is often inconsistent, which makes it difficult to determine which values are the most current or most accurate. Not having correct information is confusing and frustrating for employees and disruptive to an organization. One primary goal of a database is to eliminate information redundancy by recording each piece of information in only one place in the database. Eliminating information redundancy saves space, makes performing information updates easier, and improves information quality.

INCREASED INFORMATION INTEGRITY (QUALITY)

Information integrity is a measure of the quality of information. Within a database environment, *integrity constraints* are rules that help ensure the quality of information. Integrity constraints can be defined and built into the database design. The database (more appropriately, the database management system, which is discussed below) ensures that users can never violate these constraints. There are two types of integrity constraints: (1) relational integrity constraints and (2) business-critical integrity constraints.

Relational integrity constraints are rules that enforce basic and fundamental information-based constraints. For example, an operational integrity constraint would not allow someone to create an order for a nonexistent customer, provide a markup percentage that was negative, or order zero pounds of raw materials from a supplier. *Business-critical integrity constraints* enforce business rules vital to an organization's success and often require more insight and knowledge than relational integrity constraints. Consider a supplier of fresh produce to large grocery chains such as Kroger. The supplier might implement a business-critical integrity constraint stating that no product returns are accepted after 15 days past delivery. That would make sense because of the chance of spoilage of the produce. These types of integrity constraints tend to mirror the very rules by which an organization achieves success.

The specification and enforcement of integrity constraints produce higher quality information that will provide better support for business decisions. Organizations that establish specific procedures for developing integrity constraints typically see a decline in information error rates and an increase in the use of organizational information.

INCREASED INFORMATION SECURITY

Information is an organizational asset. Like any asset, the organization must protect its information from unauthorized users or misuse. As systems become increasingly complex and more available over the Internet, security becomes an even bigger issue. Databases offer many security features including passwords, access levels, and access controls. Passwords provide authentication of the user who is gaining access to the system. Access levels determine who has access to the different types of information, and access controls determine what type of access they have to the information. For example, customer service representatives might need read-only access to customer order information so they can answer customer order inquiries; they might not have or need the authority to change or delete order information. Managers might require access to employee files, but they should have access only to their own employees' files, not the employee files for the entire company. Various security features of databases can ensure that individuals have only certain types of access to certain types of information.

Databases can increase personal security as well as information security. The Chicago Police Department (CPD) has relied on a crime-fighting system called Citizen and Law Enforcement Analysis and Reporting (CLEAR). CLEAR electronically streamlines the way detectives enter and access critical information to help them solve crimes, analyze crime patterns, and ultimately promote security in a proactive manner. The CPD enters 650,000 new criminal cases and 500,000 new arrests into CLEAR each year.[15]

Database Management Systems

Ford's European plant manufactures more than 5,000 vehicles a day and sells them in over 100 countries worldwide. Every component of every model must conform to complex European standards, including passenger safety standards and pedestrian and environmental protection standards. These standards govern each stage of Ford's manufacturing process from design to final production. The company needs to obtain many thousands of different approvals each year to comply with the standards. Overlooking just one means the company cannot sell the finished vehicle, which brings the production line to a standstill and could potentially cost Ford up to 1 million euros per day. Ford built the Homologation Timing System (HTS), based on a relational database, to help it track and analyze these standards. The reliability and high performance of the HTS have helped Ford substantially reduce its compliance risk.[16]

A database management system is used to access information from a database. A *database management system (DBMS)* is software through which users and application programs interact with a database. The user sends requests to the DBMS and the DBMS performs the actual manipulation of the information in the database. There are two primary ways that users can interact with a DBMS: (1) directly and (2) indirectly, as displayed in Figure 7.2. In either case, users access the DBMS and the DBMS accesses the database.

DATA-DRIVEN WEB SITES

The pages on a Web site must change according to what a site visitor is interested in browsing. Consider for example, a company selling sports cars. A database is

FIGURE 7.2

Interacting Directly and Indirectly with a Database through a DBMS

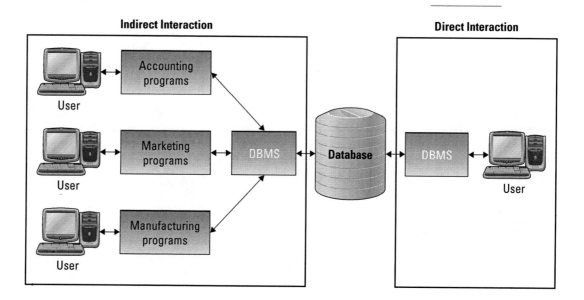

created with information on each of the currently available cars (e.g., make, model, engine details, year, a photograph, etc.). A visitor to the Web site clicks on Porsche, for example, enters the price range he or she is interested in, and hits "Go." The visitor is presented with information on available cars within the price range and an invitation to purchase or request more information from the company. Via a secure administration area on the Web site, the company has the ability to modify, add, or remove cars to the database.[17]

A **data-driven Web site** is an interactive Web site kept constantly updated and relevant to the needs of its customers through the use of a database. Data-driven Web sites are especially useful when the site offers a great deal of information, products, or services. Web site visitors are frequently angered if they are buried under an avalanche of information when searching a Web site. A data-driven Web site invites visitors to select and view what they are interested in by inserting a query. The Web site analyzes the query and then custom builds a Web page in real-time that satisfies the query. Figure 7.3 displays a Wikipedia user querying business intelligence and the database sending back the appropriate Web page that satisfies the user's request.[18]

Data-Driven Web Site Business Advantages

When building a Web site, ask two primary questions to determine if the Web site needs a database:

1. How often will the content change?
2. Who will be making the content changes?

For a general informational Web site with static information, it is best to build a "static" Web site—one that a developer can update on an as-needed basis, perhaps a few times a year. A static Web site is less expensive to produce and typically meets business needs.

For a Web site with continually changing information—press releases, new product information, updated pricing, etc.—it is best to build a data-driven Web site. Figure 7.4 displays the many advantages associated with a data-driven Web site.[19]

FIGURE 7.3

Wikipedia—Data-Driven Web Site

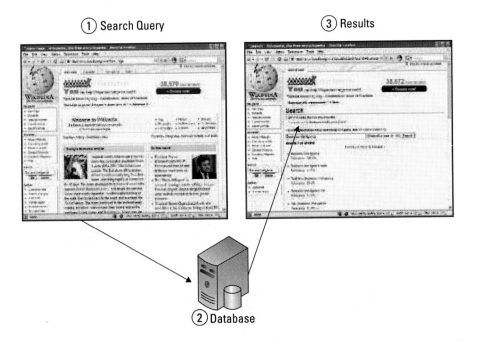

① Search Query   ③ Results

② Database

Data-Driven Web Site Advantages

- **Development:** Allows the Web site owner to make changes any time—all without having to rely on a developer or knowing HTML programming. A well-structured, data-driven Web site enables updating with little or no training.

- **Content management:** A static Web site requires a programmer to make updates. This adds an unnecessary layer between the business and its Web content, which can lead to misunderstandings and slow turnarounds for desired changes.

- **Future expandability:** Having a data-driven Web site enables the site to grow faster than would be possible with a static site. Changing the layout, displays, and functionality of the site (adding more features and sections) is easier with a data-driven solution.

- **Minimizing human error:** Even the most competent programmer charged with the task of maintaining many pages will overlook things and make mistakes. This will lead to bugs and inconsistencies that can be time consuming and expensive to track down and fix. Unfortunately, users who come across these bugs will likely become irritated and may leave the site. A well-designed, data-driven Web site will have "error trapping" mechanisms to ensure that required information is filled out correctly and that content is entered and displayed in its correct format.

- **Cutting production and update costs:** A data-driven Web site can be updated and "published" by any competent data-entry or administrative person. In addition to being convenient and more affordable, changes and updates will take a fraction of the time that they would with a static site. While training a competent programmer can take months or even years, training a data-entry person can be done in 30 to 60 minutes.

- **More efficient:** By their very nature, computers are excellent at keeping volumes of information intact. With a data-driven solution, the system keeps track of the templates, so users do not have to. Global changes to layout, navigation, or site structure would need to be programmed only once, in one place, and the site itself will take care of propagating those changes to the appropriate pages and areas. A data-driven infrastructure will improve the reliability and stability of a Web site, while greatly reducing the chance of "breaking" some part of the site when adding new areas.

- **Improved stability:** Any programmer who has to update a Web site from "static" templates must be very organized to keep track of all the source files. If a programmer leaves unexpectedly, it could involve re-creating existing work if those source files cannot be found. Plus, if there were any changes to the templates, the new programmer must be careful to use only the latest version. With a data-driven Web site, there is peace of mind, knowing the content is never lost—even if your programmer is.

FIGURE 7.4

Data-Driven Web Site Advantages

Data-Driven Business Intelligence

Companies can gain business intelligence by viewing the data accessed and analyzed from their Web site. Figure 7.5 displays how running queries or using analytical tools, such as a Pivot Table, on the database that is attached to the Web site can offer insight into the business, such as items browsed, frequent requests, items bought together, etc.

Integrating Information among Multiple Databases

Until the 1990s, each department in the United Kingdom's Ministry of Defense (MOD) and Army headquarters had its own systems, each system had its own database, and sharing information among the departments was difficult. Manually inputting the same information multiple times into the different systems was also time consuming and inefficient. In many cases, management could not even compile the information it required to answer questions and make decisions.

The Army solved the problem by integrating its systems, or building connections between its many databases. These integrations allow the Army's multiple systems to automatically communicate by passing information between the databases, eliminating the need for manual information entry into multiple systems because after entering the information once, the integrations send the information immediately to all other databases. The integrations not only enable the different departments to share information, but have also dramatically increased the quality of the

FIGURE 7.5

BI in a Data-Driven Web Site

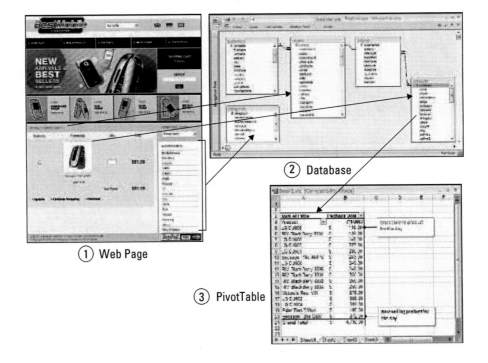

① Web Page

② Database

③ PivotTable

information. The Army can now generate reports detailing its state of readiness and other vital issues, nearly impossible tasks before building the integrations among the separate systems.[20]

An *integration* allows separate systems to communicate directly with each other. Similar to the UK's Army, an organization will probably maintain multiple systems, with each system having its own database. Without integrations, an organization will (1) spend considerable time entering the same information in multiple systems and (2) suffer from the low quality and inconsistency typically embedded in redundant information. While most integrations do not completely eliminate redundant information, they can ensure the consistency of it across multiple systems.

An organization can choose from two integration methods. The first is to create forward and backward integrations that link processes (and their underlying databases) in the value chain. A *forward integration* takes information entered into a given system and sends it automatically to all downstream systems and processes. A *backward integration* takes information entered into a given system and sends it automatically to all upstream systems and processes.

Figure 7.6 demonstrates how this method works across the systems or processes of sales, order entry, order fulfillment, and billing. In the order entry system, for example, an employee can update the information for a customer. That information, via the integrations, would be sent upstream to the sales system and downstream to the order fulfillment and billing systems.

Ideally, an organization wants to build both forward and backward integrations, which provide the flexibility to create, update, and delete information in any of the systems. However, integrations are expensive and difficult to build and maintain and most organizations build only forward integrations (sales through billing in Figure 7.6). Building only forward integrations implies that a change in the initial system (sales) will result in changes occurring in all the other systems. Integration of information is not possible for any changes occurring outside the initial system, which again can result in inconsistent organizational information. To address this issue, organizations can enforce business rules that all systems, other than the initial system, have read-only access to the integrated information. This will require

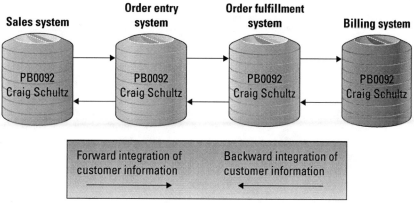

FIGURE 7.6

A Forward and Backward Customer Information Integration Example

users to change information in the initial system only, which will always trigger the integration and ensure that organizational information does not get out of sync.

The second integration method builds a central repository for a particular type of information. Figure 7.7 provides an example of customer information integrated using this method across four different systems in an organization. Users can create, update, and delete customer information only in the central customer information database. As users perform these tasks on the central customer information database, integrations automatically send the new and/or updated customer information to the other systems. The other systems limit users to read-only access of the customer information stored in them. Again, this method does not eliminate redundancy— but it does ensure consistency of the information among multiple systems.

FIGURE 7.7

Integrating Customer Information among Databases

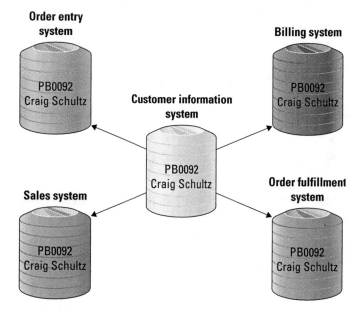

Chapter Seven Case: Keeper of the Keys

More than 145,000 consumers nationwide were placed at risk by a recent data theft at database giant ChoicePoint. Criminals tricked the company by posing as legitimate businesses to gain access to the various ChoicePoint databases, which contain a treasure trove of consumer data, including names, addresses, Social Security numbers, credit reports, and other information. At least 50 suspicious accounts had been opened in the name of nonexistent debt collectors, insurance agencies, and other companies, according to the company.

Without a doubt, databases are one of the most important IT tools that organizations use today. Databases contain large repositories of detailed data. When a transaction occurs, a sale, for example, a database stores every detail of the transaction including customer name, customer address, credit card number, products purchased, discounts received, and so on.

Organizations must carefully manage their databases. This management function includes properly organizing the information in these repositories in the most efficient way, ensuring that no erroneous information ever enters the databases, and—most important—protecting the information from thieves and hackers.

Information is a valuable commodity, and, sadly, this makes it a target for theft. Organizations store large amounts of customer information including Social Security numbers, credit card numbers, and bank account numbers—just think of the information stored at eBay, Amazon, or the IRS. When someone steals personal information (not necessarily by taking it from the person, but rather stealing it from a company), that person becomes a victim of identity theft. Consider this short list of organizations that have lost information and the huge numbers of customers affected.

- Bank of America: 1.2 million customers.
- CardSystems: 40 million customers.
- Citigroup: 3.9 million customers.
- DSW Shoe Warehouse: 1.4 million customers.
- TJX Companies: 45.6 million customers.
- Wachovia: 676,000 customers.

Adding up the numbers, almost 90 million people had their personal information either stolen or lost through organizations.

Business Accountability in Data Security

Companies may soon face stiff penalties for wayward data security practices. Massachusetts is considering legislation that would require companies to pay for any costs associated with a data breach of their IT systems. This move to protect customer data in Massachusetts comes at a fitting time, as two prominent retailers in the area, TJX Companies and Stop & Shop, wrestle with the aftermath of significant breaches that have exposed some of their customers to fraud.

Much of the expense associated with stopping fraudulent activity, such as canceling or reissuing credit or debit cards, stopping payment, and refunding customers, has been absorbed by the banks issuing credit or debit cards to the victims. The merchant banks that allow businesses such as TJX and Stop & Shop stores to accept credit and debit card transactions are penalized with fines from Visa, MasterCard, and other credit card organizations if the merchants they work with are found to violate the payment card industry's data security standards.

But the businesses who have had customer data stolen have largely suffered only from the costs to offer customers free credit-monitoring services and to repair a tarnished public image. In the case of popular retailers, this tarnish is easily polished away when juicy sales incentives are offered to get customers back.

Massachusetts House Bill 213, sponsored by Rep. Michael Costello, proposes to amend the Commonwealth's general laws to include a section that would require any corporation or other commercial entity whose sensitive customer information is stolen to notify customers about the data breach and also make companies liable to card-issuing banks for the costs those banks incur because of the breach and any subsequent fraudulent activity. This would include making businesses cover the costs to cancel or reissue cards, stop payments or block transactions with respect to any such account, open or reopen an account, and issue any refund or credit made to any customer of the bank as a result of unauthorized transactions.

The Massachusetts legislation is a key step in compelling companies to invest in better data security. Passage of this bill would put Massachusetts ahead of other states in terms of protecting customer data and spreading out the penalties so that both financial institutions and retailers have incentives to improve security. Security vendors are likely to be watching Massachusetts very closely, as the bill also would create an urgent need for companies doing business in that state to invest in ways to improve their ability to protect customer data. If the companies will not do this on their own, then holding them accountable for their customers' financial losses may be just what is needed to stop the next data breach from occurring. [21]

Questions

1. How many organizations have your personal information, including your Social Security number, bank account numbers, and credit card numbers?
2. What information is stored at your college? Is there a chance your information could be hacked and stolen from your college?
3. What can you do to protect yourself from identity theft?
4. Do you agree or disagree with changing laws to hold the company where the data theft occurred accountable? Why or why not?
5. What impact would holding the company liable where the data theft occurred have on large organizations?
6. What impact would holding the company liable where the data theft occurred have on small businesses?

<< TECHNOLOGY PLUG-IN POINTERS

Review Technology Plug-In T5 "Designing Database Applications" for an overview of the steps to follow while designing a small database application, including defining entity classes, identifying primary and foreign keys, and completing the first three steps of normalization (up through and including eliminating many-to-many relationships).

Review Technology Plug-In T6 "Basic Skills Using Access" for a comprehensive tutorial on how to create tables and define relationships..

Accessing Organizational Information—Data Warehouse

LEARNING OUTCOMES

8.1. Describe the roles and purposes of data warehouses and data marts in an organization.

8.2. Compare the multidimensional nature of data warehouses (and data marts) with the two-dimensional nature of databases.

8.3. Identify the importance of ensuring the cleanliness of information throughout an organization.

8.4. Explain the relationship between business intelligence and a data warehouse.

Accessing Organizational Information

Applebee's Neighborhood Grill & Bar posts annual sales in excess of $3.2 billion and is actively using information from its data warehouse to increase sales and cut costs. The company gathers daily information for the previous day's sales into its data warehouse from 1,500 restaurants located in 49 states and seven countries. Understanding regional preferences, such as patrons in Texas preferring steaks more than patrons in New England, allows the company to meet its corporate strategy of being a neighborhood grill appealing to local tastes. The company has found tremendous value in its data warehouse by being able to make business decisions about customers' regional needs. The company also uses data warehouse information to perform the following:

- Base labor budgets on actual number of guests served per hour.
- Develop promotional sale item analysis to help avoid losses from overstocking or understocking inventory.
- Determine theoretical and actual costs of food and the use of ingredients.[22]

History of Data Warehousing

In the 1990s as organizations began to need more timely information about their business, they found that traditional operational information systems were too cumbersome to provide relevant data efficiently and quickly. Operational systems typically include accounting, order entry, customer service, and sales and are not appropriate for business analysis for the following reasons:

- Information from other operational applications is not included.
- Operational systems are not integrated, or not available in one place.
- Operational information is mainly current—does not include the history that is required to make good decisions.
- Operational information frequently has quality issues (errors)—the information needs to be cleansed.

- Without information history, it is difficult to tell how and why things change over time.
- Operational systems are not designed for analysis and decision support.[23]

During the latter half of the 20th century, the numbers and types of databases increased. Many large businesses found themselves with information scattered across multiple platforms and variations of technology, making it almost impossible for any one individual to use information from multiple sources. Completing reporting requests across operational systems could take days or weeks using antiquated reporting tools that were designed to execute the business rather than run the business. From this idea, the data warehouse was born as a place where relevant information could be held for completing strategic reports for management. The key here is the word *strategic* as most executives were less concerned with the day-to-day operations than they were with a more overall look at the model and business functions.

A key idea within data warehousing is to take data from multiple platforms/technologies (as varied as spreadsheets, databases, and word files) and place them in a common location that uses a common querying tool. In this way operational databases could be held on whatever system was most efficient for the operational business, while the reporting/strategic information could be held in a common location using a common language. Data warehouses take this a step further by giving the information itself commonality by defining what each term means and keeping it standard. An example of this would be gender, which can be referred to in many ways (Male, Female, M/F, 1/0), but should be standardized on a data warehouse with one common way of referring to each sex (M/F).[24]

This design makes decision support more readily available without affecting day-to-day operations. One aspect of a data warehouse that should be stressed is that it is *not* a location for *all* of a business's information, but rather a location for information that is interesting, or information that will assist decision makers in making strategic decisions relative to the organization's overall mission.

Data warehousing is about extending the transformation of data into information. Data warehouses offer strategic level, external, integrated, and historical information so businesses can make projections, identify trends, and decide key business issues. The data warehouse collects and stores integrated sets of historical information from multiple operational systems and feeds them to one or more data marts. It may also provide end-user access to support enterprisewide views of information.[25]

Data Warehouse

Data Warehouse Fundamentals

A **data warehouse** is a logical collection of information—gathered from many different operational databases—that supports business analysis activities and decision-making tasks. The primary purpose of a data warehouse is to aggregate information throughout an organization into a single repository in such a way that employees can make decisions and undertake business analysis activities. Therefore, while databases store the details of all transactions (for instance, the sale of a product) and events (hiring a new employee), data warehouses store that same information but in an aggregated form more suited to supporting decision-making tasks. Aggregation, in this instance, can include totals, counts, averages, and the like. Because of this sort of aggregation, data warehouses support only analytical processing.

The data warehouse modeled in Figure 8.1 compiles information from internal databases or transactional/operational databases and external databases through **extraction, transformation, and loading (ETL),** which is a process that extracts information from internal and external databases, transforms the information using a common set of enterprise definitions, and loads the information into a data warehouse. The data warehouse then sends subsets of the information to data marts. A **data mart** contains a subset of data warehouse information. To distinguish between

Data Warehouse Model

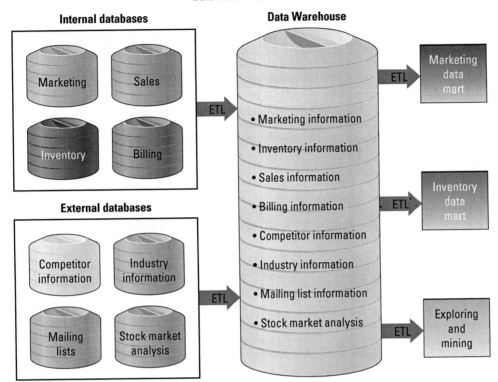

FIGURE 8.1

Model of a Typical Data Warehouse

data warehouses and data marts, think of data warehouses as having a more organizational focus and data marts as having focused information subsets particular to the needs of a given business unit such as finance or production and operations.

Lands' End created an organizationwide data warehouse so all its employees could access organizational information. Lands' End soon found out that there could be "too much of a good thing." Many of its employees would not use the data warehouse because it was simply too big, too complicated, and had too much irrelevant information. Lands' End knew there was valuable information in its data warehouse, and it had to find a way for its employees to easily access the information. Data marts were the perfect solution to the company's information overload problem. Once the employees began using the data marts, they were ecstatic at the wealth of information. Data marts were a huge success for Lands' End.[26]

MULTIDIMENSIONAL ANALYSIS AND DATA MINING

A relational database contains information in a series of two-dimensional tables. In a data warehouse and data mart, information is multidimensional, meaning it contains layers of columns and rows. For this reason, most data warehouses and data marts are *multidimensional databases*. A *dimension* is a particular attribute of information. Each layer in a data warehouse or data mart represents information according to an additional dimension. A **cube** is the common term for the representation of multidimensional information. Figure 8.2 displays a cube (cube *a*) that represents store information (the layers), product information (the rows), and promotion information (the columns).

Once a cube of information is created, users can begin to slice and dice the cube to drill down into the information. The second cube (cube *b*) in Figure 8.2 displays a slice representing promotion II information for all products, at all stores. The

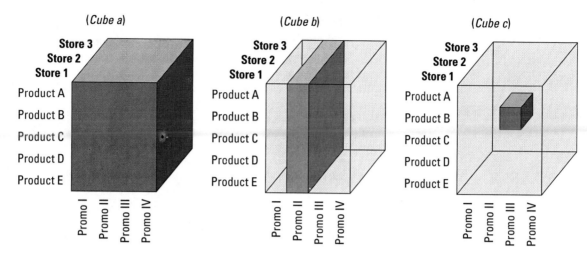

(Cube a)   (Cube b)   (Cube c)

FIGURE 8.2

A Cube of Information for Performing a Multidimensional Analysis on Three Different Stores, for Five Different Products, and Four Different Promotions

third cube (cube *c*) in Figure 8.2 displays only information for promotion III, product B, at store 2. By using multidimensional analysis, users can analyze information in a number of different ways and with any number of different dimensions. For example, users might want to add dimensions of information to a current analysis including product category, region, and even forecasted versus actual weather. The true value of a data warehouse is its ability to provide multidimensional analysis that allows users to gain insights into their information.

Data warehouses and data marts are ideal for off-loading some of the querying against a database. For example, querying a database to obtain an average of sales for product B at store 2 while promotion III is under way might create a considerable processing burden for a database, essentially slowing down the time it takes another person to enter a new sale into the same database. If an organization performs numerous queries against a database (or multiple databases), aggregating that information into a data warehouse could be beneficial.

Data mining is the process of analyzing data to extract information not offered by the raw data alone. For example, Ruf Strategic Solutions helps organizations employ statistical approaches within a large data warehouse to identify customer segments that display common traits. Marketers can then target these segments with specially designed products and promotions.[27]

Data mining can also begin at a summary information level (coarse granularity) and progress through increasing levels of detail (drilling down), or the reverse (drilling up). To perform data mining, users need data-mining tools. *Data-mining tools* use a variety of techniques to find patterns and relationships in large volumes of information and infer rules from them that predict future behavior and guide decision making. Data-mining tools for data warehouses and data marts include query tools, reporting tools, multidimensional analysis tools, statistical tools, and intelligent agents.

Sega of America, one of the largest publishers of video games, uses a data warehouse and statistical tools to distribute its annual advertising budget of more than $50 million. With its data warehouse, product line specialists and marketing strategists "drill" into trends of each retail store chain. Their goal is to find buying trends that help them determine which advertising strategies are working best and how to reallocate advertising resources by media, territory, and time.[28]

INFORMATION CLEANSING OR SCRUBBING

Maintaining quality information in a data warehouse or data mart is extremely important. The Data Warehousing Institute estimates that low quality information costs

U.S. businesses $600 billion annually. That number may seem high, but it is not. If an organization is using a data warehouse or data mart to allocate dollars across advertising strategies (such as in the case of Sega of America), low quality information will definitely have a negative impact on its ability to make the right decision.[29]

To increase the quality of organizational information and thus the effectiveness of decision making, businesses must formulate a strategy to keep information clean. This is the concept of information cleansing or scrubbing. ***Information cleansing or scrubbing*** is a process that weeds out and fixes or discards inconsistent, incorrect, or incomplete information.

Specialized software tools use sophisticated algorithms to parse, standardize, correct, match, and consolidate data warehouse information. This is vitally important because data warehouses often contain information from several different databases, some of which can be external to the organization. In a data warehouse, information cleansing occurs first during the ETL process and second on the information once it is in the data warehouse. Companies can choose information cleansing software from several different vendors including Oracle, SAS, Ascential Software, and Group 1 Software. Ideally, scrubbed information is error free and consistent.

Dr Pepper/Seven Up, Inc., was able to integrate its myriad databases in a data warehouse (and subsequently data marts) in less than two months, giving the company access to consolidated, clean information. Approximately 600 people in the company regularly use the data marts to analyze and track beverage sales across multiple dimensions, including various distribution routes such as bottle/can sales, fountain food-service sales, premier distributor sales, and chain and national accounts. The company is now performing in-depth analysis of up-to-date sales information that is clean and error free.[30]

Looking at customer information highlights why information cleansing is necessary. Customer information exists in several operational systems. In each system all details of this customer information could change from the customer ID to contact information (see Figure 8.3). Determining which contact information is accurate and correct for this customer depends on the business process that is being executed.

Figure 8.4 displays a customer name entered differently in multiple operational systems. Information cleansing allows an organization to fix these types of inconsistencies and cleans the information in the data warehouse. Figure 8.5 displays the typical events that occur during information cleansing.

Achieving perfect information is almost impossible. The more complete and accurate an organization wants its information to be, the more it costs (see Figure 8.6). The trade-off for perfect information lies in accuracy versus completeness. Accurate information means it is correct, while complete information means there are no blanks. A birth date of 2/31/10 is an example of complete but inaccurate information

FIGURE 8.3

Contact Information in Operational Systems

Billing

Contact: Hans Hultgren 555-1211

The billing system has "accounts payable" customer contact information.

Customer Service

Contact: Anne Logan 555-1288
Contact: Deborah Bridge 555-6543

The customer service system has the "product customer contact information.

Marketing

Contact: Paul Bauer 555-2211
Contact: Don McCubbrey 555-3434

Sales

Contact: Paul Bauer 555-2211
Contact: Don McCubbrey 555-3434

The marketing and sales system has "decision maker" customer contact information.

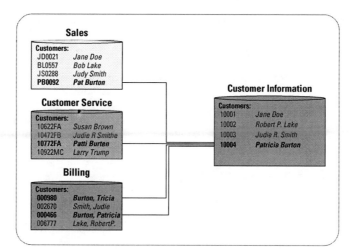

FIGURE 8.4

Standardizing Customer Name from Operational Systems

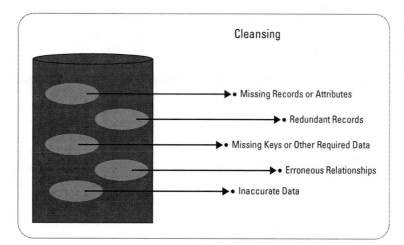

FIGURE 8.5

Information Cleansing Activities

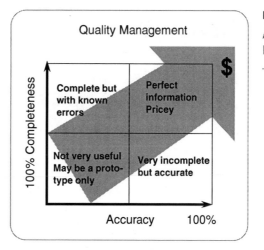

FIGURE 8.6

Accurate and Complete Information

(February 31 does not exist). An address containing Denver, Colorado, without a ZIP code is an example of incomplete information that is accurate. For their information, most organizations determine a percentage high enough to make good decisions at a reasonable cost, such as 85 percent accurate and 65 percent complete.

98

Baltzan–Phillips–Haag:
Business Driven
Technology, Third Edition

II. Exploring Business
Intelligence

8. Accessing
Organizational Information
— Data Warehouse

© The McGraw–Hill
Companies, 2009

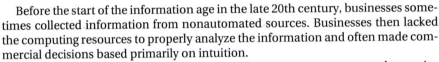

Business Intelligence

**Business
Intelligence**

Business intelligence (BI) refers to applications and technologies that are used to gather, provide access to, and analyze data and information to support decision-making efforts. An early reference to business intelligence occurs in Sun Tzu's book titled *The Art of War*. Sun Tzu claims that to succeed in war, one should have full knowledge of one's own strengths and weaknesses and full knowledge of the enemy's strengths and weaknesses. Lack of either one might result in defeat. A certain school of thought draws parallels between the challenges in business and those of war, specifically:

■ Collecting information.

■ Discerning patterns and meaning in the information.

■ Responding to the resultant information.[31]

Before the start of the information age in the late 20th century, businesses sometimes collected information from nonautomated sources. Businesses then lacked the computing resources to properly analyze the information and often made commercial decisions based primarily on intuition.

As businesses started automating more and more systems, more and more information became available. However, collection remained a challenge due to a lack of infrastructure for information exchange or to incompatibilities between systems. Reports sometimes took months to generate. Such reports allowed informed long-term strategic decision making. However, short-term tactical decision making continued to rely on intuition.

In modern businesses, increasing standards, automation, and technologies have led to vast amounts of available information. Data warehouse technologies have set up repositories to store this information. Improved ETL has increased the speedy collecting of information. Business intelligence has now become the art of sifting through large amounts of data, extracting information, and turning that information into actionable knowledge.

ENABLING BUSINESS INTELLIGENCE

Competitive organizations accumulate business intelligence to gain sustainable competitive advantage, and they may regard such intelligence as a valuable core competence in some instances. The principal BI enablers are technology, people, and corporate culture.[32]

Technology

Even the smallest company with BI software can do sophisticated analyses today that were unavailable to the largest organizations a generation ago. The largest companies today can create enterprisewide BI systems that compute and monitor metrics on virtually every variable important for managing the company. How is this possible? The answer is technology—the most significant enabler of business intelligence.

People

Understanding the role of people in BI allows organizations to systematically create insight and turn these insights into actions. Organizations can improve their decision making by having the right people making the decisions. This usually means a manager who is in the field and close to the customer rather than an analyst rich in data but poor in experience. In recent years "business intelligence for the masses" has been an important trend, and many organizations have made great strides in providing sophisticated yet simple analytical tools and information to a much larger user population than previously possible.

Culture

A key responsibility of executives is to shape and manage corporate culture. The extent to which the BI attitude flourishes in an organization depends in large part on the organization's culture. Perhaps the most important step an organization can take to encourage BI is to measure the performance of the organization against a set of key indicators. The actions of publishing what the organization thinks are the most important indicators, measuring these indicators, and analyzing the results to guide improvement display a strong commitment to BI throughout the organization.

OPENING CASE STUDY QUESTIONS

1. Determine how Wikipedia could use a data warehouse to improve its business operations.

2. Explain why Wikipedia must cleanse or scrub the information in its data warehouse.

3. Explain how a company could use information from Wikipedia to gain business intelligence.

Chapter Eight Case: Mining the Data Warehouse

According to a Merrill Lynch survey in 2006, business intelligence software and data-mining tools were at the top of CIOs' technology spending list. Following are a few examples of how companies are using data warehousing and data-mining tools to gain valuable business intelligence.

Ben & Jerry's

These days, when we all scream for ice cream, Ben & Jerry's cuts through the din by using integrated query, reporting, and online analytical processing technology from BI software vendor Business Objects. Through an Oracle database and with BI from Business Objects, Ben & Jerry's tracks the ingredients and life of each pint. If a consumer calls in with a complaint, the consumer affairs staff matches the pint with which supplier's milk, eggs, cherries, or whatever did not meet the organization's near-obsession with quality.

The BI tools let Ben & Jerry's officials access, analyze, and act on customer information collected by the sales, finance, purchasing, and quality-assurance departments. The company can determine what milk customers prefer in the making of the ice cream. The technology helped Ben & Jerry's track more than 12,500 consumer contacts in 2005. The information ranged from comments about the ingredients used in ice cream to queries about social causes supported by the company.

California Pizza Kitchen

California Pizza Kitchen (CPK) is a leading casual dining chain in the premium pizza segment with a recognized consumer brand and an established, loyal customer base. Founded in 1985, there are currently more than 130 full-service restaurants in over 26 states, the District of Columbia, and five foreign countries.

Before implementing its BI tool, Cognos, CPK used spreadsheets to plan and track its financial statements and line items. The finance team had difficulty managing the volumes of data, complex calculations, and constant changes to the spreadsheets. It took several weeks of two people working full time to obtain one version of the financial statements and future forecast. In addition, the team was limited by the software's inability to link cells and calculations across multiple spreadsheets, so updating other areas of corporate records became a time-consuming task. With Cognos, quarterly forecasting cycles have been reduced from eight days to two days. The finance team can now spend more time reviewing the results rather than collecting and entering the data.

Noodles & Company

Noodles & Company has more than 70 restaurants throughout Colorado, Illinois, Maryland, Michigan, Minnesota, Texas, Utah, Virginia, and Wisconsin. The company recently purchased Cognos BI tools to help implement reporting standards and communicate real-time operational information to field management throughout the United States.

Before implementing the first phase of the Cognos solution, IT and finance professionals spent days compiling report requests from numerous departments including sales and marketing, human resources, and real estate. Since completing phase one, operational Cognos reports are being accessed on a daily basis through the Noodles & Company Web site. This provides users with a single, 360-degree view of the business and consistent reporting throughout the enterprise.

Noodles & Company users benefit from the flexible query and reporting capabilities, allowing them to see patterns in the data to leverage new business opportunities. Cognos tools can pull information directly from a broad array of relational, operational, and other systems.[33]

Questions

1. Explain how Ben & Jerry's is using business intelligence tools to remain successful and competitive in a saturated market.
2. Identify why information cleansing is critical to California Pizza Kitchen's business intelligence tool's success.
3. Illustrate why 100 percent accurate and complete information is impossible for Noodles & Company to obtain.
4. Describe how each of the companies above is using BI to gain a competitive advantage.

TECHNOLOGY PLUG-IN POINTERS>>

Review **Technology Plug-In T3 "Problem Solving Using Excel"** for a comprehensive tutorial on how to create and sort a list in a workbook, use filters, organize and analyze entries by using subtotals, and create summary information by using pivot tables and pivot charts.

Review **Technology Plug-In T7 "Problem Solving Using Access"** for a comprehensive tutorial on using the query-by-example tool to select data from a table or tables, as well as to sort and filter data.

UNIT SUMMARY

The five common characteristics of quality information include accuracy, completeness, consistency, uniqueness, and timeliness. The costs to an organization of having low quality information can be enormous and could result in revenue losses and ultimately business failure. Databases maintain information about various types of objects, events, people, and places and help to alleviate many of the problems associated with low quality information such as redundancy, integrity, and security.

A data warehouse is a logical collection of information—gathered from many different operational databases—that supports business analysis activities and decision-making tasks. Data marts contain a subset of data warehouse information. Organizations gain tremendous insight into their business by mining the information contained in data warehouses and data marts.

Understanding the value of information is key to business success. Employees must be able to optimally access and analyze organizational information. The more knowledge employees have concerning how the organization stores, maintains, provides access to, and protects information the better prepared they will be when they need to use that information to make critical business decisions.

KEY TERMS

Analytical information,   75
Attribute,   81
Backward integration,   88
Business Intelligence (BI),   98
Business-critical integrity constraint,   84
Cube,   94
Database,   80
Database management system (DBMS),   85
Data-driven Web site,   86
Data mart,   93
Data mining,   95
Data-mining tool,   95

Data warehouse,   93
Entity,   81
Extraction, transformation, and loading (ETL),   93
Foreign key,   81
Forward integration,   88
Hierarchical database model,   81
Information cleansing or scrubbing,   96
Information granularity,   73
Information integrity,   84
Integration,   88
Integrity constraint,   84
Logical view,   83

Network database model,   81
Performance,   83
Physical view,   83
Primary key,   81
Real-time information,   75
Real-time system,   75
Redundancy,   84
Relational database model,   81
Relational integrity constraint,   84
Scalability,   83
Transactional information,   74

Harrah's—Gambling Big on Technology

The large investment made by Harrah's Entertainment Inc. in its information technology strategy has been tremendously successful. The results of Harrah's investment include:

- 10 percent annual increase in customer visits.
- 33 percent increase in gross market revenue.
- Yearly profits of over $208 million.
- Highest three-year ROI (return on investment) in the industry.
- A network that links over 42,000 gaming machines in 26 casinos across 12 states.
- Rated number six of the 100 best places to work in IT for 2003 by *ComputerWorld* magazine.
- Recipient of 2000 Leadership in Data Warehousing Award from the Data Warehousing Institute (TDWI), the premier association for data warehousing.

The casino industry is highly competitive. Bill Harrah was a man ahead of his time when he opened his first bingo parlor in 1937 with the commitment of getting to know each one of his customers. In 1984, Phil Satre, president and CEO of Harrah's, continued a commitment to customers. In search of its competitive advantage, Harrah's invested in an enterprisewide technology infrastructure to maintain Bill Harrah's original conviction: "Serve your customers well and they will be loyal."

Harrah's Commitment to Customers

Harrah's recently implemented its patented Total Rewards™ program to help build strong relationships with its customers. The program rewards customers for their loyalty by tracking their gaming habits across its 26 properties and currently maintains information on over 19 million customers, information the company uses to analyze, predict, and maximize each customer's value.

One major reason for the company's success is Harrah's implementation of a service-oriented strategy. Total Rewards allows Harrah's to give every customer the appropriate amount of personal attention, whether it's leaving sweets in the hotel room or offering free meals. Total Rewards works by providing each customer with an account and a corresponding card that the player swipes each time he or she plays a casino game. The program collects information on the amount of time the customers gamble, their total winnings and losses, and their betting strategies. Customers earn points based on the amount of time they spend gambling, which they can then exchange for comps such as free dinners, hotel rooms, tickets to shows, and even cash.

Total Rewards helps employees determine which level of service to provide each customer. When a customer makes a reservation at Harrah's, the service representative taking the call can view the customer's detailed information including the customer's loyalty level, games typically played, past winnings and losses, and potential net worth. If the service representative notices that the customer has a Diamond loyalty level, for example, the service representative knows that customer should never have to wait in line and should always receive free upgrades to the most expensive rooms.

"Almost everything we do in marketing and decision making is influenced by technology," says Gary Loveman, Harrah's chief operating officer. "The prevailing wisdom in this business is that the attractiveness of property drives customers. Our approach is different. We stimulate demand by knowing our customers. For example, if one of our customers always vacations at Harrah's in April, they will receive a promotion in February redeemable for a free weekend in April."

Gaining Business Intelligence with a Data Warehouse

Over 90 million customers visit Harrah's each year, and tracking a customer base larger than the population of Australia is a challenge. To tackle it, Harrah's began developing a system called WINet (Winner's Information Network). WINet links all Harrah's properties, allowing the company to collect and share customer information on an enterprisewide basis. WINet collects customer information from all the company transactions, game machines, and hotel management and reservations systems and places the information in a central data warehouse. Information in the data warehouse includes both customer and gaming information recorded in hourly increments. The marketing department uses the data warehouse to analyze customer information for patterns and insights, which allows it to create individualized marketing programs for each customer based on spending habits. Most important, the data warehouse allows the company to make business decisions based on information, not intuition.

Casinos traditionally treat customers as though they belong to a single property, typically the place the customer most frequently visits. Harrah's was the first casino to realize the potential of rewarding customers for visiting more than one property. Today, Harrah's has found that customers who visit more than one of its properties represent the fastest growing revenue segment. In the first two years of the Total Rewards program, the company received a $100 million increase in revenue from customers who gambled at more than one casino.

Harrah's also uses business intelligence to determine gaming machine performance. Using the data warehouse, Harrah's examines the performance and cost structure of each individual gaming machine. The company can quickly identify games that do not deliver optimal operational performance and can make a decision to move or replace the games. The capability to assess the performance of each individual slot machine has provided Harrah's with savings in the tens of millions of dollars. CIO Tim Stanley stated, "As we leverage more data from our data warehouse and increase the use and sophistication of our decision science analytical tools, we expect to have many new ways to improve customer loyalty and satisfaction, drive greater revenues, and decrease our costs as part of our ongoing focus on achieving sustainable profitability and success."

Information Security and Privacy

Some customers have concerns about Harrah's information collection strategy since they want to keep their gambling information private. The good news for these customers is that casinos are actually required to be more mindful of privacy concerns than most companies. For example, casinos cannot send marketing material to any underage persons. To adhere to strict government regulations, casinos must ensure that the correct information security and restrictions are in place. Many other companies actually make a great deal of money by selling customer information. Harrah's will not be joining in this trend since its customer information is one of its primary competitive advantages.

The Future of Harrah's

Harrah's current systems support approximately $140,000 in revenue per hour (that's almost $25 million weekly). In the future, Harrah's hopes to become device-independent by allowing employees to access the company's data warehouse via PDAs, handheld computers, and even cell phones. "Managing relationships with customers is incredibly important to the health of our business," Stanley says. "We will apply whatever technology we can to do that."[26]

Questions

1. Identify the effects poor information might have on Harrah's service-oriented business strategy.
2. Summarize how Harrah's uses database technologies to implement its service-oriented strategy.
3. Harrah's was one of the first casino companies to find value in offering rewards to customers who visit multiple Harrah's locations. Describe the effects on the company if it did not build any integrations among the databases located at each of its casinos.
4. Estimate the potential impact to Harrah's business if there is a security breach in its customer information.
5. Explain the business effects if Harrah's fails to use data-mining tools to gather business intelligence.
6. Identify three different types of data marts Harrah's might want to build to help it analyze its operational performance.
7. Predict what might occur if Harrah's fails to clean or scrub its information before loading it into its data warehouse.
8. How could Harrah's use data mining to increase revenue?

✳ UNIT CLOSING CASE TWO

Searching for Revenue—Google

Google founders Sergey Brin and Larry Page recently made *Forbes* magazine's list of world billionaires. The company is famous for its highly successful search engine.

How Google Works

Figure Unit 2.1 displays the life of an average Google query. The Web server sends the query to the index servers. The content inside the index server is similar to the index at the back of a book—it tells which pages contain the words that match any particular query term. Then the query travels to the document servers, which actually retrieve the stored documents and generate snippets to describe each search result. Finally, the search engine returns the results to the user. All these activities occur within a fraction of a second.

Google consists of three distinct parts:

1. The Web crawler, known as Googlebot, finds and retrieves Web pages and passes them to the Google indexer. Googlebot functions much like a Web browser. It sends a request for a Web page to a Web server, downloads the entire page, and then hands it off to Google's indexer. Googlebot can request thousands of different Web pages simultaneously.
2. The indexer indexes every word on each page and stores the resulting index of words in a huge database. This index is sorted alphabetically by search term, with each index

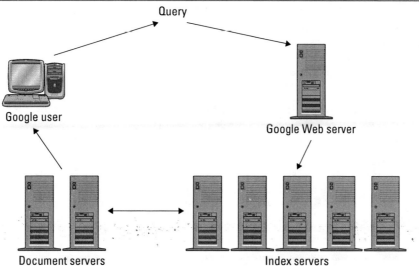

FIGURE UNIT 2.1

How Google Works

Query

Google user

Google Web server

Document servers

Index servers

entry storing a list of documents in which the term appears and the location within the text where it occurs. Indexing the full text of Web pages allows Google to go beyond simply matching single search terms. Google gives more priority to pages that have search terms near each other and in the same order as the query. Google can also match multi-word phrases and sentences.

3. The query processor compares the search query to the index and recommends the documents that it considers most relevant. Google considers over a hundred factors in determining which documents are most relevant to a query, including the popularity of the page, the position and size of the search terms within the page, and the proximity of the search terms to one another. The query processor has several parts, including the user interface (search box), the "engine" that evaluates queries and matches them to relevant documents, and the results formatter.

Selling Words

Google's primary line of business is its search engine; however, the company does not generate revenue from people using its site to search the Internet. It generates revenue from the marketers and advertisers that are paying to place their ads on the site.

Around 200 million times each day, people from all over the world access Google to perform searches. AdWords, a part of the Google site, allows advertisers to bid on common search terms. The advertisers simply enter in the keywords they want to bid on and the maximum amounts they want to pay per click, per day. Google then determines a price and a search ranking for those keywords based on how much other advertisers are willing to pay for the same terms. Pricing for keywords can range from 5 cents to $3 a click. A general search term like "tropical vacation" costs less than a more specific term like "Hawaiian vacation." Whoever bids the most for a term appears in a sponsored advertisement link either at the top or along the side of the search-results page.

Paid search is the ultimate in targeted advertising because consumers type in exactly what they want. One of the primary advantages of paid search Web programs such as AdWords is that customers do not find it annoying, as is the problem with some forms of Web advertising such as banner ads and pop-up ads. According to the Interactive Advertising Bureau, overall industry revenues from paid search surpassed banner ads in the third quarter of 2003.

"A big percentage of queries we get are commercial in nature," confirms Salar Kamangar, Google's director of product management. "It is a marketplace where the advertisers tell us about themselves by telling us how much each lead is worth. They have an incentive to bid how much they really want to pay, because if they underbid, their competitors will get more traffic."

Kamangar came up with the AdWords concept and oversees that part of the business today. Ad-Words, which launched in 2005, accounts for the vast majority of Google's annual revenue and the company has over 150,000 advertisers in its paid-search program, up from zero in 2002.

Expanding Google

Google has a secret weapon working for its research and development department—hackers. Hackers actually develop many of the new and unique ways to expand Google. The company elicits hacker ideas through its application program interface (API), a large piece of the Google code. The API enables developers to build applications around the Google search engine. By making the API freely available, Google has inspired a community of programmers that are extending Google's capabilities. "It's working," states Nelson Minar, who runs the API effort. "We get clever hacks, educational uses, and wacky stuff. We love to see people do creative things with our product." A few of the successful user-developed applications include:

- **Banana Slug**—www.bananaslug.com. For customers who hit a dead end with Google search, the site adds a random word to search text that generates surprising results.
- **Cookin' with Google**—www.researchbuzz.org. Enter the ingredients that are in the fridge and the site returns potential recipes for those ingredients.
- **Google Alert**—www.googlealert.com. Google Alert automatically searches the Web for information on a topic and returns the results by e-mail.
- **RateMyProfessors.com**—www.ratemyprofessors.com. The goal of this site was to create a place where students could rank their teachers. However, too many jokesters typing in false professor names such as "Professor Harry Leg" and "Professor Ima Dog" left the information on the site questionable. The developers turned to the Google API to create an automatic verification tool. If Google finds enough mentions in conjunction with a professor or university then it considers the information valid and posts it to the Web site.

Stopping Google

As part of its Google Print Library Project, the company is working to scan all or parts of the book collections of the University of Michigan, Harvard University, Stanford University, the New York Public Library, and Oxford University. It intends to make those texts searchable on Google and to sell advertisements on the Web pages.

The Authors Guild filed a lawsuit against Google, alleging that its scanning and digitizing of library books constitutes a massive copyright infringement. "This is a plain and brazen violation of copyright law," Nick Taylor, president of the New York-based Authors Guild, said in a statement about the lawsuit, which is seeking class-action status. "It's not up to Google or anyone other than the authors, the rightful owners of these copyrights, to decide whether and how their works will be copied."

In response, Google defended the program in a company blog posting. "We regret that this group chose to sue us over a program that will make millions of books more discoverable to the world—especially since any copyright holder can exclude their books from the program," wrote Susan Wojcicki, vice president of product management. "Google respects copyright. The use we make of all the books we scan through the Library Project is fully consistent with both the fair use doctrine under U.S. copyright law and the principles underlying copyright law itself, which allow everything from parodies to excerpts in book reviews."[35]

Questions

1. Determine if Google's search results are examples of transactional or analytical information.

2. Describe the impact on Google's business if the search information it presented to its customers was of low quality.

3. Explain how the Web site RateMyProfessors.com solved its problem of poor information.
4. Identify the different types of entity classes that might be stored in Google's indexing database.
5. Identify how Google might use a data warehouse to improve its business.
6. Explain why Google would need to cleanse the information in its data warehouse.
7. Identify a data mart that Google's marketing and sales department might use to track and analyze its AdWords revenue.

✳ MAKING BUSINESS DECISIONS

1. Improving Information Quality

HangUps Corporation designs and distributes closet organization structures. The company operates five different systems: order entry, sales, inventory management, shipping, and billing. The company has severe information quality issues including missing, inaccurate, redundant, and incomplete information. The company wants to implement a data warehouse containing information from the five different systems to help maintain a single customer view, drive business decisions, and perform multidimensional analysis. Identify how the organization can improve its information quality when it begins designing and building its data warehouse.

2. Information Timeliness

Information timeliness is a major consideration for all organizations. Organizations need to decide the frequency of backups and the frequency of updates to a data warehouse. In a team, describe the timeliness requirements for backups and updates to a data warehouse for

- Weather tracking systems.
- Car dealership inventories.
- Vehicle tire sales forecasts.
- Interest rates.
- Restaurant inventories.
- Grocery store inventories.

3. Entities and Attributes

Martex Inc. is a manufacturer of athletic equipment and its primary lines of business include running, tennis, golf, swimming, basketball, and aerobics equipment. Martex currently supplies four primary vendors including Sam's Sports, Total Effort, The Underline, and Maximum Workout. Martex wants to build a database to help it organize its products. In a group, identify the different types of entity classes and the related attributes that Martex will want to consider when designing the database.

4. Integrating Information

You are currently working for the Public Transportation Department of Chatfield. The department controls all forms of public transportation including buses, subways, and trains. Each department has about 300 employees and maintains its own accounting, inventory, purchasing, and human resource systems. Generating reports across departments is a difficult task and usually involves gathering and correlating the information from the many different systems. It typically takes about two weeks to generate the quarterly balance sheets and profit and loss statements. Your team has been asked to compile a report recommending what the Public Transportation Department of Chatfield can do to alleviate its information and system issues. Be sure that your report addresses the various reasons departmental reports are presently difficult to obtain as well as how you plan to solve this problem.

5. Explaining Relational Databases

You have been hired by Vision, a start-up recreational equipment company. Your manager, Holly Henningson, is unfamiliar with databases and their associated business value. Holly has asked you to create a report detailing the basics of databases. Holly would also like you to provide a detailed explanation of relational databases along with their associated business advantages.

★ APPLY YOUR KNOWLEDGE

1. Determining Information Quality Issues

Real People is a magazine geared toward working individuals that provides articles and advice on everything from car maintenance to family planning. *Real People* is currently experiencing problems with its magazine distribution list. Over 30 percent of the magazines mailed are returned because of incorrect address information, and each month it receives numerous calls from angry customers complaining that they have not yet received their magazines. Below is a sample of *Real People*'s customer information. Create a report detailing all of the issues with the information, potential causes of the information issues, and solutions the company can follow to correct the situation.

ID	First Name	Middle Initial	Last Name	Street	City	State	ZIP Code
433	M	J	Jones	13 Denver	Denver	CO	87654
434	Margaret	J	Jones	13 First Ave.	Denver	CO	87654
434	Brian	F	Hoover	Lake Ave.	Columbus	OH	87654
435	Nick	H	Schweitzer	65 Apple Lane	San Francisco	OH	65664
436	Richard	A		567 55th St.	New York	CA	98763
437	Alana	B	Smith	121 Tenny Dr.	Buffalo	NY	142234
438	Trevor	D	Darrian	90 Fresrdestil	Dallas	TX	74532

2. Mining the Data Warehouse

Alana Smith is a senior buyer for a large wholesaler that sells different types of arts and crafts to greeting card stores such as Hallmark. Alana's latest marketing strategy is to send all of her customers a new line of hand-made picture frames from Russia. Alana's data support her decision for the new line. Her analysis predicts that the frames should sell an average of 10 to 15 per store, per day. Alana is excited about the new line and is positive it will be a success.

One month later Alana learns that the frames are selling 50 percent below expectations and averaging between five and eight frames sold daily in each store. Alana decides to access the company's data warehouse to determine why sales are below expectations. Identify several different dimensions of data that Alana will want to analyze to help her decide what is causing the problems with the picture frame sales.

3. Cleansing Information

You are working for BI, a start-up business intelligence consulting company. You have a new client that is interested in hiring BI to clean up its information. To determine how good your work is, the client would like your analysis of the following spreadsheet.

CUST ID	First Name	Last Name	Address	City	State	ZIP	Phone	Last Order Date
233620	Christopher	Lee	12421 W Olympic Blvd	Los Angeles	CA	75080-1100	(972)680-7848	4/18/2002
233621	Bruce	Brandwen	268 W 44th St	New York	PA	10036-3906	(212)471-6077	5/3/2002
233622	Glr	Johnson	4100 E Dry Creek Rd	Littleton	CO	80122-3729	(303)712-5461	5/6/2002
233623	Dave	Owens	466 Commerce Rd	Staunton	VA	24401-4432	(540)851-0362	3/19/2002
233624	John	Coulbourn	124 Action St	Maynard	MA	1754	(978)987-0100	4/24/2002
233629	Dan	Gagliardo	2875 Union Rd	Cheektowaga	NY	14227-1461	(716)558-8191	5/4/2002
23362	Damanceee	Allen	1633 Broadway	New York	NY	10019-6708	(212)708-1576	
233630	Michael	Peretz	235 E 45th St	New York	NY	10017-3305	(212)210-1340	4/30/2002
							(608)238-9690	
233631	Jody	Veeder	440 Science Dr	Madison	WI	53711-1064	X227	3/27/2002
233632	Michael	Kehrer	3015 SSE Loop 323	Tyler	TX	75701	(903)579-3229	4/28/
233633	Erin	Yoon	3500 Carillon Pt	Kirkland	WA	98033-7354	(425)897-7221	3/25/2002
233634	Madeline	Shefferly	4100 E Dry Creek Rd	Littleton	CO	80122-3729	(303)486-3949	3/33/2002
233635	Steven	Conduit	1332 Enterprise Dr	West Chester	PA	19380-5970	(610)692-5900	4/27/2002
233636	Joseph	Kovach	1332 Enterprise Dr	West Chester	PA	19380-5970	(610)692-5900	4/28/2002
233637	Richard	Jordan	1700 N	Philadelphia	PA	19131-4728	(215)581-6770	3/19/2002
233638	Scott	Mikolajczyk	1655 Crofton Blvd	Crofton	MD	21114-1387	(410)729-8155	4/28/2002
233639	Susan	Shragg	1875 Century Park E	Los Angeles	CA	90067-2501	(310)785-0511	4/29/2002
233640	Rob	Ponto	29777 Telegraph Rd	Southfield	MI	48034-1303	(810)204-4724	5/5/2002
233642	Lauren	Butler	1211 Avenue Of The Americas	New York	NY	10036-8701	(212)852-7494	4/22/2002
233643	Christopher	Lee	12421 W Olympic Blvd	Los Angeles	CA	90064-1022	(310)689-2577	3/25/2002
233644	Michelle	Decker	6922 Hollywood Blvd	Hollywood	CA	90028-6117	(323)817-4655	5/8/2002
233647	Natalia	Galeano	1211 Avenue Of The Americas	New York	NY	10036-8701	(646)728-6911	4/23/2002
233648	Bobbie	Orchard	4201 Congress St	Charlotte	NC	28209-4617	(704)557-2444	5/11/2002
233650	Ben	Konfino	1111 Stewart Ave	Bethpage	NY	11714-3533	(516)803-1406	3/19/2002
233651	Lenee	Santana	1050 Techwood Dr NW	Atlanta	GA	30318-KKRR	(404)885-2000	3/22/2002
233652	Lauren	Monks	7700 Wisconsin Ave	Bethesda	MD	20814-3578	(301)771-4772	3/19/2005
233653	Mark	Woolley	10950 Washington Blvd	Culver City	CA	90232-4026	(310)202-2900	4/20/2002
233654	Stan	Matthews	1235 W St NE	Washington	DC	20018-1107	(202)608-2000	3/25/2002

4. Different Dimensions

The focus of data warehousing is to extend the transformation of data into information. Data warehouses offer strategic level, external, integrated, and historical information so businesses can make projections, identify trends, and make key business decisions. The data warehouse collects and stores integrated sets of historical information from multiple operational systems and feeds them to one or more data marts. It may also provide end-user access to support enterprisewide views of information.

Project Focus

You are currently working on a marketing team for a large corporation that sells jewelry around the world. Your boss has asked you to look at the following dimensions of data to determine which ones you want in your data mart for performing sales and market analysis (see Figure AYK.1). As a team, categorize the different dimensions ranking them from 1 to 5, with 1 indicating that the dimension offers the highest value and must be in your data mart and 5 indicating that the dimension offers the lowest value and does not need to be in your data mart.

FIGURE AYK.1

Data Warehouse Data

Dimension	Value (1–5)	Dimension	Value (1–5)
Product number		Season	
Store location		Promotion	
Customer net worth		Payment method	
Number of sales personnel		Commission policy	
Customer eating habits		Manufacturer	
Store hours		Traffic report	
Salesperson ID		Customer language	
Product style		Weather	
Order date		Customer gender	
Product quantity		Local tax information	
Ship date		Local cultural demographics	
Current interest rate		Stock market closing	
Product cost		Customer religious affiliation	
Customer's political affiliation		Reason for purchase	
Local market analysis		Employee dress code policy	
Order time		Customer age	
Customer spending habits		Employee vacation policy	
Product price		Employee benefits	
Exchange rates		Current tariff information	
Product gross margin			

5. Understanding Search

Pretend that you are a search engine. Choose a topic to query. It can be anything such as your favorite book, movie, band, or sports team. Search your topic on Google, pick three or four pages from the results, and print them out. On each printout, find the individual words from your query (such as "Boston Red Sox" or "The Godfather") and use a highlighter to mark each word with color. Do that for each of the documents that you print out. Now tape those documents on a wall, step back a few feet, and review your documents. If you did not know what the rest of a page said and could only judge by the colored words, which document do you think would be most relevant? Is there anything that would make a document look more relevant? Is it better to have the words be in a large heading or to occur several times in a smaller font? Do you prefer it if the words are at the top or the bottom of the page? How often do the words need to appear? Come up with two or three things you would look for to see if a document matched a query well. This exercise mimics search engine processes and should help you understand why a search engine returns certain results over others.

U N I T 4

Building Innovation

UNIT FOUR OPENING CASE

eBay—The Ultimate E-Business

Pierre Omidyar was just 28 when he sat down over a long holiday weekend to write the original computer code for what eventually became an Internet super brand—the auction site eBay. Omidyar viewed auctions as a fair mechanism for Internet commerce where sellers could set their minimum prices, and buyers could then determine an item's market value by bidding up to what they were willing to pay. A novel feedback system could allow buyers and sellers to rate each other, helping minimize fraud by enabling the community to police itself. "I really wanted to give the individual the power to be a producer as well. It was letting the users take responsibility for building the community," Omidyar would later explain.

The site launched on Labor Day, September 4, 1995, under the title of Auction Web, soon to be renamed after the site's domain name—eBay.com (a shortening of Echo Bay, Omidyar's consulting firm). The service was free at first, but started charging to cover Internet service provider costs.

A National Marketplace

Omidyar's auction Web site, eBay.com, took off. It provided something novel that its users craved: an efficient national marketplace with a strong community built on fairness and trust. A photography student looking for a used camera could choose from models across the nation and trust the timely delivery of the product. The owner of a vintage clothing store could sell to collectors nationwide. The community would expose a deceptive or fraudulent user and ban them from the marketplace.

Entrepreneurs in record numbers began setting up shop on eBay. According to a survey conducted for eBay by ACNielsen International Research, more than 1 million people support themselves by selling items on eBay, up from 75,000 in 2002. In addition to these professional eBay sellers, another 1.5 million individuals supplement their income by selling on eBay.

The stock market value of Omidyar's innovative company grew to $2 billion in just three years, and his site's staying power as an economic engine was evident. Jeffrey Skoll, a Stanford MBA, joined the company in 1996 after the site was already profitable. In March 1998, Meg Whitman took over as president and CEO. In September 1998, eBay launched a successful public offering, making both Omidyar and Skoll billionaires—three years after Omidyar created eBay. As of 2005, Omidyar's 214 million eBay shares were worth about $8 billion.

Collaborating with eBay

This e-business is collaborating with marketplace, payment, and communication companies that add value for its customers.

Marketplace—The U.S. Postal Service

People who sell items on eBay all have one thing in common: They need to ship their goods to their customers. To support this growing economic force, eBay and the U.S. Postal Service created an innovative economic and educational opportunity.

The Postal Service's bread and butter—first-class mail—is beset by rising costs and falling use. E-mail and faxes have reduced the amount of mail sent each day, but the Postal Service still bears the cost of delivering to every business and home, six days a week. Package shipping, however, remains a profitable and booming business, as evidenced by the number and earnings of private shippers in the market.

The Postal Service offers free boxes and heavy-duty envelopes for shippers using overnight or priority mail. To make it easier for those in the vanguard of the new, digital economy, the Postal Service will pick up shipments from the sender, and its Web site sells mailing labels with postage included that can be printed out from a home computer. Over 20 million shipping labels with postage were printed via the eBay/Postal Service link in 2005. Customers can also link to the United Parcel Service site, but eBay does not have a formal relationship with Federal Express.

Payment—PayPal

Founded in 1998, PayPal, an eBay company, enables any individual or business with an e-mail address to securely, easily, and quickly send and receive payments online. PayPal's service builds on the existing financial infrastructure of bank accounts and credit cards and utilizes the world's most advanced proprietary fraud prevention systems to create a safe, global, real-time payment solution.

PayPal has quickly become a global leader in online payment solutions with 96 million account members worldwide. Buyers and sellers on eBay, online retailers, online businesses, as well as traditional off-line businesses are transacting with PayPal, available in 55 countries.

Communication—Skype

Skype, a global Internet communications company, allows people everywhere to make free, unlimited, superior quality voice calls via its innovative peer-to-peer software.

Since its launch in August 2003, Skype has been downloaded more than 163 million times in 225 countries and territories. Fifty-four million people are registered to use Skype's free services, with over 3 million simultaneous users on the network at any one time. Skype adds about 150,000 users a day.

In September 2005, eBay acquired Skype for approximately $2.6 billion, anticipating that Skype will streamline and improve communications between buyers and sellers as it is integrated into the eBay marketplace. Buyers will gain an easy way to talk to sellers quickly and get the information they need, and sellers can more easily build relationships. The auction company hopes the acquisition will strengthen its global marketplace and payments platform, while opening several new lines of business and creating significant new opportunities for the company.

Unforeseen Dangers of Collaboration

"Communications is at the heart of e-commerce and community," said Meg Whitman. "By combining the two leading e-commerce franchises, eBay and PayPal, with the leader in Internet voice communications, Skype, we will create an extraordinarily powerful environment for business on the Net."

In October 2005, one month after eBay's acquisition of Skype, a press release discussed two critical flaws in Skype's software, one of which could allow malicious hackers to take control of compromised systems and another that could allow attackers to crash the client software. While fixes for the issues were being addressed, businesses asked their users to refrain from using voice services based on proprietary protocols like Skype while on corporate networks because of network security issues. Perhaps Skype might not be the collaborative tool of choice for eBay.[1]

Introduction

One of the biggest forces changing business is the Internet. Technology companies like Intel and Cisco were among the first to seize the Internet to overhaul their operations. Intel deployed Web-based automation to liberate its 200 salesclerks from tedious order-entry positions. Instead, salesclerks concentrate on customer relationship management functions such as analyzing sales trends and pampering customers. Cisco handles 75 percent of its sales online, and 45 percent of online orders never touch employees' hands. This type of Internet-based ordering has helped Cisco hike productivity by 20 percent over the past few years.[2]

E-business is the conducting of business on the Internet, not only buying and selling, but also serving customers and collaborating with business partners. Organizations realize that putting up simple Web sites for customers, employees, and partners does not create an e-business. E-business Web sites must create a buzz, much as Amazon has done in the book-selling industry. E-business Web sites must be innovative, add value, and provide useful information. In short, the site must build a sense of community and collaboration, eventually becoming the port of entry for business. This unit focuses on the opportunities and advantages found with developing collaborative partnerships in e-business and includes:

- **Chapter Thirteen**—Creating Innovative Organizations.
- **Chapter Fourteen**—E-Business.
- **Chapter Fifteen**—Creating Collaborative Partnerships.
- **Chapter Sixteen**—Integrating Wireless Technology in Business.

CHAPTER 15

Creating Collaborative Partnerships

Teams, Partnerships, and Alliances

To be successful—and avoid being eliminated by the competition—an organization must constantly undertake new initiatives, address both minor and major problems, and capitalize on significant opportunities. To support these activities, an organization often will create and utilize teams, partnerships, and alliances because the expertise needed is beyond the scope of a single individual or organization. These teams, partnerships, and alliances can be formed internally among a company's employees or externally with other organizations (see Figure 15.1).

Businesses of all sizes and in all markets have witnessed the benefits of leveraging their IT assets to create competitive advantage. Whereas information technology efforts in the past were aimed at increasing operational efficiency, the advent and proliferation of network-based computing (the Internet being the most visible, but not only, example) has enabled organizations to build systems with which all sorts of communities can interact. The ultimate result will allow organizations to do business with customers, business partners, suppliers, governments and regulatory agencies, and any other community relevant to their particular operation or activity.

Solution People

FIGURE 15.1

Teams, Partnerships, and Alliances Within and External to an Organization

In the same way that organizations use internal teams, they are increasingly forming alliances and partnerships with other organizations. The **core competency** of an organization is its key strength, a business function that it does better than any of its competitors. Apple Computer is highly regarded for its strength in product design, while Accenture's core competency is the design and installation of information systems. A **core competency strategy** is one in which an organization chooses to focus specifically on what it does best (its core competency) and forms partnerships and alliances with other specialist organizations to handle nonstrategic business processes. Strategic alliances enable businesses to gain competitive advantages through access to a partner's resources, including markets, technologies, and people. Teaming up with another business adds complementary resources and capabilities, enabling participants to grow and expand more quickly and efficiently, especially fast-growing companies that rely heavily on outsourcing many areas of their business to extend their technical and operational resources. In the outsourcing process, they save time and boost productivity by not having to develop their own systems from scratch. They are then free to concentrate on innovation and their core business.

Information technology makes such business partnerships and alliances easier to establish and manage. An **information partnership** occurs when two or more organizations cooperate by integrating their IT systems, thereby providing customers with the best of what each can offer. The advent of the Internet has greatly increased the opportunity for IT-enabled business partnerships and alliances. Amazon developed a profitable business segment by providing e-business outsourcing services to other retailers that use Amazon's Web site software. Some well-known retailers partnering with Amazon include Office Depot and Target.[26]

Collaboration Systems

Collaboration

Heineken USA has shortened its inventory cycle time for beer production and distribution from three months to four weeks. By using its collaborative system to forecast demand and expedite shipping, the company has dramatically cut inventory levels and shipping costs while increasing sales.

Over the past few years most business processes have changed on various dimensions (e.g., flexibility, interconnectivity, coordination style, autonomy) because of market conditions and organizational models. Frequently, information is located within physically separated systems as more and more organizations spread their reach globally. This creates a need for a software infrastructure that enables collaboration systems.

A **collaboration system** is an IT-based set of tools that supports the work of teams by facilitating the sharing and flow of information. Collaboration solves specific business tasks such as telecommuting, online meetings, deploying applications, and remote project and sales management (see Figure 15.2).

Collaboration systems allow people, teams, and organizations to leverage and build upon the ideas and talents of staff, suppliers, customers, and business partners. It involves unique business challenges that:

- Include complex interactions between people who may be in different locations and desire to work across function and discipline areas.
- Require flexibility in work process and the ability to involve others quickly and easily.
- Call for creating and sharing information rapidly and effortlessly within a team.

Most organizations collaborate with other companies in some capacity. Consider the supplier-customer relationship, which can be thought of in terms of a continuous life cycle of engagement, transaction, fulfillment, and service activities. Rarely do companies excel in all four life cycle areas, either from a business process or from a technology-enabled aspect. Successful organizations identify and invest in their core competencies, and outsource or collaborate for those competencies that are not core to them. Collaboration systems fall into one of two categories:

1. **Unstructured collaboration** (sometimes referred to as **information collaboration**) includes document exchange, shared whiteboards, discussion forums, and e-mail. These functions can improve personal productivity, reducing the time spent searching for information or chasing answers.

2. **Structured collaboration** (or **process collaboration**) involves shared participation in business processes, such as workflow, in which knowledge is hard-coded as rules. This is beneficial in terms of improving automation and the routing of information.

Regardless of location or format—be it unstructured or structured—relevant accurate information must be readily and consistently available to those who need it anytime, anywhere, and on any device. The integration of IT systems enables an organization to provide employees, partners, customers, and suppliers with the ability to access, find, analyze, manage, and collaborate on content. The collaboration can be done across a wide variety of formats, languages, and platforms. Figure 15.3 illustrates many of the typical collaborative functions within most organizations.

Lockheed Martin Aeronautics Company's ability to share complex project information across an extended supply chain in real time was key in its successful bid for a $19 billion Department of Defense (DoD) contract to build 21 supersonic stealth fighters. New government procurement rules require defense contractors to communicate effectively to ensure that deadlines are met, costs are controlled, and projects are managed throughout the life cycle of the contract.[27]

FIGURE 15.2

Collaborative Business Areas

FIGURE 15.3

Typical Collaborative Business Functions

Function	Collaborator(s)	Business Function(s)
Planning and forecasting	Supplier, customer	Real-time information sharing (forecast information and sales information)
Product design	Supplier, customer	Document exchange, computer-aided design (CAD)
Strategic sourcing	Supplier	Negotiation, supplier performance management
Component compatibility testing	Supplier	Component compatibility
Pricing	Supplier, customer	Pricing in supply chain
Marketing	Supplier, customer	Joint/cooperative marketing campaigns, branding
Sales	Customer	Shared leads, presentations, configuration and quotes
Make-to-order	Customer	Requirements, capabilities, contract terms
Order processing	Supplier, customer	Order solution
Fulfillment: Logistics and service	Supplier, customer	Coordination of distribution
International trade logistics	Customer	Document exchange, import/export documents
Payment	Customer	Order receipt, invoicing
Customer service/support	Supplier, customer	Shared/split customer support

In anticipation of the contract, the Fort Worth, Texas, unit of Lockheed Martin Corporation developed a real-time collaboration system that can tie together its partners, suppliers, and DoD customers via the Internet. The platform lets participants collectively work on product design and engineering tasks as well as supply chain and life cycle management issues. Lockheed will host all transactions and own the project information. The platform will let DoD and Lockheed project managers track the daily progress of the project in real time. This is the first major DoD project with such a requirement. The contract, awarded to the Lockheed unit and partners Northrop Grumman Corp. and BAE Systems, is the first installment in what could amount to a $200 billion program for 3,000 jet fighters over 40 years. The strengths of the collaboration process lie with the integration of many systems, namely:[29]

- Knowledge management systems
- Content management systems
- Workflow management systems
- Groupware systems

Knowledge Management Systems

Knowledge management (KM) involves capturing, classifying, evaluating, retrieving, and sharing information assets in a way that provides context for effective decisions and actions. It is best to think of KM in the broadest context. Succinctly put, KM is the process through which organizations generate value from their intellectual and knowledge-based assets. Most often, generating value from such assets involves codifying what employees, partners, and customers know, and sharing that information among employees, departments, and even with other companies to devise best practices. The definition says nothing about technology; while KM is often facilitated by IT, technology by itself is not KM.

Think of a golf caddie as a simplified example of a knowledge worker. Good caddies do more than carry clubs and track down wayward balls. When asked, a good caddie will give advice to golfers, such as, "The wind makes the ninth hole play 15 yards longer." Accurate advice may lead to a bigger tip at the end of the day. The golfer, having derived a benefit from the caddie's advice, may be more likely to play that course again. If a good caddie is willing to share what he knows with other caddies, then they all may eventually earn bigger tips. How would KM work to make this happen? The caddie master may decide to reward caddies for sharing their knowledge by offering them credits for pro shop merchandise. Once the best advice is collected, the course manager would publish the information in notebooks (or make it available on PDAs) and distribute them to all the caddies. The end result of a well-designed KM program is that everyone wins. In this case, caddies get bigger tips and deals on merchandise, golfers play better because they benefit from the collective experience of caddies, and the course owners win because better scores lead to repeat business.[30]

KM IN BUSINESS

KM has assumed greater urgency in American business over the past few years as millions of baby boomers prepare to retire. When they punch out for the last time, the knowledge they gleaned about their jobs, companies, and industries during their long careers will walk out with them—unless companies take measures to retain their insights. In addition, CIOs who have entered into outsourcing agreements must address the thorny issue of transferring the knowledge of their full-time staff members, who are losing their jobs because of an outsourcing deal, to the outsourcer's employees.[31]

Knowledge can be a real competitive advantage for an organization. Information technology can distribute an organization's knowledge base by interconnecting people and digitally gathering their expertise. The primary objective of knowledge management is to be sure that a company's knowledge of facts, sources of information, and solutions are readily available to all employees whenever it is needed.

Such knowledge management requires that organizations go well beyond providing information contained in spreadsheets, databases, and documents. It must include expert information that typically resides in people's heads. A **knowledge management system (KMS)** supports the capturing, organization, and dissemination of knowledge (i.e., know-how) throughout an organization. It is up to the organization to determine what information qualifies as knowledge.

Knowledge Management

EXPLICIT AND TACIT KNOWLEDGE

Not all information is valuable. Individual companies must determine what information qualifies as intellectual and knowledge-based assets. In general, intellectual and knowledge-based assets fall into one of two categories: explicit or tacit. As a rule, **explicit knowledge** consists of anything that can be documented, archived, and codified, often with the help of IT. Examples of explicit knowledge are assets such as patents, trademarks, business plans, marketing research, and customer lists.

Tacit knowledge is the knowledge contained in people's heads. The challenge inherent in tacit knowledge is figuring out how to recognize, generate, share, and manage knowledge that resides in people's heads. While information technology in the form of e-mail, instant messaging, and related technologies can help facilitate the dissemination of tacit knowledge, identifying it in the first place can be a major obstacle. Shadowing and joint problem solving are two best practices for transferring or re-creating tacit knowledge inside an organization.[32]

Shadowing

With shadowing, less experienced staff observe more experienced staff to learn how the more experienced counterparts approach their work. Dorothy Leonard and Walter Swap, two knowledge management experts, stress the importance of having the protégé discuss his or her observations with the expert to deepen the dialog and crystallize the knowledge transfer.

Joint Problem Solving

Another sound approach is joint problem solving by expert and novice. Because people are often unaware of how they approach problems or do their work and therefore cannot automatically generate step-by-step instructions for doing whatever they do, having a novice and expert work together on a project will bring the expert's approach to light. The difference between shadowing and joint problem solving is that shadowing is more passive. With joint problem solving, the expert and the novice work hand in hand on a task.[33]

Information is of little use unless it is analyzed and made available to the right people, at the right place, and at the right time. To get the most value from intellectual assets, knowledge must be shared. An effective KMS system should help do one or more of the following:

- Foster innovation by encouraging the free flow of ideas.
- Improve customer service by streamlining response time.
- Boost revenues by getting products and services to market faster.

- Enhance employee retention rates by recognizing the value of employees' knowledge.
- Streamline operations and reduce costs by eliminating redundant or unnecessary processes.

A creative approach to knowledge management can result in improved efficiency, higher productivity, and increased revenues in practically any business function. Figure 15.4 indicates the reasons organizations launch KMS.

Software is helping ChevronTexaco Corporation improve how it manages the assets in oil fields by enabling employees in multiple disciplines to easily access and share the information they need to make decisions. ChevronTexaco teams of 10 to 30 people are responsible for managing the assets, such as the drilling equipment, pipelines, and facilities, for a particular oil field. Within each team, earth scientists and various engineers with expertise in production, reservoir, and facilities work together to keep the oil field up and running. Each member of the asset team needs to communicate with other members to make decisions based on the collection and analysis of huge amounts of information from various departments. Individual team members can look at information from the perspective of their own department.

This has helped ChevronTexaco achieve a 30 percent productivity gain, a 50 percent improvement in safety performance, and more than $2 billion in operating cost reductions. Through KMSs, ChevronTexaco has restructured its gasoline retailing business and now drills oil and gas wells faster and cheaper.[34]

Not every organization matches ChevronTexaco's success with KM. Numerous KM projects have failed over the past few years, generating an unwillingness to undertake—or even address—KM issues among many organizations. However, KM is an effective tool if it is tied directly to discrete business needs and opportunities. Beginning with targeted projects that deliver value quickly, companies can achieve the success that has proved elusive with many big-bang approaches. Successful KM projects typically focus on creating value in a specific process area, or even just for a certain type of transaction. Companies should start with one job at a time—preferably the most knowledge-oriented one—and build KM into a job function in a way that

FIGURE 15.4

Key Reasons Organizations Launch Knowledge Management Systems

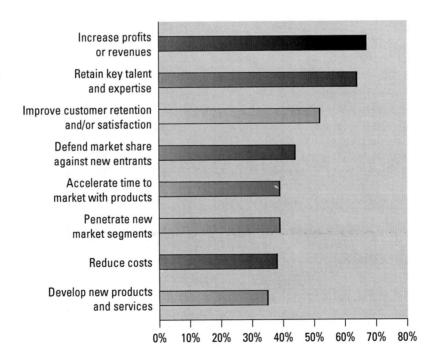

actually helps employees do their work better and faster, then expand to the next most knowledge-intensive job, and so on. Celebrating even small success with KM will help build a base of credibility and support for future KM projects.[35]

KM TECHNOLOGIES

KM is not a purely technology-based concept. Organizations that implement a centralized database system, electronic message board, Web portal, or any other collaborative tool in the hope that they have established a KMS are wasting both their time and money.

Although tools don't make a KMS, such a system does need tools, from standard, off-the-shelf e-mail packages to sophisticated collaboration tools designed specifically to support community building and identity. Generally, KMS tools fall into one or more of the following categories:[36]

- Knowledge repositories (databases).
- Expertise tools.
- E-learning applications.
- Discussion and chat technologies.
- Search and data mining tools.

KM AND SOCIAL NETWORKING

Companies that have been frustrated by traditional KM efforts are increasingly looking for ways to find out how knowledge flows through their organization, and social networking analysis can show them just that. *Social networking analysis (SNA)* is a process of mapping a group's contacts (whether personal or professional) to identify who knows whom and who works with whom. In enterprises, it provides a clear picture of how far-flung employees and divisions work together and can help identify key experts in the organization who possess the knowledge needed to, say, solve a complicated programming problem or launch a new product.

M&M maker Mars used SNA to identify how knowledge flows through its organizations, who holds influence, who gives the best advice, and how employees share information. The Canadian government's central IT unit used SNA to establish which skills it needed to retain and develop, and to determine who, among the 40 percent of the workforce that was due to retire within five years, had the most important knowledge and experience to begin transferring to others.[37]

SNA is not a replacement for traditional KM tools such as knowledge databases or portals, but it can provide companies with a starting point for how best to proceed with KM initiatives. As a component to a larger KM strategy, SNA can help companies identify key leaders and then set up a mechanism, such as communities of practice, so that those leaders can pass on their knowledge to colleagues. To identify experts in their organizations, companies can use software programs that track e-mail and other kinds of electronic communication.[38]

Content Management Systems

A *content management system* provides tools to manage the creation, storage, editing, and publication of information in a collaborative environment. As a Web site grows in size and complexity, the business must establish procedures to ensure that things run smoothly. At a certain point, it makes sense to automate this process and use a content management system to manage this effectively. The content management system marketplace is complex, incorporating document management, digital asset management, and Web content management. Figure 15.5 highlights the three primary types of content management systems. Figure 15.6 lists the major content management system vendors.

Common Types of Content Management Systems	
Document management system (DMS)	DMS—Supports the electronic capturing, storage, distribution, archiving, and accessing of documents. A DMS optimizes the use of documents within an organization independent of any publishing medium (for example, the Web). A DMS provides a document repository with information about other information. The system tracks the editorial history of each document and its relationships with other documents. A variety of search and navigation methods are available to make document retrieval easy. A DMS manages highly structured and regulated content, such as pharmaceutical documentation.
Digital asset management (DAM) system	DAM—Though similar to document management, DAM generally works with binary rather than text files, such as multimedia file types. DAM emphasizes file manipulation and conversion, for example, converting GIF files to JPEG.
Web content management (WCM) system	WCM—Adds an additional layer to document and digital asset management that enables publishing content both to intranets and to public Web sites. In addition to maintaining the content itself, WCM systems often integrate content with online processes like e-business systems.

FIGURE 15.5

Common Types of Content Management Systems

WORKING WIKIS

Wikis are Web-based tools that make it easy for users to add, remove, and change online content. *Business wikis* are collaborative Web pages that allow users to edit documents, share ideas, or monitor the status of a project. Most people are familiar with Wikipedia, one of the largest online collaboration Web sites. Employees also use wikis to collaborate; for example, companies such as Intel, Motorola, IBM, and Sony use them for a host of tasks, from setting internal meeting agendas to posting documents related to new products. Many companies rely on wikis to engage customers in ongoing discussions about products. Wikis for Motorola and T-Mobile handsets serve as continually updated user guides. TV networks including ABC and CBS are creating fan wikis that let viewers interact with each other as they unravel mysteries from such shows as *Lost* and *CSI: Crime Scene Investigation*.[39]

A handful of tech-savvy employees at two very different European companies began dabbling in the use of wikis and witnessed a rapid spread of wikis at both companies—Finnish handset-maker Nokia and London- and Frankfurt-based

FIGURE 15.6

Major Content Management System Vendors

Vendors	Strengths	Weaknesses	Costs
Documentum www.documentum.com	Document and digital asset management	Personalization features not as strong as competitors	Major components start at less than $100,000
FatWire www.fatwire.com	Web content management	May not scale to support thousands of users	SPARK, $25,000; Update Engine, $70,000 and up
InterWoven www.interwoven.com	Collaboration, enterprise content management	Requires significant customization	InterWoven 5 Platform, $50,000; average cost for a new customer, $250,000
Percussion www.percussion.com	Web content management	May not scale to support thousands of users	Rhythmyx Content Manager, about $150,000
Stellent www.stellent.com	Document conversion to Web-ready formats	Engineering for very large implementations with thousands of users	Content and Collaboration Servers, $50,000 to $250,000 each
Vignette www.vignette.com	Personalization	Document management and library services are not as robust as others	V6 Multisite Content Manager, $200,000 and up; V6 Content Suite, $450,000 and up

investment bank Dresdner Kleinwort. Nokia estimates at least 20 percent of its 68,000 employees use wiki pages to update schedules and project status, trade ideas, edit files, and so on. "It's a reversal of the normal way things are done," says Stephen Johnston, senior manager for corporate strategy at Nokia, who helped pioneer the technology. Where Nokia once bought outside software to help foster collaboration, now "some of the most interesting stuff is emerging from within the company itself," says Johnston.

It is a similar tale at Dresdner Kleinwort. A few pioneers in the IT department at its London office sent a program called Socialtext to several groups to see how it might be used to facilitate different IT tasks. The wiki program spread so quickly that Dresdner Kleinwort decided to launch its own corporate wiki. By October 2006, the bank's 5,000 employees had created more than 6,000 individual pages and logged about 100,000 hits on the company's official wiki.

The experience of Nokia and Dresdner Kleinwort offer insight into how to nurture the use of a radically new technology to change the way organizations work. Clearly, not everyone recognizes the value of wikis right way. The initial efforts at Dresdner, for example, confused employees and had to be refined to make the technology easier to use. More important than tweaking the technology was a simple edict from one of the proponents: Do not send e-mails, use the wiki. Gradually, employees embraced the use of the wiki, seeing how it increased collaboration and reduced time-consuming e-mail traffic.[40]

Workflow Management Systems

A *workflow* defines all the steps or business rules, from beginning to end, required for a business process. Therefore, *workflow management systems* facilitate the automation and management of business processes and control the movement of work through the business process. Work activities can be performed in series or in parallel and involve people and automated computer systems. In addition, many workflow management systems allow the opportunity to measure and analyze the execution of the process because workflow systems allow the flow of work between individuals and/or departments to be defined and tracked. Workflow software helps automate a range of business tasks and electronically route the right information to the right people at the right time. Users are notified of pending work, and managers can observe status and route approvals through the system quickly.

There are two primary types of workflow systems: messaging-based and database-based. *Messaging-based workflow systems* send work assignments through an e-mail system. The workflow system automatically tracks the order for the work to be assigned and, each time a step is completed, the system automatically sends the work to the next individual in line. For example, each time a team member completes a piece of the project, the system would automatically send the document to the next team member.

Database-based workflow systems store documents in a central location and automatically ask the team members to access the document when it is their turn to edit the document. Project documentation is stored in a central location and team members are notified by the system when it is their turn to log in and work on their portion of the project.

Either type of workflow system helps to present information in a unified format, improves teamwork by providing automated process support, and allows team members to communicate and collaborate within a unified environment. Figure 15.7 lists some typical features associated with workflow management systems.

New York City was experiencing a record number of claims, ranging from injuries resulting from slips on sidewalks to medical malpractice at city hospitals. The city processes over 30,000 claims and incurs $250 million in claim costs annually.

Workflow Feature	Description
Process definition tool	A graphical or textual tool for defining a business process. Each activity within the process is associated with a person or a computer application. Rules are created to determine how the activities progress across the workflow and which controls are in place to govern each activity.
Simulation, prototyping, and piloting	Some systems allow workflow simulation or create prototype and/or pilot versions of a particular workflow to test systems on a limited basis before going into production.
Task initiation and control	The business process defined above is initiated and the appropriate resources (either human and/or IT related) are scheduled and/or engaged to complete each activity as the process progresses.
Rules-based decision making	Rules are created for each step to determine how workflow-related information is to be processed, routed, tracked, and controlled. As an example, one rule might generate e-mail notifications when a condition has been met. Another rule might implement conditional routing of documents and tasks based on the content of fields.
Document routing	In simple systems, this is accomplished by passing a file or folder from one recipient to another (e.g., an e-mail attachment). In sophisticated systems, document routing is completed by checking the documents in and out of a central repository. Both systems might allow for "redlining" of the documents so that each person in the process can add their own comments without affecting the original document.
Applications to view and manipulate information	Word-processors, spreadsheets, and production systems are used to allow workers to create, update, and view information.
Work list	Current tasks are quickly identified along with such things as a due date, goal date, and priority by using work lists. In some systems, an anticipated workload is displayed as well. These systems analyze where jobs are in the workflow and how long each step should take, and then estimate when various tasks will reach a worker's desk.
Task automation	Computerized tasks are automatically invoked. These might include such things as letter writing, e-mail notices, or execution of production systems. Task automation often requires customization of the basic workflow product.
Event notification	Employees can be notified when certain milestones occur or when workload increases.
Process monitoring	The workflow system can provide an organization with valuable information on current workload, future workload, bottlenecks (current or potential), turn-around time, or missed deadlines.
Tracking and logging of activities	Information about each step can be logged. This might include such things as start and completion times, worker(s) assigned to the task, and key status fields. Later, this information can be used to analyze the process or to provide evidence that certain tasks were in fact completed.

FIGURE 15.7

Workflow Management System Features

Claims are generally filed with the Comptroller's Office, which investigates them and offers to settle meritorious claims. The New York City Comptroller's Office, with the assistance of its consultants Xerox and Universal Systems Inc., utilized a workflow management system to enhance revenues and decrease operating costs. With the implementation of the Omnibus Automated Image Storage Information System (OAISIS) for processing contracts and claims, New York City will save over $20 million. Numerous city organizations were involved in the workflow management system, including Bureau of Law and Adjustment, Office of Contracts/Administration, Management and Accounting Systems, and Bureau of Information Systems.[41]

In supporting all these organizations, the system performs many functions that were previously labor-intensive and detracted from the quality and efficiency of investigations. The workflow management system screens claims to determine accordance with statutory requirements. Acknowledgment letters are generated automatically, with little or no resource allocation involved in assignment of claims or routing of claims to specific work locations. Status letters are automatically generated by the system for certain claim types, thus allowing the Comptroller's Office to keep claimants informed two months, five months, and one year from the date of their filing. All this is done automatically by the workflow management system.

Workflow management systems allow management to schedule individual systematic claim reviews without disrupting the investigation. Management can also see the entire claim process graphically and determine bottlenecks. Deployment of additional resources to needed areas occurs without a management analysis of a particular process problem.

Groupware Systems

Groupware is software that supports team interaction and dynamics including calendaring, scheduling, and videoconferencing. Organizations can use this technology to communicate, cooperate, coordinate, solve problems, compete, or negotiate. While traditional technologies like the telephone qualify as groupware, the term refers to a specific class of technologies relying on modern computer networks, such as e-mail, newsgroups, videophones, and chat rooms. Groupware systems fall along two primary categories (see Figure 15.8):

1. Users of the groupware are working together at the same time (real-time or synchronous groupware) or different times (asynchronous groupware).

2. Users are working together in the same place (colocated or face-to-face) or in different places (non-colocated or distance).

The groupware concept integrates various systems and functionalities into a common set of services or a single (client) application. In addition, groupware can represent a wide range of systems and methods of integration. Figure 15.9 displays the advantages groupware systems offer an organization over single-user systems.

Lotus Notes is one of the world's leading software solutions for collaboration that combines messaging, groupware, and the Internet. The structure of Notes allows it to track, route, and manage documents. Systems that lend themselves to Notes involve tracking, routing, approval, document management, and organization.[42]

Toyota developed an intranet system to promote information sharing within the company and to raise productivity. Unfortunately, the company's conventional e-mail system became overloaded, generating problems. Users did not receive incoming messages and were not able to send messages. Individual departments had introduced their own e-mail systems, which were not always compatible. Messages to other mail systems, including those outside the company, experienced delays. To deal with these difficulties, Toyota's information systems

	Same time "Synchronous"	**Different time** "Asynchronous"
Same place "Colocated"	Presentation support	Shared computers
Different place "Distance"	Videophones, Chat	E-mail, Workflow

FIGURE 15.8

Groupware Systems

FIGURE 15.9

Groupware Advantages

Groupware System Advantages
Facilitating communication (faster, easier, clearer, more persuasive)
Enabling telecommuting
Reducing travel costs
Sharing expertise
Forming groups with common interests where it would not be possible to gather a sufficient number of people face-to-face
Saving time and cost in coordinating group work
Facilitating group problem solving

department reviewed the e-mail system and restructured it so that e-mail, now recognized as an important communication tool, is utilized more effectively in business transactions.[43]

VIDEOCONFERENCING

A *videoconference* is a set of interactive telecommunication technologies that allow two or more locations to interact via two-way video and audio transmissions simultaneously. It has also been called visual collaboration and is a type of groupware. Videoconferencing uses telecommunications of audio and video to bring people at different sites together for a meeting. This can be as simple as a conversation between two people in private offices (point-to-point) or involve several sites (multi-point) with more than one person in large rooms at different sites. Besides the audio and visual transmission of people, videoconferencing can be used to share documents, computer-displayed information, and whiteboards.[44]

Simple analog videoconferences could be established as early as the invention of the television. Such videoconferencing systems consisted of two closed-circuit television systems connected via cable. During the first manned space flights, NASA used two radio frequency (UHF or VHF) links, one in each direction. TV channels routinely use this kind of videoconferencing when reporting from distant locations, for instance. Then mobile links to satellites using special trucks became rather common (see Figure 15.10 for an example of videoconferencing).

FIGURE 15.10

Videoconferencing

Videoconferencing is now being introduced to online networking Web sites to help businesses form profitable relationships quickly and efficiently without leaving their place of work. Several factors support business use of videoconferencing, including:[45]

- Over 60 percent of face-to-face communication is nonverbal. Therefore, an enriched communications tool such as videoconferencing can promote an individual's or a team's identity, context, and emotional situation.

- 56 percent of business professionals waste an estimated 30 minutes a day using inefficient communication methods, costing businesses an estimated $297 billion annually.

- The latest technology is available with reliable and easy-to-use conferencing, fostering collaboration at meetings.

- Enterprises that fail to use modern communications technologies run the very real risk of falling behind their competition.[35]

WEB CONFERENCING

Web conferencing blends audio, video, and document-sharing technologies to create virtual meeting rooms where people "gather" at a password-protected Web site. There, they can chat in conference calls or use real-time text messages. They can mark up a shared document as if it were a blackboard, and even watch live software demos or video clips.

Perhaps the biggest surprise about Web conferencing is its simplicity. Users only need to set up an account and download a few small software files. The best part about a Web conference is that attendees do not have to have the same hardware or software. Every participant can see what is on anyone else's screen, regardless of the application being used (see Figure 15.11 for an example of Web conferencing).[46]

Even with its video features, Web conferencing is not quite like being there—or like being in a sophisticated (and pricey) videoconferencing facility. Still, professionals can accomplish more sitting at their desks than in an airport waiting to make travel connections. A growing number of companies are offering Web conferencing. Leaders in this industry include WebEx, SameTime 2, and Elluminate Live.

FIGURE 15.11

Web Conferencing

INSTANT MESSAGING

E-mail is by far the dominant collaboration application, but real-time collaboration tools like instant messaging are creating a new communication dynamic within organizations. *Instant messaging* (sometimes called *IM* or *IMing*) is a type of communications service that enables someone to create a kind of private chat room with another individual in order to communicate in real time over the Internet. In 1992, AOL deployed IM to the consumer market, allowing users to communicate with other IMers through a buddy list. Most of the popular instant messaging programs provide a variety of features, such as:

- Web links: Share links to favorite Web sites.
- Images: Look at an image stored on someone else's computer.
- Sounds: Play sounds.
- Files: Share files by sending them directly to another IMer.
- Talk: Use the Internet instead of a phone to talk.
- Streaming content: Receive real-time or near-real-time stock quotes and news.
- Instant messages: Receive immediate text messages.

Commercial vendors such as AOL and Microsoft offer free instant messaging tools. Real-time collaboration, such as instant messaging, live Web conferencing, and screen or document sharing, creates an environment for decision making. AOL, Microsoft's MSN, and Yahoo! have begun to sell enterprise versions of their instant messaging services that match the capabilities of business-oriented products like IBM's Lotus Sametime. Figure 15.12 demonstrates the IM application presence within IT systems.

IBM Lotus software has released new versions of its real-time collaboration platform, IBM Lotus Instant Messaging and IBM Lotus Web Conferencing, plus its mobile counterpart, IBM Lotus Instant Messaging Everyplace. These built-for-business products let an organization offer presence awareness, secure instant messaging, and Web conferencing. The products give employees instant access to colleagues and company information regardless of time, place, or device.[47]

The bigger issue in collaboration for organizations is cultural. Collaboration brings teams of people together from different regions, departments, and even companies—people who bring different skills, perceptions, and capabilities. A formal collaboration strategy helps create the right environment as well as the right systems for team members.

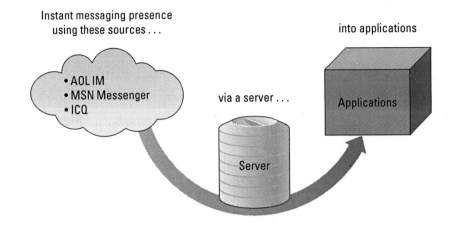

FIGURE 15.12

Instant Messaging Application

OPENING CASE STUDY QUESTIONS

1. Identify which systems eBay could use to collaborate internally.

2. Explain which Internet technologies have facilitated the way in which eBay collaborates with both its customers and business partners.

3. List the four collaboration systems discussed in this chapter and rank them in order of importance to eBay's business.

4. Describe how eBay could leverage the power of a knowledge management system for its employees and for its customers.

Chapter Fifteen Case: DreamWorks Animation Collaboration

Hewlett-Packard (HP) and DreamWorks Animation SKG were the first to introduce a collaboration studio for simulating face-to-face business meetings across long distances. Vyomesh Joshi, executive vice president at HP, and Jeffrey Katzenberg, CEO of DreamWorks, officially unveiled the HP Halo Collaboration Studio in New York City in 2005. Halo enables people in different locations to communicate in a vivid, face-to-face environment in real time. Whether across a country or across the ocean, users can see and hear one another's physical and emotional reactions to conversation and information.

By giving participants the remarkable sense that they are in the same room, the Halo Collaboration Studio is already transforming the way businesses such as PepsiCo, Advanced Micro Devices, and DreamWorks communicate across the globe. Halo significantly increases team effectiveness, provides faster decision-making capabilities, and decreases the need for travel.

"The HP Halo Collaboration Studio enables remote teams to work together in a setting so lifelike that participants feel as though they are in the same room," said Joshi. "To create this experience, HP is harnessing its expertise in color science, imaging, and networking in this new category of innovation. It is something we believe will not only disrupt the traditional videoconferencing market, but will also change the way people work in a global market."

Early in the production of the animated film *Shrek 2,* DreamWorks realized a significant return on investment using the Halo technology. By connecting its California teams in Glendale and Redwood City, DreamWorks was able to speed up many aspects of the production.

"In 2002, while we were producing *Shrek 2,* we realized that DreamWorks needed face-to-face collaboration between key creative talent in different locations," said Katzenberg. "We weren't satisfied with the available videoconferencing systems, so we designed a collaboration solution that would fulfill our needs. HP took the system and turned it into Halo, which is now the only solution on the market that allows this kind of effective communication."

Halo Connection

To connect via Halo, organizations purchase at least two Halo rooms set up for six people each. Three plasma displays in each room enable participants to see those they are collaborating with in life-size images. The rooms come equipped with studio-quality audio and lighting, and participants use a simple on-screen user interface to begin collaborating with just a few mouse clicks.

An intricate software control system ensures Halo rooms work easily and seamlessly together. The control system also provides precise image and color calibration, so participants see each other as they appear in real life. A dedicated HP Halo Video Exchange Network provides a high-bandwidth experience with imperceptible delays between Halo studios worldwide.

To ensure a 24x7 connection and eliminate the need for enterprises to manage the operation and maintenance of a Halo room, services offered include network operations and management, remote diagnostics and calibration, concierge, equipment warranty, and ongoing service and repair.

Participants can easily share documents and data directly from their notebook PCs with individuals in other rooms using a collaboration screen mounted above the plasma displays. The rooms also contain a high-magnification camera that enables individuals to zoom in on objects on a table, revealing the finest of details and color shading, and a phone that opens a conference call line to those not in one of the Halo rooms.

"We believe there is a personal connection that comes with Halo that just clearly doesn't come from any other kind of technology we've used in the past," said Steve Reinemund, CEO of PepsiCo. "Halo is one of the best investments we've made to improve the effectiveness of our business and work/life balance for our people."[48]

Questions

1. How could companies use Halo to increase their business efficiency?
2. Explain how a company like PepsiCo can use Halo to gain a competitive advantage in its industry.
3. How can knowledge management be increased by using a product such as Halo?
4. Why would a company like DreamWorks, that is not IT focused, be interested in collaboration technology?

UNIT SUMMARY

In a remarkably short time, the Internet has grown from a virtual playground into a vital, sophisticated medium for business, more specifically, e-business. Online consumers are flooding to the Internet, and they come with very high expectations and a degree of control that they did not have with traditional bricks-and-mortar companies. The enticement of doing business online must be strengthened by the understanding that, to succeed online, businesses will have to be able to deliver a satisfying and consistent customer experience, building brand loyalty and guaranteeing high rates of customer retention.

Strategic alliances enable businesses to gain competitive advantage(s) through access to a partner's resources, including markets, technologies, and people. Teaming up with another business adds complementary resources and capabilities, enabling participants to grow and expand more quickly and efficiently.

KEY TERMS

Application programming interforce (API) 193
Bluetooth, 216
Brick-and-mortar business, 191
Business-to-business (B2B), 190
Business-to-consumer (B2C), 190
Business wiki 206
Click-and-mortar business, 191
Collaboration system, 200
Consumer-to-business (C2B), 190
Consumer-to-consumer (C2C), 190
Content management system, 205
Core competency, 200
Core competency strategy, 200
Database-based workflow system, 207
Digital asset management system (DAM), 206
Digital Darwinism, 179
Digital divide, 183
Disruptive technology, 179
Document management system (DMS), 206
E-business, 178, 189

E-business model, 189
E-commerce, 189
Electronic marketplace (e-marketplace), 191
E-mall, 192
E-shop (e-store, e-tailer), 191
Explicit knowledge, 203
Geographic information system (GIS), 220
Global positioning system (GPS), 219
Groupware, 209
Hypertext transport protocol (HTTP), 182
Information partnership, 200
Information reach, 183
Information richness, 183
Instant messaging (IM or IMing), 211
Internet, 181
Knowledge management (KM), 202
Knowledge management system (KMS), 203
Messaging-based workflow system, 207
Mashup editor 194
Microwave transmitter, 219
Protocol, 182

Pure-play (virtual) business, 191
Radio frequency identification (RFID), 217
RFID tag, 217
Semantic Web 185
Service oriented architecture (SOA) 186
Social networking analysis (SNA), 205
Structured collaboration (process collaboration), 201
Sustaining technology, 179
Tacit knowledge, 203
Unstructured collaboration (information collaboration), 201
Videoconference 210
Web 2.0, 184
Web content management system (WCM), 206
Web conferencing 211
Web mashup 193
Wiki 206
Wireless fidelity (wi-fi), 214
Workflow, 207
Workflow management system, 207
World Wide Web (WWW), 182

Improving Highway Safety through Collaboration

Information on traffic-related deaths and accidents are two to three years out of date in some states, making it difficult to devise new safety regulations, rebuild unsafe roads, develop safer automobiles, and improve emergency services. Systems used by federal, state, and local agencies to collect and share information need to be overhauled, and the U.S. Department of Transportation's National Highway Traffic Safety Administration said it would ask Congress for $300 million over the next six years to upgrade them.

The goal is to eliminate antiquated paper-based reporting systems and implement a nationwide initiative to automate and synchronize the collection and sharing of information. The information will include vehicle-related injuries, associated health care costs, safety stops, driver licenses, vehicle registration, and adjudicated violations.

Safer Driving

Federal highway safety officials want $300 million to finance:

- Wireless communications equipment to facilitate electronic information collection and transmission during traffic safety stops.
- Real-time information transfer and editing processes to update driver's license or vehicle registration information from traffic stops or crash sites.
- Centralized access to query all traffic record databases.
- Standardized search capabilities on common queries and information transmission using XML formats.

Few states have the capability to capture and transmit traffic record and crash information electronically, and those that do are limited, said Joseph Carra, director of the National Center for Statistics and Analysis at the highway safety agency. "Today, the information is written and stored in files. It's a paper process. The files are sent to the state office, whose clerks input the information into proprietary computer systems. And there it sits."

Collaborating

Better information will save lives and money, says the federal highway safety administration. About 43,220 people were killed on the nation's highways in 2003, and another 2.9 million suffered serious injuries. Traffic accidents in 2000, the latest year for which information is available, cost the U.S. economy about $230 billion, the agency says.

The wide-ranging proposal calls for standardized formats to improve information sharing among various government agencies and private groups, more sophisticated sensors in cars and along highways to gather detailed information on crashes, and wireless handheld devices to let police officers check for outstanding warrants on drivers, among other ideas. Federal funding will encourage states to adopt federal standards. Many states, suffering from a slow economy and declining tax revenues, have not been able to fund upgrades themselves. Some, however, have projects under way.

Revamping Texas

Texas is about halfway done with an IT project to build a crash-records information system, a joint initiative between its Department of Public Safety and the Texas Department of Transportation. When completed, police officers will be able to file accident reports via the Web, and other state agencies will be able to electronically link their systems with it and share information.

Texas has been working on the crash-records system for several years. The state has a $9.9 million contract with IBM to build an information warehouse using a DB2 Universal Database, WebSphere Application Server, Tivoli Storage Manager, and MQ-Series, its message-queuing product. IBM says Florida, Arizona, and New Mexico are considering similar systems.

The Texas system is replacing a decades-old one that is "archaic and in need of many changes," said Carol Rawson, deputy division director for the traffic operations division with the state transportation department. The old system requires time-consuming manual entry of around 850,000 accident forms a year, as well as manual cross-checking and validation to ensure the information is correct. Because the process took so long, the state's accident information is backlogged some 30 months. "This is all about safety," Rawson said. "The way you tell if a road is safe is you look at accident information. So that information is critical."[67]

Questions

1. How are collaboration tools helping to save lives in Texas?
2. How could a police department use groupware to help with collaboration on accident reports?
3. Describe how a police department could use workflow systems to help with accident reports and health-care-related issues.
4. What would be the impact on lives if a state fails to implement collaboration tools to help track and analyze highway accidents?
5. How could police departments use wireless technologies to operate more efficiently and effectively?

★ UNIT CLOSING CASE TWO

Amazon.com—Not Your Average Bookstore

Jeffrey Bezos, CEO and founder of Amazon.com, is running what some people refer to as the "world's biggest bookstore." The story of Bezos's virtual bookstore teaches many lessons about online business. Out of nowhere, this digital bookstore turned an industry upside down.

What happened here was more than just creating a Web site. Bezos conceived and implemented an intelligent, global digital business. Its business is its technology; its technology is its business. Shocking traditional value chains in the book-selling industry, Amazon opened thousands of virtual bookstores in its first few months of operation.

Bezos graduated from Princeton and was the youngest vice president at Banker's Trust in New York. He had to decide if he would stay and receive his 1994 Wall Street bonus or leave and start a business on the Internet. "I tried to imagine being 80 years old, looking back on my life. I knew that I would hardly regret having missed the 1994 Wall Street bonus. But having missed being part of the Internet boom—that would have really hurt," stated Bezos. One evening he compiled a list of 20 products he believed would sell on the Internet. Books, being small-ticket items that are easy and inexpensive to ship, were on the top of the list. It was also apparent that no bookstore could conceivably stock more than a fraction of the 5 million books published annually. Bezos, who had never sold a book in his life, developed a strategic plan for selling books on the Internet. Amazon launched three years later. In the fall of 1994, Amazon filled its first book order—personally packaged by Bezos and his wife.

Amazon's E-Business Strategy

Amazon does not operate any physical stores. All of its sales occur through its Web site. It is consistently pushing the technological envelope in its search to provide a satisfying, personalized experience for its customers. What started as a human-edited list of product suggestions morphed into a sophisticated computer-generated recommendation engine. The company captures the comments and recommendations of buyers for site visitors to read—similar to the friendly salesperson in a store offering advice on which books to buy. The Web site tracks customer traffic, the number of visitors who access the site, how long they stay, what pages they click on, and so forth. The company uses the information to evaluate buying and selling patterns and the success of promotions. Amazon has quickly become a model success story for e-businesses around the globe.

Amazon retains customers with Web site features such as personalized recommendations, online customer reviews, and "1-click ordering"—the creation of a true one-stop shopping establishment where customers can find anything they want to buy online. Through the Amazon.com Auctions, zShops (independent third-party sellers), and more recently the Amazon.com Marketplace (where customers can sell used items), the company is able to offer its customers almost everything.

Shaping Amazon's Future

Amazon released a free Web service that enables its business partners (whom Amazon calls "associates") to interact with its Web site. More specifically, this Web service allows its partners to access catalog data, to create and populate an Amazon.com shopping cart, and even to initiate the checkout process. In 16 months, the company inspired 30,000 associates to invent new ways to extend Amazon's visibility on the Internet. With over 30 million customers, Amazon has become a household brand.[68]

Questions

1. How has Amazon used technology to revamp the book-selling industry?
2. Is Amazon using disruptive or sustaining technology to run its business?
3. What is Amazon's e-business model?
4. How is Amazon using collaboration to improve its business?
5. What are some of the business challenges facing Amazon?
6. How can Amazon use wireless technology to improve its business?

MAKING BUSINESS DECISIONS

1. Everybody Needs an Internet Strategy

An Internet strategy addresses the reasons businesses want to "go online." "Going online" because it seems like the right thing to do now or because everyone else is doing it is not a good enough reason. A business must decide how it will best utilize the Internet for its particular needs. It must plan for where it wants to go and how best the Internet can help shape that vision. Before developing a strategy, a business should spend time on the Internet, see what similar businesses have, and what is most feasible, given a particular set of resources. Think of a new online business opportunity and answer the following questions:

a. Why do you want to put your business online?
b. What benefits will going online bring?
c. What effects will Internet connectivity have on your staff, suppliers, and customers?

2. Searching for Disruption

Scheduler.com is a large corporation that develops software that automates scheduling and record keeping for medical and dental practices. Scheduler.com currently holds 48 percent of its market share, has more than 8,700 employees, and operates in six countries. You are the vice president of product development at Scheduler.com. You have just finished reading *The Innovator's Dilemma* by Clayton Christensen and you are interested in determining what types of disruptive technologies you can take advantage of, or should watch out for, in your industry. Use the Internet to develop a presentation highlighting the types of disruptive technologies you have found that have the potential to give the company a competitive advantage or could cause the company to fail.

3. Leveraging the Competitive Value of the Internet

Physical inventories have always been a major cost component of business. Linking to suppliers in real time dramatically enhances the classic goal of inventory "turn." The Internet provides a multitude of opportunities for radically reducing the costs of designing, manufacturing, and selling goods and services. E-mango.com, a fruit e-marketplace, must take advantage of these opportunities or find itself at a significant competitive disadvantage. Identify the disadvantages that confront E-mango.com if it does not leverage the competitive value of the Internet.

4. Assessing Internet Capabilities

Hoover's Rentals is a small privately owned business that rents sports equipment in Denver, Colorado. The company specializes in winter rentals including ski equipment, snowboarding equipment, and snowmobile equipment. Hoover's has been in business for 20 years and, for the first time, it is experiencing a decline in rentals. Brian Hoover, the company's owner, is puzzled by the recent decreases. The snowfall for the last two years has been outstanding, and the ski resorts have opened earlier and closed later than most previous years. Reports say tourism in the Colorado area is up, and the invention of loyalty programs has significantly increased the number of local skiers. Overall, business should be booming. The only reason for the decrease in sales might be the fact that big retailers such as Wal-Mart and Gart Sports are now renting winter sports equipment. Brian would like your team's help in determining how he can use the Internet to help his company increase sales and decrease costs to compete with these big retailers.

5. Gaining Efficiency with Collaboration

During the past year, you have been working for a manufacturing firm to help improve its supply chain management by implementing enterprise resource planning and supply chain management systems. For efficiency gains, you are recommending that the manufacturing firm should be turning toward collaborative systems. The firm has a need to share intelligent plans and forecasts with supply chain partners, reduce inventory levels, improve working capital, and reduce manufacturing changeovers. Given the technologies presented to you in this unit, what type of system(s) would you recommend to facilitate your firm's future needs?

6. Collaboration on Intranets

MyIntranet.com is a worldwide leader providing online intranet solutions. The MyIntranet.com online collaboration tool is a solution for small businesses and groups inside larger organizations that need to organize information, share files and documents, coordinate calendars, and enable efficient collaboration, all in a secure, browser-based environment. MyIntranet.com has just added conferencing and group scheduling features to its suite of hosted collaboration software. Explain why infrastructure integration is critical to the suite of applications to function within this environment.

7. Finding Innovation

Along with disruptive technologies, there are also disruptive strategies. The following are a few examples of companies that use disruptive strategies to gain competitive advantages:

- Circuit City, Best Buy—These two disrupted the consumer electronics departments of full-service and discount department stores, which has sent them up-market into higher margin goods.
- Ford—Henry Ford's Model T was so inexpensive that he enabled a much larger population of people, who historically could not afford cars, to own one.
- JetBlue—Whereas Southwest Airlines initially followed a strategy of new-market disruption, JetBlue's approach is low-end disruption. Its long-range viability depends on the major airlines' motivation to run away from the attack, as integrated steel mills and full-service department stores did.
- McDonald's—The fast-food industry has been a hybrid disrupter, making it so inexpensive and convenient to eat out that it created a massive wave of growth in the "eating out" industry. McDonald's earliest victims were mom-and-pop diners.

There are numerous other examples of corporations that have used disruptive strategies to create competitive advantages. In a team, prepare a presentation highlighting three additional companies that used disruptive strategies to gain a competitive advantage.

8. Communicating with Instant Messages

You are working for a new start-up magazine, *Jabber Inc.,* developed for information professionals that provides articles, product reviews, case studies, evaluation, and informed opinions. You need to collaborate on news items and projects, and exchange data with a variety of colleagues inside and outside the *Jabber Inc.* walls. You know that many companies are now embracing the instant messaging technology. Prepare a brief report for the CIO that will explain the reasons IM is not just a teenage fad, but also a valuable communications tool that is central to everyday business.

✱ APPLY YOUR KNOWLEDGE

1. Working Together

Upon execution of a business process, a workflow system dictates the presentation of the information, tracks the information, and maintains the information's status. For example, the following highlights the common steps performed during a team project:

1. Find out what information and deliverables are required for the project and the due date.
2. Divide the work among the team members.
3. Determine due dates for the different pieces of work.
4. Compile all the completed work together into a single project.

One of the hardest parts of a team project is getting team members to complete their work on time. Often one team member cannot perform his or her work until another team member has finished. This situation causes work to sit idle waiting for a team member to pick it up to either approve it, continue working on it, or reformat it. Workflow systems help to automate the process of presenting and passing information around a team.

Project Focus

You have just received an assignment to work on a group project with 10 other students. The project requires you to develop a detailed business plan for a business of your choice. The types of activities you will need to perform include market analysis, industry analysis, growth opportunities, Porter's Five Forces analysis, financial forecasts, competitive advantage analysis, and so on. For your project, determine the following:

1. How could you use collaboration tools to facilitate the sharing of information and the completion of the project?
2. What advantages can your group gain from using groupware?
3. What advantages can your group gain from using IM?
4. How could you use a workflow system to manage the tasks for the group members?
5. Describe a few of the biggest issues you anticipate experiencing during the group project. Identify ways that you can resolve these issues using collaboration tools.

2. Internet Groceries

E-Grocery, founded in 2007, is an online grocery shopping and delivery service. The company caters to thousands of customers in the Phoenix, Seattle, and Denver areas. Established on the idea that people will buy groceries over the Internet, e-Grocery offers over 25,000 items.

Ninety percent of e-Grocery's orders come in via computer; the rest are received by fax. Orders are received at the central office in Lakewood, Colorado, and then distributed by e-mail to a local affiliate store. The store receives the order, the delivery address, and a map to the order location. A store employee designated to online orders will fill, deliver, and collect for the order. E-Grocery members are charged actual shelf prices, plus a per-order charge of $5.00 or 5 percent of the order amount, whichever is greater. Members also receive additional benefits such as electronic coupons, customer discounts, recipes, and tips.

Project Focus

The company is using interactive technology to change the shopping experience. The success of e-Grocery lies within many areas. Analyze the e-Grocery business model using the questions below. Feel free to think outside the box to develop your own analysis of online grocery shopping and e-business models.

1. What is e-Grocery's e-business model?
2. How does e-Grocery compete with traditional retailers?
3. What value can e-Grocery offer as a true competitive advantage in this marketplace?
4. What is the threat of new entrants in this market segment?
5. How is e-Grocery using technology to change the shopping experience?

6. What are the logistics for making e-Grocery profitable?

7. How does e-Grocery profit from online customer interaction?

8. What kinds of e-business strategies can e-Grocery's marketing department use to help grow its business?

9. What are some of the benefits and challenges facing e-Grocery?

3. Getting Personal

Consider Sally Albright, the reigning queen of customization in the movie *When Harry Met Sally*. Take, for example, the scene where she orders pie a la mode: "I'd like the pie heated. And I don't want the ice cream on top; I want it on the side. And I'd like strawberry instead of vanilla if you have it. If not, then no ice cream, just whipped cream, but only if it's real." Particular, yes, but Sally knew what she liked—and was not afraid to ask for it.

Project Focus

A growing number of online retailers are letting you have it your way, too. Choose a company highlighted in Figure AYK.1 and create your own product. Was the Web site easy to use? Would this service entice you as a customer to make a purchase over a generic product? If you could personalize a product what would it be and how would the Web site work?

4. Express Yourself

One of the most popular Web sites among students is MySpace, a site that allows students to express themselves by personalizing their home page. What is your favorite band? Who is your favorite author? What is your favorite movie? You can find out a lot about a person by finding out the answers to these questions.

Project Focus

Build a Web site dedicated to your favorite band, book, or movie. Your Web site must contain all of the following:

- An image.
- Two different size headings.
- Different sizes and colors of text.

FIGURE AYK.1

Customization Companies

Company	Product
Tommy Hilfiger, custom.tomm.com	Premium-cotton chinos and jeans ($98)
Lands' End, www.landsend.com	Utilitarian jeans and chinos made of luxurious twill in traditional silhouettes ($59)
JCPenney, www.custom.jcpenney.com	Substantial twill pants in classic cuts ($44)
Ralph Lauren Polo, www.polo.com	Everything from basic polos to oxford shirts ($80)
TIMBUK2; www.timbuk2.com	Hip nylon messenger bags ($105)
L.L. Bean,www.llbean.com	Sturdy and colorful books, totes, and messenger bags ($70)
Nike, www.nikeid.com	Full range of athletic shoes and accessories ($90)
VANS, www.vans.com	Classic "Old Skool" lace-up or slip-on sneakers ($50)
Converse, www.converseone.com	Custom Chuck Taylors, the company's most classic style ($60)

- Two horizontal rules.
- Text that is bolded, underlined, and/or italicized.
- A textured background.
- A link to a Web site.
- A link to your e-mail.
- One numbered and one unnumbered list.

5. Creating a Presence

More than 1 billion people are on the Internet. Having an Internet presence is critical for any business that wants to remain competitive. Businesses need their Web sites to create a "buzz" to attract customers. E-business Web sites must be innovative, stimulating, add value, and provide useful information. In short, the site must build a sense of community and collaboration, eventually becoming the "port of entry" for business.

Project Focus

You are applying for a job at BagEm, a start-up e-business devoted to selling custom book bags that does not have any physical stores and only sells bags over the Internet. You are up against several other candidates for the job. BagEm has asked you to use your business expertise and Web site development skills to design and build a potential Web site. The candidate with the best Web site will be awarded the job. Good luck!

6. GoGo Gadgets

Now that wi-fi and other types of high-speed wireless networks are becoming common, devices using that technology are multiplying rapidly. Wireless gadgets run the gamut from cell phones to kitchen appliances and digital cameras. Here are some of the hottest new wireless broadband gadgets.

- Samsung's $3,499 POPCON refrigerator will feature a wi-fi enabled, detachable screen that can function as a TV. The fridge also can be programmed to remember products' expiration dates and generate alerts when the milk is getting old.
- The Nokia 770 Internet Tablet is small enough to fit in a pocket. It comes with a 4.13-inch-wide touch screen that can be used to access the Web over a wi-fi network. The $350 device can also access the Web via a cell phone with a Bluetooth connection.
- Motorola's latest E815 mobile phone operates over Verizon Wireless's new EVDO (Evolution Data Optimized) wireless network, offering speeds comparable to digital subscriber line (DSL). The phone can even record and play back video clips. It also features a built-in MP3 digital music player.
- Hop-On's just-announced HOP 1515 may look like a typical cell phone, but it actually makes calls over wi-fi networks. Typically sold with a $20 to $30 monthly service plan, the phone allows for unlimited over-the-Web international and long-distance calling. The $39 HOP 1515 is sold through wi-fi hotspot operators, wireless carriers, and retailers.
- Eastman Kodak's EasyShare-One is a digital camera with wi-fi capabilities, allowing users to share their snapshots wirelessly. You will be able to snap a photo and immediately show it to a friend on a wi-fi-enabled PC or TV.

Project Focus

A dizzying array of new wireless technologies now promises to make today's wi-fi networks seem like poky dial-up connections by comparison. These new technologies will extend the reach of wireless networks, not just geographically but also into new uses in the home and office.

1. Research the Internet and discover new wireless devices that entrepreneurs and established companies can use to improve their business.

2. Explain how businesses can use these devices to create competitive advantages, streamline production, and improve productivity.

7. WAP

Wireless Internet access is quickly gaining popularity among people seeking high-speed Internet connections when they are away from their home or office. The signal from a typical wireless access point (WAP) only extends for about 300 feet in any direction, so the user must find a "hotspot" to be able to access the Internet while on the road. Sometimes hotspots are available for free or for a small fee.

You work for a sales company, SalesTek, which has a salesforce of 25 representatives and customers concentrated in Denver, Colorado; Salt Lake City, Utah; and Santa Fe, New Mexico. Your sales representatives are constantly on the road and they require 24×7 Internet access.

Project Focus

You have been asked to find hotspots for your colleagues to connect to while they are on the road. It is critical that your salesforce can access the Internet 24×7 to connect with customers, suppliers, and the corporate office. Create a document detailing how your mobile workforce will be able to stay connected to the Internet while traveling. Here are a few tips to get you started:

1. Use Web sites such as www.wifinder.com and www.jiwire.com to determine which commercial hotspots would be the most appropriate for your salesforce and the commercial network service that these hotspots use.

2. Research the Web sites of two or three commercial networks that seem most appropriate to discover more about pricing and services. (Hint: T-Mobile is one example.)

3. Use www.wifinder.com and www.wififreespot.com to determine how many free public hotspots are available in these cities. Are there enough for your company to rely on them or should you use a commercial wi-fi system. If so, which one?

4. You might also research www.fon.com to see alternative methods of using home broadband connections to stay connected.

8. Securing Your Home Wireless Network

These days wireless networking products are so ubiquitous and inexpensive that anyone can easily build a wireless network with less than $100 worth of equipment. However, wireless networks are exactly that—wireless—they do not stop at walls. In fact, wireless networks often carry signals more than 300 feet from the wireless router. Living in an apartment, dorm, condominium, or house means that you might have dozens of neighbors who can access your wireless network.

It is one thing to let a neighbor borrow a lawn mower, but it is another thing to allow a neighbor to access a home wireless network. There are several good reasons for not sharing a home wireless network including:

- It may slow Internet performance.
- It allows others to view files on your computers and spread dangerous software such as viruses.
- It allows others to monitor the Web sites you visit, read your e-mail and instant messages as they travel across the network, and copy your user names and passwords.
- It allows others to send spam or perform illegal activities with your Internet connection.[69]

Securing a home wireless network is invaluable and allows you to enable security features that can make it difficult for uninvited guests to connect through your wireless network. Create a document detailing all of the features you can use to secure a home wireless network.

9. Weather Bots

Warren Jackson, an engineering graduate student at the University of Pennsylvania, was not interested in the weather until he started investigating how the National Weather Service collected weather data. The weather service has collected most of its information using weather balloons that carry a device to measure items such as pressure, wind speed, and humidity. When the balloon reaches about 100,000 feet and pressure causes it to pop, the device falls and lands a substantial distance from its launch point. The National Weather Service and researchers sometimes look for the $200 device, but of the 80,000 sent up annually, they write off many as lost.

Convinced there had to be a better way, Warren began designing a GPS-equipped robot that launches a parachute after the balloon pops and brings the device back down to Earth, landing it at a predetermined location set by the researchers. The idea is so inventive that the Penn's Weiss Tech House, a university organization that encourages students to innovate and bring their ideas to market, awarded Warren and some fellow graduate engineering students first prize in its third annual PennVention Contest. Warren won $5,000 and access to expert advice on prototyping, legal matters, and branding.[70]

Project Focus

GPS and GIS can be used in all sorts of devices, in many different industries, for multiple purposes. You want to compete, and win first prize, in the PennVention next year. Create a product, using a GPS or GIS, that is not currently in the market today that you will present at the fourth annual PennVention.

10. Wireless Networks and Streetlamps

Researchers at Harvard University and BBN Technologies have designed CitySense, a wireless network capable of reporting real-time sensor data across the entire city of Cambridge, Massachusetts. CitySense is unique because it solves a constraint on previous wireless networks—battery life. The network mounts each node on a municipal streetlamp, where it draws power from city electricity. Researchers plan to install 100 sensors on streetlamps throughout Cambridge by 2011, using a grant from the National Science Foundation. Each node will include an embedded PC running the Linux operating system, an 802.11 wi-fi interface, and weather sensors.

One of the challenges in the design was how the network would allow remote nodes to communicate with the central server at Harvard and BBN. CitySense will do that by letting each node form a mesh with its neighbors, exchanging data through multiple-hop links. This strategy allows a node to download software or upload sensor data to a distant server hub using a small radio with only a 1-kilometer range.[71]

Project Focus

You are responsible for deploying a CitySense network around your city. What goals would you have for the system besides monitoring urban weather and pollution? What other benefits could a CitySense network provide? How could local businesses and citizens benefit from the network? What legal and ethical concerns should you understand before deploying the network? What can you do to protect your network and your city from these issues?

11. Sharptooth Incorporated

Stephen Kern is the founder and CEO of Sharptooth, a small business that buys and sells comic strips to magazines and newspapers around the country. Some of Sharptooth's artists have made it big and are syndicated in hundreds of magazines and newspapers, while others are new to the industry. Stephen started in the business as an artist and began contracting with other artists when he realized he had a knack for promoting and marketing comic materials. His artistic background is great for spotting talented young artists, but not so great for running the business.

Project Focus

Stephen recently began selling comics to new forms of media such as blog sites, Web sites, and other online tools. Stephen has hired you to build him a new system to track all online comic sales. You quickly notice that Stephen has a separate system for each of his different lines of business including newspaper sources, magazine sources, billboard sources, and now online sources. You notice that each system works independently to perform its job of creating, updating, and maintaining sales information, but you are wondering how Stephen operates his business as a whole. Create a list of issues Stephen will encounter if he continues to run his business with four separate systems performing the same operations. What could happen to Stephen's business if he cannot correlate the details of each? Be sure to highlight at least 10 issues where separate systems could cause Stephen problems.

12. Wiki Debate

Wikipedia is a multilingual, Web-based, free content encyclopedia project. Wikipedia is written collaboratively by volunteers from all around the world. With rare exceptions, its articles can be edited by anyone with access to the Internet, simply by clicking a line to edit the page. The name Wikipedia is a portmanteau of the words *wiki* (a type of collaborative Web site) and *encyclopedia.* Since its creation in 2001, Wikipedia has grown rapidly into one of the largest reference Web sites.

In every article, links guide users to associated articles, often with additional information. Anyone is welcome to add information, cross-references, or citations, as long as they do so within Wikipedia's editing policies and to an appropriate standard. One need not fear accidentally damaging Wikipedia when adding or improving information, as other editors are always around to advise or correct obvious errors, and Wikipedia's software, known as MediaWiki, is carefully designed to allow easy reversal of editorial mistakes.[72]

Project Focus

A group of people believe the end of Wikipedia is close as people use the tool to self-promote. Some believe that Wikipedia will fail in four years, crushed under the weight of an automated assault by marketers and others seeking online traffic. Eric Goldman, a professor at the Santa Clara University School of Law, argues that Wikipedia will see increasingly vigorous efforts to subvert its editorial process, much as Digg has seen. As marketers become more determined and turn to automated tools to alter Wikipedia entries to generate online traffic, Goldman predicts Wikipedians will burn out trying to keep entries clean. Goldman writes that Wikipedia will enter a death spiral where the rate of junkiness will increase rapidly until the site becomes a wasteland. Alternatively, to prevent this death spiral, Wikipedia will change its core open-access architecture, increasing the database's vitality by changing its mission somewhat.

Create a paper discussing where you think the future of Wikipedia is headed.

13. Secure Collaboration

As the methods and modes of communication continue to evolve, challenges will mount for businesses trying to secure their data and for law enforcement looking to monitor communications as part of their investigations. That was the theme of the keynote speech that Sun Microsystems' chief security officer and renowned cryptographer Whitfield Diffie delivered at the AT&T Cyber Security Conference.

The growth of virtual communities across the Web as a communications channel creates a double-edged sword in this respect. Second Life and other virtual communities offer a growing abundance of information, although this information will ultimately need to be protected if virtual communities are to grow as meaningful channels of business-to-business and business-to-customer communication.

Diffie believes that with millions of people joining Second Life and companies building facilities there, it may be that virtual communities become the preferred medium of human communication. This growing volume of information opens the opportunity to use virtual communities as a source of intelligence, and communications will always be spied on.

Of course, the volume of businesses present in virtual communities such as Second Life will have to grow before they become a meaningful source of information. Once this happens, though, watch out. Diffie believes that communication always outstrips the ability to protect it. Who would be interested in gathering intelligence floating through virtual communities? The answer is businesses, governments (domestic and foreign), and reporters—the same entities that have adapted every other form of communication preceding the Web. Diffie feels the future will be a golden age for intelligence.[73]

Project Focus

As we create new and better ways to collaborate, what happens to information security?

UNIT

5 Transforming Organizations

UNIT FIVE OPENING CASE

The Digital Hospital

For years, health care has missed the huge benefits that information technology has bestowed upon the rest of the economy. During the 1990s, productivity in health care services declined, according to estimates from Economy.com Inc. That is a huge under-achievement in a decade of strong gains from the overall economy. This is beginning to change as hospitals, along with insurers and the government, are stepping up their IT investments. Hospitals are finally discarding their clumsy, sluggish first-generation net-works and are beginning to install laptops, software, and Internet technologies.

Hackensack University Medical Center in Hackensack, New Jersey, is one of the nation's most aggressive technology adopters, investing $72 million in IT projects since 1998. The IT investments are paying off for the hospital with patient mortality rates decreasing—down 16 percent in four years—and quality of care and productiv-ity increasing. The most important piece of Hackensack's digital initiatives is the net-worked software that acts as the hospital's central nervous system. Using wireless laptops, nurses log in to the system to record patient information and progress. Doctors tap into the network via wireless devices to order prescriptions and lab tests. Everything is linked, from the automated pharmacy to the X-ray lab, eliminating the need for faxes, phone calls, and other administrative hassles. Figure Unit 5.1 displays the hospital's IT systems development projects.

Health care spending accounts for 15 percent of the U.S. economy, or $1.7 trillion. It is so gargantuan that any efficiency gains will affect the overall economy. Dr. David Brailer, President George W. Bush's point man on health IT initiatives, predicts that IT investments will lead to $140 billion a year in cost savings by 2014. More important than saving money is saving lives. Poor information kills some 7,000 Americans each year just by missing drug-interaction problems, according to the National Academy of Sciences

FIGURE UNIT 5.1

Hospital IT Systems
Development Projects

Hackensack University Medical Center's IT Projects
■ Patients can use 37-inch plasma TVs in their rooms to surf the Internet for information about their medical conditions. They can also take interactive classes about their condition and find out how to take care of themselves after discharge.
■ From virtually anywhere in the world, physicians can make their hospital rounds with the help of a life-size robot, Mr. Rounder. Using laptops with joysticks and Web links, doctors drive the robot around the hospital to confer by remote video with patients and other doctors. When a blizzard prevented Dr. Garth Ballantynes from reaching the hospital, he used Mr. Rounder to make his rounds from his home 82 miles away.
■ Pocket-sized PCs that hook wirelessly into the hospital's network allow doctors the freedom to place pharmacy orders and pull up medical records from anywhere in the hospital.
■ Nurses use wireless laptops to record patients' vitals signs, symptoms, and medications. Doctors can sign into the same central system from the laptops to order prescriptions and lab tests and read their patient's progress.
■ The hospital's internal Web site stores all of its medical images. Doctors can view crystal-clear digital versions of their patients' X-rays, MRIs, and CT scans from any computer in or out of the hospital.
■ A giant robot named Robbie, equipped with arms, reads prescriptions entered into the hospital's computer system and then grabs medications stored on pegs on the wall. The pills are then dropped into containers that are marked for each patient.

Institute of Medicine. Hospital errors result in 100,000 deaths annually. Early evidence indicates that proper technology can reduce this amount. Hospitals using electronic prescription systems have seen 80 percent fewer prescription errors.[1]

Introduction

In a competitive business climate, an organization's ability to efficiently align resources and business activities with strategic objectives can mean the difference between succeeding and just surviving. To achieve strategic alignment, organizations increasingly manage their systems development efforts and project planning activities to monitor performance and make better business decisions. Fast-growing companies outsource many areas of their business to extend their technical and operational resources. By outsourcing, they save time and boost productivity by not having to develop their own systems from scratch. They are then free to concentrate on innovation and their core business. The chapters in Unit 5 are:

- **Chapter Seventeen**—Building Software to Support an Agile Organization.
- **Chapter Eighteen**—Outsourcing in the 21st Century.
- **Chapter Nineteen**—Developing a 21st Century Organization.

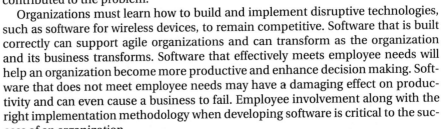

CHAPTER

17

Building Software to Support an Agile Organization

LEARNING OUTCOMES

17.1. Identify the business benefits associated with successful software development.

17.2. Describe the seven phases of the systems development life cycle.

17.3. Summarize the different software development methodologies.

17.4. Explain project management and its three interdependent variables.

Systems Development

Archtv 2

Nike's SCM system failure, which spun out of control to the tune of $400 million, is legendary. Nike blamed the system failure on its SCM vendor i2 Technologies. Nike stated that i2 Technologies' demand and supply planning module created serious inventory problems. The i2 deployment, part of a multimillion-dollar e-business upgrade, caused Nike CEO Philip Knight to famously say, "This is what we get for our $400 million?" The SCM vendor saw its stock plummet with the Nike disaster, along with its reputation. I2's chief marketing officer, Katrina Roche, asserted that Nike failed to use the vendor's implementation methodology and templates, which contributed to the problem.[2]

Organizations must learn how to build and implement disruptive technologies, such as software for wireless devices, to remain competitive. Software that is built correctly can support agile organizations and can transform as the organization and its business transforms. Software that effectively meets employee needs will help an organization become more productive and enhance decision making. Software that does not meet employee needs may have a damaging effect on productivity and can even cause a business to fail. Employee involvement along with the right implementation methodology when developing software is critical to the success of an organization.

Software development problems often lead to high-profile disasters. Hershey Food's glitch in its ERP implementation made the front page of *The Wall Street Journal* and cost the company millions of dollars. Hershey said computer problems with its SAP software system created a backlog of orders, causing slower deliveries, and resulting in lower earnings. Statistics released in 2006 by the National Research Council show that U.S. companies spent $250 billion in 2005 to repair damage caused by software defects.[3]

If software does not work, the organization will not work. Traditional business risk models typically ignored software development, largely because most organizations considered the impact from software and software development on the business to be minor. In the digital age, however, software success, or failure, can lead directly to business success, or failure. Almost every large organization in the world relies on software, either to drive its business operations or to make its products work. As organizations' reliance on software grows, so do the business-related consequences of software successes and failures including:

- **Increase or decrease revenues**—Organizations have the ability to directly increase profits by implementing successful IT systems. Organizations can also lose millions when software fails or key information is stolen or compromised.

   Nike's poorly designed supply chain management software delayed orders, increased excess inventories, and caused third-quarter earnings to fall 24 percent below expectations.

- **Repair or damage to brand reputation**—Technologies such as CRM can directly enhance a company's brand reputation. Software can also severely damage a company's reputation if it fails to work as advertised or has security vulnerabilities that affect its customers' trust.

   H&R Block customers were furious when the company accidentally placed its customers' passwords and Social Security numbers on its Web site.

- **Prevent or incur liabilities**—Technology such as CAT scans, MRIs, and mammograms can save lives. Faulty technology used in airplanes, automobiles, pacemakers, or nuclear reactors can cause massive damage, injury, or death.

   The parent company of bankrupt pharmaceutical distributor FoxMeyer sued SAP for $500 million over ERP software failure that allegedly crippled its operations.

- **Increase or decrease productivity**—CRM and SCM software can directly increase a company's productivity. Large losses in productivity can also occur when software malfunctions or crashes.

   The Standish Group estimates that defective software code accounted for 45 percent of computer-system downtime and cost U.S. companies $100 billion in lost productivity in 2003 alone.[4]

The lucrative advantages of successful software implementations provide significant incentives to manage software development risks. But according to the Standish Group's Chaos report, more than half the software development projects undertaken in the United States come in late or over budget and the majority of successful projects maintain fewer features and functions than originally specified. Organizations also cancel around 33 percent of these projects during development. Understanding the basics of software development, or the systems development life cycle, will help organizations avoid potential software development pitfalls and ensure that software development efforts are successful.[5]

Developing Software—The Systems Development Life Cycle (SDLC)

Information systems are the support infrastructure that helps an organization change quickly when adapting to shifting business environments and markets. Many factors must come together to develop successful software. This chapter focuses on the *systems development life cycle (SDLC),* also known as the software life cycle or the application life cycle, which is the overall process for developing information systems from planning and analysis through implementation and maintenance (see Figure 17.1).

1. **Planning**—The *planning phase* involves establishing a high-level plan of the intended project and determining project goals. Planning is the first and most critical phase of any systems development effort an organization undertakes, regardless of whether the effort is to develop a system that allows customers to

FIGURE 17.1

The Systems Development Life Cycle

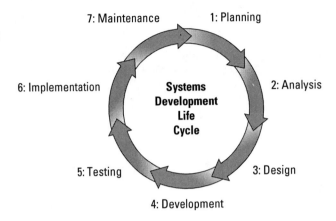

7: Maintenance   1: Planning

6: Implementation   **Systems Development Life Cycle**   2: Analysis

5: Testing   3: Design

4: Development

System Development

order products over the Internet, determine the best logistical structure for warehouses around the world, or form a strategic information alliance with another organization. Organizations must carefully plan the activities (and determine why they are necessary) to be successful.

2. **Analysis**—The *analysis phase* involves analyzing end-user business requirements and refining project goals into defined functions and operations of the intended system. *Business requirements* are the detailed set of business requests that the system must meet in order to be successful. The analysis phase is obviously critical. A good start is essential, and the organization must spend as much time, energy, and resources as necessary to perform a detailed, accurate analysis.

3. **Design**—The *design phase* involves describing the desired features and operations of the system including screen layouts, business rules, process diagrams, pseudo code, and other documentation.

4. **Development**—The *development phase* involves taking all of the detailed design documents from the design phase and transforming them into the actual system. In this phase the project transitions from preliminary designs to the actual physical implementation.

5. **Testing**—The *testing phase* involves bringing all the project pieces together into a special testing environment to test for errors, bugs, and interoperability and verify that the system meets all of the business requirements defined in the analysis phase.

   According to a report issued in June 2003 by the National Institute of Standards and Technology (NIST), defective software costs the U.S. economy an estimated $59.5 billion each year. Of that total, software users incur 64 percent of the costs and software developers 36 percent. NIST suggests that improvements in testing could reduce this cost significantly—by about a third, or $22.5 billion—but that testing improvements would not eliminate most software errors.[6]

6. **Implementation**—The *implementation phase* involves placing the system into production so users can begin to perform actual business operations with the system.

7. **Maintenance**—Maintaining the system is the final sequential phase of any systems development effort. The *maintenance phase* involves performing changes, corrections, additions, and upgrades to ensure the system continues to meet the business goals. This phase continues for the life of the system because the system must change as the business evolves and its needs change, demanding constant monitoring, supporting the new system with frequent minor changes (for example, new reports or information capturing), and reviewing the system to be sure it is moving the organization toward its strategic goals.

The London Stock Exchange is among the most admired equity exchanges in the world, not only for its long-standing position in the financial community, but also for its technology deployment and infrastructure. The London Stock Exchange must have a solid architecture because it processes over 15 million real-time messages per day (with peaks of 2,000 messages per second). In choosing a new technology infrastructure on which to ride into the future, the London Stock Exchange focused a great deal of its efforts on requiring vendors to meet benchmarks across a broad range of metrics. Below are just a few.

- **Guaranteed performance**—In financial trading, information is valuable only if it reaches traders within the first second.

- **Development costs**—Reduced development costs and development cycle times mean more productivity. Ian Homan, head of technology for the London Stock Exchange, estimates that implementation of the new infrastructure occurred in one-fifth to one-third the time it would have taken to implement other vendor infrastructures.

- **Scalability**—According to David Lester, CIO for the London Stock Exchange, "We want to be able to extend it and make it richer. Investment decisions of this kind aren't made carelessly and the ability to scale to our future needs was a critical factor."[7]

Software Development Methodologies

Today, systems are so large and complex that teams of architects, analysts, developers, testers, and users must work together to create the millions of lines of custom-written code that drive enterprises. For this reason, developers have created a number of different system development life cycle methodologies including *waterfall; rapid application development (RAD); extreme programming;* and *agile.* The oldest of these, and the best known, is the waterfall methodology: a sequence of phases in which the output of each phase becomes the input for the next (see Figure 17.2).

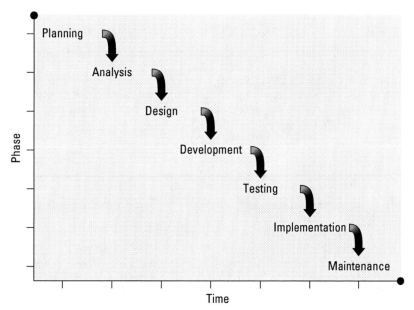

FIGURE 17.2

The Traditional Waterfall Methodology

WATERFALL METHODOLOGY

The traditional *waterfall methodology* is a sequential, activity-based process in which each phase in the SDLC is performed sequentially from planning through implementation and maintenance. The waterfall methodology is one of the oldest software development methods and has been around for more than 30 years. The success rate for software development projects that follow this approach is only about 1 in 10. One primary reason for such a low success rate is that the waterfall methodology does not sufficiently consider the level of uncertainty in new projects and the creativity required to complete software development projects in several aspects:

- **The business problem:** Any flaws in accurately defining and articulating the business problem in terms of what the business users actually require flow onward to the next phase.

- **The plan:** Managing costs, resources, and time constraints is difficult in the waterfall sequence. What happens to the schedule if a programmer quits? How will a schedule delay in a specific phase impact the total cost of the project? Unexpected contingencies may sabotage the plan.

- **The solution:** The waterfall methodology is problematic in that it assumes users can specify all business requirements in advance. Defining the appropriate IT infrastructure that is flexible, scalable, and reliable is a challenge. The final IT infrastructure solution must meet not only current but also future needs in terms of time, cost, feasibility, and flexibility. Vision is inevitably limited at the head of the waterfall.

Unfortunately, business requirements change as the business changes, which calls for considerable feedback and iterative consultation for all business requirements. Essentially, software is "soft" and it must be easily changed and manipulated to meet the changing dynamics of an organization. As people's understanding of the business problems evolve, so must the software. For this reason, it is counterproductive to define all requirements precisely upfront since, by the time the software goes into production, which can be several months or even years after completing the initial analysis phase, chances are the business problems have changed as well as the business.[8]

RAPID APPLICATION DEVELOPMENT METHODOLOGY (RAD)

In response to the faster pace of business, rapid application development has become a popular route for accelerating systems development. *Rapid application development (RAD) (*also called *rapid prototyping) methodology* emphasizes extensive user involvement in the rapid and evolutionary construction of working prototypes of a system to accelerate the systems development process. The fundamentals of RAD include:

- Focus initially on creating a prototype that looks and acts like the desired system.
- Actively involve system users in the analysis, design, and development phases.
- Accelerate collecting the business requirements through an interactive and iterative construction approach.[9]

A *prototype* is a smaller-scale representation or working model of the users' requirements or a proposed design for an information system. The prototype is an essential part of the analysis phase when using the RAD methodology.

PHH Vehicle Management Services, a Baltimore fleet-management company with over 750,000 vehicles, wanted to build an enterprise application that opened the entire vehicle information database to customers over the Internet. To build the application quickly, the company abandoned the traditional waterfall approach.

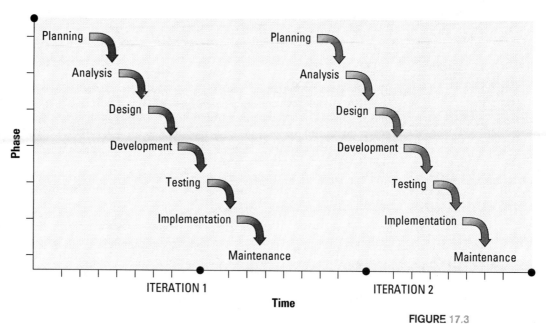

FIGURE 17.3

The Iterative Approach

Instead, a team of 30 developers began prototyping the Internet application, and the company's customers evaluated each prototype for immediate feedback. The development team released new prototypes that incorporated the customers' feedback every six weeks. The PHH Interactive Vehicle application went into production seven months after the initial work began. Over 20,000 customers, using a common browser, can now access the PHH Interactive site at any time from anywhere in the world to review their accounts, analyze billing information, and order vehicles.[10]

EXTREME PROGRAMMING METHODOLOGY

Extreme programming (XP) methodology breaks a project into tiny phases, and developers cannot continue on to the next phase until the first phase is complete. The primary difference between the waterfall and XP methodologies is that XP divides its phases into iterations with user feedback. The waterfall approach develops the entire system, whereas XP develops the system in iterations (see Figure 17.3). XP is a lot like a jigsaw puzzle; there are many small pieces. Individually the pieces make no sense, but when they are combined (again and again) an organization can gain visibility into the entire new system.

Microsoft Corporation developed Internet Explorer and Netscape Communications Corporation developed Communicator using extreme programming. Both companies did a nightly compilation (called a build) of the entire project, bringing together all the current components. They established release dates and expended considerable effort to involve customers in each release. The extreme programming approach allowed both Microsoft and Netscape to manage millions of lines of code as specifications changed and evolved over time. Most important, both companies frequently held user design reviews and strategy sessions to solicit and incorporate user feedback.[11]

XP is a significant departure from traditional software development methodologies, and many organizations in different industries have developed successful software using it. One reason for XP's success is its stress on customer satisfaction. XP empowers developers to respond to changing customer and business requirements, even late in the systems development life cycle, and XP emphasizes teamwork. Managers, customers, and developers are all part of a team dedicated to delivering quality software. XP implements a simple, yet effective way to enable groupware-style development. The XP methodology promotes quickly being able to respond to changing requirements and technology.

AGILE METHODOLOGY

The *agile methodology,* a form of XP, aims for customer satisfaction through early and continuous delivery of useful software components. Agile is similar to XP but with less focus on team coding and more on limiting project scope. An agile project sets a minimum number of requirements and turns them into a deliverable product. Agile means what it sounds like: fast and efficient; small and nimble; lower cost; fewer features; shorter projects.

The Agile Alliance is a group of software developers whose mission is to improve software development processes and whose manifesto includes the following tenets:

- Early and continuous delivery of valuable software will satisfy the customer.
- Changing requirements, even late in development, are welcome.
- Businesspeople and developers must work together daily throughout the project.
- Projects should be built around motivated individuals. Give them the environment and support they need, and trust them to get the job done.
- The best architectures, requirements, and designs emerge from self-organizing teams.
- At regular intervals, the team should reflect on how to become more effective, then tune and adjust behavior accordingly.[12]

Look for development and operational models that suit the organization's culture but move toward the perpetual beta. On the development side, use agile, iterative approaches, and on the operations side, consider best practice–centered models, such as the Information Technology Infrastructure Library (ITIL). The *Information Technology Infrastructure Library (ITIL)* is a framework of best practice approaches intended to facilitate the delivery of high quality IT services. ITIL outlines an extensive set of management procedures that are intended to support businesses in achieving both high financial quality and value in IT operations. These procedures are supplier-independent and have been developed to provide guidance across the breadth of IT infrastructure, development, and operations. ITIL is published in a series of books (hence the term *Library*), each of which covers a core area within IT management.

Developing Successful Software

The Gartner Group estimates that 65 percent of agile projects are successful. This success rate is extraordinary compared to the 10 percent success rate of waterfall projects. The following are the primary principles an organization should follow for successful agile software development.[13]

SLASH THE BUDGET

Small budgets force developers and users to focus on the essentials. Small budgets also make it easier to kill a failing project. For example, imagine that a project that has already cost $20 million is going down the tubes. With that much invested, it is tempting to invest another $5 million to rescue it rather than take a huge loss. All too often, the system fails and the company ends up with an even bigger loss.

Jim Johnson, chairman of The Standish Group, says he forced the CIO of one Fortune 500 company to set a $100,000 ceiling on all software development projects.

There were no exceptions to this business rule without approval from the CIO and CEO. Johnson claims the company's project success rate went from 0 percent to 50 percent.[14]

IF IT DOESN'T WORK, KILL IT

Bring all key stakeholders together at the beginning of a project and as it progresses bring them together again to evaluate the software. Is it doing what the business wants and, more important, requires? Eliminate any software that is not meeting business expectations. This is called triage, and it's "the perfect place to kill a software project," said Pat Morgan, senior program manager at Compaq's Enterprise Storage Group. He holds monthly triage sessions and says they can be brutal. "At one [meeting], engineering talked about a cool process they were working on to transfer information between GUIs. No one in the room needed it. We killed it right there. In our environment, you can burn a couple of million dollars in a month only to realize what you're doing isn't useful."[15]

KEEP REQUIREMENTS TO A MINIMUM

Start each project with what the software must absolutely do. Do not start with a list of everything the software should do. Every software project traditionally starts with a requirements document that will often have hundreds or thousands of business requirements. The Standish Group estimates that only 7 percent of the business requirements are needed for any given application. Keeping requirements to a minimum also means that scope creep and feature creep must be closely monitored. *Scope creep* occurs when the scope of the project increases. *Feature creep* occurs when developers add extra features that were not part of the initial requirements. Both scope creep and feature creep are major reasons software development fails.[16]

TEST AND DELIVER FREQUENTLY

As often as once a week, and not less than once a month, complete a part of the project or a piece of software. The part must be working and it must be bug-free. Then have the customers test and approve it. This is the agile methodology's most radical departure from traditional development. In some traditional software projects, the customers did not see any working parts or pieces for years.

ASSIGN NON-IT EXECUTIVES TO SOFTWARE PROJECTS

Non-IT executives should coordinate with the technical project manager, test iterations to make sure they are meeting user needs, and act as liaisons between executives and IT. Having the business side involved full-time will bring project ownership and a desire to succeed to all parties involved. SpreeRide, a Salt Lake City market research outfit, used the agile methodology to set up its company's Web site. The project required several business executives designated full-time. The company believes this is one of the primary reasons that the project was successfully deployed in less than three months.[17]

Project Managing the Systems Development Effort

No one would think of building an office complex by turning loose 100 different construction teams to build 100 different rooms, with no single blueprint or agreed-upon vision of the completed structure. Yet this is precisely the situation in which many large organizations find themselves when managing systems development

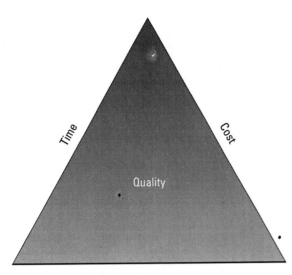

FIGURE 17.4

Project Management
Interdependent Variables

projects. Organizations routinely overschedule their resources (human and otherwise), develop redundant projects, and damage profitability by investing in non-strategic efforts that do not contribute to the organization's bottom line. Project management offers a strategic framework for coordinating the numerous activities associated with organizational projects.

According to the Project Management Institute, ***project management*** is the application of knowledge, skills, tools, and techniques to project activities in order to meet or exceed stakeholder needs and expectations from a project. ***Project management software*** specifically supports the long-term and day-to-day management and execution of the steps in a project (such as building a new warehouse or designing and implementing a new IT system).

Project management is essential to the success of almost every aspect of IT. Without it, projects tend to be delayed, over budget, and often never reach completion. Horizon Blue Cross Blue Shield of New Jersey, a $6-billion-plus health insurance provider, allocated several hundred million dollars to IT over a five-year period to tackle tasks such as consolidating five enterprise software platforms, managing compliance with regulatory offices, and simplifying new product development. These IT initiatives involve hundreds of skilled people working on hundreds of concurrently developing projects. Horizon's executives needed to gain visibility into all projects, subsets of projects, and existing and planned projects collectively. The company considered a rigorous and formalized project management strategy fundamental to the project's success.

Horizon decided to implement IT project management software from Business Engine Inc. to manage its projects. The software collects information through standardized templates created for Microsoft Project, which are stored in an enterprise database and then fed into Business Engine's analytical tool, called Ben. Each user can then view and manipulate spreadsheets and graphs, share documents, track revisions, and run what-if scenarios in a personalized digital dashboard view. With the help from Business Engine, Horizon is managing IT projects and assets as if they were investments, tracking their performance against business goals, assessing their individual return and value to the company, and helping sort out which projects require greater attention and resources and which require reduced attention and resources. Horizon found itself ahead of schedule on over 70 percent of its IT projects.[18]

Figure 17.4 displays the relationships between the three primary variables in any project—(1) time, (2) cost, and (3) scope. These three variables are interdependent. For example, decreasing a project's time frame means either increasing the cost of the project or decreasing the scope of the project to meet the new deadline. Increasing a project's scope means either increasing the project's time frame or increasing the project's cost—or both—to meet the increased scope changes. Project management is the science of making intelligent trade-offs between time, cost, and scope. All three of the factors combined determine a project's quality.

Benjamin Franklin's timeless advice—by failing to prepare, you prepare to fail—especially applies to many of today's software development projects. A recent survey concluded that the failure rate of IT projects is much higher in organizations that do not exercise disciplined project management. Figure 17.5 displays the top six reasons IT projects fail, according to *Information Week*'s research survey of 150 IT managers.[19]

A successful project is typically on time, within budget, meets the business's requirements, and fulfills the customer's needs. The Hackett Group, an Atlanta-based

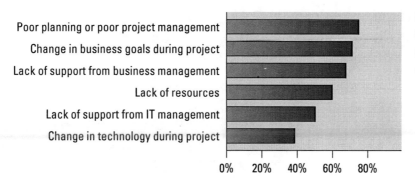

FIGURE 17.5

Why IT Projects Fall Behind Schedule or Fail

consultancy, analyzed its client database (which includes 2,000 companies, including 81 Fortune 100 companies) and discovered:

■ Three in 10 major IT projects fail.

■ 21 percent of the companies state that they cannot adjust rapidly to market changes.

■ One in four validate a business case for IT projects after completion.[20]

Nicolas Dubuc, collaborative project manager at Rhodia Inc., a $6 billion worldwide manufacturer of specialty chemicals, uses Microsoft's software to develop project management templates and methodologies for its 18 divisions. "We're designing a platform for rapid application development that will enhance opportunities for innovation," Dubuc said.

Today, the leaders in the project management software market include Microsoft, Primavera, Oracle, and SAP. Microsoft Project is the core project management tool for many organizations and dominates with more than 8 million users and over 80 percent of the market share. Figure 17.6 displays the growth in project management software. If an organization wants to deliver successful, quality software on time and under budget, it must take advantage of project management software.[21]

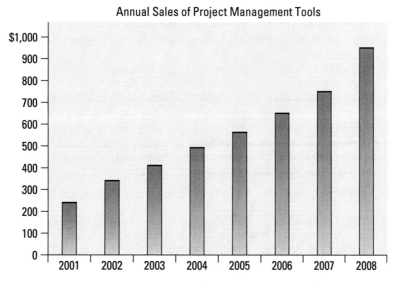

FIGURE 17.6

Growth for Project Management Software

OPENING CASE STUDY QUESTIONS

1. How are hospitals using new software to improve their operations?

2. List and describe the seven phases in the systems development life cycle and determine which phase is most important to a hospital when developing new systems.

3. Review the primary principles of successful software development and list them in order of importance for Hackensack University Medical Center's business strategy.

4. Why is building agile software important to Hackensack University Medical Center?

5. Assess the impact to a hospital if it decided to use the waterfall methodology to build its customers' information systems.

Chapter Seveenteen Case: Transforming the Entertainment Industry—Netflix

The online DVD rental pioneer Netflix is transforming the movie business with its unique business model and streamlined shipping strategy. Netflix is quickly becoming one of Hollywood's most promising new business partners and is experiencing staggering growth with over 1 million subscribers, accounting for 3 to 5 percent of all U.S. home video rentals.

Typically, traditional video rental stores focus on major films and ignore older movies and smaller titles with niche audiences. Netflix is turning that idea upside down by offering a serious market for every movie, not just blockbusters. How? Netflix attributes its success to its proprietary software, called the Netflix Recommendation System, which constantly suggests movies a customer might like, based on how the customer rates any of the 15,000 titles in the company's catalog. Beyond recommendations, Netflix has figured out how to get DVDs from one subscriber to the next with unbelievable efficiency.

Netflix operates by allowing its 3.5 million subscribers to rent unlimited videos for $9.99 a month, as long as they have no more than three DVDs rented at a time. Currently there are more than 5 million discs in the hands of its customers at any given time, with an average of 500,000 DVDs shipped out of the company's 36 leased distribution centers daily. To handle the rental logistics for its 10 million-DVD library the company created a proprietary supply chain management system.

As with any change or market advance, when new competition invades, existing competitors will not stand still. Walmart.com recently launched its own version of the Netflix model; it has already built six distribution centers, and is charging less per month for the same services offered by Netflix. Blockbuster purchased a similar service called FilmCaddy and is deciding how it will promote the service nationally. Other companies threatening to steal Netflix's market share are satellite and cable companies that now offer on-demand movies. To remain disruptive, Netflix will need to analyze its competition and strategize new ways to continue to increase subscriptions and revenues.

Netflix's Value Proposition

A crucial competitive weapon for maintaining its market share (estimated at two-thirds of online rentals) is new, homegrown software that improves upon the Oracle database the company uses to automate the DVD distribution process. The software consults the database to match a customer request with the movies in inventory. Based on algorithms devised to maximize delivery time by mail, the application decides which distribution center will fulfill each movie. The program then generates a "pull list" for workers at each center to fulfill the orders and ship them to customers.

Blockbuster, with 1 million online subscribers and 5,700 retail stores, is attacking with similar technology to orchestrate DVD delivery by mail from the chain's stores. Central to the Blockbuster strategy is the integration of 28 systems into one that feeds data about online orders to retail locations quickly.[22]

Questions

1. Assess the business-related consequences of a failure in Netflix's proprietary supply chain management system.

2. List and describe the seven phases in the systems development life cycle and determine which phase you think is most important to Netflix when it is developing software.

3. Determine the primary differences between the waterfall development methodology and the agile development methodology. Which methodology would you recommend Netflix use and why?

4. Why would prototyping be a good idea for Netflix if it decides to build a CRM system?

5. Given $10,000, would you recommend purchasing Netflix or Blockbuster stock?

BUSINESS PLUG-IN POINTER

Review **Business Plug-In B14 "Systems Development"** for in-depth coverage of the SDLC and its associated activities including performing feasibility studies, gathering business requirements, analyzing a buy versus build decision, designing and building systems, writing and performing testing, supporting users, etc.

Review **Business Plug-In B15 "Project Management"** for an overview of the fundamentals of project management including prioritizing projects and developing project plans, along with a detailed look at risk management and change management.

TECHNOLOGY PLUG-IN POINTER

Review **Technology Plug-In T11 "Creating Web Pages Using Dreamweaver"** for a tour of using Dreamweaver to create Web pages. Dreamweaver allows anyone with limited Web page design experience to create, modify, and maintain full-featured, professional-looking pages without having to learn how to code all the functions and features from scratch.

Review **Technology Plug-In T12 "Creating Gantt Charts with Excel and Microsoft Project"** for a quick and efficient way to manage projects. Excel and Microsoft Project are great for managing all phases of a project, creating templates, collaborating on planning processes, tracking project progress, and sharing information with all interested parties.

UNIT SUMMARY

An organization must remain competitive in this quick-paced, constantly changing, global business environment. It must implement technology that is adaptive, disruptive, and transformable to meet new and unexpected customer needs. Focusing on the unexpected and understanding disruptive technologies can give an organization a competitive advantage.

Organizations need software that users can transform quickly to meet the requirements of the rapidly changing business environment. Software that effectively meets employee needs will help an organization become more productive and make better decisions. Software that does not meet employee needs may have a damaging effect on productivity. Employee involvement along with using the right implementation methodology in developing software is critical to the success of an organization.

Four areas of focus for organizations heading into the 21st century are IT infrastructure, security, e-business (mobility), and integration. Information technology has rapidly expanded from a backroom resource providing competitive advantage (e.g., cost, time, quality) to a front-office resource (e.g., marketing, sales) that is a competitive necessity. The dynamic business and technical environment of the 21st century is driving the need for technology infrastructures and applications architecture that are increasingly flexible, integrated, and maintainable (while always providing functionality, cost effectiveness, timeliness, and security).

 KEY TERMS

Agile methodology, 246
Analysis phase, 242
Business process outsourcing (BPO), 255
Business requirement, 242
Design phase, 242
Development phase, 242
Electronic tagging, 261
Extreme programming (XP) methodology, 245
Feature creep, 247
Implementation phase, 242
Information Technology Infrastructure Library (ITIL), 246

Insourcing (in-house development), 252
IT infrastructure, 258
Maintenance phase, 242
Mobile commerce (m-commerce), 261
Offshore outsourcing 255
Outsourcing 253
Planning phase, 241
Project management, 248
Project management software, 248
Prototype, 244

Radio frequency identification (RFID), 261
Rapid application development (RAD) (also called rapid prototyping) methodology, 244
Scope creep, 247
Systems development life cycle (SDLC), 241
Telematics, 261
Testing phase, 242
Waterfall methodology, 244

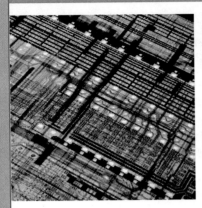

RFID—Future Tracking

The elementary school that required students to wear radio frequency identification (RFID) tags to track their movements ended the program because the company that developed the technology pulled out. "I'm disappointed; that's about all I can say at this point," stated Ernie Graham, the superintendent and principal of Brittan Elementary School. "I think I let my staff down."

The tags, developed by California-based technology company InCom Corp., were introduced in January 2005. Students were required to wear identification cards around their necks with their picture, name, and grade and a wireless transmitter that beamed ID numbers to a teacher's handheld computer when the children passed under an antenna posted above a classroom door. The school instituted the system, without parental input, to simplify attendance-taking and potentially reduce vandalism and improve student safety. "I'm happy for now that kids are not being tagged, but I'm still fighting to keep it out of our school system," said parent Dawn Cantrall, who filed a complaint with the American Civil Liberties Union. "It has to stop here."

While many parents criticized the tags for violating privacy and possibly endangering children's health, some parents supported the plan. "Technology scares some people; it's a fear of the unknown," parent Mary Brower said. "Any kind of new technology has the potential for misuse, but I feel confident the school is not going to misuse it."

Tracking Children

Children's sleepwear with radio frequency identification tags sewn into the seams hit stores in early 2006. Made by Lauren Scott California, the nightgowns and pajamas will be one of the first commercial RFID-tagged clothing lines sold in the United States.

The PJs are designed to keep kids safe from abductions, says proprietor Lauren Scott, who licensed the RFID technology from SmartWear Technologies Inc., a maker of personal-security systems. Readers positioned in doorways and windows throughout a house scan tags within a 30-foot radius and trigger an alarm when boundaries are breached.

A pamphlet attached to the garment informs customers that the sleepwear is designed to help prevent child abductions. It directs parents to a Web site that explains how to activate and encode the RFID tag with a unique digital identification number. The site also provides information on a $500 home-installed system that consists of RFID readers and a low-frequency encoder that connects through a USB port to a computer. Parents can sign up to include data about their children, including photos, in the SmartWear database. That information can be shared with law enforcement agencies or the Amber Alert system if a child disappears.

SmartWear has several other projects in the works including an extended-range RFID tag that can transmit signals up to 600 feet. The tag could be inserted into law enforcement and military uniforms or outerwear, such as ski jackets, and used to find a missing or lost person or to recover and identify a body.

Plastic RFID

A typical RFID tag costs 40 cents, making price a barrier for many potential applications. Start-up OrganicID is creating a plastic RFID tag that it expects will reduce the price to a penny or less. CEO Klaus Dimmler hopes to market the plastic tags, which will operate in the 13.56-MHz range, by 2008.[40]

Questions

1. What are some advantages and disadvantages of tagging students with RFID tags?
2. What are some advantages and disadvantages of tagging children's pajamas with RFID tags?
3. Do you agree or disagree that tagging students with RFID tags is a violation of privacy rights? Explain why.
4. Do you agree or disagree that tagging children's pajamas with RFID tags is a violation of privacy rights? Explain why.
5. Describe the relationship between privacy rights and RFID.
6. Determine a way that schools could use RFID tags without violating privacy rights.

✳ UNIT CLOSING CASE TWO

Masters of Innovation, Technology, and Strategic Vision

Several companies are emerging as leaders on the intensely competitive playing field of e-business. *Wired* magazine highlights The Wired 40—companies driven by innovative thinking, not marketplace brawn, that demonstrate a mastery of tomorrow's business essentials including innovation, technology, strategic vision, global reach, and networked communication.

BusinessWeek magazine highlights The Web Smart 50—companies that are using technology to develop new e-business opportunities in the areas of collaboration, customer service, customization, streamlining, management, and cutting-edge technology. Cross-referencing the two lists reveals seven outstanding companies that are included in both The Wired 40 and The Web Smart 50:

▪ Amazon.com
▪ Charles Schwab

- Cisco
- Dell
- IBM
- Sony
- Wal-Mart

Amazon.com—It's a Mall World after All

- Ranked seventh on The Wired 40.
- Featured on The Web Smart 50 under "Cutting Edge."

"Amazon.com and you're done!" was the e-business pioneer's slogan. Critics of Amazon.com said that CEO Jeff Bezos should have stuck with books; his online store would soon crumple under the debt it had taken on to expand into other goods. Jeff Bezos proved the critics wrong by reducing Amazon.com's debt while doubling its revenue growth rate.

In 2003, Amazon.com opened its site to independent developers, allowing merchants to use its gold-standard e-business technology to build their own stores on top of Amazon's. To date, over 35,000 software developers have created programs from building customized Web stores to checking prices from handheld devices. Currently, other retailers now account for 22 percent of all items sold on Amazon.com. Amazon.com continues to prove critics wrong and is demonstrating that a Web site can be the best storefront location of all.

Charles Schwab—Trading Places

- Ranked 37th on The Wired 40.
- Featured on The Web Smart 50 under "Customer Service."

Charles Schwab, the full-service investment firm, continues to shock the investment industry by using technology innovations to transform its business. The company invested $20 million on Web technology to build the Schwab Equity Rating System, a computer-generated online service that offers recommendations for the buying and selling of over 3,000 stocks. The system allows Schwab to avoid the $20-million-a-year cost of hiring new analysts and avoid conflicts of interest between analysts and business, something to watch in the wake of Wall Street scandals.

Charles Schwab also rolled out Web-based services for financial advisers. Collaboration between Schwab and independent financial advisers gives retail investors the best of both worlds.

Cisco—The Network Connection

- Ranked 11th on The Wired 40.
- Featured on The Web Smart 50 under "Cutting Edge."

Cisco, with its flat revenue and steady profit, has become a cash machine in less than two decades. The company is continuing to transform to ensure it is evolving as the Internet evolves. First, it is switching 35,000 employees and consultants to Voice-over-IP (VOIP) Internet-enabled telephone systems. Cisco workers worldwide now use Internet phones, cutting down on telephony services by $300,000 monthly.

Second, the company is changing its lines of business. John Chambers, the CEO of Cisco, understands that the market for routers and switches, which account for 70 percent of Cisco's sales, is headed for stagnation. To combat this, the company is investing 40 percent of its research and development dollars into areas that constitute a mere 15 percent of sales: optical and storage networking, wireless communications, security software, and VOIP. Cisco promises to be ready for companies that want to start investing in next-generation networks.

Baltzan–Phillips–Haag:
Business Driven
Technology, Third Edition

V. Transforming
Organizations

Unit Summary

© The McGraw–Hill
Companies, 2009

167

Dell—Just-in-Time Hardware

- Ranked 15th on The Wired 40.
- Featured on The Web Smart 50 under "Cutting Edge."

Dell's core PC business is still "disruptive" (cutting edge) as the company installs robots to automate its e-business network. By installing robots on the assembly lines that process orders from the Web, the company can build 900 computers an hour, increasing output by over 40 percent. At Dell's plant in Nashville, assembly line robots retrieve online orders and fetch all of the required components to build the custom PCs. This new setup requires half as many workers and operates at three times the speed. The plant churns out one computer every four seconds.

Dell has a reputation for shattering every industry it targets. When the personal computer went from branded gizmo to commodity, Dell polished its famous strategy—assemble on demand, deliver high value at low cost, sell directly to customers—and drove IBM out of the PC market and Compaq into HP's arms. Dell is now focusing on attacking the server sector (of which it claims nearly a quarter), the workstation niche (where it has Sun on the run), the networking arena (where Cisco is looking vulnerable), and the consulting business specializing in systems integration.

IBM—The Ultimate IT Outsource

- Ranked fourth on The Wired 40.
- Featured on The Web Smart 50 under "Collaboration."

Perhaps IBM's acronym should stand for It's Been Morphing. The 92-year-old company proved as nimble as a start-up by supporting Linux and promoting it as an enterprise-friendly solution. IBM is now promoting "e-business on demand," which envisions computing as a utility: Switch it on when needed and pay only for what is used. The services will allow everything including offering organizations the ability to expand at will.

IBM is also creating an online collaboration system for employees that has cut training costs by $375 million annually and travel expenses by $20 million annually. IBM's intranet allows its 300,000 workers to brainstorm. Web jams, big sessions with over 1,000 employees, encourage the free flow of ideas. Many organizations are now looking to IBM for expertise in the area of intranet development. IBM hopes to become to computing what "Ma Bell" once was to telephones.

Sony—That's Home Entertainment!

- Ranked 16th on The Wired 40.
- Featured on The Web Smart 50 under "Collaboration."

CEO Nobuyuki Idei sees Sony's future in home networks that beam files among PCs, TVs, and portables. That means melding the company's music and video departments, which currently deliver more than half the company's profit. Nobuyuki Idei is restructuring the organization by moving away from departmental silos into a more seamless organization.

Wal-Mart—Retail-o-rama

- Ranked 13th on The Wired 40.
- Featured on The Web Smart 50 under "Collaboration."

Wal-Mart squeezes big brands for low prices and passes the savings on to consumers. Then it pumps suppliers for information that will help it give shoppers what they want, when they want it. The newest technology innovation the company is pursuing to help streamline its supply chain is "smart tags," which will be placed in every product case for its top 100 suppliers.

The tags will track product in every phase of the supply chain, allowing the company to know exactly where every product is and increase its ability to keep its shelves stocked. Analysts expect Wal-Mart to reap pretax savings of as much as $8 billion by 2007.

CEO Lee Scott is focusing on several other new investments including branding products like dog food and moving into pharmaceuticals, financial services, and DVD rentals. Global expansion continues: Wal-Mart has more stores in Mexico (551) than in its two biggest states, Texas and Florida, combined, plus 486 others in the United Kingdom, Brazil, China, and South Korea. Wal-Mart promises to continue to redefine efficiency in retailing.[41]

Questions

1. Which one of the seven companies has the most disruptive technology that is capable of making the greatest impact on business?
2. How has Amazon used technology to change the bookselling industry in the 21st century?
3. Choose one of the seven companies and create a Porter's Five Forces analysis to highlight potential issues the company might face in the 21st century.
4. List and describe the seven phases in the systems development life cycle and determine which phase is most important to Cisco when it is developing software.
5. Review the primary principles of successful software development and prioritize them in order of importance for Sony.
6. Why is building agile software important for all seven companies?
7. What potential systems might Dell want to outsource?
8. Discuss the pitfalls Wal-Mart might encounter if it decided to outsource its SCM system.

✱ MAKING BUSINESS DECISIONS

1. Selecting a Systems Development Methodology

Exus Incorporated is an international billing outsourcing company. Exus currently has revenues of $5 billion, over 3,500 employees, and operations on every continent. You have recently been hired as the CIO. Your first task is to increase the software development project success rate, which is currently at 20 percent. To ensure that future software development projects are successful, you want to standardize the systems development methodology across the entire enterprise. Currently, each project determines which methodology it uses to develop software.

Create a report detailing three additional system development methodologies that were not covered in this text. Compare each of these methodologies to the traditional waterfall approach. Finally, recommend which methodology you want to implement as your organizational standard. Be sure to highlight any potential roadblocks you might encounter when implementing the new standard methodology.

2. Transforming an Organization

Your college has asked you to help develop the curriculum for a new course titled "Building a 21st Century Organization." Use the materials in this text, the Internet, and any other resources to outline the curriculum that you would suggest the course cover. Be sure to include your reasons why the material should be covered and the order in which it should be covered.

3. Approving a Project

You are working in the IT development team for Gear International, a privately held sports and recreational equipment manufacturer. To date, you have spent the majority of your career developing applications for your corporate intranet. Your team has an idea to add an application that allows employees to learn about corporate athletic teams, register online, determine team schedules, post team statistics, etc. Your supervisor likes your idea and would like your team to prepare a short presentation with 5 to 10 slides that she can use to convince senior management to approve the project. Be sure to list benefits of the project along with your suggested methodology to help guarantee the project's development success.

4. Patrolling by Remote

Today's gadgets offer all-weather, all-knowing, anytime, anyplace. Whether you are trying to keep tabs on your children, your new home theater, or your streaming audio, here are a few wireless tools you can use around your house.

- **Wi-fi camera**—A five-inch-high Wireless Observer lets you take pictures at regular intervals or in response to motion and you can access it anytime through a Web browser (www.veo.com).
- **Security sensor**—This detector system alerts you to break-ins and errant pop flies. Its dual sensors record vibration and acoustic disturbances—signs of a shattered window—to help avoid false alarms. (www.getintellisense.com).
- **GPS tracking device**—Total Parental Information Awareness is here. Lock this GPS locator to your kids' wrist and whenever you want to check on them just query Wherify's Web page. It pinpoints their location on a street map and displays an aerial photo (www.wherify.com).
- **Wireless speakers**—Sony's versatile 900-MHz speakers connect the RF receiver to your stereo, TV, or PC, and get crystal-clear audio anywhere within 150 feet (www.sonystyle.com).

In a group, create a document discussing how these new wireless technologies could potentially change the business arena and list at least one company for each technology that should view these new products as potential threats.

5. Saving Failing Systems

Signatures Inc. specializes in producing personalized products for companies, such as coffee mugs and pens with company logos. The company generates over $40 million in annual revenues and has more than 300 employees. The company is in the middle of a large multimillion-dollar SCM implementation and has just hired your Project Management Outsourcing firm to take over the project management efforts. On your first day, your team is told that the project is failing for the following reasons:

- The project is using the traditional waterfall methodology.
- The SDLC was not followed and the developers decided to skip the testing phase.
- A project plan was developed during the analysis phase, but the old project manager never updated or followed the plan.

In a group determine what your first steps would be to get this project back on track.

APPLY YOUR KNOWLEDGE

1. Connecting Components

Components of a solid enterprise architecture include everything from documentation to business concepts to software and hardware. Deciding which components to implement and how to implement them can be a challenge. New IT components are released daily, and business needs continually change. An enterprise architecture that meets your organization's needs today may not meet those needs tomorrow. Building an enterprise architecture that is scalable, flexible, available, accessible, and reliable is key to your organization's success.

Project Focus

You are the enterprise architect for a large clothing company called Xedous. You are responsible for developing the initial enterprise architecture. Create a list of questions you will need answered to develop your architecture. Below are examples of a few questions you might ask.

- What are the company's growth expectations?
- Will systems be able to handle additional users?
- How long will information be stored in the systems?
- How much customer history must be stored?
- What are the organization's business hours?
- What are the organization's backup requirements?

2. Back on Your Feet

You are working for GetSmart, a document creation company for legal professionals. Due to the highly sensitive nature of the industry, employees must store all work on the network drive and are not allowed to back up the data to a CD, flash drive, or any other type of external storage including home computers. The company has been following this policy for the last three years without any issues. You return to work Monday morning after a long weekend to find that the building was struck by lightning destroying several servers. Unfortunately, the backup strategy failed and all of the data from your department has been lost.

When the head of the company demanded an explanation as to why there were no individual backups, he was shown the company policy he had signed not once but three times. The head of IT along with four of his cronies who had developed this ridiculous policy were fired.

Project Focus

You have been placed on a committee with several of your peers to revamp the backup and recovery policies and create a new disaster recovery plan. You must create policies and procedures that will preserve the sensitive nature of the documents, while ensuring the company is safe from disasters. Be sure to address a worst-case scenario where the entire building is lost.

3. GEM Athletic Center

First Information Corporation is a large consulting company that specializes in systems analysis and design. The company has over 2,000 employees and first-quarter revenues reached $15 million. The company prides itself on maintaining an 85 percent success rate for all project implementations. The primary reason attributed to the unusually high project success rate is the company's ability to define accurate, complete, and high quality business requirements.

The GEM Athletic Center located in Cleveland, Ohio, is interested in implementing a new payroll system. The current payroll process is manual and takes three employees two days each month to complete. The GEM Athletic Center does not have an IT department and is outsourcing the entire procurement, customization, and installation of the new payroll system to First Information Corporation.

Project Focus

You have been working for First Information for a little over one month. Your team has just been assigned the GEM Athletic Center project and your first task is to define the initial business requirements for the development of the new payroll system.

1. Review the testimony of three current GEM Athletic Center accounting employees who detail the current payroll process along with their wish list for the new system. Use the files MaggieCleaver.doc, AnneLogan.doc, JimPoulos.doc.
2. Review the Characteristics of Good Business Requirements document (Business-Requirements.doc) that highlights several techniques you can use to develop solid business requirements.
3. After careful analysis, create a report detailing the business requirements for the new system. Be sure to list any assumptions, issues, or questions in your document.

Data Folder: Chapter 19_AYK 3

4. Confusing Coffee

Business requirements are the detailed set of business requests that any new system must meet in order to be successful. A sample business requirement might state, "The system must track all customer sales by product, region, and sales representative." This requirement states what the system must do from the business perspective, giving no details or information on how the system is going to meet this requirement.

Project Focus

You have been hired to build an employee payroll system for a new coffee shop. Review the following business requirements and highlight any potential issues.

- All employees must have a unique employee ID.
- The system must track employee hours worked based on employee's last name.
- Employees must be scheduled to work a minimum of eight hours per day.
- Employee payroll is calculated by multiplying the employee's hours worked by $7.25.
- Managers must be scheduled to work morning shifts.
- Employees cannot be scheduled to work more than eight hours per day.
- Servers cannot be scheduled to work morning, afternoon, or evening shifts.
- The system must allow managers to change and delete employees from the system.

5. Picking Projects

You are a project management contractor attempting to contract work at a large telecommunications company, Hex Incorporated. Your interview with Debbie Fernandez, the senior vice president of IT, went smoothly. The last thing Debbie wants to see from you before she makes her final hiring decision is a prioritized list of the projects below. You are sure to land the job if Debbie is satisfied with your prioritization.

Project Focus

Create a report for Debbie prioritizing the following projects and be sure to include the business justifications for your prioritization.

- Upgrade accounting system.
- Develop employee vacation tracking system.

- Enhance employee intranet.
- Cleanse and scrub data warehouse information.
- Performance test all hardware to ensure 20 percent growth scalability.
- Implement changes to employee benefits system.
- Develop backup and recovery strategy.
- Implement supply chain management system.
- Upgrade customer relationship management system.
- Build executive information system for CEO.

6. Keeping Time

Time Keepers Inc. is a small firm that specializes in project management consulting. You are a senior project manager, and you have recently been assigned to the Tahiti Tanning Lotion account. The Tahiti Tanning Lotion company is currently experiencing a 10 percent success rate (90 percent failure rate) on all internal IT projects. Your first assignment is to analyze one of the current project plans being used to develop a new CRM system (see Figure AYK.1).

Project Focus

1. Review the project plan and create a document listing the numerous errors in the plan. Be sure to also provide suggestions on how to fix the errors.
2. If you have access to Microsoft Project, open the file BadProject.mpp. Fix the errors you found in question 1 directly to BadProject.mpp. (If you are new to using Microsoft Project, review the document MSProjectGuidelines.doc for an overview of several tips for using Microsoft Project.)

FIGURE AYK.1

Sample Project Plan

Data Folder: Chapter 19_AYK 6

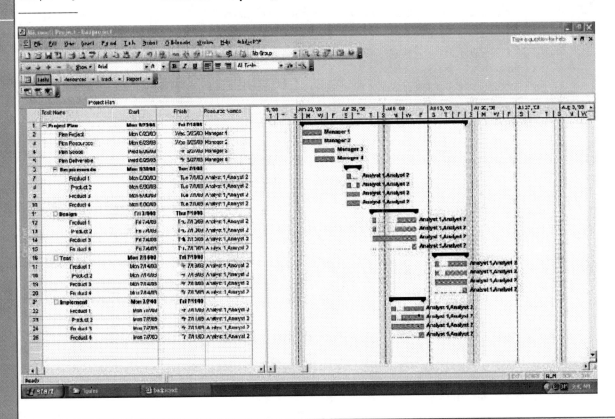

7. Growing, Growing, Gone

You are the founder of Black Pearl, a small comic book start-up. The good news is Black Pearl has found tremendous success. You have 34 employees in a creative, yet functional, office in downtown Chicago. The comics you produce are of extremely high quality. The artwork is unmatched and the story lines are compelling, gripping, and addictive, according to your customers. Your comics are quickly becoming a cult classic and Black Pearl customers are extremely loyal. You produce all of the comics and sell them in your store and via the Internet to individuals all over the United States.

Project Focus

You had vision when you started Black Pearl. You knew the potential of your business model to revamp the comic industry. You purchased high-end computers and customizable software to support your operations. Now, you are faced with a new dilemma. You have a large international following and you have decided to pursue international opportunities. You would like to open stores in Japan, France, and Brazil during the next year. To determine if this is possible, you need to evaluate your current systems to see if they are flexible and scalable enough to perform business internationally. You know that you are going to run into many international business issues. Create a list of questions you need to answer to determine if your systems are capable of performing international business.

8. The Virtualization Opportunity

Virtualization makes good business sense. Organizations recognize the opportunity to use virtualization to break down the silos that keep applications from sharing infrastructure and that contribute to chronic underutilization of IT resources. Virtualization can help an organization simultaneously reduce costs, increase agility, and make IT more responsive to the needs of the business. So for many organizations, the question is not, "Should we virtualize?" Instead, the question is, "How can we transition to a virtualized environment in a predictable, cost-effective manner?"

Project Focus

You are the CFO for Martello's, a food distribution organization with locations in Chicago, New York, and San Francisco. Your CIO, Jeff Greenwald, has given you a proposal for a budget of $2 million to convert the organization to a virtualized environment. You are unfamiliar with virtualization, how it works, and the long-term goals it will satisfy for the company. You have a meeting with Jeff tomorrow and you want to be able to discuss his proposal. Use the Internet to research virtualization to prepare for your meeting. Once you have a solid understanding of virtualization, create a report detailing your decision to grant or deny Jeff's budget proposal.

PLUG-IN

B1

Business Basics

Introduction

A sign posted beside a road in Colorado states, "Failing to plan is planning to fail." Playnix Toys posted the sign after successfully completing its 20th year in the toy business in Colorado. The company's mission is to provide a superior selection of high-end toys for children of all ages. When the company began, it generated interest by using unique marketing strategies and promotions. The toy business has a lot of tough competition. Large chain stores such as Wal-Mart and Target offer toys at deep discount prices. Finding the right strategy to remain competitive is difficult in this industry, as FAO Schwarz discovered when it filed for bankruptcy after 143 years in the toy business.[1]

This plug-in introduces basic business fundamentals beginning with the three most common business structures—sole proprietorship, partnership, and corporation. It then focuses on the internal operations of a corporation including accounting, finance, human resources, sales, marketing, operations/production, and management information systems.

Types of Business

Businesses come in all shapes and sizes and exist to sell products or perform services. Businesses make profits or incur losses. A *profit* occurs when businesses sell products or services for more than they cost to produce. A *loss* occurs when

Baltzan–Phillips–Haag:
Business Driven
Technology, Third Edition

Business Plug–Ins

B1: Business Basics

© The McGraw–Hill
Companies, 2009

175

businesses sell products or services for less then they cost to produce. Businesses typically organize in one of the following types:

1. Sole proprietorship
2. Partnership
3. Corporation

SOLE PROPRIETORSHIP

The *sole proprietorship* is a business form in which a single person is the sole owner and is personally responsible for all the profits and losses of the business. The sole proprietorship is the quickest and easiest way to set up a business operation. No prerequisites or specific costs are associated with starting a sole proprietorship. A simple business license costing around $25 from the local county clerk is all that is required to start a sole proprietorship. The person who starts the sole proprietorship is the sole owner.[2]

PARTNERSHIP

Partnerships are similar to sole proprietorships, except that this legal structure allows for more than one owner. Each partner is personally responsible for all the profits and losses of the business. Similar to the sole proprietorship, starting a partnership is a relatively easy process since there are no prerequisites or specific costs required. When starting a partnership, it is wise to have a lawyer draft a partnership agreement. A *partnership agreement* is a legal agreement between two or more business partners that outlines core business issues. Partnership agreements typically include:

- Amount of capital each partner expects to contribute. *Capital* represents money whose purpose is to make more money, for example, the money used to buy a rental property or a business.
- Duties and responsibilities expected from each partner.
- Expectations for sharing profits and losses.
- Partners' salary requirements.
- Methods for conflict resolution.
- Methods for dissolving the partnership.[3]

Limited Partnership

A *limited partnership* is much like a general partnership except for one important fundamental difference; the law protects the limited partner from being responsible for all of the partnership's losses. The limited partner's legal liability in the business is limited to the amount of his or her investment. The limited partnership enables this special type of investor to share in the partnership profits without being exposed to its losses in the event the company goes out of business. However, this protection exists only as long as the limited partner does not play an active role in the operation of the business.

CORPORATION

The corporation is the most sophisticated form of business entity and the most common among large companies. The *corporation* (also called *organization, enterprise,* or *business*) is an artificially created legal entity that exists separate and apart from those individuals who created it and carry on its operations. In a corporation, the business entity is separate from the business owners. *Shareholder* is another term for business owners. An important advantage of using a corporation as a business form is

that it offers the shareholders limited liability. **_Limited liability_** means that the shareholders are not personally liable for the losses incurred by the corporation. In most instances, financial losses incurred by a corporation are limited to the assets owned by the corporation. Shareholders' personal assets, such as their homes or investments, cannot be claimed to pay off debt or losses incurred by the corporation.

There are two general types of corporations—for profit and not for profit. **_For profit corporations_** primarily focus on making money and all profits and losses are shared by the business owners. **_Not for profit_** (or **_nonprofit_**) **_corporations_** usually exist to accomplish some charitable, humanitarian, or educational purpose, and the profits and losses are not shared by the business owners. Donations to nonprofit businesses may be tax deductible for the donor. Typical examples include hospitals, colleges, universities, and foundations.[4]

Eleanor Josaitis is a tiny 72-year-old woman who co-founded the Detroit civil-rights group Focus: HOPE. Focus: HOPE, founded in 1968, began as a food program serving pregnant women, new mothers, and their children. Josaitis has built the nonprofit organization from a basement operation run by a handful of friends into a sprawling 40-acre campus in Detroit that now employs over 500 people, boasts more than 50,000 volunteers and donors, and has helped over 30,000 people become gainfully employed.

Josaitis and her team developed a technical school to help job seekers gain certifications in IT support. They operate a machinists' training program that funnels people into the employment pipeline at local automotive companies. The organization also teams up with local universities to help disadvantaged students receive college educations, and it runs a child care center to make sure all these opportunities are available to working and single parents. Josaitis states that the most courageous act she has performed in her life occurred 36 years ago when she turned off her television, got up off the couch, and decided to do something. "You have to have the guts to try something, because you won't change a thing by sitting in front of the TV with the clicker in your hand," Josaitis said.[5]

Forming a corporation typically costs several hundred dollars in fees, and the owners must file a charter within the respective state. The charter typically includes:

- Purpose of the intended corporation.
- Names and addresses of the incorporators.
- Amount and types of stock the corporation will be authorized to issue.
- Rights and privileges of the shareholders.

FIGURE B1.1

Reasons Businesses Choose to Incorporate

Reasons Businesses Choose to Incorporate	
Limited liability	In most instances, financial losses or judgments against the corporation are limited to the assets owned by the corporation.
Unlimited life	Unlike sole proprietorships and partnerships, the life of the corporation is not dependent on the life of a particular individual or individuals. It can continue indefinitely until it accomplishes its objective, merges with another business, or goes bankrupt. Unless stated otherwise, it could go on indefinitely.
Transferability of shares	It is easy to sell, transfer, or give the ownership interest in a corporation to another person. The process of divesting sole proprietorships or partnerships can be cumbersome and costly. Property has to be re-titled, new deeds drawn, and other administrative steps taken any time the slightest change of ownership occurs. With a corporation, all of the individual owners' rights and privileges are represented by the shares of stock they own. Corporations can quickly transfer ownership by simply having the shareholders endorse the back of each stock certificate to another party.
Ability to raise investment capital	It is easy to attract new investors into a corporate entity because of limited liability and the easy transferability of ownership.

	Sole Proprietorship	Partnership	Corporation
Licensing	Local license, $25–$100	Partnership agreement, legal fees	Articles of incorporation through the Secretary of State
Income	Business flows directly into personal income	Distributions taken by partners, as agreed by partners	Business and personal earnings separate, depending on corporate structure
Liability	Owner is liable	Owners are liable	Only business is liable

FIGURE B1.2

Comparison of Business Structures

The most common reason for incurring the cost of setting up a corporation is the recognition that the shareholder is not legally liable for the actions of the corporation. Figure B1.1 displays the primary reasons businesses choose to incorporate.

The Limited Liability Corporation (LLC)

The *limited liability corporation (LLC)* is a hybrid entity that has the legal protections of a corporation and the ability to be taxed (one time) as a partnership. A company can form an LLC for any lawful business as long as the nature of the business is not banking, insurance, and certain professional service operations. By simply filing articles of organization with the respective state agency, an LLC takes on a separate identity similar to a corporation, but without the tax problems of the corporation. Figure B1.2 summarizes the primary differences between the three most common business structures.[6]

Internal Operations of a Corporation

The majority of corporations use different specialized departments to perform the unique operations required to run the business. These departments commonly include accounting, finance, human resources, sales, marketing, operations/production, and management information systems (see Figure B1.3).

Accounting

The *accounting department* provides quantitative information about the finances of the business including recording, measuring, and describing financial information. People tend to use the terms *accounting* and *bookkeeping* synonymously;

COMMON DEPARTMENTS FOUND IN A CORPORATION

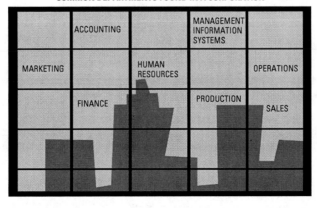

FIGURE B1.3

Departmental Structure of a Typical Organization

178 Baltzan–Phillips–Haag:
Business Driven
Technology, Third Edition

Business Plug-Ins

B1: Business Basics

© The McGraw–Hill
Companies, 2009

Accounting
/
managerial Financial

however, the two are different. **Bookkeeping** is the actual recording of the business's transactions, without any analysis of the information. **Accounting** analyzes the transactional information of the business so the owners and investors can make sound economic decisions.

The two primary types of accounting are financial and managerial. **Financial accounting** involves preparing financial reports that provide information about the business's performance to external parties such as investors, creditors, and tax authorities. Financial accounting must follow strict guidelines known as Generally Accepted Accounting Principles (GAAP). **Managerial accounting** involves analyzing business operations for internal decision making and does not have to follow any rules issued by standard-setting bodies such as GAAP.[7]

FINANCIAL STATEMENTS

All businesses operate using the same basic element, the transaction. A **transaction** is an exchange or transfer of goods, services, or funds involving two or more people. Each time a transaction occurs a source document captures all of the key data involved with the transaction. The **source document** describes the basic transaction data such as its date, purpose, and amount and includes cash receipts, canceled checks, invoices, customer refunds, employee time sheet, etc. The source document is the beginning step in the accounting process and serves as evidence that the transaction occurred. **Financial statements** are the written records of the financial status of the business that allow interested parties to evaluate the profitability and solvency of the business. **Solvency** represents the ability of the business to pay its bills and service its debt. The financial statements are the final product of the accountant's analysis of the business transactions. Preparing the financial statements is a major undertaking and requires a significant amount of effort. Financial statements must be understandable, timely, relevant, fair, and objective in order to be useful. The four primary financial statements include:

■ Balance sheet.

■ Income statement.

■ Statement of owner's equity.

■ Statement of cash flows.[8]

Balance Sheet

The **balance sheet** gives an accounting picture of property owned by a company and of claims against the property on a specific date. The balance sheet is based on the fundamental accounting principle that assets = liabilities + owner's equity. An **asset** is anything owned that has value or earning power. A **liability** is an obligation to make financial payments. **Owner's equity** is the portion of a company belonging to the owners. The left (debit) side of a balance sheet states assets. The right (credit) side shows liabilities and owners' equity. The two sides must be equal (balance). The balance sheet is like a snapshot of the position of an individual or business at one point in time (see Figure B1.4).[9]

Income Statement

The **income statement** (also referred to as **earnings report, operating statement,** and **profit-and-loss (P&L) statement**) reports operating results (revenues minus expenses) for a given time period ending at a specified date. **Revenue** refers to the amount earned resulting from the delivery or manufacture of a product or from the rendering of a service. Revenue can include sales from a product or an amount received for performing a service. **Expenses** refer to the costs incurred in operating and maintaining a business. The income statement reports a company's **net income,** or the amount of money remaining after paying taxes (see Figure B1.5).[10]

ASSETS		LIABILITIES	
Current Assets		**Current Liabilities**	
Cash	$ 250,000	Accounts Payable	$ 150,000
Securities	$ 30,000	Loans (due < 1 year)	$ 750,000
Accounts Receivable	$ 1,500,000	Taxes	$ 200,000
Inventory	$ 2,920,000		
		Long-term Liabilities	
Fixed Assets	$ 7,500,000	Loans (due > 1 year)	$ 2,500,000
		Total Liabilities	$ 3,600,000
		Owner's Equity	$ 8,600,000
Total Assets	**$12,200,000**	**Total Liabilities + Owner's Equity**	**$12,200,000**

ASSETS = LIABILITIES + OWNER'S EQUITY

FIGURE B1.4

Balance Sheet Example

Income Statement	
Revenue (Sales)	$60,000,000
Cost of Goods Sold	$30,000,000
Gross Profit	$30,000,000
(Sales – Cost of Goods Sold)	
Operating Expenses	$7,000,000
Profit Before Taxes	$23,000,000
(Gross Profit – Operating Expenses)	
Taxes	$18,000,000
Net Profit (or Loss)	**$5,000,000**

FIGURE B1.5

Income Statement Example

Statement of Owner's Equity

The *statement of owner's equity* (also called the *statement of retained earnings* or *equity statement*) tracks and communicates changes in the shareholder's earnings. Profitable organizations typically pay the shareholders dividends. *Dividends* are a distribution of earnings to shareholders.

Statement of Cash Flows

Cash flow represents the money an investment produces after subtracting cash expenses from income. The *statement of cash flows* summarizes sources and uses of cash, indicates whether enough cash is available to carry on routine operations, and offers an analysis of all business transactions, reporting where the firm obtained its cash and how it chose to allocate the cash. The cash flow statement shows where money comes from, how the company is going to spend it, and when the company will require additional cash. Companies typically project cash flow statements on a monthly basis for the current year and a quarterly basis for the next two to five years. A *financial quarter* indicates a three-month period (four quarters per year). Cash flow statements become less valid over time since numerous assumptions are required to project into the future.[11]

When it comes to decreasing expenses and managing a company's cash flow, managers need to look at all costs. Ben Worthen, executive vice president and CIO of Manufacturers Bank in Los Angeles, states that everyone notices the million-dollar negotiation; however, a couple of thousand dollars here and there are just as important. When attempting to cut costs, Worthen listed every contract the bank had. He saved $5,000 by renegotiating a contract with the vendor who watered the plants, a vendor that most employees did not even know existed. He also saved $50,000 by renegotiating the contract with the bank's cleaning agency. "You need to think of everything when cutting costs," Worthen said. "$5,000 buys three or four laptops for salespersons."[12]

Finance

Finance deals with the strategic financial issues associated with increasing the value of the business while observing applicable laws and social responsibilities. Financial decisions include such things as:

- How the company should raise and spend its capital.
- Where the company should invest its money.
- What portion of profits will be paid to shareholders in the form of dividends.
- Whether the company should merge with or acquire another business.

Financial decisions are short term (usually up to one year), medium term (one to seven years), or long term (more than seven years). The typical forms of financing include loans (debt or equity) or grants. Financing may be required for immediate use in business operations or for an investment.[13]

FINANCIAL ANALYSIS

Different financial ratios are used to evaluate a company's performance. Companies can gain additional insight into their performance by comparing financial ratios against other companies in their industry. A few of the more common financial ratios include:

- **Internal rate of return (IRR)**—the rate at which the net present value of an investment equals zero.
- **Return on investment (ROI)**—indicates the earning power of a project and is measured by dividing the benefits of a project by the investment.
- **Cash flow analysis**—a means to conduct a periodic check on the company's financial health. A projected cash flow statement estimates what the stream of money will be in coming months or years, based on a history of sales and expenses. A monthly cash flow statement reveals the current state of affairs. The ability to perform a cash flow analysis is an essential skill for every business owner; it can be the difference between being able to open a business and being able to stay in business.
- **Break-even analysis**—a way to determine the volume of business required to make a profit at the current prices charged for the products or services. For example, if a promotional mailing costs $1,000 and each item generates $50 in revenue, the company must generate 20 sales to break even and cover the cost of the mailing. The *break-even point* is the point at which revenues equal costs. The point is located by performing a break-even analysis. All sales over the break-even point produce profits; any drop in sales below that point will produce losses (see Figure B1.6).[14]

Human Resources

Human resources (HR) includes the policies, plans, and procedures for the effective management of employees (human resources). HR typically focuses on the following:

- Employee recruitment.
- Employee selection.

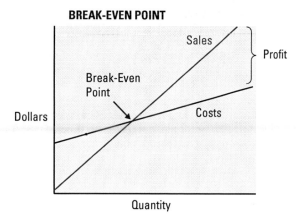

FIGURE B1.6

Break-Even Analysis

- Employee training and development.
- Employee appraisals, evaluations, and rewards.
- Employee communications.

The primary goal of HR is to instill employee commitment by creating an environment of shared values, innovation, flexibility, and empowerment. Most organizations recognize that focusing on strong HR practices that foster employee growth and satisfaction can significantly contribute to achieving business success. The most obvious way HR practices create business success is through quality employee selection. Hiring the right employee who suits the company's culture is difficult. Organizations create employee value by implementing employment practices such as training, skill development, and rewards. An organization that focuses on HR creates valuable employees with strategic business competencies.[15]

MANAGEMENT TECHNIQUES

There may be no such thing as a best practice for managing people. Numerous management techniques are used by all different types of managers in a variety of industries. For example, Sears and Nordstrom are legends in the retailing industry; however, their approaches to HR are completely different. Sears is one of the pioneering companies in the science of employee selection, relying on some of the most sophisticated selection tests in American industry. Sears employees receive extensive training in company practices; management tracks employee attitudes and morale through frequent and rigorous employee surveys. The company provides its sales representatives, who work on salary rather than commission, with intensive training in Sears products, the company's operating systems, and sales techniques.

Nordstrom operates with virtually no formal personnel practices. Its hiring is decentralized, using no formal selection tests. Managers look for applicants with experience in customer contact, but the main desirable quality appears to be pleasant personalities and motivation. The company has only one rule in its personnel handbook: "Use your best judgment at all times." Individual salesclerks virtually run their areas as private stores. Nordstrom maintains a continuous stream of programs to motivate employees to provide intensive service, but it offers very little training. Its commission-based payroll system makes it possible for salesclerks to earn sizable incomes. Nordstrom sales personnel are ranked within each department according to their monthly sales; the most successful are promoted (almost all managers are promoted from within the company) and the least successful are terminated.[16]

Sears and Nordstrom are both highly successful retailers, yet they operate using widely different recruitment policies. One of the biggest success factors for any business is the company's management and personnel. Employees must possess certain critical skills for the company to succeed. The HR department takes on the important task of hiring, training, evaluating, rewarding, and terminating employees. Effective HR goes far beyond executing a standard set of policies and procedures; it requires questioning and understanding the relationships between choices in managing people, the strategies and goals of the organization, and the possibilities presented by the external environment. Today's competitive environment features rapid technological change, increasingly global markets, and a diverse workforce comprising not just men and women with different sorts of career objectives, but also potential workers from diverse cultural and ethnic backgrounds. HR must ensure that the choices made in managing people are made sensibly and with clear purposes in mind.

Sales

Sales is the function of selling a good or service and focuses on increasing customer sales, which increases company revenues. A salesperson has the main activity of selling a product or service. Many industries require a license before a salesperson can sell the products, such as real estate, insurance, and securities.

A common view of the sales department is to see the salespersons only concerned with making the sale now, without any regard to the cost of the sale to the business. This is called the hard sell, where the salesperson heavily pushes a product (even when the customer does not want the product) and where price cuts are given even if they cause financial losses for the company. A broader view of the sales department sees it as taking on the task of building strong customer relationships where the primary emphasis is on securing new customers and keeping current customers satisfied. Many sales departments are currently focusing on building strong customer relationships.

THE SALES PROCESS

FIGURE B1.7

The Sales Process

Figure B1.7 depicts the typical sales process, which begins with an opportunity and ends with billing the customer for the sale. An opportunity is a name of a potential customer who might be interested in making a purchase (opportunities are also

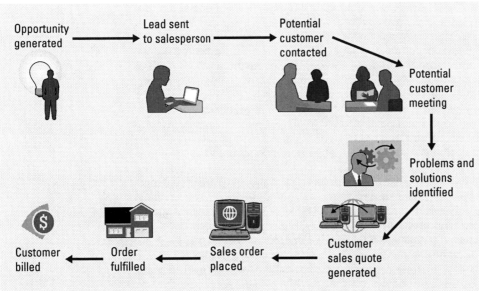

Sales Process

called *leads*). The company finds opportunities from a variety of sources such as mailing lists and customer inquiries. The name is sent to a salesperson who contacts the potential customer and sets up a meeting to discuss the products. During the meeting, all problems and issues are identified and resolved, and the salesperson generates a quote for the customer. If the customer decides to accept the quote, a sales order is placed. The company fulfills the order and delivers the product, and the process ends when the customer is billed.

MARKET SHARE

Sales figures offer a good indication of how well a company is performing. For example, high sales volumes typically indicate that a company is performing well. However, they do not always indicate how a firm is performing relative to its competitors. For example, changes in sales might simply reflect shifts in market size or in economic conditions. A sales increase might occur because the market increased in size, not because the company is performing better.

Measuring the proportion of the market that a firm captures is one way to measure a firm's performance relative to its competitors. This proportion is the firm's *market share* and is calculated by dividing the firm's sales by the total market sales for the entire industry. For example, if a firm's total sales (revenues) were $2 million and the sales for the entire industry were $10 million, the firm would have captured 20 percent of the total market, or have a 20 percent market share.

Many video game products launch with great enthusiasm and die a quick death such as Sega's GameGear and DreamCast, Atari's Lynx, and Nintendo's Virtual Boy. Video game consoles die quickly when only a limited number of game publishers sign up to supply games for the particular product. Producing video game products is a tough competitive business in a finicky market.

Sony released its first handheld video game player, the PSP (for PlayStation Portable), to go up against the market leader Nintendo's GameBoy, which uses pricey cartridges for games. Instead of pricey cartridges, the PSP plays inexpensive mini disks to bring PlayStation2-quality graphics to the relatively primitive handheld market. When Sony announced the PSP, game publishers raced to get a piece of the action, and Sony had 89 companies contracted to build games within a few weeks. In contrast, when Nokia launched its N-Gage game device, it struggled to land five game publishers. Electronic Arts, the world's biggest game publisher, has declared that the PSP will be the biggest driver of growth in the video game market for the next five years. For a new video game product heading into an uncertain and high-stakes market, that is the ultimate vote of confidence.[17]

Reasons to Increase Market Share

Many organizations seek to increase their market share because many individuals associate market share with profitability. Figure B1.8 indicates the primary reasons organizations seek to increase their market share.

Reasons to Increase Market Share
Economies of scale—An organization can develop a cost advantage by selling additional products or higher volumes.
Sales growth in a stagnant industry—If an industry stops growing, an organization can increase its sales by increasing its market share.
Reputation—A successful organization with a solid reputation can use its clout to its advantage.
Increased bargaining power—Larger organizations have an advantage in negotiating with suppliers and distributors.

FIGURE B1.8

Reasons to Increase Market Share

FIGURE B1.9

Ways to Increase Market Share

Ways to Increase Market Share

Product—An organization can change product attributes to provide more value to the customer. Improving product quality is one example.

Price—An organization can decrease a product's price to increase sales. This strategy will not work if competitors are willing to match discounts.

Place (Distribution)—An organization can add new distribution channels. This allows the organization to increase the size of its market, which should increase sales.

Promotion—An organization can increase spending on product advertising, which should increase sales. This strategy will not work if competitors also increase advertising.

FIGURE B1.10

Reasons Not to Increase Market Share

Reasons Not to Increase Market Share

If an organization is near its production capacity and it experiences an increase in market share, it could cause the organization's supply to fall below its demand. Not being able to deliver products to meet demand could damage the organization's reputation.

Profits could decrease if an organization gains market share by offering deep discounts or by increasing the amount of money it spends on advertising.

If the organization is not prepared to handle the new growth, it could begin to offer shoddy products or less attentive customer service. This could result in the loss of its professional reputation and valuable customers.

Ways to Increase Market Share

A primary way to increase market share is by changing one of the following variables: product, price, place, or promotion (see Figure B1.9). It is common to refer to these four variables as the marketing mix, discussed in detail below.[18]

Reasons Not to Increase Market Share

Surprisingly, it is not always a good idea to increase an organization's market share. Figure B1.10 offers a few reasons increasing an organization's market share can actually decrease an organization's revenues.[19]

Marketing

Marketing is the process associated with promoting the sale of goods or services. The marketing department supports the sales department by creating promotions that help sell the company's products. *Marketing communications* seek to build product or service awareness and to educate potential consumers on the product or service.

Jenny Ming, president of Old Navy, a division of Gap Inc., believes that unique marketing ideas for Old Navy's original designs heavily contributed to the success of the $6.5 billion brand. Ideas come from anywhere, and Ming found one of the company's most successful products when she was dropping her daughter off at school. It was pajama day at school, and all of the girls were wearing pajama bottoms with a tank top. Ming began wondering why they even created and sold pajama tops; nobody seemed to wear them. The company, having problems selling pajama sets, quickly introduced "just bottoms," a line of pajama bottoms selling at $15. A full pajama set cost $25. Along with the bottoms, the company offered tank tops in different colors so the customer could mix and match the items. The company built a huge business from the "just bottoms" line. Ming encourages her staff to look for marketing and product opportunities everywhere, even in the most unlikely of places.[20]

MARKETING MIX

The classic components of marketing include the four Ps in the marketing mix: product, price, place, and promotion. The **marketing mix** includes the variables that marketing managers can control in order to best satisfy customers in the target market (see Figure B1.11). The organization attempts to generate a positive response in the target market by blending these four marketing mix variables in an optimal manner.

Figure B1.12 summarizes the primary attributes involved with each decision made in the marketing mix.[21]

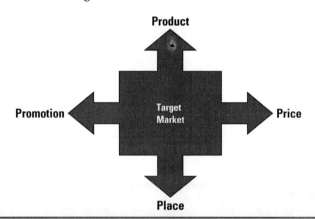

FIGURE B1.11

The Marketing Mix

1.	**Product** — the physical product or service offered to the consumer. Product decisions include function, appearance, packaging, service, warranty, etc.
2.	**Price** — takes into account profit margins and competitor pricing. Pricing includes list price, discounts, financing, and other options such as leasing.
3.	**Place** (distribution) — associated with channels of distribution that serve as the means for getting the product to the target customers. Attributes involved in place decisions include market coverage, channel member selection, logistics, and levels of service.
4.	**Promotion** — related to communication to and selling to potential consumers. An organization can perform a break-even analysis when making promotion decisions. If an organization knows the value of each customer, it can determine whether additional customers are worth the coast of acquisition. Attributes involved in promotion decisions involve advertising, public relations, media types, etc.

Product	Price	Place (Distribution)	Promotion
Quality	Discount	Channel	Advertising
Brand	Financing	Market	Sales
Appearance	Lease	Location	Public relations
Package		Logistics	Marketing message
Function		Service Level	Media type
Warranty			Budget
Service/Support			

FIGURE B1.12

Common Attributes Involved with Each P in the Marketing Mix

CUSTOMER SEGMENTATION

Market segmentation is the division of a market into similar groups of customers. It is not always optimal for an organization to offer the same marketing mix to vastly different customers. Market segmentation makes it possible for organizations to tailor the marketing mix for specific target markets, hence better satisfying its customer needs. Not all attributes of the marketing mix need to be changed for each market segment. For example, one market segment might require a discounted price, while another market segment might require better customer service. An organization uses marketing research, market trends, and managerial judgment when deciding the optimal way to segment a market. Market segmentation typically includes:

- **Geographic segmentation**—based on regional variables such as region, climate, population density, and population growth rate.
- **Demographic segmentation**—based on variables such as age, gender, ethnicity, education, occupation, income, and family status.
- **Psychographic segmentation**—based on variables such as values, attitudes, and lifestyles.
- **Behavioral segmentation**—based on variables such as usage rate, usage patterns, price sensitivity, and brand loyalty.[22]

THE PRODUCT LIFE CYCLE

The *product life cycle* includes the four phases a product progresses through during its life cycle including introduction, growth, maturity, and decline. An organization's marketing of a product will change depending on its stage in the product life cycle. An organization can plot a product's profits as a function of the product life cycle (see Figure B1.13).

Joanne Bischmann, vice president, Harley-Davidson Inc., is still awed by the lengths customers will go to display their commitment to Harley-Davidson products. Recently, she saw a man who had tattooed a portrait of the four founding fathers along with their 100th anniversary logo on his back. When Bischmann was hired, her manager told her the following, "This will be the best job you're ever going to have because it isn't just about working at a company that makes motorcycles. The founding fathers actually seep out of the walls here." After 15 years with the company, Bischmann agrees with that statement. She always receives calls asking for the Harley-Davidson manual on how to keep customers passionate. Unfortunately, there is no manual. According to Bischmann, Harley-Davidson is a brand that none can own individually; it is more like a tribe, and its members carry on its traditions so it will be here for future generations.[23]

Operations/Production

Operations management (also called *production management*) includes the methods, tasks, and techniques organizations use to produce goods and services. The operations department oversees the transformation of input resources (i.e., labor, materials, and machines) into output resources (i.e., products and services). The operations department is critical because it manages the physical processes by which companies take in raw materials, convert them into products, and distribute them to customers. The operations department generally ranks high in the responsibilities of general management.

BUSINESS PROCESS REENGINEERING

A *business process* is a standardized set of activities that accomplishes a specific task, such as processing a customer's order. *Business process reengineering (BPR)* is the analysis and redesign of workflow within and between enterprises. In

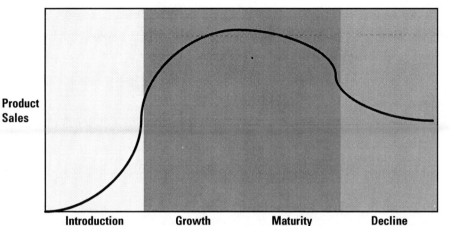

FIGURE B1.13
The Product Life Cycle

Product Sales

| Introduction | Growth | Maturity | Decline |

- **Introduction Stage**—The organization seeks to build product awareness and develop the product's market. The organization will use the marketing mix to help impact the target market. Product branding and quality level are established.

- **Growth Stage**—The organization seeks to build brand preference and increase market share. The organization maintains or increases the quality of the product and might add additional features or better customer service. The organization typically enjoys increases in demand with little competition allowing the price to remain constant.

- **Maturity Stage**—The strong growth in sales diminishes. Competition begins to appear with similar products. The primary objective at this point is to defend market share while maximizing profits. Some companies enhance product features to differentiate the product in the market.

- **Decline Stage**—Sales begin to decline. At this point, the organization has several options. It can maintain the product, possibly rejuvenating it by adding new features and finding new uses. It can reduce costs and continue to offer it, possibly to a loyal niche segment. It can discontinue the product, liquidating remaining inventory or selling it to another firm that is willing to continue the product.

business process reengineering, the project team starts with a clean sheet of paper and redesigns the process to increase efficiency and effectiveness. The project team does not take anything for granted and questions all the aspects of the process and the business. The reengineering project team obtains dramatic process improvement by redesigning processes that cross departments.

Most of the major opportunities for process improvement exist in cross-departmental processes. Information technology usually plays a key role in process improvement by making possible a radically faster and almost paperless process. However, IT is only an enabling factor. A classic reengineering project example is the accounts payable process at Ford. Through BPR, Ford reduced the number of people required to perform the process from 500 to 125.[24]

TRANSFORMING CORPORATIONS

Complete transformation of an organization, or an entire industry, is the ultimate goal of successful business process reengineering. Figure B1.14 displays a matrix that has project scope on one axis and project speed on the other. For a project with a relatively narrow scope where the speed is fast, reengineering occurs. Fast speed with broad scope may be a turnaround situation requiring downsizing and tough decision making. A project with a relatively slow speed and narrow scope results in continuous improvement. In the upper right-hand corner of Figure B1.14, where the project scope is broad and the time frame for achieving that change is longer, the term *transformation* is appropriate.

FIGURE B1.14

Organizational Transformation through BPR

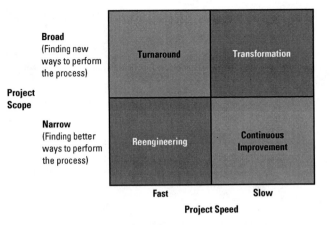

Progressive Insurance offers a great example of a corporation that transformed its entire industry by reengineering the insurance claims process. Progressive Insurance has seen phenomenal growth in an otherwise staid auto insurance market. Progressive's growth came not through acquisitions or mergers—the stuff that puts CEOs on the front page of *The Wall Street Journal*—but through substantial innovations in everyday operations. Progressive reengineered the insurance claim process. When a customer has an auto accident, Progressive representatives are on hand 24 hours a day to take the call and schedule a claims adjustor. The claims adjustor works out of a mobile van, enabling a nine-hour turnaround rather than the industry standard of 10 to 17 days. The Progressive adjustor prepares an estimate on the spot and will, in most cases, write the customer a check immediately and even offer a ride home.

What provoked this innovation? Progressive says it was the strong connection it has to its customers, its willingness to listen to customers' frustrations, and the common sense to act on those frustrations by changing the core of its business operations. As a result of customer feedback, the company did not merely tweak the details of the claims adjustment process. It dramatically rewrote the process, resulting in significant cost savings for the company. More important, however, the hassle-free claims process keeps customers happy and loyal, reducing the significant burden of constantly replacing lapsed customers with new ones.[25]

Management Information Systems

Information technology (IT) is a field concerned with the use of technology in managing and processing information. Information technology is a broad subject concerned with technology and other aspects of managing and processing information, especially in large organizations. In particular, IT deals with the use of electronic computers and computer software to convert, store, protect, process, transmit, and retrieve information. For that reason, computer professionals are often called IT specialists, and the division that deals with software technology is often called the IT department.

Management information systems is a business function just as marketing, finance, operations, and human resources management are business functions. Formally defined, *management information systems (MIS)* is a general name for the business function and academic discipline covering the application of people technologies, and procedures—collectively called information systems—to solve business problems. Other names for MIS include information services (IS), management information services (MIS), or managed service provider (MSP). In business, MIS supports business processes and operations, decision making, and competitive strategies. MIS involves collecting, recording, storing, and basic processing of information including:

- Accounting records such as sales, purchase, investment, and payroll information, processed into financial statements such as income statements, balance sheets, ledgers, management reports, and so on.

- Operations records such as inventory, work-in-process, equipment repair and maintenance, supply chain, and other production/operations information, processed into production schedules, production controllers, inventory systems, and production monitoring systems.

- Human resources records such as personnel, salary, and employment history information, processed into employee expense reports and performance-based reports.

- Marketing records such as customer profiles, customer purchase histories, marketing research, advertising, and other marketing information, processed into advertising reports, marketing plans, and sales activity reports.

- Strategic records such as business intelligence, competitor analysis, industry analysis, corporate objectives, and other strategic information, processed into industry trends reports, market share reports, mission statements, and portfolio models.

The bottom line is that management information systems use all of the above to implement, control, and monitor plans, strategies, tactics, new products, new business models, or new business ventures. Unit 1 covers IT and MIS in detail.

The study of business begins with understanding the different types of businesses including a sole proprietorship, partnership, or a corporation. Figure B1.15 highlights seven departments found in a typical business.

All of these departments must be able to execute activities specific to their business function and also be able to work with the other departments to create synergies throughout the entire business.

- **Accounting** provides quantitative information about the finances of the business including recording, measuring, and describing financial information.

- **Finance** deals with the strategic financial issues associated with increasing the value of the business, while observing applicable laws and social responsibilities.

- **Human resources (HR)** includes the policies, plans, and procedures for the effective management of employees (human resources).

- **Sales** is the function of selling a good or service and focuses on increasing customer sales, which increases company revenues.

- **Marketing** is the process associated with promoting the sale of goods or services. The marketing department supports the sales department by creating promotions that help sell the company's products.

- **Operations management** (also called **production management**) includes the methods, tasks, and techniques organizations use to produce goods and services. Transportation (also called logistics) is part of operations management.

- **Management information systems (MIS)** is a general name for the business function and academic discipline covering the application of people technologies, and procedures—collectively called information systems—to solve business problems.

FIGURE B1.15

Common Departments in a Business

✳ KEY TERMS

Accounting, 280
Accounting department, 279
Asset, 280
Balance sheet, 280
Bookkeeping, 280
Break-even point, 282
Business process, 283
Business process reengineering (BPR), 288
Capital, 277
Corporation (also called, organization, enterprise, or business), 277
Dividend, 281
Expense, 280
Finance, 282
Financial accounting, 280
Financial quarter, 281
Financial statement, 280
For profit corporation, 278
Human resources (HR), 282
Income statement (also referred to as earnings report, operating statement,

and profit-and-loss (P&L) statement), 280
Information technology (IT), 290
Liability, 280
Limited liability, 278
Limited liability corporation (LLC), 279
Limited partnership, 277
Loss, 276
Management information systems (MIS), 290
Managerial accounting, 280
Marketing, 286
Marketing communication, 286
Marketing mix, 287
Market segmentation, 288
Market share, 285
Net income, 280
Not for profit (or nonprofit) corporation, 278
Operations management (also called production management), 288
Owner's equity, 280

Partnership, 277
Partnership agreement, 277
Product life cycle, 288
Profit, 276
Revenue, 280
Sales, 284
Shareholder, 277
Sole proprietorship, 277
Solvency, 280
Source document, 280
Statement of cash flow, 281
Statement of owner's equity (also called the statement of retained earnings or equity statement), 281
Transaction, 280

✳ CLOSING CASE ONE

Battle of the Toys—FAO Schwarz Is Back!

German immigrant Frederick Schwarz established FAO Schwarz, a premier seller of fine toys, in 1862. After moving between several store locations in Manhattan, the growing company settled at 745 Fifth Avenue in 1931. FAO Schwarz soon became a toy institution, despite the impending Depression.

Unfortunately, the New York institution closed its doors in 2004 after its owner, FAO Inc., filed for bankruptcy twice in 2003. The company ran into trouble because it could not compete with the deep discounts offered on toys at chain stores like Wal-Mart and Target. All the stores in the FAO chain were closed.

Some people believe that FAO Schwarz was its own worst enemy. The company sold Sesame Street figures for $9 while the same figure at a discount store went for less than $3.

In 2004, the New York investment firm D. E. Shaw & Co. bought the rights to the FAO Schwarz name and reopened the Manhattan and Las Vegas stores. The grand reopening of the New York store occurred on November 25, 2004, during the Macy's Thanksgiving Day parade. It appears that the company has learned from its previous mistakes and is moving forward with a new business strategy of offering high-end, hard-to-find toys and products along with outstanding customer service.

Jerry Welch, FAO chief executive officer, states the company based its new business strategy on offering customers—local, visitors, and Internet—a unique shopping experience in which they can spend thousands of dollars or just twenty, but still purchase an exclusive item. The store no longer carries any items from top toymakers Hasbro Inc. or Lego. The only toys it carries from Mattel Inc. are Hot Wheels and limited-edition Barbie dolls, starting at $130 for the Bridal Barbie dressed in a Badgley Mischka designer wedding gown and chandelier earrings. A few of the items the store is offering include:

- $20 made-to-order Hot Wheels car that a child can custom design via a computer.
- $50,000 miniature Ferrari with a full leather interior, fiberglass body, three-speed transmission, and working sound system that travels up to 24 kilometers an hour and is not recommended for children six and under.
- $15,000 stuffed elephant.
- $150,000 6.7-meter-long piano keyboard, which premiered in the Tom Hanks movie *Big*.
- Baby dolls that are arranged in incubators and sold by staff wearing nurses' uniforms.

Welch said, "FAO is a 142-year-old brand that, because of our location on Fifth Avenue, people all over the world know. So we start out with great recognition and what we've done here is pull together something that you just can't find anywhere else in the world. Everything here is made by small, unique manufacturers from all over the world." Welch is confident the stores will be richly profitable for its new owners because they have stopped offering mainstream products found in rival stores to generate sales volume. The new owners have returned to a business strategy focusing on quality and exclusivity that were the hallmark of the original store.

The Future of the Toy Store Playing Field

Toys 'R' Us began slashing prices during the 2004 holiday season in a last-ditch effort to fight off intense price competition from big discounters like Wal-Mart and Target. Toys 'R' Us CEO John Eyler stated the company would not be outdone on pricing, during the holiday sales rush, though he cautioned he was not planning to engage in a price war. There have been several reports that the company might leave the toy business to focus on its more profitable Babies 'R' Us unit. Toys 'R' Us lost $25 million for the three months ended in October 2004. The company lost $46 million in the same period the year earlier. The decrease in losses can be attributed to a big cost-cutting effort.

Kurt Barnard of Barnard's *Retail Trend Report* stated that Toys 'R' Us is destined for oblivion—it cannot stand up to the discounters. Toymakers like Mattel and Hasbro, whose profits have also suffered from Wal-Mart's market power, have given Toys 'R' Us a hand by offering it 21 exclusive items not available at other stores.

Toy manufacturers fear that greater monopoly power from Wal-Mart will force them to slash their profit margins. Wal-Mart carries fewer items than toy stores like Toys 'R' Us, which could lead to fewer choices for consumers.

FAO's new owners believe that Wal-Mart cannot compare with the atmosphere now offered at FAO Schwarz, a true toy heaven. The company is hoping that its new business strategy will allow it to move beyond the battle of the toy stores. Toys 'R' Us will need to find new ways to compete with discounters like Wal-Mart and Target.[26]

Questions

1. Why did FAO Inc. have to declare bankruptcy?
2. Describe the issues with FAO's original business model.
3. Identify the toy retailer's new business model. Do you believe it will keep the new company in business? Why or why not?
4. What strategy can Toys 'R' Us follow that will help it compete with big discount chains like Wal-Mart and Target?

CLOSING CASE TWO

Innovative Managers	
Jeffrey Immelt, General Electric (GE)	■ Repositioned GE's portfolio with major acquisitions in health care, entertainment, and commercial finance ■ Created a more diverse, global, and customer-driven culture
Steven Reinemund, PepsiCo	■ Developed strong and diverse leadership that helped PepsiCo tap new markets ■ Attained consistent double-digit growth through product innovation and smart marketing
Steven Spielberg, Jeffrey Katzenberg, and David Geffen, DreamWorks SKG	■ Computer-animated *Shrek 2* set a record with a gross of $437 million ■ IPO pulled in $812 million
Robert Nardelli, Home Depot	■ Turned a $46 billion company focused on big stores into a $70 billion chain with urban, suburban, and international outlets ■ Drive for efficiency, such as centralizing purchasing and investing in technology, pushed margins above 30 percent
John Henry, Boston Red Sox	■ Broke the most fabled curse in sports, when the Boston Red Sox won the team's first World Championship since 1918 ■ Sold out all 81 home games for the first time in team history
Phil Knight, Nike	■ Transformed a volatile, fad-driven marketing and design icon into a more shareholder-friendly company

FIGURE B1.16

Innovative Business Managers

Innovative Business Managers

BusinessWeek magazine recognized several innovative managers who have demonstrated talent, vision, and the ability to identify excellent opportunities (see Figure B1.16).

Jeffrey Immelt, General Electric (GE)

When Jeffrey Immelt took over as CEO of General Electric, he had big shoes to fill. The former CEO, Jack Welch, had left an unprecedented record as one of the top CEOs of all time. Immelt proved his ability to run the company by creating a customer-driven global culture that spawns innovation and embraces technology. The company was forecasting earnings to increase 17 percent in 2005.

Steven Reinemund, PepsiCo

Steven Reinemund has turned PepsiCo into a $27 billion food and beverage giant. "To be a leader in consumer products, it's critical to have leaders who represent the population we serve," states Reinemund, who created a diverse leadership group that defines the strategic vision for the company. Reinemund also takes a major role in mentoring and teaching his employees and demands that all senior executives do the same. The payoff: consistent double-digit earnings and solid sales at a time when many of the company's staple products—potato chips and soft drinks—are under attack for fears about childhood obesity and health concerns.

Steven Spielberg, Jeffrey Katzenberg, and David Geffen, DreamWorks

The DreamWorks studio, founded in 1994 by Steven Spielberg, Jeffrey Katzenberg, and David Geffen, suffered through its share of early bombs. Finally, the studio discovered a green ogre named Shrek and quickly became the hottest studio this side of Pixar Animation. DreamWorks Animation turned a $187 million loss in 2003 into a $196 million profit in 2004, with revenues of $1.1 billion. DreamWorks plans to release two animation films per year, each taking almost four years to produce.

Robert Nardelli, Home Depot

Robert Nardelli took several risks when he became CEO of Home Depot. First, he allocated $14 billion into upgrading merchandise, renovating outdated stores, and investing in new technology such as self-checkout lanes and cordless scan guns. Second, Nardelli expanded into Mexico, China, and other regions, tapping the growing homeowner market. Finally, Nardelli bet big on carrying products for aging baby boomers who wanted to spruce up their empty nests. The moves are paying off. The company sits on $3.4 billion in cash. With 2005 revenues headed to $80 billion, Home Depot is the number two U.S. retailer after Wal-Mart.

John Henry, Boston Red Sox

John Henry earned his fortune in the global futures market by developing a proprietary futures-trading system that consistently produced double-digit returns. Henry's new system, Sabermetrics, helped him reverse the most fabled curse in sports history by leading the Boston Red Sox to the team's first World Championship since 1918. Sabermetrics mines baseball statistics to find under-valued players while avoiding long contracts for aging stars whose performance is likely to decline. With the help of Sabermetrics, Henry has built one of the most effective teams in baseball.

Philip Knight, Nike

Philip Knight, who got his start by selling Japanese sneakers from the trunk of his car, built the $12 billion sports behemoth Nike. Knight and his team transformed high-performance sports equipment into high-fashion gear and forever changed the rules of sports marketing with huge endorsement contracts and in-your-face advertising. Then, just as suddenly, Nike lost focus. In early 2000, kids stopped craving the latest sneaker, the company's image took a huge hit from its labor practices, sales slumped, and costs soared.

Thus began Knight's second act. He revamped management and brought in key outsiders to oversee finances and apparel lines. Knight devoted more energy to developing new information systems. Today, Nike's earnings are less volatile and less fad-driven. In 2004, Nike's earnings increased $1 billion.[27]

Questions

1. Choose one of the companies listed above and explain how it has achieved business success.
2. Why is it important for all of DreamWorks' functional business areas to work together? Provide an example of what might happen if the DreamWorks marketing department failed to work with its sales department.
3. Why is marketing important to an organization like the Boston Red Sox? Explain where Major League Baseball is in the product life cycle.
4. Which types of financial statements are most important to Home Depot's business?
5. Identify the marketing mix and why customer segmentation is critical to PepsiCo's business strategy.
6. Explain business process reengineering and how a company like GE can use it to improve operations.

✱ MAKING BUSINESS DECISIONS

1. Setting Up a Business

Your friend, Lindsay Harvey, is going to start her own chocolate shop, called Chocolate-By-Design. Lindsay is an expert candy maker and one of the city's top pastry chefs. Lindsay has come to you for advice on what type of business Chocolate-By-Design should be—a sole proprietorship, partnership, or corporation. Create a report comparing the three different types of businesses, along with your recommendation for Chocolate-By-Design's business structure.

2. Guest Lecturing on Business

As a recent college graduate, your favorite professor, Dr. Henning, has asked you to come back and guest lecture at his introduction to business course. Create a presentation defining the different departments in a typical business, what roles each play, and why it is important that they all work together.

3. Expanding Markets

J. R. Cash created a small business selling handmade cowboy boots, and within a year his business is booming. J. R. currently builds all of the boots in his store and takes orders over the phone and from walk-in customers. There is currently a three-month waiting list for boots. J. R. is not sure how to grow his business and has come to you for advice. Describe the reasons and ways some businesses increase market share and why J. R. might choose not to increase his market share.

4. Segmenting Customers

Due to your vast marketing experience, you have been hired by a new company, Sugar, to perform a strategic analysis on chewing gum. The company wants to understand the many market segments for the different brands, flavors, sizes, and colors of gum. Create an analysis of the different market segments for chewing gum. What market segment would you recommend Sugar pursue?

5. Product Life Cycle

An associate, Carl Grotenhuis, has developed a new brand of laundry detergent called Clean. Carl wants your opinion on his potential to enter and dominate the laundry detergent market. Using the product life cycle create a recommendation for Carl's new product.

6. Redesigning a Business

Tom Walton is the new CEO for Lakeside, a large cereal manufacturing company. Tom's predecessor had run the company for 50 years and did little in terms of process improvement; in fact, his motto was "if it isn't broke, why fix it." Tom wants to take advantage of technology to create new processes for the entire company. He believes that improving operations will increase efficiency and lower costs.

Tom has a major hurdle to overcome before he can begin revamping the company—its employees. Many of the employees have worked at the company for decades and are comfortable with the motto "if it isn't broke, why fix it." Develop a plan Tom can use to communicate to his employees the potential value gained from business process reengineering.

PLUG-IN
B2

Business Process

1. Describe business processes and their importance to an organization.
2. Differentiate between customer facing processes and business facing processes.
3. Compare the continuous process improvement model and business process re-engineering.
4. Describe the importance of business process modeling (or mapping) and business process models.
5. Explain business process management along with the reason for its importance to an organization.

Introduction

The benefits of business process improvement vary, but a rough rule of thumb is that it will, at a minimum, double the gains of a project by streamlining outdated practices, enhancing efficiency, promoting compliance and standardization, and making an organization more agile. Business process improvement involves three key steps:

1. Measure what matters to most customers.
2. Monitor the performance of key business processes.
3. Assign accountability for process improvement.

Comprehensive business process management systems help organizations model and define complete business processes, implement those processes integrated with existing systems, and provide business leaders with the ability to analyze, manage, and improve the execution of processes in real time.[1]

Examining Business Processes

Waiting in line at a grocery store is a great example of the need for process improvement. In this case, the "process" is called checkout, and the purpose is to pay for and bag groceries. The process begins when a customer steps into line and ends

Baltzan–Phillips–Haag:
Business Driven
Technology, Third Edition

Business Plug–Ins

B2: Business Process

© The McGraw–Hill
Companies, 2009

197

when the customer receives the receipt and leaves the store. The *process* steps are the activities the customer and store personnel do to complete the transaction. A **business process** is a standardized set of activities that accomplish a specific task, such as processing a customer's order. Business processes transform a set of inputs into a set of outputs (goods or services) for another person or process by using people and tools. This simple example describes a customer checkout process. Imagine other business processes: developing new products, building a new home, ordering clothes from mail-order companies, requesting new telephone service from a telephone company, administering Social Security payments, and so on.

Examining business processes helps an organization determine bottlenecks and identify outdated, duplicate, and smooth running processes. To stay competitive, organizations must optimize and automate their business processes. To identify which business processes need to be optimized, the organization must clearly understand its business processes, which typically have the following important characteristics:

- The processes have internal and external users.
- A process is cross-departmental. Departments are functional towers of expertise, but processes cut across departments.
- The processes occur across organizations.
- The processes are based on how work is done in the organization.
- Every process should be documented and fully understood by everyone participating in the process.
- Processes should be modeled to promote complete understanding.[2]

A business process can be viewed as a "value chain." By contributing to the creation or delivery of a product or service, each step in a process should add value to the preceding step. For example, one step in the product development process consists of conducting market acceptance tests. This step adds value by ensuring that the product meets the needs of the market before the product or service is finalized. A tremendous amount of learning and improvement can result from the documentation and examination of the input-output linkages. However, between every input and every output is a process. Knowledge and improvement can only be completed by peeling the layers of the onion and examining the processes through which inputs are converted into outputs. Figure B2.1 displays several sample business processes.[3]

Some processes (such as a programming process) may be contained wholly within a single department. However, most processes (such as ordering a product) are cross-departmental, spanning the entire organization. Figure B2.2 (on page 302) displays the different categories of cross-departmental business processes. **Customer facing processes** result in a product or service that is received by an organization's external customer. **Business facing processes** are invisible to the external customer but essential to the effective management of the business and include goal setting, day-to-day planning, performance feedback, rewards, and resource allocation.[4]

UNDERSTANDING THE IMPORTANCE OF BUSINESS PROCESSES

Organizations are only as effective as their business processes. Developing logical business processes can help an organization achieve its goals. For example, an automobile manufacturer might have a goal to reduce the time it takes to deliver a car to a customer. The automobile manufacturer cannot hope to meet this goal with an inefficient ordering process or a convoluted distribution process. Sales representatives might be making mistakes when completing order forms, data-entry clerks might not accurately code order information, and dock crews might be inefficiently loading cars onto trucks. All of these errors increase the time it will take

FIGURE B2.1

Sample Business Processes

Sample Business Processes
ACCOUNTING BUSINESS PROCESSES ■ Accounts payable ■ Accounts receivable ■ Bad/NSF checks ■ Bank account reconciliation ■ Cash receipts ■ Check requests ■ Check signing authority ■ Depreciation ■ Invoice billings ■ Petty cash ■ Month-end closing procedures
CUSTOMER SERVICE BUSINESS PROCESSES ■ Customer satisfaction survey ■ Customer service contact/complaint handling ■ Guarantee customer service satisfaction ■ Postsale customer follow-up ■ Warranty and service policies
ENVIRONMENTAL BUSINESS PROCESSES ■ Environmental protection ■ Hazardous waste management ■ Air/water/soil resource management
FINANCE BUSINESS PROCESSES ■ Account collection ■ Bank loan applications ■ Banking policy and relations ■ Business plans and forecasts ■ Customer credit approval and credit terms ■ Exercise of incentive stock options ■ Property tax assessments ■ Release of financial or confidential information ■ Stock transactions ■ Weekly financial and six-week cash flow reports
HUMAN RESOURCES BUSINESS PROCESSES ■ Board of directors and shareholders meetings, minutes, and protocol ■ Disabilities employment policies ■ Drug-free workplace employment policies ■ Employee hiring policies ■ Employee orientation ■ Family and medical leave act ■ Files and records management ■ Health care benefits ■ Paid and unpaid time off ■ Pay and payroll matters ■ Performance appraisals and salary adjustments ■ Resignations and terminations ■ Sexual harassment policies ■ Training/tuition reimbursement ■ Travel and entertainment ■ Workplace rules and guidelines ■ Workplace safety

Sample Business Processes
MANAGEMENT INFORMATION SYSTEMS BUSINESS PROCESSES
■ Disaster recovery procedures
■ Backup/recovery procedures
■ Service agreements, emergency services, and community resources
■ Emergency notification procedures
■ Office and department recovery
■ User workstation standards
■ Use of personal software
■ Computer security incident reporting
■ Control of computer virus programs
■ Computer user/staff training plan
■ Internet use policy
■ E-mail policy
■ Computer support center
MANUFACTURING BUSINESS PROCESSES
■ Assembly manuals
■ Bill of materials
■ Calibration for testing and measuring equipment
■ FDA inspections
■ Manufacturing change orders
■ Master parts list and files
■ Serial number designation
■ Quality control for finished goods
■ Quality assurance audit procedure
SALES AND MARKETING BUSINESS PROCESSES
■ Collection of sales tax
■ Copyrights and trademarks
■ Marketing plans model number
■ Designation public relations
■ Return of goods from customers
■ Sales leads
■ Sales order entry
■ Sales training
■ Trade shows
SHIPPING, PURCHASING, AND INVENTORY CONTROL BUSINESS PROCESSES
■ Packing, storage, and distribution
■ Physical inventory procedures
■ Purchasing procedures
■ Receiving, inspection, and stocking of parts and materials
■ Shipping and freight claims
■ Vendor selection, files, and inspections

FIGURE B2.1

(Continued)

to get the car to the customer. Improving any one of these business processes can have a significant effect on the total distribution process, made up of the order entry, production scheduling, and transportation processes.

IBM Business Consulting Services helped Bank of America's card services division identify $40 million of simplification and cost savings projects over two years by improving business processes to identify opportunities, eliminate redundancies, consolidate systems/applications, and remove duplicate processes. Within the card services and e-commerce division were several fragmented strategies and IT architectures. These were consolidated and simplified to streamline the business area and provide better and faster response to customer demand.

The scope of the IT strategy and architecture business process realignment project included all consumer card segments (including military, school, airlines, etc.), ATM cards and services, and e-commerce.[5]

FIGURE B2.2

Customer Facing, Industry-Specific, and Business Facing Processes

Customer Facing Processes	Industry-Specific Customer Facing Processes	Business Facing Processes
Marketing and sales	Banking—loan processing	Strategic planning
Product development	Insurance—claims processing	Tactical planning
Service development	Government—grant allocation	Budgeting
Manufacturing	Retail—merchandise return	Training
Distribution	Restaurant—food preparation	Purchasing
Billing	Airline—baggage handling	
Order processing	Hotel—reservation handling	
Customer service		

Business Process Improvement

Improving business processes is paramount for businesses to stay competitive in today's marketplace. Over the past 10 to 15 years, companies have been forced to improve their business processes because customers are demanding better products and services; if they do not receive what they want from one supplier, they have many others to choose from (hence the competitive issue for businesses). Figure B2.3 displays several opportunities for business process improvement.

Many organizations began business process improvement with a continuous improvement model. A ***continuous process improvement model*** attempts to understand and measure the current process, and make performance improvements accordingly. Figure B2.4 illustrates the basic steps for continuous process improvement. Organizations begin by documenting what they do today, establish some way to measure the process based on what customers want, perform the process, measure the results, and then identify improvement opportunities based on the collected information. The next step is to implement process improvements, and then measure the performance of the new process. This loop repeats over and over again and is called continuous process improvement. It might also be called business process improvement or functional process improvement.[6]

This method for improving business processes is effective to obtain gradual, incremental improvement. However, several factors have accelerated the need to improve business processes. The most obvious is technology. New technologies (like the Internet and wireless) rapidly bring new capabilities to businesses, thereby raising the competitive bar and the need to improve business processes dramatically.

Another apparent trend is the opening of world markets and increased free trade. Such changes bring more companies into the marketplace, adding to the competition. In today's marketplace, major changes are required just to stay in the game. As a result, companies have requested methods for faster business process improvement. Also, companies want breakthrough performance changes, not just incremental

Business Process Improvement Examples
Eliminate duplicate activities
Combine related activities
Eliminate multiple reviews and approvals
Eliminate inspections
Simplify processes
Reduce batch sizes
Process in parallel
Implement demand pull
Outsource inefficient activities
Eliminate movement of work
Organize multifunctional teams
Design cellular workplaces
Centralize/decentralize

FIGURE B2.3

Opportunities for Business Process Improvement

FIGURE B2.4

Continuous Process Improvement Model

Document As-Is Process → Establish Measures → Follow Process → Measure Performance → Identify and Implement Improvements

Baltzan–Phillips–Haag:
Business Driven
Technology, Third Edition

Business Plug–Ins

B2: Business Process

© The McGraw–Hill
Companies, 2009

201

FIGURE B2.5

Business Process
Reengineering Model

changes, and they want it now. Because the rate of change has increased for everyone, few businesses can afford a slow change process. One approach for rapid change and dramatic improvement is business process reengineering (BPR).

BUSINESS PROCESS REENGINEERING (BPR)

An organization must continuously revise and reexamine its decisions, goals, and targets to improve its performance. A bank may have many activities, such as investing, credit cards, loans, and so on, and it may be involved in cross-selling (e.g., insurance) with other preferred vendors in the market. If the credit card department is not functioning in an efficient manner, the bank might reengineer the credit card business process. This activity, *business process reengineering (BPR),* is the analysis and redesign of workflow within and between enterprises. BPR relies on a different school of thought than continuous process improvement. *In the extreme,* BPR assumes the current process is irrelevant, does not work, or is broken and must be overhauled from scratch. Such a clean slate enables business process designers to disassociate themselves from today's process and focus on a new process. It is like the designers projecting themselves into the future and asking: What should the process look like? What do customers want it to look like? What do other employees want it to look like? How do best-in-class companies do it? How can new technology facilitate the process?[7]

Figure B2.5 displays the basic steps in a business process reengineering effort. It begins with defining the scope and objectives of the reengineering project, then goes through a learning process (with customers, employees, competitors, non-competitors, and new technology). Given this knowledge base, the designers can create a vision for the future and design new business processes by creating a plan of action based on the gap between current processes, technologies, and structures, and process vision. It is then a matter of implementing the chosen solution. The Department of Defense (DoD) is an expert at reengineering business process. Figure B2.6 highlights the Department of Defense's best-in-class suggestions for a managerial approach to a reengineering effort.[8]

FIGURE B2.6

Managerial Approach to
Reengineering Projects

Managerial Approach to Reengineering Projects
1. **Define the scope.** Define functional objectives; determine the management strategy to be followed in streamlining and standardizing processes; and establish the process, data, and information systems baselines from which to begin process improvement.
2. **Analyze.** Analyze business processes to eliminate non-value-added processes; simplify and streamline processes of little value; and identify more effective and efficient alternatives to the process, data, and system baselines.
3. **Evaluate.** Conduct a preliminary, functional, economic analysis to evaluate alternatives to baseline processes and select a preferred course of action.
4. **Plan.** Develop detailed statements of requirements, baseline impacts, costs, benefits, and schedules to implement the planned course of action.
5. **Approve.** Finalize the functional economic analysis using information from the planning data, and present to senior management for approval to proceed with the proposed process improvements and any associated data or system changes.
6. **Execute.** Execute the approved process and data changes, and provide functional management oversight of any associated information system changes.

Business Process Design

After choosing the method of business process improvement that is appropriate for the organization, the process designers must determine the most efficient way to begin revamping the processes. To determine whether each process is appropriately structured, organizations should create a cross-functional team to build process models that display input-output relationships among process-dependent operations and departments. They should create business process models documenting a step-by-step process sequence for the activities that are required to convert inputs to outputs for the specific process.

Business process modeling (or ***mapping***) is the activity of creating a detailed flow chart or process map of a work process showing its inputs, tasks, and activities, in a structured sequence. A ***business process model*** is a graphic description of a process, showing the sequence of process tasks, which is developed for a specific purpose and from a selected viewpoint. A set of one or more process models details the many functions of a system or subject area with graphics and text and its purpose is to:

- Expose process detail gradually and in a controlled manner.
- Encourage conciseness and accuracy in describing the process model.
- Focus attention on the process model interfaces.
- Provide a powerful process analysis and consistent design vocabulary.[9]

A process model typically displays activities as boxes and uses arrows to represent data and interfaces. Process modeling usually begins with a functional process representation of *what* the process problem is or an As-Is process model. ***As-Is process models*** represent the current state of the operation that has been mapped, without any specific improvements or changes to existing processes. The next step is to build a To-Be process model that displays *how* the process problem will be solved or implemented. ***To-Be process models*** show the results of applying change improvement opportunities to the current (As-Is) process model. This approach ensures that the process is fully and clearly understood before the details of a process solution are decided. The To-Be process model shows *how* the *what* is to be realized. Figure B2.7 displays the As-Is and To-Be process models for ordering a hamburger.

Analyzing As-Is business process models leads to success in business process reengineering since these diagrams are very powerful in visualizing the activities, processes, and data flow of an organization. As-Is and To-Be process models are integral in process reengineering projects. Figure B2.8 illustrates an As-Is process model of an order-filling process developed by a process modeling team representing all departments that contribute to the process. The process modeling team traces the process of converting the input (orders) through all the intervening steps until the final required output (payment) is produced. The map shows how all departments are involved as the order is processed.[10]

It is easy to become bogged down in excessive detail when creating an As-Is process model. The objective is to aggressively eliminate, simplify, or improve the

FIGURE B2.7

As-Is and To-Be Process Model for Ordering a Hamburger

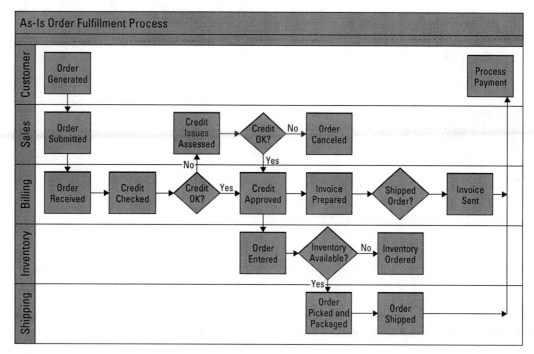

FIGURE B2.8

As-Is Process Model for Order Entry

To-Be processes. Successful process improvement efforts result in positive answers to the key process design or improvement question: Is this the most efficient and effective process for accomplishing the process goals? This process modeling structure allows the team to identify all the critical interfaces, overlay the time to complete various processes, start to define the opportunities for process simulation, and identify disconnects (illogical, missing, or extraneous steps) in the processes. Figure B2.9 displays sample disconnects in the order filling process in Figure B2.8.

The team then creates a To-Be process model, which reflects a disconnect-free order fulfillment process (see Figure B2.10). Disconnects fixed by the new process include

- Direct order entry by sales, eliminating sales administration.
- Parallel order processing and credit checking.
- Elimination of multiple order-entry and order-logging steps.[11]

The consulting firm KPMG Peat Marwick uses process modeling as part of its business reengineering practice. Recently the firm helped a large financial services company slash costs and improve productivity in its Manufactured Housing Finance Division. Turnaround time for loan approval was reduced by half, using 40 percent fewer staff members.

Issues in the As-Is Order Process Model

- Sales representatives take too long to submit orders.
- There are too many process steps.
- Sales administration slows down the process by batch-processing orders.
- Credit checking is performed for both old and new customers.
- Credit checking holds up the process because it is done before (rather than concurrently with) order picking.

FIGURE B2.9

Issues in the As-Is Process Model for Order Entry

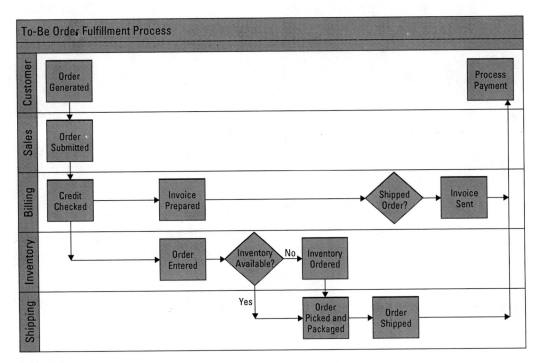

To-Be Order Fulfillment Process

FIGURE B2.10

To-Be Process Model for Order Entry

Modeling helped the team analyze the complex aspects of the project. "In parts of the loan origination process, a lot of things happen in a short period of time," according to team leader Bob Karrick of KPMG. "During data capture, information is pulled from a number of different sources, and the person doing the risk assessment has to make judgment calls at different points throughout the process. There is often a need to stop, raise questions, make follow-up calls, and so on and then continue with the process modeling effort. Modeling allows us to do a thorough analysis that takes into account all these decision points and variables."[12]

SELECTING A PROCESS TO REENGINEER

An organization can reengineer its cross-departmental business processes or an individual department's business processes according to its needs. When selecting a business process to reengineer, wise organizations will focus on those core processes that are critical to their performance, rather than marginal processes that have little impact. Reengineering practitioners can use several criteria to determine the importance of the process:

- Is the process broken?
- Is it feasible that reengineering of this process will succeed?
- Does it have a high impact on the agency's strategic direction?
- Does it significantly impact customer satisfaction?
- Is it antiquated?
- Does it fall far below best-in-class?
- Is it crucial for productivity improvement?
- Will savings from automation be clearly visible?
- Is the return on investment from implementation high and preferably immediate?[13]

Business Process Management (BPM)

A key advantage of technology is its ability to improve business processes. Working faster and smarter has become a necessity for companies. Initial emphasis was given to areas such as production, accounting, procurement, and logistics. The next big areas to discover technology's value in business process were sales and marketing automation, customer relationship management, and supplier relationship management. Some of these processes involve several departments of the company and some are the result of real-time interaction of the company with its suppliers, customers, and other business partners. The latest area to discover the power of technology in automating and reengineering business process is business process management. *Business process management (BPM)* integrates all of an organization's business process to make individual processes more efficient. BPM can be used to solve a single glitch or to create one unifying system to consolidate a myriad of processes.

Many organizations are unhappy with their current mix of software applications and dealing with business processes that are subject to constant change. These organizations are turning to BPM systems that can flexibly automate their processes and glue their enterprise applications together. Figure B2.11 displays the key reasons organizations are embracing BPM technologies.

BPM technologies effectively track and orchestrate the business process. BPM can automate tasks involving information from multiple systems, with rules to define the sequence in which the tasks are performed as well as responsibilities, conditions, and other aspects of the process (see Figure B2.12 for BPM benefits). BPM not only allows a business process to be executed more efficiently, but it also provides the tools to measure performance and identify opportunities for improvement—as well as to easily make changes in processes to act upon those opportunities such as:

- Bringing processes, people, and information together.
- Identifying the business processes is relatively easy. Breaking down the barriers between business areas and finding owners for the processes are difficult.
- Managing business processes within the enterprise and outside the enterprise with suppliers, business partners, and customers.
- Looking at automation horizontally instead of vertically.[14]

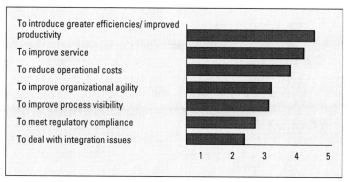

Scale 1 to 5 where 1 = not important and 5 = very important

FIGURE B2.11

Key Reasons for BPM

FIGURE B2.12

Benefits of BPM

BPM Benefits
■ Update processes in real time
■ Reduce overhead expenses
■ Automate key decisions
■ Reduce process maintenance cost
■ Reduce operating cost
■ Improve productivity
■ Improve process cycle time
■ Improve forecasting
■ Improve customer service

IS BPM FOR BUSINESS OR IT?

A good BPM solution requires two great parts to work together as one. Since BPM solutions cross application and system boundaries, they often need to be sanctioned and implemented by the IT organization, while at the same time BPM products are business tools that business managers need to own. Therefore, confusion often arises in companies as to whether business or IT managers should be responsible for driving the selection of a new BPM solution.

The key requirement for BPM's success in an organization is the understanding that it is a collaboration of business and IT, and thus both parties need to be involved in evaluating, selecting, and implementing a BPM solution. IT managers need to understand the business drivers behind the processes, and business managers need to understand the impact the BPM solution may have on the infrastructure. Generally, companies that have successfully deployed BPM solutions are those whose business and IT groups have worked together as a cohesive team.

All companies can benefit from a better understanding of their key business processes, analyzing them for areas of improvement and implementing improvements. BPM applications have been successfully developed to improve complex business issues of some medium- to large-sized companies. Like many large-scale implementation projects, BPM solutions are most successful in companies with a good understanding of their technology landscape and management willing to approach business in a new way. BPM solutions are truly driven by the business process and the company's owners.

Effective BPM solutions allow business owners to manage many aspects of the technology through business rules they develop and maintain. Companies that cannot support or manage cultural and organizational changes may lack positive BPM results.[15]

Tool Name	Company Name
BPM Suite	Ultimus
Process Suite	Stalfware
Business Manager	Savvion
Pega Rules Process Commander	PegaSystem
E Work Vision	MetaStorm
Team Works	Lombardi Software
Intalio	Intalio
Bizflow	Handysoft
FugeoBPM	Fugeo
Business Process Manager	Filenet

FIGURE B2.13

Popular BPM Tools

BPM TOOLS

Business process management tools are used to create an application that is helpful in designing business process models and also helpful in simulating, optimizing, monitoring, and maintaining various processes that occur within an organization. Many tasks are involved in achieving a goal, and these tasks are done either manually or with the help of software systems. For example, if an organization needs to buy a software application that costs $6 million, then a request has to be approved by several authorities and managers. The request approval may be done manually. However, when a person applies for a loan of $300,000, several internal and external business processes are triggered to find out details about that person before approving the loan. For these activities the BPM tool creates an application that coordinates the manual and automated tasks. Figure B2.13 displays several popular BPM tools.[16]

BPM RISKS AND REWARDS

If an organization is considering BPM, it must be aware of the risks involved in implementing these systems. One factor that commonly derails a BPM project has nothing to do with technology and everything to do with people. BPM projects involve cultural and organizational changes that companies must make to support the new management approach required for success. Where 10 area leaders once controlled 10 pieces of an end-to-end process, now a new group is involved in implementing a BPM solution across all these areas. Suddenly the span of control is consolidated and all are accountable to the whole process, not just one piece of the puzzle.

The added benefit of BPM is not only a technology solution, but also a business solution. BPM is a new business architecture and approach to managing the process and enabling proactive, continuous improvement. The new organizational structure and roles created to support BPM help maximize the continuous benefits to ensure success.

An IT director from a large financial services company gave this feedback when asked about his experience in using a BPM solution to improve the company's

Critical Success Factors for BPM Projects
1. **Understand reengineering.**   ■ Understand business process fundamentals.   ■ Know what reengineering is.   ■ Differentiate and integrate process improvement approaches.
2. **Build a business and political case.**   ■ Have necessary and sufficient business (mission delivery) reasons for reengineering.   ■ Have the organizational commitment and capacity to initiate and sustain reengineering.   ■ Secure and sustain political support for reengineering projects.
3. **Adopt a process management approach.**   ■ Understand the organizational mandate and set mission strategic directions and goals cascading to process-specific goals and decision making across and down the organization.   ■ Define, model, and prioritize business processes important for mission performance.   ■ Practice hands-on senior management ownership of process improvement through personal involvement, responsibility, and decision making.   ■ Adjust organizational structure to better support process management initiatives.   ■ Create an assessment program to evaluate process management.
4. **Measure and track performance continuously.**   ■ Create organizational understanding of the value of measurement and how it will be used.   ■ Tie performance management to customer and stakeholder current and future expectations.
5. **Practice change management and provide central support.**   ■ Develop human resource management strategies to support reengineering.   ■ Build information resources management strategies and a technology framework to support process change.   ■ Create a central support group to assist and integrate reengineering efforts and other improvement efforts across the organization.   ■ Create an overarching and project-specific internal and external communication and education program.
6. **Manage reengineering projects for results.**   ■ Have a clear criterion to select what should be reengineered.   ■ Place the project at the right level with a defined reengineering team purpose and goals.   ■ Use a well-trained, diversified, expert team to ensure optimum project performance.   ■ Follow a structured, disciplined approach for reengineering.

FIGURE B2.14

Critical Success Factors for BPM Projects

application help desk process. "Before BPM, the company's application help desk was a manual process, filled with inefficiencies, human error, and no personal accountability. In addition, the old process provided no visibility into the process. There was absolutely no way to track requests, since it was all manual. Business user satisfaction with the process was extremely low. A BPM solution provided a way for the company to automate, execute, manage, and monitor the process in real time. The biggest technical challenge in implementation was ensuring that the user group was self-sufficient. While the company recognized that the IT organization is needed, it wanted to be able to maintain and implement any necessary process changes with little reliance on IT. It views process management as empowering the business users to maintain, control, and monitor the process. BPM goes a long way to enable this process."[17]

CRITICAL SUCCESS FACTORS

In a publication for the National Academy of Public Administration, Dr. Sharon L. Caudle identified six critical success factors that ensure government BPM initiatives achieve the desired results (see Figure B2.14).[18]

FIGURE B2.15

E-Business Process Model

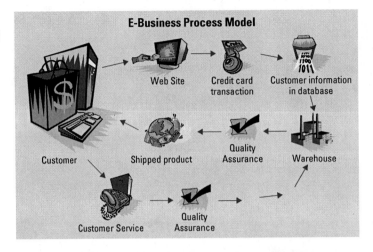

Business Process Modeling Examples

A picture is worth a thousand words. Just ask Wayne Kendrick, a system analyst for Mobil Oil Corporation in Dallas, Texas. Kendrick, whose work involves planning and designing complex processes, was scheduled to make a presentation to familiarize top management with a number of projects his group was working on. "I was given 10 minutes for my presentation, and I had 20 to 30 pages of detailed documentation to present. Obviously, I could not get through it all in the time allocated." Kendrick turned to business process models to help communicate his projects. "I think people can relate to pictures better than words," Kendrick said. He applied his thinking to his presentation by using Microsoft's Visio to create business process models and graphs to represent the original 30 pages of text. "It was an effective way to get people interested in my projects and to quickly see the importance of each project," he stated. The process models worked and Kendrick received immediate approval to proceed with all of his projects. Figures B2.15 through B2.21 offer examples of business process models.[19]

FIGURE B2.16

Online Banking Business Process Model

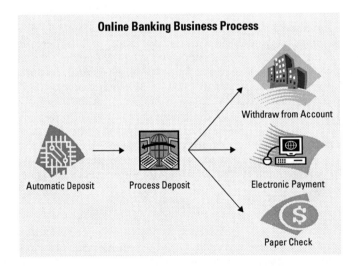

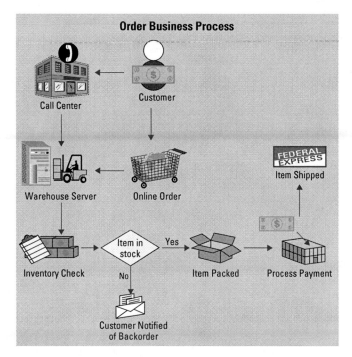

FIGURE B2.17

Customer Order Business Process Model

Purchase an Item on eBay Business Process

- Decides to Purchase Item
- Reviews Auction Listing
- Places Bid
- Wins Bid
- Receives Invoice
- Pays Invoice
- Receives Item
- Rates Seller
- Ends Sale

FIGURE B2.18

eBay Buyer Business Process Model

Sell an Item on eBay Business Process

- Decides to Sell Item
- Lists Item on eBay
- Sets Initial Price
- Sets Auction Length
- Invoices Winning Bid
- Receives Payment
- Ships Item
- Rates Buyer
- Ends Sale

FIGURE B2.19

eBay Seller Business Process Model

FIGURE B2.20

Customer Service
Business Process Model

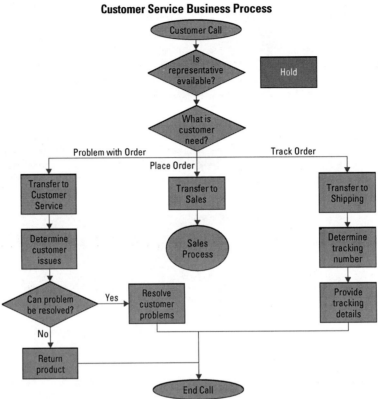

Customer Service Business Process

FIGURE B2.21

Business Process
Improvement Model

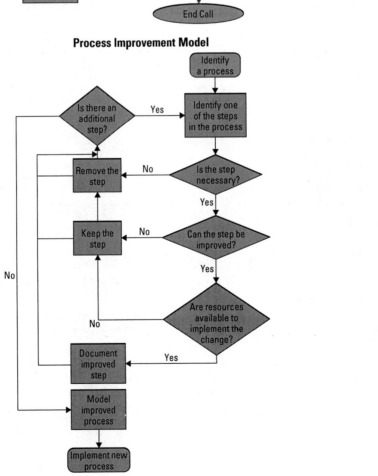

Process Improvement Model

* PLUG-IN SUMMARY

Investment in continuous process improvement, business process reengineering, or business process management is the same as any other technology-related investment. Planning the project properly, setting clear goals, educating those people who have to change their mind-set once the system is implemented, and retaining strong management support will help with a successful implementation generating a solid return on investment.

Organizations must go beyond the basics when implementing business process improvement and realize that it is not a one-time project. Management and improvement of end-to-end business processes is difficult and requires more than a simple, one-time effort. Continuously monitoring and improving core business processes will guarantee performance improvements across an organization.

* KEY TERMS

As-Is process model, 304
Business facing process, 299
Business process, 299
Business process management (BPM), 307
Business process management tool, 308

Business process model, 304
Business process modeling (or mapping), 304
Business process reengineering (BPR), 303

Continuous process improvement model, 302
Customer facing process, 299
To-Be process model, 304

* CLOSING CASE ONE

Streamlining Processes at Adidas

The Adidas name resonates with athletes and retail consumers worldwide. Registered as a company in 1949, the company differentiated itself during the 1960s by supporting all athletes who were committed to raising performance levels, including athletes in what some considered fringe sports such as high jumping. During a banner year in 1996, the "three stripes company" equipped 6,000 Olympic athletes from 33 countries. Those athletes won 220 medals, including 70 gold, and helped increase immediate apparel sales by 50 percent.

In 1997, Adidas acquired the Salomon Group, which included the Salomon, Taylor Made, and Bonfire brands. Today, Adidas-Salomon strives to be the global leader in the sporting goods industry with a wide range of products that promote a passion for competition and a sports-oriented lifestyle. Its strategy is simple: continuously strengthen its brands and products to improve its competitive position and financial performance.

Adidas-Salomon competes in an environment as relentless as that of the Olympics. Staying in the forefront requires the support of world-class technology. Over the past 15 years, Adidas-Salomon transformed itself from a manufacturing organization to a global sports brand manager with 14,000 employees located around the world. Previously, Adidas-Salomon operated in a decentralized manner, and each operating unit chose software that suited its geography and internal preferences. The company believed that implementing and creating common processes, especially in its sales organization, would help it establish global direction. With common processes, the company could streamline and automate its business operations—improving flexibility, scalability, and visibility across the extended enterprise. Overall, system integration would translate into faster time to market, higher revenue, and lower costs.

Adidas-Salomon reviewed its IT systems and associated information. One finding was that the company needed to develop a better solution for business process integration and establish an easy way to automate new applications throughout the enterprise. Such an infrastructure required Adidas-Salomon to impose a common business process platform that would allow the company's operating units to remain flexible in meeting their own particular needs and goals.

Adidas-Salomon identified several major business requirements for the project. First, it wanted to automate business events and reduce the manual effort required to exchange data between internal and external parties. Second, Adidas-Salomon needed to develop a cost-effective solution that would be simple to use, maintain, and update in the future. Last, the company wanted to enable real-time data exchange among the key Adidas-Salomon business processes.

"We considered many metrics, and it was clear that TIBCO Software had the breadth and depth of product offering backed by a strong reputation," said Garry Semetka, head of development and integration services in global application development at Adidas-Salomon. With its desired infrastructure in place, Adidas-Salomon standardized on TIBCO products and moved toward real-time business process management of its internal supply chain. The company now publishes and makes the most of events when they occur on key systems, giving the most current, valuable information to business processes and decision makers.[20]

Questions

1. Describe business processes and their importance for Adidas-Salomon.
2. Identify a few examples of customer facing processes and business facing processes at Adidas-Salomon.
3. How could Adidas-Salomon use continuous process improvement and business process reengineering to remain competitive?
4. How can a business process management tool help Adidas-Salomon remain at the top of its game?

 CLOSING CASE TWO

3Com Optimizes Product Promotion Processes

Product promotions, such as rebates or subsidized promotional items, can serve as excellent marketing and sales tools to drive increased revenues by providing incentives for customers to purchase select items. However, when you are a leading global networking provider like 3Com that serves thousands of channel partners and customers, such promotions must be easily managed and executed.

To gain better control over the creation and execution of its product promotions, 3Com used Savvion's business process automation and management platform to build a Web-based system that streamlines the approval and management workflow of product promotions offered to distributors and resellers. "We needed to ensure that our product promotions were attractive to our channel partners while also being manageable in terms of execution," said Ari

Bose, CIO at 3Com. "Using Savvion BusinessManager, we were able to quickly put a process in place that speeds approval and enhances awareness of product promotions to generate opportunities for increased revenue."

Promoting Effective Promotions

The Savvion BusinessManager-based promotions system provides significant time and cost savings by replacing former inefficient and uncontrollable e-mail processes. Instead of informally sending promotion ideas around for approval, employees now use the automated system as a centralized location to manage the workflow involved in proposing new promotions and ensuring all needed approvals are in place before promotion details are shared on the 3Com partner and reseller Web site.

The promotions system automatically routes proposed promotions to each department that is required to sign off on the promotion, including marketing, promotions communications, and claims administration. The streamlined system also immediately notifies all key parties once new promotions are approved, increasing visibility and revenue opportunities through improved communication with 3Com sales representatives, distributors, and resellers.

Adding Muscle to Management

An important feature of the new system is the automatic auditing of each step taken. The company can easily establish an audit trail, increasing accountability as approvals are given. The structured process also ensures that approved promotions are manageable from an administrative perspective.

In addition, the system tracks promotion fulfillment, enforcing associated terms and conditions such as purchasing limits or available supplies—tracking that was previously almost impossible to do, creating numerous management headaches. The promotions system is also integrated with another BusinessManager-developed process that generates special price quotes (SPQs) for 3Com channel partners, creating built-in checks and balances to prevent the approval of an SPQ while a promotion is being offered for the same product.

The system also provides extensive reporting capabilities that 3Com now uses to gain a better understanding of all offered promotions, authorizations, and potential financial impacts. These online reports replace manually created Excel spreadsheets, enabling departments to generate reports on the fly for enhanced strategic planning.

Bottom-Line Benefits

Greater visibility of product promotions is yielding significant opportunities for increased revenue at 3Com. Sales representatives are immediately notified when promotions are approved, improving internal communications and enabling representatives to share promotion details with resellers and distributors more quickly to foster increased sales. Other business benefits delivered by the automated promotions system include the following:

- Real-time monitoring features enable 3Com employees to check the status of a promotion's approval at any time.
- Greater efficiency in the approval cycle and streamlined communications increase employee productivity, providing significant time and cost savings.
- Claims processing is also more effective because of the structured approval process, delivering additional savings.
- Increased visibility enables 3Com to reduce reserve spending by having a clearer idea of channel response to each promotion.
- Order and efficiency come to previously chaotic manual processes.[21]

Questions

1. Describe business processes and their importance to 3Com's business model.
2. How can 3Com use continuous process improvement to become more efficient?
3. How can 3Com use business process reengineering to become more efficient?
4. Describe the importance of business process modeling (or mapping) and business process models for 3Com.
5. How did 3Com use business process management software to revamp its business?

★ MAKING BUSINESS DECISIONS

1. Discovering Reengineering Opportunities

In an effort to increase efficiency, your college has hired you to analyze its current business processes for registering for classes. Analyze the current business processes from paying tuition to registering for classes and determine which steps in the process are:

- Broken
- Redundant
- Antiquated

Be sure to define how you would reengineer the processes for efficiency.

2. Modeling a Business Process

Do you hate waiting in line at the grocery store? Do you find it frustrating when you go to the movie store and cannot find the movie you wanted to rent? Do you get annoyed when the pizza delivery person brings you the wrong order? This is your chance to reengineer the annoying process that drives you crazy. Choose a problem you are currently experiencing and reengineer the process to make it more efficient. Be sure to provide an As-Is and To-Be process model.

3. Revamping Business Processes

The following is the sales order business process for MusicMan. Draw the As-Is process model based on the following narrative:

1. A customer submits an order for goods to MusicMan, a music retailer, through an online mechanism such as a browser-based order form. The customer supplies his or her name, the appropriate e-mail address, the state to which the order will be shipped, the desired items (IDs and names), and the requested quantities.
2. The order is received by a processing system, which reads the data and appends an ID number to the order.
3. The order is forwarded to a customer service representative, who checks the customer's credit information.
4. If the credit check fails, the customer service representative is assigned the task of notifying the customer to obtain correct credit information, and the process becomes manual from this point on.
5. If the credit check passes, the system checks a database for the current inventory of the ordered item, according to the item ID, and it compares the quantity of items available with the quantity requested.

6. If the amount of stock is not sufficient to accommodate the order, the order is placed on hold until new inventory arrives. When the system receives notice of new incoming inventory, it repeats step 5 until it can verify that the inventory is sufficient to process the order.

7. If the inventory is sufficient, the order is forwarded simultaneously to a shipping agent who arranges shipment and an accounting agent who instructs the system to generate an invoice for the order.

8. If the system encounters an error in processing the input necessary to calculate the total price for the invoice, including state sales tax, the accounting agent who initiated the billing process is notified and prompted to provide the correct information.

9. The system calculates the total price of the order.

10. The system confirms that the order has been shipped and notifies the customer via e-mail.

11. At any point in the transaction before shipping, the order can be canceled by notification from the customer.

4. Revamping Accounts

The accounting department at your company deals with the processing of critical documents. These documents must arrive at their intended destination in a secure and efficient manner. Such documents include invoices, purchase orders, statements, purchase requisitions, financial statements, sales orders, and quotes.

The current processing of documents is done manually, which causes a negative ripple effect. Documents tend to be misplaced or delayed through the mailing process. Unsecured documents are vulnerable to people making changes or seeing confidential documents. In addition, the accounting department incurs costs such as preprinted forms, inefficient distribution, and storage. Explain BPM and how it can be used to revamp the accounting department.

Hardware and Software

Introduction

Managers need to determine what types of hardware and software will satisfy their current and future business needs, the right time to buy the equipment, and how to protect their IT investments. This does not imply that managers need to be experts in all areas of technology; however, building a basic understanding of hardware and software can help them make the right IT investment choices.

Information technology (IT) is a field concerned with the use of technology in managing and processing information. Information technology can be composed of the Internet, a personal computer, a cell phone that can access the Web, a personal digital assistant, or presentation software. All of these technologies help to perform specific information processing tasks. There are two basic categories of information technology: hardware and software. *Hardware* consists of the physical devices associated with a computer system. *Software* is the set of instructions that the hardware executes to carry out specific tasks. Software, such as Microsoft Excel, and various hardware devices, such as a keyboard and a monitor, interact to create a spreadsheet or a graph. This plug-in covers the basics of computer hardware and software including terminology, business uses, and common characteristics.

Hardware Basics

In many industries, exploiting computer hardware is key to gaining a competitive advantage. Frito-Lay gained a competitive advantage by using handheld devices

Six Hardware Components	
Central processing unit (CPU)	The actual hardware that interprets and executes the program (software) instructions and coordinates how all the other hardware devices work together.
Primary storage	The computer's main memory, which consists of the random access memory (RAM), the cache memory, and the read-only memory (ROM) that is directly accessible to the central processing unit (CPU).
Secondary storage	The equipment designed to store large volumes of data for long-term storage (e.g., diskette, hard drive, memory card, CD).
Input devices	The equipment used to capture information and commands (e.g., keyboard, scanner).
Output devices	The equipment used to see, hear, or otherwise accept the results of information processing requests (e.g., monitor, printer).
Communication devices	The equipment used to send information and receive it from one location to another (e.g., modem).

FIGURE B3.1

Hardware Components of a Computer System

to track the strategic placement and sale of items in convenience stores. Sales representatives could track sale price, competitor information, the number of items sold, and item location in the store all from their handheld device.[1]

A ***computer*** is an electronic device operating under the control of instructions stored in its own memory that can accept, manipulate, and store data. A computer system consists of six hardware components (see Figure B3.1). Figure B3.2 displays how these components work together to form a computer system.

CENTRAL PROCESSING UNIT

The dominant manufacturers of CPUs today include Intel (with its Celeron and Pentium lines for personal computers) and Advanced Micro Devices (AMD) (with its Athlon series). AMD was initially dismissed as a company that simply cloned current chips, producing processors that mimic the features and capabilities of those from industry leader Intel. However, over the past few years, AMD has begun introducing innovative CPUs that are forcing Intel into the unfamiliar position of reacting to competition. AMD led the way in transforming the processor market by creating chips that handle 64 bits of data at a time, up  from 32 bits. It also broke new territory when it became the first provider of dual-core processors for the server market. Hector Ruiz, chairman and CEO of AMD, stated, "In our position there is only one thing we can do: Stay close to our customers and end users, understand what they need and want, and then simply out-innovate the competition. Innovation is at the center of our ability to succeed. We cannot win by just copying the competition."[2]

The ***central processing unit (CPU)*** (or ***microprocessor***) is the actual hardware that interprets and executes the program (software) instructions and coordinates how all the other hardware devices work together. The CPU is built on a small flake of silicon and can contain the equivalent of several million transistors. CPUs are unquestionably one of the 20th century's greatest technological advances.

A CPU contains two primary parts: control unit and arithmetic/logic unit. The ***control unit*** interprets software instructions and literally tells the other hardware

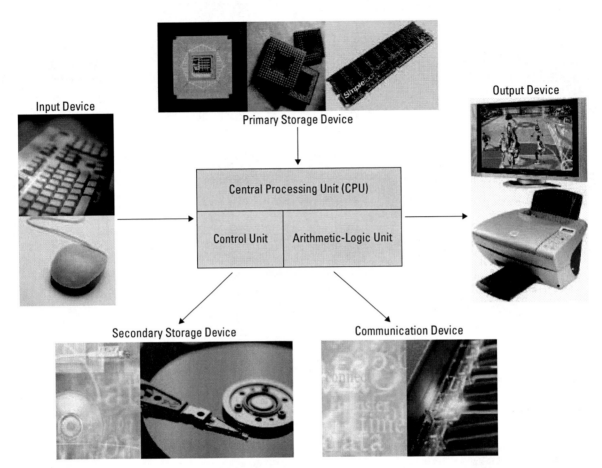

Input Device

Primary Storage Device

Output Device

Central Processing Unit (CPU)

Control Unit | Arithmetic-Logic Unit

Secondary Storage Device

Communication Device

FIGURE B3.2

How the Hardware Components Work Together

devices what to do, based on the software instructions. The ***arithmetic-logic unit (ALU)*** performs all arithmetic operations (for example, addition and subtraction) and all logic operations (such as sorting and comparing numbers). The control unit and ALU perform different functions. The control unit obtains instructions from the software. It then interprets the instructions, decides which tasks other devices perform, and finally tells each device to perform the task. The ALU responds to the control unit and does whatever it dictates, performing either arithmetic or logic operations.

The number of CPU cycles per second determines how fast a CPU carries out the software instructions; more cycles per second means faster processing, and faster CPUs cost more than their slower counterparts. CPU speed is usually quoted in megahertz and gigahertz. ***Megahertz (MHz)*** is the number of millions of CPU cycles per second. ***Gigahertz (GHz)*** is the number of billions of CPU cycles per second. Figure B3.3 displays the factors that determine CPU speed.

Advances in CPU Design

Chip makers are pressing more functionality into CPU technology. Most CPUs are ***complex instruction set computer (CISC) chips,*** which is a type of CPU that can recognize as many as 100 or more instructions, enough to carry out most computations directly. ***Reduced instruction set computer (RISC) chips*** limit the number of instructions the CPU can execute to increase processing speed. The idea of RISC is to reduce the instruction set to the bare minimum, emphasizing the instructions used most of the time and optimizing them for the fastest possible execution. A RISC processor runs faster than a CISC processor.

CPU Speed Factors
Clock speed—the speed of the internal clock of a CPU that sets the pace at which operations proceed within the computer's internal processing circuitry. Clock speed is measured in megahertz (MHz) and gigahertz (GHz). Faster clock speeds bring noticeable gains in microprocessor-intensive tasks, such as recalculating a spreadsheet.
Word length—number of bits (0s and 1s) that can be processed by the CPU at any one time. Computers work in terms of bits and bytes using electrical pulses that have two states: on and off. A *binary digit (bit)* is the smallest unit of information that a computer can process. A bit can be either a 1 (on) or a 0 (off). A group of eight bits represents one natural language character and is called a *byte.*
Bus width—the size of the internal electrical pathway along which signals are sent from one part of the computer to another. A wider bus can move more data, hence faster processing.
Chip line width—the distance between transistors on a chip. The shorter the chip line width the faster the chip since more transistors can be placed on a chip and the data and instructions travel short distances during processing.

FIGURE B3.3

Factors That Determine CPU Speed

In the next few years, better performance, systems management capabilities, virtualization, security, and features to help track computer assets will be built directly into the CPU (see Figure B3.4). *Virtualization* is a protected memory space created by the CPU allowing the computer to create virtual machines. Each virtual machine can run its own programs isolated from other machines.

PRIMARY STORAGE

Primary storage is the computer's main memory, which consists of the random access memory (RAM), cache memory, and the read-only memory (ROM) that is directly accessible to the CPU.

Random Access Memory

Random access memory (RAM) is the computer's primary working memory, in which program instructions and data are stored so that they can be accessed directly by the CPU via the processor's high-speed external data bus.

RAM is often called read/write memory. In RAM, the CPU can write and read data. Most programs set aside a portion of RAM as a temporary work space for data so that one can modify (rewrite) as needed until the data are ready for printing or storage on secondary storage media, such as a hard drive or memory key. RAM does not retain its contents when the power to the computer is switched off, hence individuals should save their work frequently. When the computer is turned off, everything in RAM is wiped clean. *Volatility* refers to RAM's

Chip Advancements
AMD: Security, virtualization, and advanced power-management technology.
IBM: Cryptography for additional security and floating point capability for faster graphics processing.
Intel: Cryptography for additional security, hardware-assisted virtualization, and Active Management Technology for asset tracking, patching, and software updates.
Sun Microsystems: Cryptography for additional security, increased speed for data transmission and receipt, and ability to run 32 computations simultaneously.

FIGURE B3.4

Chip Advancements by Manufacturer

complete loss of stored information if power is interrupted. RAM is volatile and its contents are lost when the computer's electric supply fails.

Cache Memory

Cache memory is a small unit of ultra-fast memory that is used to store recently accessed or frequently accessed data so that the CPU does not have to retrieve this data from slower memory circuits such as RAM. Cache memory that is built directly into the CPU's circuits is called primary cache. Cache memory contained on an external circuit is called secondary cache.

Read Only Memory (ROM)

Read-only memory (ROM) is the portion of a computer's primary storage that does not lose its contents when one switches off the power. ROM contains essential system programs that neither the user nor the computer can erase. Since the computer's internal memory is blank during start-up, the computer cannot perform any functions unless given start-up instructions. These instructions are stored in ROM.

Flash memory is a special type of rewriteable read-only memory (ROM) that is compact and portable. *Memory cards* contain high-capacity storage that holds data such as captured images, music, or text files. Memory cards are removable; when one is full the user can insert an additional card. Subsequently, the data can be downloaded from the card to a computer. The card can then be erased and used again. Memory cards are typically used in digital devices such as cameras, cellular phones, and personal digital assistants (PDA). *Memory sticks* provide nonvolatile memory for a range of portable devices including computers, digital cameras, MP3 players, and PDAs.

SECONDARY STORAGE

Storage is a hot area in the business arena as organizations struggle to make sense of exploding volumes of data. Storage sales grew more than 16 percent to nearly $8 billion in 2004, according to IDC market research. *Secondary storage* consists of equipment designed to store large volumes of data for long-term storage. Secondary storage devices are nonvolatile and do not lose their contents when the computer is turned off. Some storage devices, such as a hard disk, offer easy update capabilities and a large storage capacity. Others, such as CD-ROMs, offer limited update capabilities but possess large storage capacities.

Storage capacity is expressed in bytes, with megabytes being the most common. A *megabyte (MB or M or Meg)* is roughly 1 million bytes. Therefore, a computer with 256 MB of RAM translates into the RAM being able to hold roughly 256 million characters of data and software instructions. A *gigabyte (GB)* is roughly 1 billion bytes. A *terabyte (TB)* is roughly 1 trillion bytes (refer to Figure B3.5).

Most standard desktops have a hard drive with storage capacity in excess of 80 GB. Hard drives for large organizational computer systems can hold in excess of 100 TB of information. For example, a typical double-spaced page of pure text is roughly 2,000 characters. Therefore, a 40 GB (40 gigabyte or 40 billion characters) hard drive can hold approximately 20 million pages of text.

Common storage devices include:

■ Magnetic medium
■ Optical medium

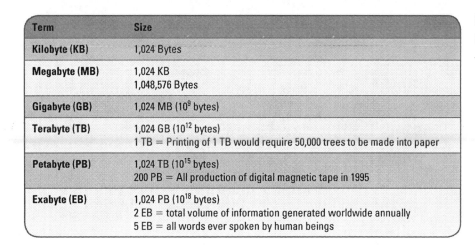

FIGURE B3.5

Binary Terms

Term	Size
Kilobyte (KB)	1,024 Bytes
Megabyte (MB)	1,024 KB 1,048,576 Bytes
Gigabyte (GB)	1,024 MB (10^9 bytes)
Terabyte (TB)	1,024 GB (10^{12} bytes) 1 TB = Printing of 1 TB would require 50,000 trees to be made into paper
Petabyte (PB)	1,024 TB (10^{15} bytes) 200 PB = All production of digital magnetic tape in 1995
Exabyte (EB)	1,024 PB (10^{18} bytes) 2 EB = total volume of information generated worldwide annually 5 EB = all words ever spoken by human beings

Magnetic Medium

Magnetic medium is a secondary storage medium that uses magnetic techniques to store and retrieve data on disks or tapes coated with magnetically sensitive materials. Like iron filings on a sheet of waxed paper, these materials are reoriented when a magnetic field passes over them. During write operations, the read/write heads emit a magnetic field that orients the magnetic materials on the disk or tape to represent encoded data. During read operations, the read/write heads sense the encoded data on the medium.

One of the first forms of magnetic medium developed was magnetic tape. ***Magnetic tape*** is an older secondary storage medium that uses a strip of thin plastic coated with a magnetically sensitive recording medium. The most popular type of magnetic medium is a hard drive. A ***hard drive*** is a secondary storage medium that uses several rigid disks coated with a magnetically sensitive material and housed together with the recording heads in a hermetically sealed mechanism. Hard drive performance is measured in terms of access time, seek time, rotational speed, and data transfer rate.

Optical Medium

Optical medium is a secondary storage medium for computers on which information is stored at extremely high density in the form of tiny pits. The presence or absence of pits is read by a tightly focused laser beam. Optical medium types include:

- **Compact disk-read-only memory (CD-ROM) drive**—an optical drive designed to read the data encoded on CD-ROMs and to transfer this data to a computer.
- **Compact disk-read-write (CD-RW) drive**—an optical drive that enables users to erase existing data and to write new data repeatedly to a CD-RW.
- **Digital video disk (DVD)**—a CD-ROM format capable of storing up to a maximum of 17 GB of data; enough for a full-length feature movie.
- **DVD-ROM drive**—a read-only drive designed to read the data encoded on a DVD and transfer the data to a computer.
- **Digital video disk-read/write (DVD-RW)**—a standard for DVD discs and player/recorder mechanisms that enables users to record in the DVD format.

CD-ROMs and DVDs offer an increasingly economical medium for storing data and programs. The overall trend in secondary storage is toward more direct-access methods, higher capacity with lower costs, and increased portability.

INPUT DEVICES

An *input device* is equipment used to capture information and commands. A keyboard is used to type in information, and a mouse is used to point and click on buttons and icons. Numerous input devices are available in many different environments, some of which have applications that are more suitable in a personal setting than a business setting. A keyboard, mouse, and scanner are the most common forms of input devices (see Figures B3.6 and B3.7).

New forms of input devices allow people to exercise and play video games at the same time. The Kilowatt Sport from Powergrid Fitness lets people combine strength training with their favorite video games. Players can choose any PlayStation or Xbox game that uses a joystick to run the elliptical trainer. After loading the game, participants stand on a platform while pushing and pulling a resistance rod in all directions to control what happens in the game. The varied movement targets muscle groups on the chest, arms, shoulders, abdomen, and back. The machine's display shows information such as pounds lifted and current resistance level, and players can use one-touch adjustment to vary the degree of difficulty.[3]

Another new input device is a stationary bicycle. A computer design team of graduate and undergraduate students at MIT built the Cyclescore, an integrated video game and bicycle. The MIT students tested current games on the market but found users would stop pedaling to concentrate on the game. To engage users, the team is designing games that interact with the experience of exercise itself, for example, monitoring heart rate and adjusting the difficulty of the game according to the user's bicycling capabilities. In one game, the player must pedal to make a hot-air balloon float over mountains, while collecting coins and shooting at random targets.[4]

OUTPUT DEVICES

An *output device* is equipment used to see, hear, or otherwise accept the results of information processing requests. Among output devices, printers and monitors are the most common; however, speakers and plotters (special printers that draw output on a page) are widely used (see Figure B3.8). In addition, output devices are responsible for converting computer-stored information into a form that can be understood.

Manual Input Devices
Joystick—widely used as an alternative to the keyboard for computer games and some professional applications, such as computer-aided design
Keyboard—provides a set of alphabetic, numeric, punctuation, symbol, and control keys
Microphone—captures sounds such as a voice for voice recognition software
Mouse—one or more control buttons housed in a palm-sized case and designed so that one can move it about on the table next to the keyboard
Pointing stick—causes the pointer to move on the screen by applying directional pressure (popular on notebooks and PDAs)
Touch screen—allows the use of a finger to point at and touch a particular function to perform
Touch pad—a form of a stationary mouse on which the movement of a finger causes the pointer on the screen to move

FIGURE B3.6

Manual Input Devices

Automated Input Devices
Bar code scanner—captures information that exists in the form of vertical bars whose width and distance apart determine a number
Digital camera—captures still images or video as a series of 1s and 0s
Magnetic ink character reader—reads magnetic ink numbers printed on checks that identify the bank, checking account, and check number
Optical-character recognition—converts text into digital format for computer input
Optical-mark recognition (OMR)—detects the presence or absence of a mark in a predetermined place (popular for multiple-choice exams)
Point-of-sale (POS)—captures information at the point of a transaction, typically in a retail environment
Radio frequency identification (RFID)—uses active or passive tags in the form of chips or smart labels that can store unique identifiers and relay this information to electronic readers

FIGURE B3.7

Automated Input Devices

Output Devices
Cathode-ray tube (CRT)—a vacuum tube that uses an electron gun (cathode) to emit a beam of electrons that illuminates phosphors on a screen as the beam sweeps across the screen repeatedly; a monitor is often called a CRT
Liquid crystal display (LCDs)—a low-powered display technology used in laptop computers where rod-shaped crystal molecules change their orientation when an electrical current flows through them
Laser printer—a printer that forms images using an electrostatic process, the same way a photocopier works
Ink-jet printer—a printer that makes images by forcing ink droplets through nozzles
Plotter—a printer that uses computer-directed pens for creating high-quality images, blueprints, schematics, etc.

FIGURE B3.8

Output Devices

A new output device based on sensor technology aims to translate American Sign Language (ASL) into speech, enabling the millions of people who use ASL to better communicate with those who do not know the rapid gesturing system. The AcceleGlove is a glove lined on the inside with sensors embedded in rings. The sensors, called accelerometers, measure acceleration and can categorize and translate finger and hand movements. Additional, interconnected attachments for the elbow and shoulder capture ASL signs that are made with full arm motion. When users wear the glove while signing ASL, algorithms in the glove's software translate the hand gestures into words. The translations can be relayed through speech synthesizers or read on a PDA-size computer screen. Inventor Jose L. Hernandez-Rebollar started with a single glove that could translate only the ASL alphabet. Now, the device employs two gloves that contain a 1,000-word vocabulary.[5]

Other new output devices are being developed every day. Needapresent.com, a British company, has developed a vibrating USB massage ball, which plugs into a computer's USB port to generate a warm massage for sore body parts during those long evenings spent coding software or writing papers. Needsapresent.com also makes a coffee cup warmer that plugs into the USB port.[6]

COMMUNICATION DEVICES

A **communication device** is equipment used to send information and receive it from one location to another. A telephone modem connects a computer to a phone line in order to access another computer. The computer works in terms of digital signals, while a standard telephone line works with analog signals. Each digital signal represents a bit (either 0 or 1). The modem must convert the digital signals of a computer into analog signals so they can be sent across the telephone line. At the other end, another modem translates the analog signals into digital signals, which can then be used by the other computer. Figure B3.9 displays the different types of modems.

Computer Categories

Supercomputers today can hit processing capabilities of well over 200 teraflops—the equivalent of everyone on earth performing 35,000 calculations per second (see Figure B3.10). For the past 20 years, federally funded supercomputing research has given birth to some of the computer industry's most significant technology breakthroughs including:

- Clustering, which allows companies to chain together thousands of PCs to build mass-market systems.
- Parallel processing, which provides the ability to run two or more tasks simultaneously and is viewed as the chip industry's future.
- Mosaic browser, which morphed into Netscape and made the Web a household name.

Federally funded supercomputers have also advanced some of the country's most dynamic industries, including advanced manufacturing, gene research in the life sciences, and real-time financial-market modeling.[7]

Carrier Technology	Description	Speed	Comments
Dial-up Access	On demand access using a modem and regular telephone line (POT).	2400 bps to 56 Kbps	■ Cheap but slow.
Cable	Special cable modem and cable line required.	512 Kbps to 20 Mbps	■ Must have existing cable access in area. ■ Bandwidth is shared.
DSL Digital Subscriber Line	This technology uses the unused digital portion of a regular copper telephone line to transmit and receive information. A special modem and adapter card are required.	128 Kbps to 8 Mbps	■ Doesn't interfere with normal telephone use. ■ Bandwidth is dedicated. ■ Must be within 5 km (3.1 miles) of telephone company switch.
Wireless (LMCS)	Access is gained by connection to a high-speed cellular like local multipoint communications system (LMCS) network via wireless transmitter/receiver.	30 Mbps or more	■ Can be used for high-speed data, broadcast TV, and wireless telephone service.
Satellite	Newer versions have two-way satellite access, removing need for phone line.	6 Mbps or more	■ Bandwidth is not shared. ■ Some connections require an existing Internet service account. ■ Setup fees can range from $500 to $1,000.

FIGURE B3.9

Comparing Modems

Computers come in different shapes, sizes, and colors. Some are small enough to carry around, while others are the size of a telephone booth. Size does not always correlate to power, speed, and price (see Figure B3.11).

MIT's Media Lab is developing a laptop that it will sell for $100 each to government agencies around the world for distribution to millions of underprivileged schoolchildren. Using a simplified sales model and some reengineering of the device helped MIT reach the $100 price point. Almost half the price of a current laptop comprises marketing, sales, distribution, and profit. Of the remaining costs, the display panel and backlight account for roughly half while the rest covers the operating system.

FIGURE B3.10

Supercomputer

Computer Category	Description	Size
Personal digital assistant (PDA)	A small handheld computer that performs simple tasks such as taking notes, scheduling appointments, and maintaining an address book and a calendar. The PDA screen is touch-sensitive, allowing a user to write directly on the screen, capturing what is written.	Fits in a person's hand
Laptop	A fully functional computer designed to be carried around and run on battery power. Laptops come equipped with all of the technology that a personal desktop computer has, yet weigh as little as two pounds.	Similar to a textbook
Tablet	A pen-based computer that provides the screen capabilities of a PDA with the functional capabilities of a laptop or desktop computer. Similar to PDAs, tablet PCs use a writing pen or stylus to write notes on the screen and touch the screen to perform functions such as clicking on a link while visiting a Web site.	Similar to a textbook
Desktop	Available with a horizontal system box (the box is where the CPU, RAM, and storage devices are held) with a monitor on top, or a vertical system box (called a tower) usually placed on the floor within a work area.	Fits on a desk
Workstation	Similar to a desktop but has more powerful mathematical and graphics processing capabilities and can perform more complicated tasks in less time. Typically used for software development, Web development, engineering, and e-business tools.	Fits on a desk
Minicomputer (midrange computer)	Designed to meet the computing needs of several people simultaneously in a small to medium-size business environment. A common type of minicomputer is a server and is used for managing internal company networks and Web sites. Minicomputers are more powerful than desktop computers but also cost more, ranging in price from $5,000 to several hundred thousand dollars.	Ranges from fitting on a desk to the size of a filing cabinet
Mainframe computer	Designed to meet the computing needs of hundreds of people in a large business environment. Mainframe computers are a step up in size, power, capability, and cost from minicomputers. Mainframes can cost in excess of $1 million. With processing speeds greater than 1 trillion instructions per second (compared to a typical desktop that can process about 2.5 billion instructions per second), mainframes can easily handle the processing requests of hundreds of people simultaneously.	Similar to a refrigerator
Supercomputer	The fastest, most powerful, and most expensive type of computer. Organizations such as NASA that are heavily involved in research and number crunching employ supercomputers because of the speed with which they can process information. Other large, customer-oriented businesses such as General Motors and AT&T employ supercomputers just to handle customer information and transaction processing.	Similar to a car

FIGURE B3.11

Computer Categories

The low-cost laptop will use a display system that costs less than $25, a 500 MHz processor from AMD, a wireless LAN connection, 1 GB of storage, and the Linux operating system. The machine will automatically connect with others. China and Brazil have already ordered 3 million and 1 million laptops, respectively. MIT's goal is to produce around 150 million laptops per year.[8]

Software Basics

Hardware is only as good as the software that runs it. Over the years, the cost of hardware has decreased while the complexity and cost of software have increased. Some large software applications, such as customer relationship management systems, contain millions of lines of code, take years to develop, and cost millions of dollars. The two main types of software are system software and application software.

SYSTEM SOFTWARE

System software controls how the various technology tools work together along with the application software. System software includes both operating system software and utility software.

Operating System Software

Linus Torvalds, a shy Finnish programmer, may seem an unlikely choice to be one of the world's top managers. However, Linux, the software project he created while a university student, is now one of the most powerful influences on the computer world. Linux is an operating system built by volunteers and distributed for free and has become one of the primary competitors to Microsoft. Torvalds coordinates Linux development with a few dozen volunteer assistants and more than 1,000 programmers scattered around the globe. They contribute code for the kernel—or core piece—of Linux. He also sets the rules for dozens of technology companies that have lined up behind Linux, including IBM, Dell, Hewlett-Packard, and Intel.

While basic versions of Linux are available for free, Linux is having a considerable financial impact. According to market researcher IDC, the total market for Linux devices and software will increase from $11 billion in 2004 to $35.7 billion by 2008.[9]

Operating system software controls the application software and manages how the hardware devices work together. When using Excel to create and print a graph, the operating system software controls the process, ensures that a printer is attached and has paper, and sends the graph to the printer along with instructions on how to print it.

Operating system software also supports a variety of useful features, one of which is multitasking. *Multitasking* allows more than one piece of software to be used at a time. Multitasking is used when creating a graph in Excel and simultaneously printing a word processing document. With multitasking, both pieces of application software are operating at the same time. There are different types of operating system software for personal environments and for organizational environments (see Figure B3.12).

Utility Software

Utility software provides additional functionality to the operating system. Utility software includes antivirus software, screen savers, and anti-spam software. Figure B3.13 displays a few types of available utility software.

FIGURE B3.12

Operating System Software

Operating System Software	
Linux	An open source operating system that provides a rich environment for high-end workstations and network servers. Open source refers to any program whose source code is made available for use or modification as users or other developers see fit.
Mac OS X	The operating system of Macintosh computers.
Microsoft Windows	Generic name for the various operating systems in the Microsoft Windows family, including Microsoft Windows CE, Microsoft Windows 98, Microsoft Windows ME, Microsoft Windows 2000, Microsoft Windows XP, Microsoft Windows NT, and Microsoft Windows Server 2003.
MS-DOS	The standard, single-user operating system of IBM and IBM-compatible computers, introduced in 1981. MS-DOS is a command-line operating system that requires the user to enter commands, arguments, and syntax.
UNIX	A 32-bit multitasking and multiuser operating system that originated at AT&T's Bell Laboratories and is now used on a wide variety of computers, from mainframes to PDAs.

APPLICATION SOFTWARE

Application software is used for specific information processing needs, including payroll, customer relationship management, project management, training, and many others. Application software is used to solve specific problems or perform specific tasks. From an organizational perspective, payroll software, collaborative software such as videoconferencing (within groupware), and inventory management software are all examples of application software (see Figure B3.14).

FIGURE B3.13

Utility Software

Types of Utility Software	
Crash-proof	Helps save information if a computer crashes.
Disk image for data recovery	Relieves the burden of reinstalling and tweaking scores of applications if a hard drive crashes or becomes irretrievably corrupted.
Disk optimization	Organizes information on a hard disk in the most efficient way.
Encrypt data	Protects confidential information from unauthorized eyes. Programs such as BestCrypt simply and effectively apply one of several powerful encryption schemes to hard drive information. Users unlock the information by entering a password in the BestCrypt control panel. The program can also secure information on rewritable optical disks or any other storage media that is assigned a drive letter.
File and data recovery	Retrieves accidental deletion of photos or documents in Windows XP by utilities such as Free Undelete, which searches designated hard drive deletion areas for recognizable data.
Text protect	In Microsoft Word, prevents users from typing over existing text after accidentally hitting the Insert key. Launch the Insert Toggle Key program, and the PC will beep whenever a user presses the Insert key.
Preventative security	Through programs such as Window Washer, erases file histories, browser cookies, cache contents, and other crumbs that applications and Windows leave on a hard drive.
Spyware	Removes any software that employs a user's Internet connection in the background without the user's knowledge or explicit permission.
Uninstaller	Can remove software that is no longer needed.

Types of Application Software	
Browser	Enables the user to navigate the World Wide Web. The two leading browsers are Netscape Navigator and Microsoft Internet Explorer.
Communication	Turns a computer into a terminal for transmitting data to and receiving data from distant computers through the telephone system.
Data management	Provides the tools for data retrieval, modification, deletion, and insertion; for example, Access, MySQL, and Oracle.
Desktop publishing	Transforms a computer into a desktop publishing workstation. Leading packages include Adobe FrameMaker, Adobe PageMaker, and QuarkXpress.
E-mail	Provides e-mail services for computer users, including receiving mail, sending mail, and storing messages. Leading e-mail software includes Microsoft Outlook, Microsoft Outlook Express, and Eudora.
Groupware	Increases the cooperation and joint productivity of small groups of co-workers.
Presentation graphics	Creates and enhances charts and graphs so that they are visually appealing and easily understood by an audience. A full-features presentation graphics package such as Lotus Freelance Graphics or Microsoft PowerPoint includes facilities for making a wide variety of charts and graphs and for adding titles, legends, and explanatory text anywhere in the chart or graph.
Programming	Possesses an artificial language consisting of a fixed vocabulary and a set of rules (called syntax) that programmers use to write computer programs. Leading programming languages include Java, C + +, C#, and .NET.
Spreadsheet	Simulates an accountant's worksheet onscreen and lets users embed hidden formulas that perform calculations on the visible data. Many spreadsheet programs also include powerful graphics and presentation capabilities to create attractive products. The leading spreadsheet application is Microsoft Excel.
Word processing	Transforms a computer into a tool for creating, editing, proofreading, formatting, and printing documents. Leading word processing applications include Microsoft Word and WordPerfect.

FIGURE B3.14

Application Software

PLUG-IN SUMMARY

Information technology (IT) is a field concerned with the use of technology in managing and processing information. IT includes cell phones, PDAs, software such as spreadsheet software, and printers. There are two categories of IT: hardware and software. The six hardware components include CPU, primary storage, secondary storage, input devices, output devices, and communication devices. Computer categories include PDAs, laptops, tablets, desktops, workstations, minicomputers, mainframe computers, and supercomputers.

Software includes system software and application software. Operating system software and utility software are the two primary types of system software. There are many forms of application software from word processing to databases.

KEY TERMS

Application software, 330
Arithmetic-logic unit (ALU), 320
Binary digit (bit), 321
Byte, 321
Cache memory, 322
Central processing unit (CPU)
  (or microprocessor), 319
Communication device, 326
Complex instruction set
  computer (CISC) chip, 320
Computer, 319
Control unit, 319
Flash memory, 322
Gigabyte (GB), 322

Gigahertz (GHz), 320
Hard drive, 323
Hardware, 318
Information technology (IT), 318
Input device, 324
Magnetic medium, 323
Magnetic tape, 323
Megabyte (MB, M, or
  Meg), 322
Megahertz (MHz), 320
Memory card, 322
Memory stick, 322
Multitasking, 329
Operating system software, 329

Output device, 324
Primary storage, 321
Random access memory
  (RAM), 321
Read-only memory (ROM), 322
Reduced instruction set
  computer (RISC) chip, 320
Secondary storage, 322
Software, 318
System software, 329
Terabyte (TB), 322
Utility software, 329
Virtualization, 321
Volatility, 321

CLOSING CASE ONE

Changing Circuits at Circuit City

When Circuit City expanded the big-box warehouse format to consumer electronics retailing in the 1980s, the company was on its way to becoming the place to go for TVs and stereos. By the late 1980s, it had sidestepped its then top competitor, Silo, and it soon put the squeeze on the likes of Tweeter and RadioShack. Circuit City was doing so well in the 1990s that business consultant Jim Collins, in his best seller *Good to Great*, wrote: "From 1982 to 1999, Circuit City generated cumulative stock returns 22 times better than the market, handily beating Intel, Wal-Mart, GE, Hewlett-Packard and Coca-Cola."

Today, Circuit City is in a markedly different position. By 2001, Best Buy had raced past the Richmond, Virginia-based chain, usurping its position as the number one consumer electronics retailer. Best Buy now has 608 stores compared with Circuit City's 599 and nearly $25 billion in revenue to Circuit City's $9.7 billion. Circuit City is ranked by consultancy Retail Forward as the

Baltzan–Phillips–Haag:
Business Driven
Technology, Third Edition

Business Plug–Ins

B3: Hardware and
Software

© The McGraw–Hill
Companies, 2009

231

number three seller of consumer electronics, behind Best Buy and Wal-Mart. "Circuit City was the 800-pound gorilla," said Joseph Feldman, a research analyst with the investment bank SG Cowen & Co. However, "they woke up one morning and Best Buy had doubled its size with the same number of stores."

Catching Best Buy

Circuit City has been trying to catch up to Best Buy, or at least cement its position as a serious contender in consumer electronics retailing. Its top executives announced plans to turn the company into a customer-focused business that delivers a personalized experience to all customers across all its channels (stores, Web, and call centers). Michael Jones, who took over as Circuit City's CIO in January 2004, speaks passionately about the high-profile role technology will play in delivering personalized customer experiences. However, before he can achieve his vision of store associates recognizing customers through their loyalty cards as soon as they enter the store, he has a lot of unglamorous groundwork to lay. Circuit City's strategy hinges on a robust IT infrastructure that makes information readily accessible to decision makers. Everything the company is doing to improve its business—from developing more effective promotions to deciding which products should be displayed at the ends of aisles in stores—hinges on data. "This is heavy analytical work. It's fact-based, data-driven," said Philip Schoonover, Circuit City's new president who was hired in October 2004 from Best Buy.

Circuit City is just starting to invest heavily in the technology needed to act on this strategy. It is upgrading its mostly proprietary point-of-sale (POS) system and building an enterprise data warehouse to replace siloed databases. However, some analysts say Circuit City's turnaround effort has been hampered by a stodgy, overly complacent leadership that lacks vision. Top executives saw the Best Buy locomotive coming but failed to react as it steamed past them. Indeed, some analysts say they doubt Circuit City will ever catch up.

Bottom-Up Changes

As part of its turnaround effort over the past few years, Circuit City has sold all of its noncore businesses to focus on its core: consumer electronics. It also has changed the pay structure for in-store employees, begun relocating stores (it closed 19), and hired new management. In addition, the company is finally starting to hone its customer-centric strategy. Circuit City is already improving the customer experience in its stores by, among other things, locating accessories and services close to big-ticket items so that customers can see more quickly what they might need to furnish their home office or outfit a home theater. For example, when a customer is looking at a high-definition television, nearby is a selection of furniture to hold the TV, the cables needed to hook it up, and DirectTV or digital cable service products. Circuit City is also making merchandising decisions based on what is important to the customer. For example, its stores are beginning to feature products deemed most important to customers on the displays at the ends of aisles. The company is trying to nail the basics of customer service by making sure that items are not out of stock.[10]

Questions

1. How would anticipating Best Buy's growth have helped Circuit City remain as an industry leader?
2. Why is keeping up with technology critical to a global company such as Circuit City?
3. Highlight some of the potential risks facing Circuit City's new business model.
4. Why is Circuit City benefiting from implementing strategic product placement techniques?

Electronic Breaking Points

What happens when someone accidentally spills a cup of hot coffee on a laptop, puts a USB memory key in a washing machine, or drops an iPod in the sand? How much abuse can electronic products take and keep on working? *PC World* tested several products to determine their breaking points.[11]

Laptop

A Gateway laptop was placed in a shoulder bag and smashed into several doors and walls. It was also dropped off a six-foot-high bookcase to simulate a drop from an airplane's overhead bin. Finally, it was knocked off a desk onto a carpeted floor without the bag. After all the abuse, the Gateway consistently rebooted and recognized the wireless network; however, the battery did become slightly dislodged and the optical drive opened.

Severe physical damage was caused when the laptop was dropped onto a hardwood floor. The laptop's screen cracked, and the black plastic molding above the keyboard cracked. Plastic splinters littered the floor, and the optical drive refused to open.

Spilling coffee in a travel-size mug onto the keyboard caused a slight sizzle, after which the Gateway's blue light winked out. The machine was quickly turned off, the battery removed, the liquid drained, the keys mopped, and the unit set aside. Unfortunately, the laptop never recovered.

Smart Phone

The PalmOne Treo 600 smart phone was stepped on, buried in the sand, bounced around in a car, and dropped off a desk onto carpeted and hardwood floors. Even though the Treo 600 was not protected by a shock-absorbent case or plastic screen cover, there were no signs of failure. Repeatedly knocking it off the desk onto a carpeted floor also left it undamaged, although the unit did turn off on several occasions.

The desk-to-hardwood-floor test produced scratches but nothing else. If dropped when in phone mode, the Treo automatically turned off. If an application was running—the calculator, for example—the device stayed on and the data remained on the screen, though a mysterious extra numeral nine appeared every time it was dropped.

MP3 Player

A 6 GB silver iPod Mini went for a bouncy car ride, was dropped on wet grass and dry pavement, was knocked off a desk onto carpeted and hardwood floors, and was finally dropped in dry sand. Bouncing inside the car caused a couple of skips. Drops on soft wet grass and carpet had no ill effect. Dropping it from the car seat to the curb and off a desk onto a hardwood floor produced a few nicks and caused songs to skip and the device to shut down repeatedly. Still, all the unit's features continued to work after the abuse, and songs played.

However, the Mini did not like the beach. Without the benefit of a protective case or plastic display covering on the unit, sand wedged under the scroll wheel, affecting all controls. Feature settings could be seen and highlighted, but the crunching sand prevented the Mini from launching them. The unit turned on but could not turn off until the iPod's automatic shutdown feature took over.

Protecting Electronic Products
Bag it. Place your product in a cushioned case or shock-absorbent travel bag. The secret is to make sure it has plenty of padding.
Get protection. Almost every technology manufacturer offers some type of warranty and equipment-replacement program. For example, Sprint provides the PCS Total Equipment Protection service, which costs $5 per month and covers loss, theft, and accidental damage to a cell phone.
Clean up spills. Try these tips to bring a laptop and data back from the dead after a spill.
1. **Disconnect the battery.** The faster the battery is disconnected the less likely components will burn out.
2. **Empty it.** Turn over the device and pour out as much liquid as possible.
3. **Open it up.** Remove the optical drive and keyboard. This can be tricky, so check the user manual for instructions. Once open, use a towel to soak up as much liquid as possible. According to Herman De Hoop, HP's technical marketing manager, you can even use a hair dryer set on cool (not hot) to dry the liquid.
4. **Leave it alone.** Let the device sit for at least 12 to 24 hours. Robert Enochs, IBM's worldwide product manager for the ThinkPad Series, warns that you should not turn the device on until all the liquid is gone and it is completely dry.
5. **Plug and pray.** Reassemble the device, and if it powers up, copy off important data, and then call the manufacturer. Even if the unit works, a professional cleaning is recommended.
6. **Enter a recovery program.** For an average price of $900, enlist the help of data recovery services like DriveSavers to rescue data from drowned hard disks.

FIGURE B3.15

How to Protect Electronic Products

Memory Stick

Lexar claims that its JumpDrive Sport 256 MB USB 2.0 Flash Drive is "built for the rugged life." A rubber cap protects the device, absorbing shock from any drops. For these experiments, the device was used without its cap. It was dropped, stepped on, buried in the sand, and knocked off a desk onto a hardwood floor. It also took a spin through the washing machine and dryer and was even run over by a car.

There is truth in advertising. Neither water, heat, sand, nor car could keep the memory stick from its appointed storage rounds. The car did squeeze the metal USB connector tip a tad tighter, but the device was still able to make contact with the USB port, and it worked perfectly.

Memory Card

The SanDisk SD 64 MB memory card is easy to misplace, but not easy to break. It was swatted off a desk onto a hardwood floor, dropped, stepped on, and buried in the sand. It also underwent a two-rinse cycle in the wash in a jeans pocket and then tumbled in the dryer for an hour on a high-heat setting. The SanDisk memory card aced every torture test.

For tips on how to protect electronic products, review Figure B3.15.

Questions

1. Identify the six hardware categories and place each product listed in the case in its appropriate category.
2. Describe the CPU and identify which products would use a CPU.
3. Describe the relationship between memory sticks and laptops. How can a user employ one to help protect information loss from the other?
4. Identify the different types of software each of the products listed in the case might use.

✳ MAKING BUSINESS DECISIONS

1. Purchasing a Computer

Dell is considered the fastest company on earth and specializes in computer customization. Connect to Dell's Web site at www.dell.com. Go to the portion of Dell's site that allows you to customize either a laptop or a desktop computer. First, choose an already prepared system and note its price and capability in terms of CPU speed, RAM size, monitor quality, and storage capacity. Now, customize that system to increase CPU speed, add more RAM, increase monitor size and quality, and add more storage capacity. What is the difference in price between the two? Which system is more in your price range? Which system has the speed and capacity you need?

2. Web-Enabled Cell Phones

When categorizing computers by size for personal needs, we focused on PDAs, laptops, and desktop computers. Other variations include Web-enabled cell phones that include instant text messaging and Web computers. For this project, you will need a group of four people, which you will then split into two groups of two. Have the first group research Web-enabled cell phones, their capabilities and costs. Have that group make a purchase recommendation based on price and capability. Have the second group do the same for Web computers. What is your vision of the future? Will we ever get rid of clunky laptops and desktops in favor of more portable and cheaper devices such as Web-enabled cell phones and Web computers? Why or why not?

3. Small Business Computers

Many different types of computers are available for small businesses. Use the Internet to find three different vendors of laptops or notebooks that are good for small businesses. Find the most expensive and the least expensive that the vendor offers and create a table comparing the different computers based on the following:

- CPU
- Memory
- Hard drive
- Optical drive
- Operating system
- Utility software
- Application software
- Support plan

Determine which computer you would recommend for a small business looking for an inexpensive laptop. Determine which computer you would recommend for a small business looking for an expensive laptop.

4. PDA Software

The personal digital assistant (PDA) market is ferocious, dynamic, and uncertain. One of the uncertainties is which operating system for PDAs will become dominant. Today, Microsoft operating systems dominate the laptop and desktop market. Research the more popular PDAs available today. What are the different operating systems? What different functionality do they offer? Are they compatible with each other? Determine which one will dominate in the future.

PLUG-IN

B4

Enterprise Architectures

Enterprise Architectures

A 66-hour failure of an FBI database that performed background checks on gun buyers was long enough to allow criminals to buy guns. The database failed at 1:00 p.m. on a Thursday and was not restored until 7:30 a.m. Sunday. The FBI must complete a gun check within three days; if it fails to do so, a merchant is free to make the sale. During this outage, any gun checks that were in progress were not finished, allowing merchants to complete those gun sales at their own discretion.[1]

To support the volume and complexity of today's user and application requirements, information technology needs to take a fresh approach to enterprise architectures by constructing smarter, more flexible environments that protect from system failures and crashes. *Enterprise architectures* include the plans for how an organization will build, deploy, use, and share its data, processes, and IT assets. A unified enterprise architecture will standardize enterprisewide hardware and software systems, with tighter links to the business strategy. A solid enterprise architecture can decrease costs, increase standardization, promote reuse of IT assets, and speed development of new systems. The end result is that the right enterprise architecture can make IT cheaper, strategic, and more responsive. The primary business goals of enterprise architectures are displayed in Figure B4.1.[2]

Enterprise architectures are never static; they continually change. Organizations use enterprise architects to help manage change. An *enterprise architect (EA)* is a person grounded in technology, fluent in business, a patient diplomat, and provides the important bridge between IT and the business. An EA is expensive and generally

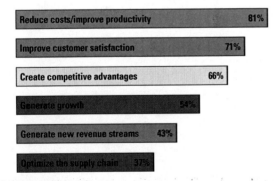

FIGURE B4.1

Primary Business Goals of Enterprise Architectures

Reduce costs/improve productivity	81%
Improve customer satisfaction	71%
Create competitive advantages	66%
Generate growth	54%
Generate new revenue streams	43%
Optimize the supply chain	37%

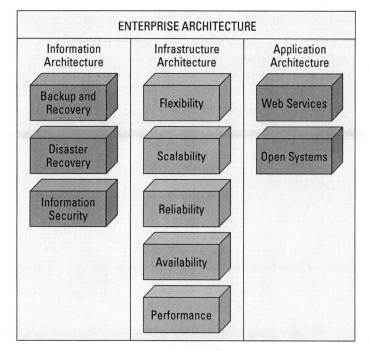

FIGURE B4.2

Three Components of Enterprise Architecture

receives a salary upward of $150,000 per year. T-Mobile International's enterprise architects review projects to ensure they are soundly designed, meet the business objectives, and fit in with the overall enterprise architecture. One T-Mobile project was to create software that would let subscribers customize the ring sounds on their cell phones. The project group assumed it would have to create most of the software from scratch. However, T-Mobile's EAs found software already written elsewhere at T-Mobile that could be reused to create the new application. The reuse reduced the development cycle time by eight months, and the new application was available in less than six weeks.[3]

Companies that have created solid enterprise architectures, such as T-Mobile, are reaping huge rewards in savings, flexibility, and business alignment. Basic enterprise architectures contain three components (see Figure B4.2).

1. *Information architecture* identifies where and how important information, like customer records, is maintained and secured.

2. *Infrastructure architecture* includes the hardware, software, and telecommunications equipment that, when combined, provide the underlying foundation to support the organization's goals.

3. *Application architecture* determines how applications integrate and relate to each other.

Information Architecture

Information architecture identifies where and how important information, like customer records, is maintained and secured. A single backup or restore failure can cost an organization more than time and money; some data cannot be re-created, and the business intelligence lost from that data can be tremendous. Chief information officers should have enough confidence that they could walk around and randomly pull out cables to prove that the systems are safe. The CIO should also be secure enough to perform this test during peak business hours. If the thought of this test makes the CIO cringe, then the organization's customers should be cringing also. Three primary areas an enterprise information architecture should focus on are:

1. Backup and recovery
2. Disaster recovery
3. Information security

BACKUP AND RECOVERY

Each year businesses lose time and money because of system crashes and failures. One way to minimize the damage of a system crash is to have a backup and recovery strategy in place. A *backup* is an exact copy of a system's information. *Recovery* is the ability to get a system up and running in the event of a system crash or failure and includes restoring the information backup. Many different types of backup and recovery media are available, including redundant storage servers, tapes, disks, and even CDs and DVDs. All the different types of backup and recovery media are reliable; their primary differences are the speed and associated costs.

A chain of more than 4,000 franchise locations, 7-Eleven Taiwan uploads backup and recovery information from its central location to all its chain locations daily. The company implemented a new technology solution by Digital Fountain that could quickly and reliably download and upload backup and recovery information to all its stores. In addition, when a connection fails during the download or upload, the technology automatically resumes the download without having to start over, saving valuable time.[4]

Organizations should choose a backup and recovery strategy that is in line with business goals. If the organization deals with large volumes of critical information, it will require daily backups, perhaps even hourly backups, to storage servers. If the organization deals with small amounts of noncritical information, then it might require only weekly backups to tapes, CDs, or DVDs. Deciding how often to back up information and what media to use is a critical business decision. If an organization decides to back up on a weekly basis, then it is taking the risk that, if a total system crash occurs, it could lose a week's worth of work. If this risk is acceptable, then a weekly backup strategy will work. If this risk is unacceptable, then the organization needs to move to a daily backup strategy. Some organizations find the risk of losing a day's worth of work too high and move to an hourly backup strategy.

Two techniques used to help in case of system failure are fault tolerance and failover. *Fault tolerance* is a computer system designed that in the event a component fails, a backup component or procedure can immediately take its place with no loss of service. Fault tolerance can be provided with software, or embedded in hardware, or provided by some combination. *Failover* is a backup operational mode in which the functions of a computer component (such as a processor, server, network, or database) are assumed by secondary system components when the primary component becomes unavailable through either failure or scheduled down time. A failover procedure involves automatically offloading tasks to a standby system component so that the procedure is as seamless as possible to the end user. Used to make systems more fault tolerant, failover is typically an integral part of mission-critical systems that must be constantly available.[5]

DISASTER RECOVERY

A northern Ohio power company, FirstEnergy, missed signs that there were potential problems in its portion of North America's electrical grid. The events that followed left an estimated 50 million people in the Northeast and Canada in the dark. The failings are laid out in the widely reported findings of a joint U.S./Canada task force that investigated the causes of the blackout and recommended what to do to avoid big-scale outages in the future. The report detailed many procedures or best practices including:

- Mind the enterprise architectures.
- Monitor the quality of computer networks that provide data on power suppliers and demand.
- Make sure the networks can be restored quickly in the case of downtime.
- Set up disaster recovery plans.
- Provide adequate staff training, including verbal communication protocols "so that operators are aware of any IT-related problems that may be affecting their situational awareness of the power grid."[6]

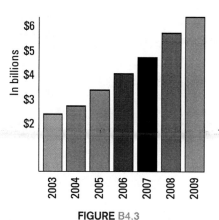

FIGURE B4.3

Financial Institutions Worldwide Spending on Disaster Recovery

Disasters such as power outages, floods, and even harmful hacking strike businesses every day. Organizations must develop a disaster recovery plan to prepare for such occurrences. A *disaster recovery plan* is a detailed process for recovering information or an IT system in the event of a catastrophic disaster such as a fire or flood. Spending on disaster recovery is rising worldwide among financial institutions (see Figure B4.3).[7]

A comprehensive disaster recovery plan takes into consideration the location of the backup information. Many organizations store backup information in an off-site facility. StorageTek specializes in providing off-site information storage and disaster recovery solutions. A comprehensive disaster recovery plan also foresees the possibility that not only the computer equipment but also the building where employees work may be destroyed. A *hot site* is a separate and fully equipped facility where the company can move immediately after a disaster and resume business. A *cold site* is a separate facility that does not have any computer equipment, but is a place where employees can move after a disaster.

A *disaster recovery cost curve* charts (1) the cost to the organization of the unavailability of information and technology and (2) the cost to the organization of recovering from a disaster over time. Figure B4.4 displays a disaster recovery cost curve and shows that where the two lines intersect is the best recovery plan in terms of cost and time. Creating an organization's disaster recovery cost curve is no small task. It must consider the cost of losing information and technology within each department or functional area, and the cost of losing information and technology across the whole enterprise. During the first few hours of a disaster, those costs will be low but become increasingly higher over time. With those costs in hand, an organization must then determine the costs of recovery. Cost of recovery during the first few hours of a disaster is exceedingly high and diminishes over time.

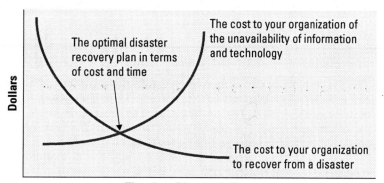

The optimal disaster recovery plan in terms of cost and time

The cost to your organization of the unavailability of information and technology

The cost to your organization to recover from a disaster

Dollars

Time from Disaster to Recovery

FIGURE B4.4

The Disaster Recovery Cost Curve

Marshall & Swift, which provides property valuation services, may be located in sunny Los Angeles, but the company barely averted a major disaster when Hurricane Charley ripped through southwest Florida. Many of the nation's largest insurance companies rely on Marshall & Swift's 200-plus servers to process claims and calculate the costs of rebuilding commercial and residential properties. Within one month of the Florida hurricane, the number of claims jumped from 20,000 to a whopping 180,000. This sudden surge in server utilization could have spelled disaster.

Fortunately, Marshall & Swift used an application performance management solution called ProactiveNet that identifies when an application or system is operating outside of its normal parameters and pinpoints the most likely source of the problem. ProactiveNet alerted the company's IT department to an improper balance of application, Web, and database servers. Some servers were being underutilized while others were being overburdened, thereby causing degradations in overall system performance. Marshall & Swift quickly began monitoring the usage patterns of each server and moved certain servers to ensure that all requests were processed in a timely matter.[8]

INFORMATION SECURITY

Security professionals are under increasing pressure to do the job right and cost-effectively as networks extend beyond organizations to remote users, partners, and customers, and to cell phones, PDAs, and other mobile devices. Regulatory requirements to safeguard data have increased. Concerns about identity theft are at an all-time high. Hacking and other unauthorized access contribute to the approximately 10 million instances of identity theft each year, according to the Federal Trade Commission. A good information architecture includes a strong information security plan, along with managing user access and up-to-date antivirus software and patches.[9]

Managing User Access

Managing user access to information is a critical piece of the information architecture. Passwords may still be the weakest link in the security chain. At Vitas Healthcare Corporation, with a workforce of 6,000 and operations across 15 states, authorized employees enter as many as a half-dozen passwords a day to access multiple systems. While it is important to maintain password discipline to secure customers' health care data, maintaining and managing the situation creates a drag on the IT department. "Our help desk spends 30 percent of their time on password management and provisioning," says John Sandbrook, senior IT director.

The company began using Fischer International Corporation's Identity Management Suite to manage passwords and comply with data-access regulations such as the Sarbanes-Oxley Act. The ID-management product includes automated audit, reporting, and compliance capabilities, plus a common platform for password management, provisioning, and self-service. With the software, Vitas can enforce stronger passwords with seven, eight, or nine characters, numbers, and capital letters that frequently change. The company anticipates curbing help-desk password time by 50 percent.[10]

Up-to-Date Antivirus Software and Patches

There is little doubt that security is a top priority for business managers, regardless of the size of their company. Among Fortune 500 companies, more than 80 percent of those surveyed described updating security procedures, tools, and services as a key business priority. That desire holds true for small, midsize, or large companies and for IT managers and corporate managers.

The main focus for most managers is preventing hackers, spammers, and other malcontents from entering their networks, and nearly two-thirds are looking to enhance their network-security-management, intrusion-detection, content-filtering, and anti-spam software. More than half also plan to upgrade their encryption software.[11]

Microsoft issues patches for its software on the second Tuesday of every month. These patches must be downloaded and installed on all systems across the entire enterprise if the company wants to keep its systems protected. At OMD, a media buying and planning subsidiary of Omnicom Group Inc., the network administrator had to manually install critical patches on all 100 servers, taking more than a week to deploy the patch across the company. Now, OMD uses automated installation software for patches and upgrades. The company purchased Altiris Management Suite for Dell servers, which let it move ahead with applying patches without taking down entire systems and balancing patch-deployment timing among servers so that all departments were not down at once during a patch install. Given everything else that security professionals need to think about, automated installation software is a welcome relief.[12]

Infrastructure Architecture

Gartner Inc. estimates that the typical Web application goes down 170 hours per year. At Illinois-based online brokerage OptionsXpress, application performance problems can have a serious impact on livelihoods. Nearly 7,000 options traders visit the OptionsXpress Web site at any given time, completing nearly 20,000 transactions a day. With all this online traffic, the brokerage's IT administrators were always up against the clock when re-creating troublesome applications offline in the development environment. The company struggled to unlock the mystery behind a troublesome trading application that was forcing traders to resubmit orders. Sometimes the application would just die and then restart itself for no apparent reason.[13]

Infrastructure architecture includes the hardware, software, and telecommunications equipment that, when combined, provide the underlying foundation to support the organization's goals. As an organization changes, its systems must be able to change to support its operations. If an organization grows by 50 percent in a single year, its systems must be able to handle a 50 percent growth rate. Systems that cannot adapt to organizational changes can severely hinder the organization's ability to operate. The future of an organization depends on its ability to meet its partners and customers on their terms, at their pace, any time of the day, in any geographic location. The following are the five primary characteristics of a solid infrastructure architecture:

1. Flexibility
2. Scalability
3. Reliability
4. Availability
5. Performance

FLEXIBILITY

Organizations must watch today's business, as well as tomorrow's, when designing and building systems. Systems must be flexible enough to meet all types of business changes. For example, a system might be designed to include the ability to handle multiple currencies and languages, even though the company is not currently performing business in other countries. When the company starts growing and performing business in new countries, the system will already have the flexibility to handle multiple currencies and languages. If the company failed to recognize that its business would someday be global, it would need to redesign all its systems to handle multiple currencies and languages, not easy once systems are up and running.

SCALABILITY

Estimating organizational growth is a challenging task. Growth can occur in a number of different forms including more customers and product lines and expansion into new markets. *Scalability* refers to how well a system can adapt to increased demands. A number of factors can create organizational growth including market, industry, and economy factors. If an organization grows faster than anticipated, it might experience all types of performance degradations, ranging from running out of disk space to a slowdown in transaction speeds. Anticipating expected—and unexpected—growth is key to building scalable systems that can support that growth.

MSNBC's Web site typically received moderate traffic. On September 11, 2001, the site was inundated with more than 91 million page views as its customers were trying to find out information about the terrorist attacks. Fortunately, MSNBC had anticipated this type of surging demand and built adaptable systems accordingly, allowing it to handle the increased page view requests.[15]

Capacity planning determines the future IT infrastructure requirements for new equipment and additional network capacity. Performing a capacity plan is one way to ensure the IT infrastructure is scalable. It is cheaper for an organization to implement an IT infrastructure that considers capacity growth at the beginning of a system launch than to try to upgrade equipment and networks after the system has been implemented. Not having enough capacity leads to performance issues and hinders the ability of knowledge workers to perform their jobs. If 100 workers are using the Internet to perform their jobs and the company purchases bandwidth that is too small and the network capacity is too small, the workers will spend a great deal of time just waiting to get information from the Internet. Waiting for an Internet site to return information is not very productive.

A computer glitch caused Delta Air Lines subsidiary Comair to cancel 1,100 flights on Christmas Day. The problem occurred when snowstorms caused the airline to ground flights, and the resulting quagmire overwhelmed its aging crew-scheduling system, causing further cancellations. Delta's crew-scheduling system is being replaced by one that can scale to handle more transactions.[16]

RELIABILITY

Reliability ensures all systems are functioning correctly and providing accurate information. Reliability is another term for accuracy when discussing the correctness of systems within the context of efficiency IT metrics. Inaccurate information processing occurs for many reasons, from the incorrect entry of data to information corruption. Unreliable information puts the organization at risk when making decisions based on the information.

AVAILABILITY

Availability (an efficiency IT metric) addresses when systems can be accessed by employees, customers, and partners. *High availability* refers to a system or component that is continuously operational for a desirably long length of time. Availability is typically measured relative to "100 percent operational" or "never failing." A widely held but difficult-to-achieve standard of availability for a system or product is known as "five 9s" (99.999 percent) availability.

Some companies have systems available 24x7 to support business operations and global customer and employee needs. With the emergence of the Web, companies expect systems to operate around the clock. A customer who finds that a Web site closes at 9:00 p.m. is not going to be a customer long.

Systems, however, must come down for maintenance, upgrades, and fixes. One challenge organizations face is determining when to schedule system downtime if the system is expected to operate continually. Exacerbating the negative impact of scheduled system downtime is the global nature of business. Scheduling maintenance during the evening might seem like a great idea, but the evening in one city is the morning somewhere else in the world, and global employees may not be able to perform their jobs if the system is down. Many organizations overcome this problem by having redundant systems, allowing the organization to take one system down by switching over to a redundant, or duplicate, system.[17]

PERFORMANCE

Performance measures how quickly a system performs a certain process or transaction (in terms of efficiency IT metrics of both speed and throughput). Not having enough performance capacity can have a devastating, negative impact on a business. A customer will wait only a few seconds for a Web site to return a request before giving up and moving on to another Web site. To ensure adaptable systems performance, capacity planning helps an organization determine future IT infrastructure requirements for new equipment and additional network capacity. It is cheaper for an organization to design and implement an IT infrastructure that envisions performance capacity growth than to update all the equipment after the system is already operational.

Abercrombie & Fitch (A&F) uses the Internet to market its distinctive image of being a fashion trendsetter to one of its largest customer segments, college students. The company designed its enterprise architecture with the help of IBM, which ensured www.abercrombie.com paralleled the same sleek but simple design of *A&F Quarterly*, the company's flagship magazine. Abercrombie & Fitch knew that its Web site had to be accessible, available, reliable, and scalable to meet the demands of its young customers. Young customers tend to be Internet savvy, and their purchasing habits vary from customers who only shop for sale items at midnight to customers who know exactly what they want immediately. The highly successful Web site gives customers not only an opportunity to shop online, but also a taste of the Abercrombie & Fitch lifestyle through downloadable MP3s, calendars, and desktop accessories.[18]

Application Architecture

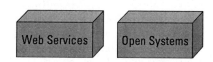

Gartner Inc. research indicates that application problems are the single largest source of downtime, causing 40 percent of annual downtime hours and 32 percent of average downtime costs. *Application architecture* determines how applications integrate and relate to each other. Advances in integration technology—primarily Web services and open systems—are providing new ways for designing more agile, more responsive enterprise architectures that provide the kind of value businesses need. With these new architectures, IT can build new business capabilities faster, cheaper, and in a vocabulary the business can understand.[19]

WEB SERVICES

Web services promise to be the next major frontier in computing. *Web services* contain a repertoire of Web-based data and procedural resources that use shared protocols and standards permitting different applications to share data and services. The major application of Web services is the integration among different applications. Before Web services, organizations had trouble with interoperability. **Interoperability** is the capability of two or more computer systems to share data and resources, even though they are made by different manufacturers. If a supply chain management (SCM) system can talk to (share information with) a customer relationship management (CRM) system, interoperability exists between the two systems. The traditional way that organizations achieved interoperability was to build integrations. Now, an organization can use Web services to perform the same task.

Verizon's massive enterprise architecture includes three different companies GTE, Bell Atlantic, and Nynex, each with its own complex systems. To find a customer record in any of the three companies' systems, Verizon turns to its search engine, called Spider. Spider is Verizon's version of Google, and it's helping Verizon's business to thrive.

Spider contains a vital customer information Web service that encapsulates Verizon's business rules, which help it to access the correct data repository when looking for customer information. Whenever a new system is built that needs to link to customer information, all the developer has to do is reuse the Web service that will link to the customer records. Because Verizon has the Web service in place as part of its enterprise architecture, development teams can build new applications within a month, as opposed to six months.[20]

Web services encompass all the technologies that are used to transmit and process information on and across a network, most specifically the Internet. It is easiest to think of an individual Web service as software that performs a specific task, with that task being made available to any user who needs its service. For example, a "Deposit" Web service for a banking system might allow customers to perform the task of depositing money to their accounts. The Web service could be used by a bank teller, by the customer at an ATM, and/or by the customer performing an online transaction through a Web browser.

The "Deposit" Web service demonstrates one of the great advantages of using the Web service model to develop applications. Developers do not have to reinvent the wheel every time they need to incorporate new functionality. A Web service is really a piece of reusable software code. A software developer can quickly build a new application by using many of these pieces of reusable code. The two primary parts of Web services are events and services.[21]

Events

Events are the eyes and ears of the business expressed in technology—they detect threats and opportunities and alert those who can act on the information. Pioneered by telecommunication and financial services companies, this involves using IT systems to monitor a business process for events that matter—a stock-out in the warehouse or an especially large charge on a consumer's credit card—and automatically alert the people best equipped to handle the issue. For example, a credit monitoring system automatically alerts a credit supervisor and shuts down an account when the system processes a $7,000 charge on a credit card with a $6,000 limit.[22]

Services

Services are more like software products than they are coding projects. They must appeal to a broad audience, and they need to be reusable if they are going to have an impact on productivity. Early forms of services were defined at too low a level in the architecture to interest the business, such as simple "Print" and "Save" services. The new services are being defined at a higher level; they describe such things as "Credit Check," "Customer Information," and "Process Payment." These services describe a valuable business process. For example, "Credit Check" has value not just for programmers who want to use that code in another application, but also for businesspeople who want to use it across multiple products—say, auto loans and mortgages—or across multiple businesses.[23]

Baltzan–Phillips–Haag:
Business Driven
Technology, Third Edition

Business Plug–Ins

B4: Enterprise
Architectures

© The McGraw–Hill
Companies, 2009

245

The trick to building services is finding the right level of granularity. T-Mobile builds services starting at the highest level and then works its way down to lower levels, helping to ensure it does not build services that no one uses. The company first built a "Send Message" Web service and then built a "Send SMS Message" Web service that sends messages in special formats to different devices such as cell phones and pagers.

Lydian Trust's enterprise architects designed a Web service called "Get Credit" that is used by several different business units for loan applications. "Get Credit" seeks out credit ratings over the Internet from the major credit bureaus. One day, one of the credit bureaus' Web servers crashed, and Lydian Trust's "Get Credit" Web service could not make a connection. Since the connection to the server was loosely linked, the system did not know what to do. "Get Credit" was not built to make more than one call. So, while it waited for a response, hundreds of loan applications sat idle.

Lydian Trust's loan officers had to work overnight to ensure that all of the applications were completed within 24 hours as promised by the company. Fortunately, Lydian Trust's customers never felt the pain; however, its employees did. Systems must be designed to deal with the existence of certain events, or the lack of an event, in a way that does not interrupt the overall business. The "Get Credit" Web service has been modified to include an automatic e-mail alert to a supervisor whenever the Web service encounters a delay.[24]

OPEN SYSTEMS

Microsoft Internet Explorer's share of the Web browser market has dipped below 90 percent because of Mozilla's Firefox, an open source Web browser. According to WebSideStory, which has been tracking the Firefox versus Internet Explorer numbers, the Mozilla-made open source browser had captured 5 percent of the U.S. market in January 2005, an increase of almost a full percentage point in a month. Firefox claimed more than 25 million copies of the browser had been downloaded in its first 15 weeks of release.[25]

An **open system** is a broad, general term that describes nonproprietary IT hardware and software made available by the standards and procedures by which their products work, making it easier to integrate them. Amazon.com embraced open source technology converting from Sun's proprietary operating system to Linux. The switch to an open source operating system, such as Linux, is simplifying the process by which Amazon.com associates can build links to Amazon.com applications into their Web sites.[26]

The designs of open systems allow for information sharing. In the past, different systems were independent of each other and operated as individual islands of control. The sharing of information was accomplished through software drivers and devices that routed data allowing information to be translated and shared between systems. Although this method is still widely used, its limited capability and added cost are not an effective solution for most organizations. Another drawback to the stand-alone system is it can communicate only with components developed by a single manufacturer. The proprietary nature of these systems usually results in costly repair, maintenance, and expansion because of a lack of competitive forces. On the other hand, open system integration is designed to:

■ Allow systems to seamlessly share information. The sharing of information reduces the total number of devices, resulting in an overall decrease in cost.

■ Capitalize on enterprise architectures. This avoids installing several independent systems, which creates duplication of devices.

■ Eliminate proprietary systems and promote competitive pricing. Often a sole-source vendor can demand its price and may even provide the customer with less than satisfactory service. Utilization of open systems allows users to purchase systems competitively.

✳ PLUG-IN SUMMARY

Companies that have created solid enterprise architectures are reaping huge rewards in savings, flexibility, and business alignment. Basic enterprise architectures contain three components:

1. Information architecture identifies where and how important information, like customer records, are maintained and secured.

2. Infrastructure architecture includes the hardware, software, and telecommunications equipment that, when combined, provide the underlying foundation to support the organization's goals.

3. Application architecture determines how applications integrate and relate to each other.

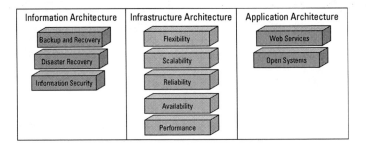

✳ KEY TERMS

Application
architecture, 339, 345
Availability, 344
Backup, 340
Capacity planning, 344
Cold site, 341
Disaster recovery cost
curve, 341

Disaster recovery plan, 341
Enterprise architect (EA), 338
Enterprise architecture, 338
Failover, 340
Fault tolerance, 340
High availability, 344
Hot site, 341
Information architecture, 339

Infrastructure architecture, 343
Interoperability, 346
Open system, 347
Performance, 345
Recovery, 340
Reliability, 344
Scalability, 344
Web service, 345

✳ CLOSING CASE ONE

Chicago *Tribune*'s Server Consolidation a Success

The *Chicago Tribune* is the seventh-largest newspaper in the country. Overhauling its data center and consolidating servers was a difficult task; however, the payoff was tremendous. The *Chicago Tribune* successfully moved its critical applications from a mishmash of mainframes and older Sun Microsystems servers to a new dual-site enterprise architecture, which has resulted in lower costs and increased reliability throughout the company.

The paper's new enterprise architecture clustered its servers over a two-mile distance, lighting up a 1Gbps dark-fiber link—an optical fiber that is in place but not yet being used—between two data centers. This architecture lets the newspaper spread the processing load between the servers while improving redundancy and options for disaster recovery.

The transfer to the new architecture was not smooth. A small piece of software written for the transition contained a coding error that caused the *Tribune*'s editorial applications to experience intermittent processing failures. As a result, the paper was forced to delay delivery to about 40 percent of its 680,000 readers and cut 24 pages from a Monday edition, costing the newspaper nearly $1 million in advertising revenue.

After editorial applications were stabilized, the *Tribune* proceeded to migrate applications for operations—the physical production and printing of the newspaper—and circulation to the new enterprise architecture. "As we gradually took applications off the mainframe, we realized that we were incurring very high costs in maintaining underutilized mainframes at two different locations," says Darko Dejanovic, vice president and CTO of the Tribune Co., which owned the *Chicago Tribune*, the *Los Angeles Times*, Long Island's *Newsday*, and about a dozen other metropolitan newspapers. "By moving from two locations to one, we've achieved several million dollars in cost savings. There's no question that server consolidation was the right move for us."

The company is excited about its new enterprise architecture and is looking to consolidate software across its newspapers. Currently, each newspaper maintains its own applications for classified advertising and billing, which means the parent company must support about 10 billing packages and the same number of classified-ad programs. Most of the business processes can be standardized. So far, the company has standardized about 95 percent of classified-ad processes and about 90 percent of advertising-sales processes. Over three years, the company will replace the disparate billing and ad applications with a single package that will be used by all business units. The different newspapers will not necessarily share the same data, but they will have the same processes and the same systems for accessing them. Over time, that will allow some of the call centers to handle calls for multiple newspapers; East Coast centers will handle the early-morning calls and West Coast centers the late-day and evening calls.

The company is looking at a few additional projects including the implementation of hardware that will allow its individual applications to run on partial CPUs, freeing up processor power and making more efficient use of disk space.[27]

Questions

1. Review the five characteristics of infrastructure architecture and rank them in order of their potential impact on the Tribune Co.'s business.
2. What is the disaster recovery cost curve? Where should the Tribune Co. operate on the curve?
3. Define backups and recovery. What are the risks to the Tribune's business if it fails to implement an adequate backup plan?
4. Why is a scalable and highly available enterprise architecture critical to current operations and future growth?
5. Identify the need for information security at the Tribune Co.
6. How could the Tribune Co. use a classified ad Web service across its different businesses?

✱ CLOSING CASE TWO

Fear the Penguin

Linux has proved itself the most revolutionary software of the past decade. Spending on Linux was reported to reach $280 million by 2006. Linus Torvalds, who wrote the kernel (the core) of the Linux operating system at age 21, posted the operating system on the Internet and invited other programmers to improve his code and users to download his operating system for free. Since then, tens of thousands of people have, making Linux perhaps the single largest collaborative project in the planet's history.

Today, Linux, if not its penguin mascot, is everywhere. You can find Linux inside a boggling array of computers, machines, and devices. Linux is robust enough to run the world's most powerful supercomputers, yet sleek and versatile enough to run inside consumer items like TiVo, cell phones, and handheld portable devices. Even more impressive than Linux's increasing prevalence in living rooms and pockets is its growth in the market for corporate computers.

Since its introduction in 1991, no other operating system in history has spread as quickly across such a broad range of systems as Linux, and it has finally achieved critical mass. According to studies by market research firm IDC, Linux is the fastest-growing server operating system, with shipments expected to grow by 34 percent per year over the next four years. With its innovative open source approach, strong security, reliability, and scalability, Linux can help companies achieve the agility they need to respond to changing consumer needs and stay ahead of the game.

Thanks to its unique open source development process, Linux is reliable and secure. A "meritocracy," a team specifically selected for their competence by the technical developer community, governs the entire development process. Each line of code that makes up the Linux kernel is extensively tested and maintained for a variety of different platforms and application scenarios.

This open collaborative approach means the Linux code base continually hardens and improves itself. If vulnerabilities appear, they get the immediate attention of experts from around the world, who quickly resolve the problems. According to Security Portal, which tracks vendor response times, it takes an average of 12 days to patch a Linux bug compared to an average of three months for some proprietary platforms. With the core resilience and reliability of Linux, businesses can minimize downtime, which directly increases their bottom line.

The Spread of Open Systems

Businesses and governments are opting for open source operating systems like Linux instead of Windows. One attendee at the Linux Desktop Consortium in 2004 was Dr. Martin Echt, a cardiologist from Albany, New York. Dr. Echt, chief operating officer of Capital Cardiology Associates, an eight-office practice, discussed his decision to shift his business from Microsoft's Windows to Linux. Dr. Echt is not your typical computer geek or Linux supporter, and he is not the only one switching to Linux.

The State Council in China has mandated that all ministries install the local flavor of Linux, dubbed Red Flag, on their PCs. In Spain, the government has installed a Linux operating system that incorporates the regional dialect. The city of Munich, despite a personal visit from Microsoft CEO Steve Ballmer, is converting its 14,000 PCs from Windows to Linux.

"It's open season for open source," declared Walter Raizner, general manager of IBM Germany. One of the biggest corporate backers of Linux, IBM has more than 75 government customers worldwide, including agencies in France, Spain, Britain, Australia, Mexico, the United States, and Japan.

The move toward Linux varies for each country or company. For Dr. Echt, it was a question of lower price and long-term flexibility. In China, the government claimed national security as a reason to move to open source code because it permitted engineers to make sure there were no security leaks and no spyware installed on its computers. In Munich, the move was largely political. Regardless of the reason, the market is shifting toward Linux.

Microsoft versus Linux

Bill Gates has openly stated that Linux is not a threat to Microsoft. According to IDC analysts, Microsoft's operating systems ship with 93.8 percent of all desktops worldwide. Ted Schadler, IDC research principal analyst, states that despite the push of lower cost Linux players into the market, Microsoft will maintain its desktop market share for the following three reasons:

1. Linux adds features to its applications that most computer users have already come to expect.
2. Linux applications might not be compatible with Microsoft applications such as Microsoft Word or Microsoft Excel.
3. Microsoft continues to innovate, and the latest version of Office is beginning to integrate word processing and spreadsheet software to corporate databases and other applications.

The Future of Linux

IDC analyst Al Gillen predicts that an open source operating system will not enjoy explosive growth on the desktop for at least six or eight years. Still, even Gillen cannot deny that Linux's penetration continues to rise, with an estimated 18 million users. Linux's market share increased from 1.5 percent at the end of 2000 to 4.2 percent at the beginning of 2004. According to IDC, by the end of 2005 it surpassed Apple's Mac OS, which has 2.9 percent of the market, as the second most popular operating system. Gartner Dataquest estimates Linux's server market share will grow seven times faster than Windows.[28]

Questions

1. How does Linux differ from traditional software?
2. Should Microsoft consider Linux a threat? Why or why not?
3. How is open source software a potential trend shaping organizations?
4. How can you use Linux as an emerging technology to gain a competitive advantage?
5. Research the Internet and discover potential ways that open source software might revolutionize business in the future.

✳ MAKING BUSINESS DECISIONS

1. Planning for Disaster Recovery

You are the new senior analyst in the IT department at Beltz, a large snack food manufacturing company. The company is located on the beautiful shoreline in Charleston, North Carolina. The company's location is one of its best and also worst features. The weather and surroundings are beautiful, but the threat of hurricanes and other natural disasters is high. Compile a disaster recovery plan that will minimize any risks involved with a natural disaster.

2. Comparing Backup and Recovery Systems

Research the Internet to find three different vendors of backup and recovery systems. Compare and contrast the three systems and determine which one you would recommend if you were installing a backup and recovery system for a medium-sized business with 3,500 employees that maintains information on the stock market. Compile your findings in a presentation that you can give to your class that details the three systems' strengths and weaknesses, along with your recommendation.

3. Ranking the -ilities

In a group, review the following list of IT infrastructure qualities and rank them in order of their impact on an organization's success. Use a rating system of 1 to 7, where 1 indicates the biggest impact and 7 indicates the least impact.

IT Infrastructure Qualities	Business Impact
Availability	
Accessibility	
Reliability	
Scalability	
Flexibility	
Performance	
Capacity Planning	

4. Designing an Enterprise Architecture

Components of a solid enterprise architecture include everything from documentation to business concepts to software and hardware. Deciding which components to implement and how to implement them can be a challenge. New IT components are released daily, and business needs continually change. An enterprise architecture that meets your organization's needs today may not meet those needs tomorrow. Building an enterprise architecture that is scalable, flexible, available, accessible, and reliable is key to your organization's success.

You are the enterprise architect (EA) for a large clothing company called Xedous. You are responsible for developing the initial enterprise architecture. Create a list of questions you will need answered to develop your architecture. Below is an example of a few of the questions you might ask.

■ What are the company's growth expectations?
■ Will systems be able to handle additional users?
■ How long will information be stored in the systems?
■ How much customer history must be stored?
■ What are the organization's business hours?
■ What are the organization's backup requirements?

PLUG-IN

B5

Networks and Telecommunications

1. Compare LANs, WANs, and MANs.
2. List and describe the four components that differentiate networks.
3. Compare the two types of network architectures.
4. Explain topology and the different types found in networks.
5. Describe TCP/IP along with its primary purpose.
6. Identify the different media types found in networks.

Networks and Telecommunications

Telecommunication systems enable the transmission of data over public or private networks. A *network* is a communications, data exchange, and resource-sharing system created by linking two or more computers and establishing standards, or protocols, so that they can work together. Telecommunication systems and networks are traditionally complicated and historically inefficient. However, businesses can benefit from today's modern network infrastructures that provide reliable global reach to employees and customers. Businesses around the world are moving to network infrastructure solutions that allow greater choice in how they go to market—solutions with global reach. Plug-In B5 takes a detailed look at key network and telecommunication technologies being integrated into businesses around the world.

Network Basics

Music is the hottest new product line at ubiquitous coffee retailer Starbucks. In Starbucks stores, customers can burn CDs while sipping coffee, thanks to the company's own online music library and increasingly sophisticated in-store network. Networks range from small two-computer networks to the biggest network of all, the Internet. A network provides two principal benefits: the ability to communicate and the ability to share. E-mail is the most popular form of network communication. Figure B5.1 highlights the three different types of networks, and Figure B5.2 graphically depicts each network type.

Network Types	
Local area network (LAN)	A computer network that uses cables or radio signals to link two or more computers within a geographically limited area, generally one building or a group of buildings. A networked office building, school, or home usually contains a single LAN. The linked computers are called workstations.
Wide area network (WAN)	A computer network that provides data communication services for business in geographically dispersed areas (such as across a country or around the world). The Internet is a WAN that spans the world.
Metropolitan area network (MAN)	A computer network that provides connectivity in a geographic area or region larger than that covered by a local area network, but smaller than the area covered by a wide area network. A college or business may have a MAN that joins the different LANs across its campus.

FIGURE B5.1

Network Types

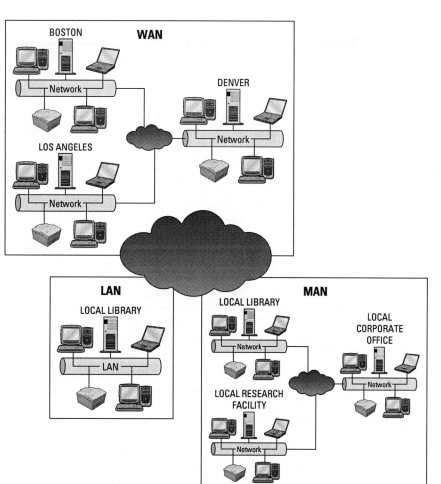

FIGURE B5.2

LAN, WAN, and MAN

Networks are differentiated by the following:

- Architecture—peer-to-peer, client/server.
- Topology—bus, star, ring, hybrid, wireless.
- Protocols—Ethernet, Transmission Control Protocol/Internet Protocol (TCP/IP).
- Media—coaxial, twisted-pair, fiber-optic.

Architecture

The two primary types of network architectures are: peer-to-peer networks and client/server networks.

PEER-TO-PEER NETWORKS

A *peer-to-peer (P2P) network* is any network without a central file server and in which all computers in the network have access to the public files located on all other workstations, as illustrated in Figure B5.3. Each networked computer can allow other computers to access its files and use connected printers while it is in use as a workstation without the aid of a server.

While Napster may be the most widely known example of a P2P implementation, it may also be one of the most narrowly focused since the Napster model takes advantage of only one of the many capabilities of P2P computing: file sharing. The technology has far broader capabilities, including the sharing of processing, memory, and storage, and the supporting of collaboration among vast numbers of distributed computers. Peer-to-peer computing enables immediate interaction among people and computer systems.[1]

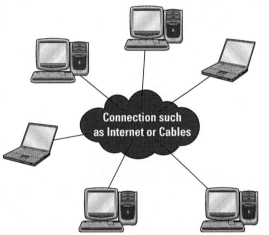

Connection such as Internet or Cables

FIGURE B5.3

Peer-to-Peer (P2P) Networks

CLIENT/SERVER NETWORKS

A *client* is a computer that is designed to request information from a server. A *server* is a computer that is dedicated to providing information in response to external requests. A *client/server network* is a model for applications in which the bulk of the back-end processing, such as performing a physical search of a database, takes place on a server, while the front-end processing, which involves communicating with the users, is handled by the clients (see Figure B5.4). A *network operating system (NOS)* is the operating system that runs a network, steering information between computers and managing security and users. The client/server model has become one of the central ideas of network computing. Most business applications written today use the client/server model.

A fundamental part of client/server architecture is packet-switching. *Packet-switching* occurs when the sending computer divides a message into a number of efficiently sized units called packets, each of which contains the address of the destination computer. Each packet is sent on the network and intercepted by routers. A *router* is an intelligent connecting device that examines each packet of data it receives and then decides which way to send it onward toward its destination. The packets arrive at their intended destination, although some may have actually traveled by different physical paths, and the receiving computer assembles the packets and delivers the message to the appropriate application. The number of network routers being installed by businesses worldwide is booming (see Figure B5.5).[2]

Eva Chen, CIO at Trend Micro, built a router that helps prevent worms and viruses from entering networks. The problem with most existing antivirus software is that it starts working after a destructive sequence of code is identified, meaning it starts doing its job only after the virus or worm has been unleashed inside

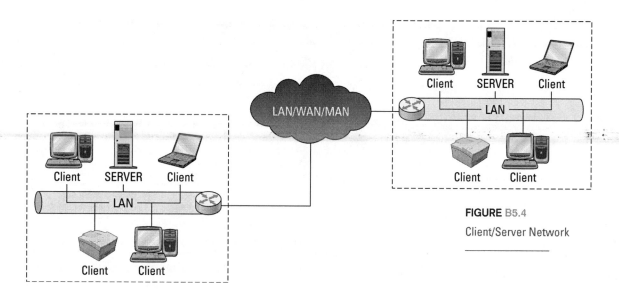

FIGURE B5.4

Client/Server Network

the network. Chen's router, the Network VirusWall, sits on the edge of a corporate network, scanning data packets and detaining those that might contain viruses or worms. Any suspicious packets are compared with up-to-the-second information from Trend Micro's virus-tracking command center. Viruses and worms are then deleted and refused entry to the network, allowing the company to perform a preemptive strike.[3]

Topology

Networks are assembled according to certain rules. Cables, for example, have to be a certain length; each cable strand can support only a certain amount of network traffic. A *network topology* refers to the geometric arrangement of the actual physical organization of the computers (and other network devices) in a network. Topologies vary depending on cost and functionality. Figure B5.6 highlights the five common topologies used in networks, and Figure B5.7 displays each topology.[4]

Protocols

A *protocol* is a standard that specifies the format of data as well as the rules to be followed during transmission. Simply put, for one computer (or computer program) to talk to another computer (or computer program) they must both be talking the same language, and this language is called a protocol.

A protocol is based on an agreed-upon and established standard, and this way all manufacturers of hardware and software that are using the protocol do so in a similar fashion to allow for interoperability. *Interoperability* is the capability of two or more computer systems to share data and resources, even though they are made by different manufacturers. The most popular network protocols used are Ethernet and Transmission Control Protocol/Internet Protocol (TCP/IP).

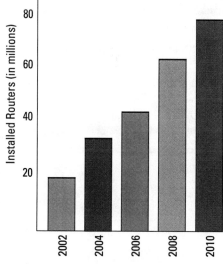

FIGURE B5.5

Worldwide Router Growth

ETHERNET

Ethernet is a physical and data layer technology for LAN networking (see Figure B5.8). Ethernet is the most widely installed LAN access method, originally developed by Xerox and then developed further by Xerox, Digital Equipment Corporation, and

FIGURE B5.6

Five Network Topologies

Network Topologies	
Bus	All devices are connected to a central cable, called the bus or backbone. Bus networks are relatively inexpensive and easy to install for small networks.
Star	All devices are connected to a central device, called a hub. Star networks are relatively easy to install and manage, but bottlenecks can occur because all data must pass through the hub.
Ring	All devices are connected to one another in the shape of a closed loop, so that each device is connected directly to two other devices, one on either side of it. Ring topologies are relatively expensive and difficult to install, but they offer high bandwidth and can span large distances.
Hybrid	Groups of star-configured workstations are connected to a linear bus backbone cable, combining the characteristics of the bus and star topologies.
Wireless	Devices are connected by a receiver/transmitter to a special network interface card that transmits signals between a computer and a server, all within an acceptable transmission range.

Intel. When it first began to be widely deployed in the 1980s, Ethernet supported a maximum theoretical data transfer rate of 10 megabits per second (Mbps). More recently, Fast Ethernet has extended traditional Ethernet technology to 100 Mbps peak, and Gigabit Ethernet technology extends performance up to 1,000 Mbps.[5]

Ethernet has survived as the major LAN technology—it is currently used for approximately 85 percent of the world's LAN-connected PCs and workstations—because its protocol has the following characteristics:

FIGURE B5.7

Network Topologies

- Is easy to understand, implement, manage, and maintain.
- Allows low-cost network implementations.

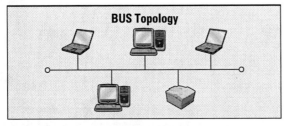

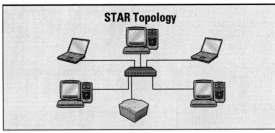

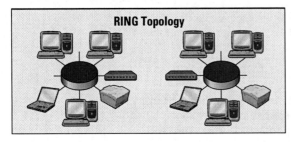

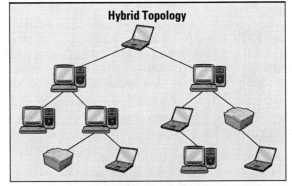

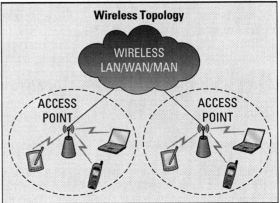

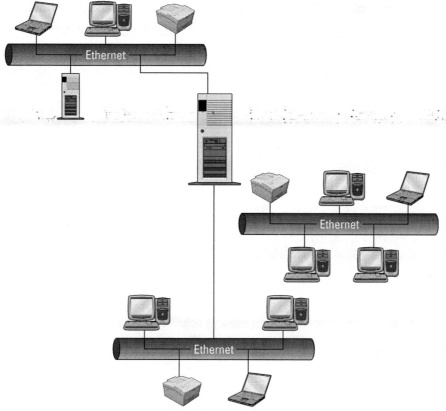

FIGURE B5.8

Ethernet Protocol

- Provides extensive flexibility for network installation.
- Guarantees successful interconnection and operation of standards-compliant products, regardless of manufacturer.[6]

TRANSMISSION CONTROL PROTOCOL/INTERNET PROTOCOL

The most common telecommunication protocol is Transmission Control Protocol/ Internet Protocol (TCP/IP), which was originally developed by the Department of Defense to connect a system of computer networks that became known as the Internet. *Transmission Control Protocol/Internet Protocol (TCP/IP)* provides the technical foundation for the public Internet as well as for large numbers of private networks. The key achievement of TCP/IP is its flexibility with respect to lower-level protocols. TCP/IP uses a special transmission method that maximizes data transfer and automatically adjusts to slower devices and other delays encountered on a network. Although more than 100 protocols make up the entire TCP/IP protocol suite, the two most important of these are TCP and IP. **TCP** provides transport functions, ensuring, among other things, that the amount of data received is the same as the amount transmitted. **IP** provides the addressing and routing mechanism that acts as a postmaster. Figure B5.9 displays TCP/IP's four-layer reference model:

- Application layer—serves as the window for users and application processes to access network services.
- Transport layer—handles end-to-end packet transportation.
- Internet layer—formats the data into packets, adds a header containing the packet sequence and the address of the receiving device, and specifies the services required from the network.
- Network interface layer—places data packets on the network for transmission.[7]

FIGURE B5.9

TCP/IP Four-Layer Reference Model

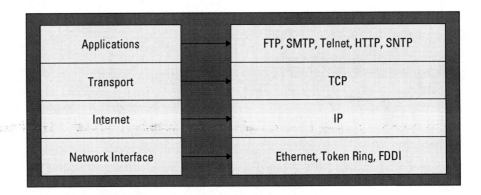

Applications	FTP, SMTP, Telnet, HTTP, SNTP
Transport	TCP
Internet	IP
Network Interface	Ethernet, Token Ring, FDDI

FIGURE B5.10

TCP/IP Applications

TCP/IP Applications	
File Transfer Protocol (FTP)	Allows files containing text, programs, graphics, numerical data, and so on to be downloaded off or uploaded onto a network.
Simple Mail Transfer Protocol (SMTP)	TCP/IP's own messaging system for e-mail.
Telnet Protocol	Provides terminal emulation that allows a personal computer or workstation to act as a terminal, or access device, for a server.
Hypertext Transfer Protocol (HTTP)	Allows Web browsers and servers to send and receive Web pages.
Simple Network Management Protocol (SNMP)	Allows the management of networked nodes to be managed from a single point.

The TCP/IP suite of applications includes five protocols—file transfer, simple mail transfer, telnet, hypertext transfer, and simple network management (see Figure B5.10).

Another communication reference model is the seven-layer Open System Interconnection (OSI) reference model. Figure B5.11 show the OSI model's seven layers.[8]

The lower layers (1 to 3) represent local communications, while the upper layers (4 to 7) represent end-to-end communications. Each layer contributes protocol functions that are necessary to establish and maintain the error-free exchange of information between network users.

For many years, users thought the OSI model would replace TCP/IP as the preferred technique for connecting multivendor networks. But the slow pace of OSI standards as well as the expense of implementing complex OSI software and having products certified for OSI interoperability will preclude this from happening.

FIGURE B5.11

Open System Interconnection Model

OSI Model
7. Application
6. Presentation
5. Session
4. Transport
3. Network
2. Data Link
1. Physical

Voice over IP (VoIP)

Originally, phone calls made over the Internet had a reputation of offering poor call quality, lame user interfaces, and low call-completion rates. With new and improved technology and IT infrastructures, Internet phone calls now offer similar quality to traditional telephone calls. Today, many consumers are making phone calls over the Internet by using voice over Internet protocol (VoIP). *Voice over IP (VoIP)* uses TCP/IP technology to transmit voice calls over long-distance telephone lines. In fact, VoIP transmits over 10 percent of all phone calls and this number is growing exponentially.

VoIP and e-mail work in similar ways. The user sends a call over the Internet in packets of audio data tagged with the same destination. VoIP reassembles the packets once they arrive at their final destination.

Numerous vendors offer VoIP services; however, the service works differently depending on the vendor's IT infrastructure. Skype pairs P2P (peer-to-peer) technology with a PC's sound card to create a voice service, which the user can use to call other Skype users. Unfortunately, the user can talk only to other Skype users. Vonage lets the user place calls to any person who has a mobile or landline (regular telephone) number. Vonage sends the call over a cable via a digital-to-analog converter. A few providers even offer an adapter for a traditional handset that plugs into a broadband modem. All of these vendors are providing VoIP, but the service and its features can vary significantly.[9]

The telecom industry expects great benefits from combining VoIP with emerging standards that allow for easier development, interoperability among systems, and application integration. This is a big change for an industry that relies on proprietary systems to keep customers paying for upgrades and new features. The VoIP and open-standards combo should produce more choices, lower prices, and new applications.

Writing voice applications may never be as common as writing computer applications. But the spread of VoIP will make it easier to manage applications and add capabilities to the voice feature set. In a decade, the telecom network "will be like getting water out of the tap," predicts Stef van Aarle, vice president of marketing and strategy at Lucent Worldwide Services. "The only time you think of it will be when it doesn't work. And software is the glue that makes it all easy to use."

Upstarts like Vonage and Skype are bringing VoIP to the masses. But a bigger opportunity lurks in the $2 billion corporate phone market. New York-based start-up Popular Telephony is offering a new VoIP technology that dramatically cuts corporate phone costs while letting workers take their office phones anywhere. Its secret: peer-to-peer software called Peerio that is built right into handsets.

CEO Dmitry Goroshevsky founded the company to bring PC economics to the office telephone system. A traditional workplace setup requires a dedicated voice network and a private branch exchange, or PBX, to connect to the outside world and can cost up to $1 million (see Figure B5.12). Cisco has been selling an IP PBX, which uses a data network for voice calls. But Popular Telephony eliminates pricey hardware. Using an ordinary PC, network administrators assign an extension to each phone. Peerio-enabled handsets, which will be sold through discount retailers and office supply stores, plug directly into a company's data network, where calls are routed through a gateway and then out. Since Peerio is based on Internet protocol, office workers can use their phones wherever there is a broadband connection. And though companies pay the usual rates to call conventional landline and mobile phone numbers, ringing up other Peerio and VoIP users will not cost a dime. A handful of licensees are manufacturing the phones.[10]

Telephone System	Typical Telecom System	IP-Based System	Peerio
Requirements	■ Phones ■ Private branch exchange (PBX) ■ Voice switches network ■ Dedicated voice network	■ Phones ■ IP PBX ■ Existing data network ■ Gateway	■ Phones ■ PC ■ Existing data ■ Gateway
Total Cost	$1,000,000	$500,000	$100,000

FIGURE B5.12

Typical Telephone Start-up Costs for a 1,000-Person Office

Media

Network transmission media refers to the various types of media used to carry the signal between computers. When information is sent across the network, it is converted into electrical signals. These signals are generated as electromagnetic waves (analog signaling) or as a sequence of voltage pulses (digital signaling). To be sent from one location to another, a signal must travel along a physical path. The physical path that is used to carry a signal between a signal transmitter and a signal receiver is called the transmission media. The two types of transmission media are wire (guided) and wireless (unguided).

WIRE MEDIA

Wire media are transmission material manufactured so that signals will be confined to a narrow path and will behave predictably. The three most commonly used types of guided media are (see Figure B5.13):

- Twisted-pair wiring
- Coaxial cable
- Fiber-optic cable

Twisted-Pair Wiring

Twisted-pair wiring refers to a type of cable composed of four (or more) copper wires twisted around each other within a plastic sheath. The wires are twisted to reduce outside electrical interference. Twisted-pair cables come in shielded and unshielded varieties. Shielded cables have a metal shield encasing the wires that acts as a ground for electromagnetic interference. Unshielded twisted-pair (UTP) is the most popular and is generally the best option for LAN networks. The quality of UTP may vary from telephone-grade wire to high-speed cable. The cable has four pairs of wires inside the jacket. Each pair is twisted with a different number of twists per inch to help eliminate interference from adjacent pairs and other electrical devices. The RJ-45 connectors on twisted-pair cables resemble large telephone connectors.[11]

Coaxial Cable

Coaxial cable is cable that can carry a wide range of frequencies with low signal loss. It consists of a metallic shield with a single wire placed along the center of a shield and isolated from the shield by an insulator. This type of cable is referred to as coaxial because it contains one copper wire (or physical data channel) that carries the signal and is surrounded by another concentric physical channel consisting of a

FIGURE B5.13

Twisted-Pair, Coaxial Cable, and Fiber-Optic

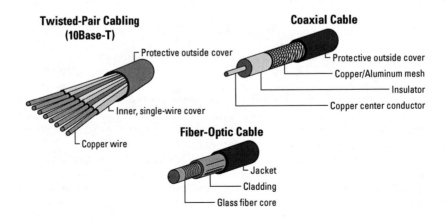

Twisted-Pair Cabling (10Base-T)
- Protective outside cover
- Inner, single-wire cover
- Copper wire

Coaxial Cable
- Protective outside cover
- Copper/Aluminum mesh
- Insulator
- Copper center conductor

Fiber-Optic Cable
- Jacket
- Cladding
- Glass fiber core

wire mesh. The outer channel serves as a ground for electrical interference. Because of this grounding feature, several coaxial cables can be placed within a single conduit or sheath without significant loss of data integrity.

Fiber-Optic Cable

Fiber optic (or *optical fiber*) refers to the technology associated with the transmission of information as light impulses along a glass wire or fiber. The 10Base-FL and 100Base-FX optical fiber cable are the same types of cable used by most telephone companies for long-distance service. Optical fiber cable can transmit data over long distances with little loss in data integrity. In addition, because data are transferred as a pulse of light, optical fiber is not subject to interference. The light pulses travel through a glass wire or fiber encased in an insulating sheath.

Optical fiber's increased maximum effective distance comes at a price. Optical fiber is more fragile than wire, difficult to split, and labor intensive to install. For these reasons, optical fiber is used primarily to transmit data over extended distances where the hardware required to relay the data signal on less expensive media would exceed the cost of optical fiber installation. It is also used where large amounts of data need to be transmitted on a regular basis.[12]

WIRELESS MEDIA

Wireless media are natural parts of the Earth's environment that can be used as physical paths to carry electrical signals. The atmosphere and outer space are examples of wireless media that are commonly used to carry signals. These media can carry such electromagnetic signals as microwave, infrared light waves, and radio waves.

Network signals are transmitted through all media as a type of waveform. When transmitted through wire and cable, the signal is an electrical waveform. When transmitted through fiber-optic cable, the signal is a light wave, either visible or infrared light. When transmitted through the Earth's atmosphere, the signal can take the form of waves in the radio spectrum, including microwaves, infrared, or visible light.

Recent advances in radio hardware technology have produced significant advancements in wireless networking devices: the cellular telephone, wireless modems, and wireless LANs. These devices use technology that in some cases has been around for decades but until recently was too impractical or expensive for widespread use.[13]

E-Business Networks

To set up an e-business even a decade ago would have required an individual organization to assume the burden of developing the entire network infrastructure. Today, industry-leading companies have developed Internet-based products and services to handle many aspects of customer and supplier interactions.

"In today's retail market, you cannot be a credible national retailer without having a robust Web site," says Dennis Bowman, senior vice president and CIO of Circuit City, who adds that customers now expect seamless retailing just as they expect stores that are clean and well stocked. For this reason, retailers are working furiously to integrate their e-business sites with their inventory and point-of-sale (POS) systems so that they can accept in-store returns of merchandise bought online and allow customers to buy on the Web and pick up in the store.[14]

Some companies, such as Best Buy, Circuit City, Office Depot, and Sears, already have their physical and online stores integrated. These companies have been the fast movers because they already had an area in their stores for merchandise pickup (usually for big, bulky items like TVs and appliances), and because long before the

FIGURE B5.14

E-Business Network Characteristics

E-Business Network Characteristics
■ Provide for the transparent exchange of information with suppliers, trading partners, and customers.
■ Reliably and securely exchange information internally and externally via the Internet or other networks.
■ Allow end-to-end integration and provide message delivery across multiple systems, in particular, databases, clients, and servers.
■ Respond to high demands with scalable processing power and networking capacity.
■ Serve as the integrator and transaction framework for both digital businesses and traditional brick-and-mortar businesses that want to leverage the Internet for any type of business.

Web they had systems and processes in place that facilitated the transfer of a sale from one store to another. Other retailers are partially integrated. Ann Taylor, Bed Bath & Beyond, Eddie Bauer, Linens 'n' Things, Macy's, REI, Target, The Gap, and others let customers return but not pick up online-ordered merchandise in stores. To take on the challenge of e-business integration, an organization needs a secure and reliable IT infrastructure for mission-critical systems (see Figure B5.14).[15]

A *virtual private network (VPN)* is a way to use the public telecommunication infrastructure (e.g., Internet) to provide secure access to an organization's network (see Figure B5.15). A *valued-added network (VAN)* is a private network, provided by a third party, for exchanging information through a high capacity connection. To date, organizations engaging in e-business have relied largely on VPNs, VANs, and other dedicated links handling electronic data interchange transactions. These traditional solutions are still deployed in the market and for many companies will likely hold a strategic role for years to come. However, conventional technologies present significant challenges:

■ By handling only limited kinds of business information, these contribute little to a reporting structure intended to provide a comprehensive view of business operations.

■ They offer little support for the real-time business process integration that will be essential in the digital marketplace.

■ Relatively expensive and complex to implement, conventional technologies make it difficult to expand or change networks in response to market shifts.[16]

FIGURE B5.15

Virtual Private Network Example

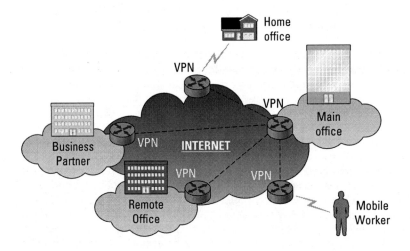

PLUG-IN SUMMARY

N etworks come in all sizes, from two computers connected to share a printer, to the Internet, which is the largest network of all, joining millions of computers of all types all over the world. In between are business networks, which vary in size from a dozen or fewer computers to many thousands. There are three primary types of networks: local area network (LAN), wide area network (WAN), and metropolitan area network (MAN). The following differentiate networks:

- Architecture—peer-to-peer, client/server.
- Topology—bus, star, ring, hybrid, wireless.
- Protocols—Ethernet, Transmission Control Protocol/Internet Protocol (TCP/IP).
- Media—coaxial, twisted-pair, fiber-optic.

 KEY TERMS

Client, 356
Client/server network, 356
Coaxial cable, 362
Ethernet, 357
Fiber optic (or optical fiber), 363
Interoperability, 357
Local area network (LAN), 355
Metropolitan area network (MAN), 355
Network, 354
Network operating system (NOS), 356

Network topology, 357
Network transmission media, 362
Packet-switching, 356
Peer-to-peer (P2P) network, 356
Protocol, 357
Router, 356
Server, 356
Telecommunication system, 354
Transmission Control Protocol/

Internet Protocol (TCP/IP), 359
Twisted-pair wiring, 362
Valued-added network (VAN), 364
Virtual private network (VPN), 364
Voice over Internet Protocol (VoIP), 360
Wide area network (WAN), 355
Wire media, 362
Wireless media, 363

 CLOSING CASE ONE

Watching Where You Step—Prada

Prada estimates its sales per year at $22 million. The luxury retailer recently spent millions on IT for its futuristic "epicenter" store—but the flashy technology turned into a high-priced hassle. The company needed to generate annual sales of $75 million by 2007 to turn a profit on its new high-tech investment.

When Prada opened its $40 million Manhattan flagship, hotshot architect Rem Koolhaas promised a radically new shopping experience. And he kept the promise—though not quite according to plan. Customers were soon enduring hordes of tourists, neglected technology, and the occasional thrill of getting stuck in experimental dressing rooms. A few of the problems associated with the store:

1. **Fickle fitting rooms**—Doors that turn from clear to opaque confuse shoppers and frequently fail to open on cue.
2. **Failed RFID**—Touch screens meant to spring to life when items are placed in the RFID "closets" are often just blank.
3. **Pointless PDAs**—Salesclerks let the handheld devices gather dust and instead check the stockroom for inventory.
4. **Neglected network**—A lag between sales and inventory systems makes the wireless network nearly irrelevant.

This was not exactly the vision for the high-end boutique when it debuted in December 2001. Instead, the 22,000-square-foot SoHo shop was to be the first of four "epicenter" stores around the world that would combine cutting-edge architecture and 21st century technology to revolutionize the luxury shopping experience. Prada poured roughly 25 percent of the store's budget into IT, including a wireless network to link every item to an Oracle inventory database in real-time using radio frequency identification (RFID) tags on the clothes. The staff would roam the floor armed with PDAs to check whether items were in stock, and customers could do the same through touch screens in the dressing rooms.

But most of the flashy technology today sits idle, abandoned by employees who never quite embraced computing chic and are now too overwhelmed by large crowds to assist shoppers with handhelds. On top of that, many gadgets, such as automated dressing-room doors and touch screens, are either malfunctioning or ignored. Packed with experimental technology, the clear-glass dressing-room doors were designed to open and close automatically at the tap of a foot pedal, then turn opaque when a second pedal sent an electric current through the glass. Inside, an RFID-aware rack would recognize a customer's selections and display them on a touch screen linked to the inventory system.

In practice, the process was hardly that smooth. Many shoppers never quite understood the pedals and disrobed in full view, thinking the door had turned opaque. That is no longer a problem, since staff members usually leave the glass opaque, but often the doors get stuck. Some of the chambers are open only to VIP customers during peak traffic times.

With the smart closets and handhelds out of commission, the wireless network in the store is nearly irrelevant, despite its considerable expense. As Prada's debt reportedly climbed to around $1 billion in late 2001, the company shelved plans for the fourth epicenter store, in San Francisco. A second store opened in Tokyo to great acclaim, albeit with different architects in a different market. Though that store incorporates similar cutting-edge concepts, architect Jacques Herzog emphasized that avant-garde retail plays well only in Japan. "This building is clearly a building for Tokyo," he told *The New York Times*. "It couldn't be somewhere else."

The multimillion-dollar technology is starting to look more like technology for technology's sake than an enhancement of the shopping experience, and the store's failings have prompted Prada to reevaluate its epicenter strategy.[17]

Questions

1. Explain how Prada was anticipating using its wireless network to help its stores operate more efficiently. What prevented the system from working correctly?
2. What could Prada have done to help its employees embrace the wireless network?
3. Would Prada have experienced the same issues if it had used a wire (guided) network instead of a wireless (unguided) network?
4. What security issues would Prada need to be aware of concerning its wireless network?
5. What should Prada do differently when designing its fourth store to ensure its success?

✳ CLOSING CASE TWO

Banks Banking on Network Security

Bank of America, Commerce Bancorp, PNC Financial Services Group, and Wachovia were victims of a crime involving a person trying to obtain customer data and sell it to law firms and debt-collection agencies. New Jersey police seized 13 computers from the alleged mastermind with 670,000 account numbers and balances. There is no indication the data were used for identity theft, but it highlights how increasingly difficult it is to protect information against such schemes as the market value of personal information grows. In the past, banks were wary of the cost or customer backlash from adopting network security technologies. Today, banks are beefing up network security as more customers begin to view security as a key factor when choosing a bank.

Bank of America

Bank of America is moving toward a stronger authentication process for its 13 million online customers. Bank of America's new SiteKey service is designed to thwart scams in which customers think they are entering data on the bank's Web site, when they are actually on a thief's site built to steal data. This occurs when a worm tells a computer to reroute the bank's URL into a browser to another site that looks exactly like the bank's.

SiteKey offers two-factor authentication. When enrolling in SiteKey, a customer picks an image from a library and writes a brief phrase. Each time the customer signs on, the image and phrase are displayed, indicating that the bank recognizes the computer the customer is using and letting the customer know that he or she is at the bank's official Web site. The customer then enters a password and proceeds. When signing on from a different computer than usual, the customer must answer one of three prearranged questions.

Wells Fargo & Company

"Out-of-wallet" questions contain information that is not found on a driver's license or ATM card. Wells Fargo is implementing a security strategy that operates based on "out-of-wallet" questions as a second factor for network password enrollment and maintenance. It is also offering network security hardware such as key fobs that change passwords every 60 seconds. Last fall, it launched a two-factor authentication pilot in which small businesses making electronic funds transfers need a key fob to complete transactions.

E-Trade Financial Corporation

E-Trade Financial Corporation provides customers holding account balances of more than $50,000 with a free Digital Security ID for network authentication. The device displays a new six-digit code every 60 seconds, which the customer must use to log on. Accounts under $50,000 can purchase the Digital Security ID device for $25.

Barclays Bank

Barclays Bank instituted online-transfer delays of between several hours and one day. The delays, which apply the first time a transfer is attempted between two accounts, are intended to give the bank time to detect suspicious activity, such as a large number of transfers from multiple accounts into a single account. The online-transfer delay was adopted in response to a wave of phishing incidents in which thieves transferred funds from victims' bank accounts into accounts owned by "mules." Mules are people who open bank accounts based on e-mail solicitations, usually under the guise of a business proposal. From the mule accounts, the thieves withdraw cash, open credit cards, or otherwise loot the account.

Barclays also offers account monitoring of customers' actions to compare them with historical profile data to detect unusual behavior. For instance, the service would alert the bank to contact the customer if the customer normally logs on from England and suddenly logs on from New York and performs 20 transactions.[18]

Questions

1. What reason would a bank have for not wanting to adopt an online-transfer delay policy?
2. Why is network security critical to financial institutions?

3. Explain the differences between the types of network security offered by the banks in the case. Which bank would you open an account with and why?

4. What additional types of network security, not mentioned in the case, would you recommend a bank implement?

5. Identity three policies a bank should implement to help it improve network information security.

✱ MAKING BUSINESS DECISIONS

1. Secure Access

Organizations that have traditionally maintained private, closed systems have begun to look at the potential of the Internet as a ready-made network resource. The Internet is inexpensive and globally pervasive: Every phone jack is a potential connection. However, the Internet lacks security. What obstacles must organizations overcome to allow secure network connections?

2. Rolling Out with Networks

As organizations begin to realize the benefits of adding a wireless component to their network, they must understand how to leverage this emerging technology. Wireless solutions have come to the forefront for many organizations with the rollout of more standard, cost-effective, and secure wireless protocols. With wireless networks, increased business agility may be realized by continuous data access and synchronization. However, with the increased flexibility comes many challenges. Develop a report detailing the benefits an organization could obtain by implementing wireless technology. Also, include the challenges that a wireless network presents along with recommendations for any solutions.

3. Wireless Fitness

Sandifer's Fitness Club is located in beautiful South Carolina. Rosie Sandifer has owned and operated the club for 20 years. The club has three outdoor pools, two indoor pools, 10 racquetball courts, 10 tennis courts, an indoor and outdoor track, along with a four-story exercise equipment and massage therapy building. Rosie has hired you as a summer intern specializing in information technology. The extent of Rosie's current technology includes a few PCs in the accounting department and two PCs with Internet access for the rest of the staff. Your first assignment is to create a report detailing networks and wireless technologies. The report should explain how the club could gain a business advantage by implementing a wireless network. If Rosie likes your report, she will hire you as the full-time employee in charge of information technology. Be sure to include all of the different uses for wireless devices the club could implement to improve its operations.

PLUG-IN

B6

Information Security

Introduction

The core units introduced *information security,* which is a broad term encompassing the protection of information from accidental or intentional misuse by persons inside or outside an organization. With current advances in technologies and business strategies such as CRM, organizations are able to determine valuable information such as who are the top 20 percent of the customers that produce 80 percent of all revenues. Most organizations view this type of information as valuable intellectual capital, and they are implementing security measures to prevent the information from walking out the door or falling into the wrong hands. This plug-in discusses how an organization can implement information security lines of defense through people first and through technology second.

The First Line of Defense—People

Adding to the complexity of information security is the fact that organizations must enable employees, customers, and partners to access information electronically to be successful in this electronic world. Doing business electronically automatically creates tremendous information security risks for organizations. Surprisingly, the biggest issue surrounding information security is not a technical issue, but a people issue.

The CSI/FBI Computer Crime and Security Survey reported that 38 percent of respondents indicated security incidents originated within the enterprise. *Insiders* are legitimate users who purposely or accidentally misuse their access to the environment and cause some kind of business-affecting incident. Most information security breaches result from people misusing an organization's information either advertently or inadvertently. For example, many individuals freely give up their passwords or write them on sticky notes next to their computers, leaving the door wide open to intruders.[1]

The director of information security at a large health care company discovered how easy it was to create an information security breach when she hired outside auditors to test her company's security awareness. In one instance, auditors found that staff members testing a new system had accidentally exposed the network to outside hackers. In another, auditors were able to obtain the passwords of 16 employees when the auditors posed as support staff; hackers frequently use such "social engineering" to obtain passwords. **Social engineering** is using one's social skills to trick people into revealing access credentials or other information valuable to the attacker. Dumpster diving, or looking through people's trash, is another way social engineering hackers obtain information.[2]

Information security policies identify the rules required to maintain information security. An **information security plan** details how an organization will implement the information security policies. Figure B6.1 is an example of the University of Denver's Information Security Plan.

FIGURE B6.1

Sample Information Security Plan

Interim Information Security Plan

This Information Security Plan ("Plan") describes the University of Denver's safeguards to protect information and data in compliance ("Protected Information") with the Financial Services Modernization Act of 1999, also known as the Gramm Leach Bliley Act, 15 U.S.C. Section 6801. These safeguards are provided to:

- Ensure the security and confidentiality of Protected Information;
- Protect against anticipated threats or hazards to the security or integrity of such information; and
- Protect against unauthorized access to or use of Protected Information that could result in substantial harm or inconvenience to any customer.

This Information Security Plan also provides for mechanisms to:

- Identify and assess the risks that may threaten Protected Information maintained by the University of Denver;
- Develop written policies and procedures to manage and control these risks;
- Implement and review the plan; and
- Adjust the plan to reflect changes in technology, the sensitivity of covered data and information and internal or external threats to information security.

Identification and Assessment of Risks to Customer Information

The University of Denver recognizes that it has both internal and external risks. These risks include, but are not limited to:

- Unauthorized access of Protected Information by someone other than the owner of the covered data and information
- Compromised system security as a result of system access by an unauthorized person
- Interception of data during transmission
- Loss of data integrity
- Physical loss of data in a disaster
- Errors introduced into the system
- Corruption of data or systems
- Unauthorized access of covered data and information by employees
- Unauthorized requests for covered data and information
- Unauthorized access through hardcopy files or reports
- Unauthorized transfer of covered data and information through third parties

The University of Denver recognizes that this may not be a complete list of the risks associated with the protection of Protected Information. Since technology growth is not static, new risks are created regularly. Accordingly, the Information Technology Department and the Office of Student Affairs will actively participate with and seek advice from an advisory committee made up of university representatives for identification of new risks. The University of Denver believes current safeguards used by the Information Technology Department are reasonable and, in light of current risk assessments, are sufficient to provide security and confidentiality to Protected Information maintained by the University.

(Continued)

Interim Information Security Plan

Information Security Plan Coordinators

The University CIO and the Vice President for Student Affairs, in consultation with an advisory committee, have been appointed as the coordinators of this Plan. They are responsible for assessing the risks associated with unauthorized transfers of covered data and information and implementing procedures to minimize those risks to the University of Denver.

Design and Implementation of Safeguards Program

Employee Management and Training

During employee orientation, each new employee in departments that handle Protected Information will receive proper training on the importance of confidentiality of Protected Information.

Physical Security

The University of Denver has addressed the physical security of Protected Information by limiting access to only those employees who have a business reason to know such information.

Information Systems

The University of Denver has policies governing the use of electronic resources and firewall and wireless policies. The University of Denver will take reasonable and appropriate steps consistent with current technological developments to make sure that all Protected Information is secure and to safeguard the integrity of records in storage and transmission. The University of Denver will develop a plan to ensure that all electronic Protected Information is encrypted in transit.

Selection of Appropriate Service Providers

Due to the specialized expertise needed to design, implement, and service new technologies, vendors may be needed to provide resources that the University of Denver determines not to provide on its own. In the process of choosing a service provider that will maintain or regularly access Protected Information, the evaluation process shall include the ability of the service provider to safeguard Protected Information. Contracts with service providers may include the following provisions:

- A stipulation that the Protected Information will be held in strict confidence and accessed only for the explicit business purpose of the contract;
- An assurance from the contract partner that the partner will protect the Protected Information it receives.

Continuing Evaluation and Adjustment

This Information Security Plan will be subject to periodic review and adjustment, especially when due to the constantly changing technology and evolving risks. The Coordinators, in consultation with the Office of General Counsel, will review the standards set forth in this policy and recommend updates and revisions as necessary. It may be necessary to adjust the plan to reflect changes in technology, the sensitivity of student/customer data and internal or external threats to information security.

FIGURE B6.1

(Continued)

The first line of defense an organization should follow is to create an information security plan detailing the various information security policies. A detailed information security plan can alleviate people-based information security issues. Figure B6.2 displays the five steps for creating an information security plan. Figure B6.3 provides the top 10 questions from Ernst & Young that managers should ask to ensure their information is secure.

The Second Line of Defense—Technology

Arkansas State University (ASU) recently completed a major network upgrade that brought gigabit-speed network capacity to every dorm room and office on its campus. The university was concerned that the new network would be a tempting playground for hackers. To reduce its fear the university decided to install intrusion detection software (IDS) from Cisco Systems to stay on top of security and potential network abuses. Whenever the IDS spots a potential security threat, such as a virus or a hacker, it alerts the central management system. The system automatically pages the IT staff, who deal with the attack by shutting off access to the system, identifying the hacker's location, and calling campus security.[3]

Five Steps for Creating an Information Security Plan	
1. Develop the information security policies	Identify who is responsible and accountable for designing and implementing the organization's information security policies. Simple, yet highly effective types of information security policies include requiring users to log off of their systems before leaving for lunches or meetings, never sharing passwords with anyone, and changing personal passwords every 60 days. The chief security officer (CSO) will typically be responsible for designing these information security policies.
2. Communicate the information security policies	Train all employees on the policies and establish clear expectations for following the policies. For example, let all employees know that they will receive a formal reprimand for leaving a computer unsecured.
3. Identify critical information assets and risks	Require the use of user IDs, passwords, and antivirus software on all systems. Ensure any systems that contain links to external networks have the appropriate technical protections such as firewalls or intrusion detection software. A *firewall* is hardware and/or software that guards a private network by analyzing the information leaving and entering the network. *Intrusion detection software (IDS)* searches out patterns in information and network traffic to indicate attacks and quickly responds to prevent any harm.
4. Test and reevaluate risks	Continually perform security reviews, audits, background checks, and security assessments.
5. Obtain stakeholder support	Gain the approval and support of the information security polices from the board of directors and all stakeholders.

Once an organization has protected its intellectual capital by arming its people with a detailed information security plan, it can begin to focus its efforts on deploying the right types of information security technologies such as the IDS installed at Arkansas State.

Organizations can deploy numerous technologies to prevent information security breaches. When determining which types of technologies to invest in, it helps to understand the three primary information security areas:

1. Authentication and authorization.

2. Prevention and resistance.

3. Detection and response.[4]

FIGURE B6.2

Creating an Information Security Plan

Top 10 Questions Managers Should Ask Regarding Information Security
1. Does the board of directors recognize information security is a board-level issue that cannot be left to the IT department alone?
2. Is there clear accountability for information security in the organization?
3. Do the board members articulate an agreed-upon set of threats and critical assets? How often do they review and update these?
4. How much is spent on information security and what is it being spent on?
5. What is the impact on the organization of a serious security incident?
6. Does the organization view information security as an enabler? (For example, by implementing effective security, could the organization increase business over the Internet?)
7. What is the risk to the business of getting a reputation for low information security?
8. What steps have been taken to ensure that third parties will not compromise the security of the organization?
9. How does the organization obtain independent assurance that information security is managed effectively?
10. How does the organization measure the effectiveness of its information security activities?

FIGURE B6.3

Top 10 Questions Managers Should Ask Regarding Information Security

AUTHENTICATION AND AUTHORIZATION

Authentication is a method for confirming users' identities. Once a system determines the authentication of a user, it can then determine the access privileges (or authorization) for that user. *Authorization* is the process of giving someone permission to do or have something. In multiple-user computer systems, user access or authorization determines such things as file access, hours of access, and amount of allocated storage space. Authentication and authorization techniques are broken down into three categories, and the most secure type involves a combination of all three:

1. Something the user knows such as a user ID and password.

2. Something the user has such as a smart card or token.

3. Something that is part of the user such as a fingerprint or voice signature.

Something the User Knows such as a User ID and Password

The first type of authentication, using something the user knows, is the most common way to identify individual users and typically consists of a unique user ID and password. However, this is actually one of the most *ineffective* ways for determining authentication because passwords are not secure. All it typically takes to crack a password is enough time. More than 50 percent of help-desk calls are password related, which can cost an organization significant money, and passwords are vulnerable to being coaxed out of somebody by a social engineer.

Identity theft is the forging of someone's identity for the purpose of fraud. The fraud is often financial fraud, to apply for and use credit cards in the victim's name or to apply for a loan. Figure B6.4 displays several examples of identity theft.

Phishing is a common way to steal identities online. *Phishing* is a technique to gain personal information for the purpose of identity theft, usually by means of fraudulent e-mail. One way to accomplish phishing is to send out e-mail messages that look as though they came from legitimate businesses such as AOL, MSN, or Amazon. The messages appear to be genuine with official-looking formats and logos. These e-mails typically ask for verification of important information like passwords and account numbers. The reason given is often that this personal

FIGURE B6.4

Examples of Identity Theft

Identity Theft Examples
An 82-year-old woman in Fort Worth, Texas, discovered that her identity had been stolen when the woman using her name was involved in a four-car collision. For 18 months, she kept getting notices of lawsuits and overdue medical bills that were really meant for someone else. It took seven years for her to get her financial good name restored after the identity thief charged over $100,000 on her 12 fraudulently acquired credit cards.
A 42-year-old retired Army captain in Rocky Hill, Connecticut, found that an identity thief had spent $260,000 buying goods and services that included two trucks, a Harley-Davidson motorcycle, and a time-share vacation home in South Carolina. The victim discovered his problem only when his retirement pay was garnished to pay the outstanding bills.
In New York, members of a pickpocket ring forged the driver's licenses of their victims within hours of snatching the women's purses. Stealing a purse typically results in around $200, if not less. But stealing the person's identity can net on average between $4,000 and $10,000.
A crime gang took out $8 million worth of second mortgages on victims' homes. It turned out the source of all the instances of identity theft came from a car dealership.
The largest identity-theft scam to date in U.S. history was broken up by police in 2002 when they discovered that three men had downloaded credit reports using stolen passwords and sold them to criminals on the street for $60 each. Many millions of dollars were stolen from people in all 50 states.

information is required for accounting or auditing purposes. Since the e-mails look authentic, up to one in five recipients respond with the information, and subsequently become victim of identity theft and other fraud. [5]

Something the User Has such as a Smart Card or Token

The second type of authentication, using something that the user has, offers a much more effective way to identify individuals than a user ID and password. Tokens and smart cards are two of the primary forms of this type of authentication. *Tokens* are small electronic devices that change user passwords automatically. The user enters his/her user ID and token displayed password to gain access to the network. A *smart card* is a device that is around the same size as a credit card, containing embedded technologies that can store information and small amounts of software to perform some limited processing. Smart cards can act as identification instruments, a form of digital cash, or a data storage device with the ability to store an entire medical record.

Something That Is Part of the User such as a Fingerprint or Voice Signature

The third kind of authentication, using something that is part of the user, is by far the best and most effective way to manage authentication. *Biometrics* (narrowly defined) is the identification of a user based on a physical characteristic, such as a fingerprint, iris, face, voice, or handwriting. Unfortunately, biometric authentication can be costly and intrusive. For example, iris scans are expensive and considered intrusive by most people. Fingerprint authentication is less intrusive and inexpensive but is also not 100 percent accurate.

PREVENTION AND RESISTANCE

Prevention and resistance technologies stop intruders from accessing intellectual capital. A division of Sony Inc., Sony Pictures Entertainment (SPE), defends itself from attacks by using an intrusion detection system to detect new attacks as they occur. SPE develops and distributes a wide variety of products including movies, television, videos, and DVDs. A compromise to SPE security could result in costing the company valuable intellectual capital as well as millions of dollars and months of time. The company needed an advanced threat management solution that would take fewer resources to maintain and require limited resources to track and respond to suspicious network activity. The company installed an advanced intrusion detection system allowing it to monitor all of its network activity including any potential security breaches.[6]

The cost of downtime or network operation failures can be devastating to any business. For example, eBay experienced a 22-hour outage that caused the company's market cap to plunge an incredible $5.7 billion. Downtime costs for businesses can vary from $100 to $1 million per hour. An organization must prepare for and anticipate these types of outages resulting most commonly from hackers and viruses. Technologies available to help prevent and build resistance to attacks include (1) content filtering, (2) encryption, and (3) firewalls.[7]

Content Filtering

Content filtering occurs when organizations use software that filters content to prevent the transmission of unauthorized information. Organizations can use content filtering technologies to filter e-mail and prevent e-mails containing sensitive information from transmitting, whether the transmission was malicious or accidental. It can also filter e-mails and prevent any suspicious files from transmitting such as potential virus-infected files. E-mail content filtering can also filter for *spam,* a form of unsolicited e-mail. Organizational losses from spam were estimated to be about $198 billion in 2007 (see Figure B6.5).[8]

FIGURE B6.5

Corporate Losses Caused by Spam Worldwide (2003 and 2007 in billions)

2003 $20.5
2007 $198

Encryption

Encryption scrambles information into an alternative form that requires a key or password to decrypt the information. If there is an information security breach and the information was encrypted, the person stealing the information will be unable to read it. Encryption can switch the order of characters, replace characters with other characters, insert or remove characters, or use a mathematical formula to convert the information into some sort of code. Companies that transmit sensitive customer information over the Internet, such as credit card numbers, frequently use encryption.

Some encryption technologies use multiple keys like public key encryption. *Public key encryption (PKE)* is an encryption system that uses two keys: a public key that everyone can have and a private key for only the recipient (see Figure B6.6). When implementing security using multiple keys, the organization provides the public key to all of its customers (end consumers and other businesses). The customers use the public key to encrypt their information and send it along the Internet. When it arrives at its destination, the organization would use the private key to unscramble the encrypted information.

Firewalls

One of the most common defenses for preventing a security breach is a firewall. A *firewall* is hardware and/or software that guards a private network by analyzing the information leaving and entering the network. Firewalls examine each message that wants entrance to the network. Unless the message has the correct markings, the firewall prevents it from entering the network. Firewalls can even detect computers communicating with the Internet without approval. As Figure B6.7 illustrates, organizations typically place a firewall between a server and the Internet.

DETECTION AND RESPONSE

The final area where organizations can allocate resources is in detection and response technologies. If prevention and resistance strategies fail and there is a

FIGURE B6.6

Public Key Encryption (PKE) System

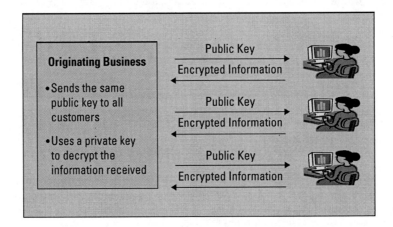

Originating Business

- Sends the same public key to all customers

- Uses a private key to decrypt the information received

Public Key
Encrypted Information

Public Key
Encrypted Information

Public Key
Encrypted Information

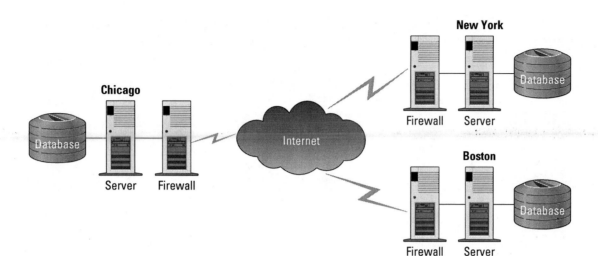

FIGURE B6.7

Sample Firewall
Architecture Connecting
Systems Located in
Chicago, New York, and
Boston

security breach, an organization can use detection and response technologies to mitigate the damage. The most common type of defense within detection and response technologies is antivirus software.

A single worm can cause massive damage. The "Blaster worm" infected over 50,000 computers worldwide. Jeffrey Lee Parson, 18, was arrested by U.S. cyber investigators for unleashing the damaging worm on the Internet. The worm replicated itself repeatedly, eating up computer capacity, but did not damage information or programs. The worm generated so much traffic that it brought entire networks down.

The FBI used the latest technologies and code analysis to find the source of the worm. Prosecutors said Microsoft suffered financial losses that significantly exceeded $5,000, the statutory threshold in most hacker cases. Parson, charged with intentionally causing or attempting to cause damage to a computer, was sentenced to 18 months in prison, three years of supervised release, and 100 hours of community service. "What you've done is a terrible thing. Aside from injuring people and their computers, you shook the foundation of technology," U.S. District Judge Marsha Pechman told Parson.

"With this arrest, we want to deliver a message to cyber-hackers here and around the world," said U.S. Attorney John McKay in Seattle. "Let there be no mistake about it, cyber-hacking is a crime. We will investigate, arrest, and prosecute cyber-hackers."[9]

Typically, people equate viruses (the malicious software) with hackers (the people). While not all types of hackers create viruses, many do. Figure B6.8 provides an overview of the most common types of hackers and viruses.

Some of the most damaging forms of security threats to e-business sites include malicious code, hoaxes, spoofing, and sniffers (see Figure B6.9).

Hackers—people very knowledgeable about computers who use their knowledge to invade other people's computers.

- **White-hat hackers**—work at the request of the system owners to find system vulnerabilities and plug the holes.
- **Black-hat hackers**—break into other people's computer systems and may just look around or may steal and destroy information.
- **Hactivists**—have philosophical and political reasons for breaking into systems and will often deface the Web site as a protest.
- **Script kiddies** or **script bunnies**—find hacking code on the Internet and click-and-point their way into systems to cause damage or spread viruses.
- **Cracker**—a hacker with criminal intent.
- **Cyberterrorists**—seek to cause harm to people or to destroy critical systems or information and use the Internet as a weapon of mass destruction.

Viruses—software written with malicious intent to cause annoyance or damage.

- **Worm**—a type of virus that spreads itself, not only from file to file, but also from computer to computer. The primary difference between a virus and a worm is that a virus must attach to something, such as an executable file, in order to spread. Worms do not need to attach to anything to spread and can tunnel themselves into computers.
- **Denial-of-service attack (DoS)**—floods a Web site with so many requests for service that it slows down or crashes the site.
- **Distributed denial-of-service attack (DDoS)**—attacks from multiple computers that flood a Web site with so many requests for service that it slows down or crashes. A common type is the Ping of Death, in which thousands of computers try to access a Web site at the same time, overloading it and shutting it down.
- **Trojan-horse virus**—hides inside other software, usually as an attachment or a downloadable file.
- **Backdoor programs**—viruses that open a way into the network for future attacks.
- **Polymorphic viruses and worms**—change their form as they propagate.

FIGURE B6.8

Hackers and Viruses

FIGURE B6.9

Security Threats to E-Business

Security Threats to E-Business
Elevation of privilege is a process by which a user misleads a system into granting unauthorized rights, usually for the purpose of compromising or destroying the system. For example, an attacker might log on to a network by using a guest account, and then exploit a weakness in the software that lets the attacker change the guest privileges to administrative privileges.
Hoaxes attack computer systems by transmitting a virus hoax, with a real virus attached. By masking the attack in a seemingly legitimate message, unsuspecting users more readily distribute the message and send the attack on to their co-workers and friends, infecting many users along the way.
Malicious code includes a variety of threats such as viruses, worms, and Trojan horses.
Spoofing is the forging of the return address on an e-mail so that the e-mail message appears to come from someone other than the actual sender. This is not a virus but rather a way by which virus authors conceal their identities as they send out viruses.
Spyware is software that comes hidden in free downloadable software and tracks online movements, mines the information stored on a computer, or uses a computer's CPU and storage for some task the user knows nothing about. According to the National Cyber Security Alliance, 91 percent of the study had spyware on their computers that can cause extremely slow performance, excessive pop-up ads, or hijacked home pages.
A **sniffer** is a program or device that can monitor data traveling over a network. Sniffers can show all the data being transmitted over a network, including passwords and sensitive information. Sniffers tend to be a favorite weapon in the hacker's arsenal.
Packet tampering consists of altering the contents of packets as they travel over the Internet or altering data on computer disks after penetrating a network. For example, an attacker might place a tap on a network line to intercept packets as they leave the computer. The attacker could eavesdrop or alter the information as it leaves the network.

PLUG-IN SUMMARY

Implementing information security lines of defense through people first and through technology second is the best way for an organization to protect its vital intellectual capital. The first line of defense is securing intellectual capital by creating an information security plan detailing the various information security policies. The second line of defense is investing in technology to help secure information through authentication and authorization, prevention and resistance, and detection and response.

KEY TERMS

Authentication, 374
Authorization, 374
Backdoor program, 378
Biometrics, 375
Black-hat hacker, 378
Content filtering, 375
Cracker, 378
Cyberterrorist, 378
Denial-of-service attack (DoS), 378
Distributed denial-of-service attack (DDoS), 378
Encryption, 376
Elevation of privilege, 378
Firewall, 373, 376

Hacker, 378
Hactivist, 378
Hoaxes, 378
Identify theft, 374
Information security, 370
Information security plan, 371
Information security policy, 371
Insider, 370
Intrusion detection software (IDS), 373
Malicious code, 378
Packet tampering, 378
Phishing, 374
Polymorphic virus and worm, 378

Public key encryption (PKE), 376
Script kiddies or script bunnies, 378
Smart card, 375
Sniffer, 378
Social engineering, 371
Spam, 375
Spoofing, 378
Spyware, 378
Token, 375
Trojan-horse virus, 378
Virus, 378
White-hat hacker, 378
Worm, 378

CLOSING CASE ONE

Thinking Like the Enemy

David and Barry Kaufman, the founders of the Intense School, recently added several security courses, including the five-day "Professional Hacking Boot Camp" and "Social Engineering in Two Days."

Information technology departments must know how to protect organizational information. Therefore, organizations must teach their IT personnel how to protect their systems, especially in light of the many new government regulations, such as the Health Insurance Portability and Accountability Act (HIPAA), that demand secure systems. The concept of sending IT professionals to a hacking school seems counterintuitive; it is somewhat similar to sending accountants to an Embezzling 101 course. The Intense School does not strive to breed the next generation of hackers, however, but to teach its students how to be "ethical" hackers: to use their skills to build better locks, and to understand the minds of those who would attempt to crack them.

The main philosophy of the security courses at the Intense School is simply "To know thy enemy." In fact, one of the teachers at the Intense School is none other than Kevin Mitnick, the famous hacker who was imprisoned from 1995 to 2000. Teaching security from the hacker's perspective, as Mitnick does, is more difficult than teaching hacking itself: A hacker just needs to know one way into a system, David Kaufman notes, but a security professional needs to know *all* of the system's vulnerabilities. The two courses analyze those vulnerabilities from different perspectives.

The hacking course, which costs $3,500, teaches ways to protect against the mischief typically associated with hackers: worming through computer systems through vulnerabilities that are susceptible to technical, or computer-based, attacks. Mitnick's $1,950 social engineering course, by contrast, teaches the more frightening art of worming through the vulnerabilities of the people using and maintaining systems—getting passwords and access through duplicity, not technology. People that take this class, or read Mitnick's book, *The Art of Deception,* never again think of passwords or the trash bin the same way.

So how does the Intense School teach hacking? With sessions on dumpster diving (the unsavory practice of looking for passwords and other bits of information on discarded papers), with field trips to case target systems, and with practice runs at the company's in-house "target range," a network of computers set up to thwart and educate students.

One feature of the Intense School that raises a few questions is that the school does not check on morals at the door: Anyone paying the tuition can attend the school. Given the potential danger that an unchecked graduate of a hacking school could represent, it is surprising that the FBI does not collect the names of the graduates. But perhaps it gets them anyhow—several governmental agencies have sent students to the school.[10]

Questions

1. How could an organization benefit from attending one of the courses offered at the Intense School?

2. What are the two primary lines of security defense and how can organizational employees use the information taught by the Intense School when drafting an information security plan?

3. Determine the differences between the two primary courses offered at the Intense School, "Professional Hacking Boot Camp" and "Social Engineering in Two Days." Which course is more important for organizational employees to attend?

4. If your employer sent you to take a course at the Intense School, which one would you choose and why?

5. What are the ethical dilemmas involved with having such a course offered by a private company?

 CLOSING CASE TWO

Hacker Hunters

Hacker hunters are the new breed of crime-fighter. They employ the same methodology used to fight organized crime in the 1980s—informants and the cyberworld equivalent of wiretaps. Daniel Larking, a 20-year veteran who runs the FBI's Internet Crime Complaint Center, taps online service providers to help track down criminal hackers. Leads supplied by the FBI and eBay helped Romanian police round up 11 members of a gang that set up fake eBay accounts and auctioned off cell phones, laptops, and cameras they never intended to deliver.

On October 26, 2004, the FBI unleashed Operation Firewall, targeting the ShadowCrew, a gang whose members were schooled in identity theft, bank account pillage, and selling illegal goods on the Internet. ShadowCrew's 4,000 gang members lived in a dozen countries and across the United States. For months, agents had been watching their every move through a clandestine gateway into their Web site, shadowcrew.com. One member turned informant called a group meeting, ensuring the members would be at home on their computers during a certain time. At 9 p.m. the Secret Service issued orders to move in on the gang. The move was synchronized around the globe to prevent gang members from warning each other via instant messages. Twenty-eight gang members in eight states and six countries were arrested, most still at their computers. Authorities seized dozens of computers and found 1.7 million credit card numbers and more than 18 million e-mail accounts.

ShadowCrew's Operations

The alleged ringleaders of ShadowCrew included Andres Mantovani, 23, a part-time community college student in Arizona, and David Appleyard, 45, a former New Jersey mortgage broker. Mantovani and Appleyard allegedly were administrators in charge of running the Web site and recruiting members. The site created a marketplace for over 4,000 gang members who bought and sold hot information and merchandise. The Web site was open for business 24 hours a day, but since most of the members held jobs, the busiest time was from 10 p.m. to 2 a.m. on Sundays. Hundreds of gang members would meet online to trade credit card information, passports, and even equipment to make fake identity documents. Platinum credit cards cost more than gold ones and discounts were offered for package deals. One member known as "Scarface" sold 115,695 stolen credit card numbers in a single trade. Overall, the gang made more than $4 million in credit card purchases over two years. ShadowCrew was equivalent to an eBay for the underworld. The site even posted crime tips on how to use stolen credit cards and fake IDs at big retailers.

The gang stole credit card numbers and other valuable information through clever tricks. One of the favorites was sending millions of phishing e-mails—messages that appeared to be from legitimate companies such as Yahoo!— designed to steal passwords and credit card numbers. The gang also hacked into corporate databases to steal account data. According to sources familiar with the investigation, the gang cracked the networks of 12 unidentified companies that were not even aware their systems had been breached.

Police Operations

Brian Nagel, an assistant director at the Secret Service, coordinated the effort to track the ShadowCrew. Allies included Britain's National High-Tech Crimes unit, the Royal Canadian Mounted Police, and the Bulgarian Interior Ministry. Authorities turned one of the high-ranking members of the gang into a snitch and had the man help the Secret Service set up a new electronic doorway for ShadowCrew members to enter their Web site. The snitch spread the word that the new gateway was a more secure way to the Web site. It was the first-ever tap of a private computer network. "We became shadowcrew.com," Nagel said. [11]

Questions

1. What types of technology could big retailers use to prevent identity thieves from purchasing merchandise?
2. What can organizations do to protect themselves from hackers looking to steal account data?
3. Authorities frequently tap online service providers to track down hackers. Do you think it is ethical for authorities to tap an online service provider and read people's e-mail? Why or why not?
4. Do you think it was ethical for authorities to use one of the high-ranking officials to trap other gang members? Why or why not?
5. In a team, research the Internet and find the best ways to protect yourself from identity theft.

✳ MAKING BUSINESS DECISIONS

1. Firewall Decisions

You are the CEO of Inverness Investments, a medium-sized venture capital firm that specializes in investing in high-tech companies. The company receives over 30,000 e-mail messages per year. On average, there are two viruses and three successful hackings against the company each year, which result in losses to the company of about $250,000. Currently, the company has antivirus software installed but does not have any firewalls.

Your CIO is suggesting implementing 10 firewalls for a total cost of $80,000. The estimated life of each firewall is about three years. The chances of hackers breaking into the system with the firewalls installed are about 3 percent. Annual maintenance costs on the firewalls is estimated around $15,000. Create an argument for or against supporting your CIO's recommendation to purchase the firewalls.

2. Drafting an Information Security Plan

Making The Grade is a nonprofit organization that helps students learn how to achieve better grades in school. The organization has 40 offices in 25 states and over 2,000 employees. The company is currently building a Web site to offer its services online. You have recently been hired by the CIO as the director of information security. Your first assignment is to develop a document discussing the importance of creating information security policies and an information security plan. Be sure to include the following:

- The importance of educating employees on information security.
- A few samples of employee information security policies.
- Other major areas the information security plan should address.
- Signs the company should look for to determine if the new site is being hacked.
- The major types of attacks the company should expect to experience.

3. Discussing the Three Areas of Security

Great Granola Inc. is a small business operating out of northern California. The company specializes in selling unique homemade granola, and its primary sales vehicle is through its Web site. The company is growing exponentially and expects its revenues to triple this year to $12 million. The company also expects to hire 60 additional employees to support its growing number of customers. Joan Martin, the CEO, is aware that if her competitors discover the recipe for her granola, or who her primary customers are, it could easily ruin her business. Joan has hired you to draft a document discussing the different areas of information security, along with your recommendations for providing a secure e-business environment.

4. College Security

Computer and online security is a growing concern for businesses of all sizes. Computer security issues range from viruses to automated Internet attacks to outright theft, the result of which is lost information and lost time. Security issues pop up in news articles daily, and most business owners understand the need to secure their businesses. Your college is no different from any other business when it comes to information security. Draft a document identifying the questions you should ask your college's CIO to ensure information security across your campus.

PLUG-IN

B7

Ethics

1. Summarize the guidelines for creating an information privacy policy.
2. Identify the differences between an ethical computer use policy and an acceptable use policy.
3. Describe the relationship between an e-mail privacy policy and an Internet use policy.
4. Explain the effects of spam on an organization.
5. Summarize the different monitoring technologies and explain the importance of an employee monitoring policy.

Introduction

The core units introduced *ethics,* which are the principles and standards that guide our behavior toward other people. Technology has created many new ethical dilemmas in our electronic society. The following are a few important concepts and terms related to ethical issues stemming from advances in technology:

- *Intellectual property*—intangible creative work that is embodied in physical form.
- *Copyright*—the legal protection afforded an expression of an idea, such as a song, video game, and some types of proprietary documents.
- *Fair use doctrine*—in certain situations, it is legal to use copyrighted material.
- *Pirated software*—the unauthorized use, duplication, distribution, or sale of copyrighted software.
- *Counterfeit software*—software that is manufactured to look like the real thing and sold as such.

The core units also introduced *privacy,* which is the right to be left alone when you want to be, to have control over your own personal possessions, and not to be observed without your consent. Privacy is related to *confidentiality,* which is the assurance that messages and information are available only to those who are authorized to view them. This plug-in takes a detailed look at *ePolicies*—policies and procedures that address the ethical use of computers and Internet usage in the business environment. These ePolicies typically address information privacy and confidentiality issues and include the following:

- Ethical computer use policy.
- Information privacy policy.
- Acceptable use policy.
- E-mail privacy policy.
- Internet use policy.
- Anti-spam policy.

Ethics

Individuals form the only ethical component of an IT system. They determine how they use IT, and how they are affected by IT. How individuals behave toward each other, how they handle information and technology, are largely influenced by their ethics. Ethical dilemmas usually arise not in simple, clear-cut situations but out of a clash between competing goals, responsibilities, and loyalties. Ethical decisions are complex judgments that balance rewards against responsibilities. Inevitably, the decision process is influenced by uncertainty about the magnitude of the outcome, by the estimate of the importance of the situation, by the perception of conflicting "right reactions," when there is more than one socially acceptable "correct" decision. Figure B7.1 contains examples of ethically questionable or unacceptable uses of information technology.

People make arguments for or against—justify or condemn—the behaviors in Figure B7.1. Unfortunately, there are few hard and fast rules for always determining what is and is not ethical. Knowing the law will not always help because what is legal might not always be ethical, and what might be ethical is not always legal. For example, Joe Reidenberg received an offer for cell phone service from AT&T Wireless. The offer revealed that AT&T Wireless had used Equifax, a credit reporting agency, to identify Joe Reidenberg as a potential customer. Overall, this strategy seemed like good business. Equifax could generate additional revenue by selling information it already owned and AT&T Wireless could identify target markets, thereby increasing response rates to its marketing campaigns. Unfortunately, by law, credit information cannot be used to sell anything. The Fair Credit Reporting Act (FCRA) forbids repurposing credit information except when the information is used for "a firm offer of credit or insurance." In other words, the only product that can be sold based on credit information is credit. A spokesman for Equifax stated that "as long as AT&T Wireless (or any company for that matter) is offering the cell

Examples of Questionable Information Technology Use
Individuals copy, use, and distribute software.
Employees search organizational databases for sensitive corporate and personal information.
Organizations collect, buy, and use information without checking the validity or accuracy of the information.
Individuals create and spread viruses that cause trouble for those using and maintaining IT systems.
Individuals hack into computer systems to steal proprietary information.
Employees destroy or steal proprietary organization information such as schematics, sketches, customer lists, and reports.

FIGURE B7.1

Ethically Questionable or Unacceptable Information Technology Use

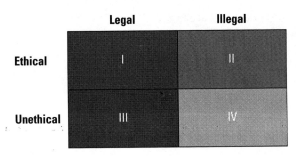

FIGURE B7.2

Acting Ethically and
Legally Are Not Always
the Same

phone service on a credit basis, such as allowing the use of the service before the consumer has to pay, it is in compliance with the FCRA."[1] But is it ethical?

This is a good example of the ethical dilemmas facing many organizations today; because technology is so new and pervasive in unexpected ways, the ethics surrounding information have not been all worked out. Figure B7.2 displays the four quadrants of ethical and legal behavior. The ideal goal for organizations is to make decisions within quadrant I that are both legal and ethical.

INFORMATION HAS NO ETHICS

Jerry Rode, CIO of Saab Cars USA, realized he had a public relations fiasco on his hands when he received an e-mail from an irate customer. Saab had hired four Internet marketing companies to distribute electronic information about Saab's new models to its customers. Saab specified that the marketing campaign be *opt-in,* implying that it would contact only the people who had agreed to receive promotions and marketing material via e-mail. Unfortunately, one of the marketing companies apparently had a different definition of opt-in and was e-mailing all customers regardless of their opt-in decision.

Rode fired the errant marketing company and immediately developed a formal policy for the use of customer information. "The customer doesn't see ad agencies and contracted marketing firms. They see Saab USA spamming them," Rode said. "Finger-pointing after the fact won't make your customers feel better."[2]

Information has no ethics. Information does not care how it is used. It will not stop itself from spamming customers, sharing itself if it is sensitive or personal, or revealing details to third parties. Information cannot delete or preserve itself. Therefore, it falls on the shoulders of those who lord over the information to develop ethical guidelines on how to manage it. Figure B7.3 provides an overview of some of the important laws that individuals must follow when they are attempting to manage and protect information.[3]

FIGURE B7.3

Established Information-
Related Laws

Established Information-Related Laws	
Privacy Act—1974	Restricts what information the federal government can collect; allows people to access and correct information on themselves; requires procedures to protect the security of personal information; and forbids the disclosure of name-linked information without permission.
Family Education Rights and Privacy Act—1974	Regulates access to personal education records by government agencies and other third parties and ensures the right of students to see their own records.
Cable Communications Act—1984	Requires written or electronic consent from viewers before cable TV providers can release viewing choices or other personally identifiable information.
Electronic Communications Privacy Act—1986	Allows the reading of communications by a firm and says that employees have no right to privacy when using the companies' computers.
Computer Fraud and Abuse Act—1986	Prohibits unauthorized access to computers used for financial institutions, the U.S. government, or interstate and international trade.

(Continued)

FIGURE B7.3

(Continued)

Established Information-Related Laws	
The Bork Bill (officially known as the Video Privacy Protection Act)—1988	Prohibits the use of video rental information on customers for any purpose other than that of marketing goods and services directly to the customer.
Communications Assistance for Law Enforcement Act—1994	Requires that telecommunications equipment be designed so that authorized government agents are able to intercept all wired and wireless communications being sent or received by any subscriber. The act also requires that subscriber call-identifying information be transmitted to a government when and if required.
Freedom of Information Act— 1967, 1975, 1994, and 1998	Allows any person to examine government records unless it would cause an invasion of privacy. It was amended in 1974 to apply to the FBI, and again in 1994 to allow citizens to monitor government activities and information gathering, and once again in 1998 to allow access to government information on the Internet.
Health Insurance Portability and Accountability Act (HIPAA)—1996	Requires that the health care industry formulate and implement regulations to keep patient information confidential.
Identity Theft and Assumption Deterrence Act—1998	Strengthened the criminal laws governing identity theft making it a federal crime to use or transfer identification belonging to another. It also established a central federal service for victims.
USA Patriot Act—2001 and 2003	Allows law enforcement to get access to almost any information, including library records, video rentals, bookstore purchases, and business records when investigating any act of terrorist or clandestine intelligence activities. In 2003, Patriot II broadened the original law.
Homeland Security Act—2002	Provided new authority to government agencies to mine data on individuals and groups including e-mails and Web site visits; put limits on the information available under the Freedom of Information Act; and gave new powers to government agencies to declare national health emergencies.
Sarbanes-Oxley Act—2002	Sought to protect investors by improving the accuracy and reliability of corporate disclosures and requires companies to (1) implement extensive and detailed policies to prevent illegal activity within the company, and (2) to respond in a timely manner to investigate illegal activity.
Fair and Accurate Credit Transactions Act—2003	Included provisions for the prevention of identity theft including consumers' right to get a credit report free each year, requiring merchants to leave all but the last five digits of a credit card number off a receipt, and requiring lenders and credit agencies to take action even before a victim knows a crime has occurred when they notice any circumstances that might indicate identity theft.
CAN-Spam Act—2003	Sought to regulate interstate commerce by imposing limitations and penalties on businesses sending unsolicited e-mail to consumers. The law forbids deceptive subject lines, headers, return addresses, etc., as well as the harvesting of e-mail addresses from Web sites. It requires businesses that send spam to maintain a do-not-spam list and to include a postal mailing address in the message.

Developing Information Management Policies

Treating sensitive corporate information as a valuable resource is good management. Building a corporate culture based on ethical principles that employees can understand and implement is responsible management. In an effort to provide guidelines for ethical information management, *CIO* magazine (along with over 100 CIOs) developed six principles for ethical information management displayed in Figure B7.4.

To follow *CIO*'s six principles for ethical information management, a corporation should develop written policies establishing employee guidelines, personnel procedures, and organizational rules. These policies set employee expectations about the organization's practices and standards and protect the organization from misuse of computer systems and IT resources. If an organization's employees use computers at work, the organization should, at a minimum, implement ePolicies. Such *ePolicies* are policies and procedures that address the ethical use of computers and Internet usage in the business environment. They typically embody the following:

- Ethical computer use policy.
- Information privacy policy.
- Acceptable use policy.
- E-mail privacy policy.
- Internet use policy.
- Anti-spam policy.[4]

ETHICAL COMPUTER USE POLICY

One of the essential steps in creating an ethical corporate culture is establishing an ethical computer use policy. An *ethical computer use policy* contains general principles to guide computer user behavior. For example, the ethical computer use policy might explicitly state that users should refrain from playing computer games during working hours. This policy ensures that the users know how to behave at work and that the organization has a published standard by which to deal with user infractions—for example, after appropriate warnings, terminating an employee who spends significant amounts of time playing computer games at work.

There are variations in how organizations expect their employees to use computers, but in any approach the overriding principle when seeking appropriate computer use should be informed consent. The users should be *informed* of the rules and, by agreeing to use the system on that basis, *consent* to abide by the rules.[5]

An organization should make a conscientious effort to ensure that all users are aware of the policy through formal training and other means. If an organization were to have only one policy, it would want it to be an ethical computer use policy since it is the starting point and the umbrella for any other policies that the organization might establish.

FIGURE B7.4

CIO Magazine's Six Principles for Ethical Information Management

Six Principles for Ethical Information Management
1. Information is a valuable corporate asset like cash, facilities, or any other corporate asset and should be managed as such.
2. The CIO is steward of corporate information and is responsible for managing it over its life cycle—from its generation to its appropriate destruction.
3. The CIO is responsible for controlling access to and use of information, as determined by governmental regulation and corporate policy.
4. The CIO is responsible for preventing the inappropriate destruction of information.
5. The CIO is responsible for bringing technological knowledge to the development of information management practices and policies.
6. The CIO should partner with executive peers to develop and execute the organization's information management policies.

INFORMATION PRIVACY POLICY

Scott Thompson is the executive vice president of Inovant, the company Visa set up to handle its technology. Thompson errs on the side of caution in regard to Visa's information: He bans the use of Visa's customer information for anything outside its intended purpose—billing.

Visa's customer information details such things as what people are spending their money on, in which stores, on which days, and even at what time of day. Sales and marketing departments around the country no doubt are salivating at any prospect of gaining access to Thompson's databases. "They would love to refine the information into loyalty programs, target markets, or even partnerships with Visa. There are lots of creative people coming up with these ideas," Thompson says. "This whole area of information sharing is enormous and growing. For the marketers, the sky's the limit." Thompson, along with privacy specialists, developed a strict credit card information policy, which the company follows. The question now is can Thompson guarantee that some unethical use of his information will not occur? Many experts do not believe that he can.[6]

In fact, in a large majority of cases, the unethical use of information happens not through the malicious scheming of a rogue marketer, but rather unintentionally. For example, information is collected and stored for some purpose, such as record keeping or billing. Then, a sales or marketing professional figures out another way to use it internally, share it with partners, or sell it to a trusted third party. The information is "unintentionally" used for new purposes. The classic example of this type of unintentional information reuse is the Social Security number, which started simply as a way to identify government retirement benefits and is now used as a sort of universal personal ID, found on everything from drivers' licenses to savings accounts.

An organization that wants to protect its information should develop an information privacy policy. An *information privacy policy* contains general principles regarding information privacy. Figure B7.5 highlights a few guidelines an organization can follow when creating an information privacy policy.[7]

FIGURE B7.5

Organizational Guidelines for Creating an Information Privacy Policy

Creating an Information Privacy Policy
1. **Adoption and implementation of a privacy policy.** An organization engaged in online activities or e-business has a responsibility to adopt and implement a policy for protecting the privacy of personal information. Organizations should also take steps that foster the adoption and implementation of effective online privacy policies by the organizations with which they interact, for instance, by sharing best practices with business partners.
2. **Notice and disclosure.** An organization's privacy policy must be easy to find, read, and understand. The policy must clearly state: ■ What information is being collected. ■ The use of information being collected. ■ Possible third-party distribution of that information. ■ The choices available to an individual regarding collection, use, and distribution of the collected information. ■ A statement of the organization's commitment to information security. ■ What steps the organization takes to ensure information quality and access.
3. **Choice and consent.** Individuals must be given the opportunity to exercise choice regarding how personal information collected from them online may be used when such use is unrelated to the purpose for which the information was collected. At a minimum, individuals should be given the opportunity to opt out of such use.
4. **Information security.** Organizations creating, maintaining, using, or disseminating personal information should take appropriate measures to assure its reliability and should take reasonable precautions to protect it from loss, misuse, or alteration.
5. **Information quality and access.** Organizations should establish appropriate processes or mechanisms so that inaccuracies in material personal information, such as account or contact information, may be corrected. Other procedures to assure information quality may include use of reliable sources, collection methods, appropriate consumer access, and protection against accidental or unauthorized alteration.

Acceptable Use Policy Stipulations
1. Not using the service as part of violating any law.
2. Not attempting to break the security of any computer network or user.
3. Not posting commercial messages to groups without prior permission.
4. Not performing any nonrepudiation.
5. Not attempting to send junk e-mail or spam to anyone who does not want to receive it.
6. Not attempting to mail bomb a site. A **mail bomb** is sending a massive amount of e-mail to a specific person or system resulting in filling up the recipient's disk space, which, in some cases, may be too much for the server to handle and may cause the server to stop functioning.

ACCEPTABLE USE POLICY

An *acceptable use policy (AUP)* is a policy that a user must agree to follow in order to be provided access to a network or to the Internet. *Nonrepudiation* is a contractual stipulation to ensure that e-business participants do not deny (repudiate) their online actions. A nonrepudiation clause is typically contained in an AUP.

It is common practice for many businesses and educational facilities to require that employees or students sign an acceptable use policy before being granted a network ID. When signing up with an Internet service provider (ISP), each customer is typically presented with an AUP, which states that they agree to adhere to certain stipulations (see Figure B7.6).[8]

E-MAIL PRIVACY POLICY

E-mail is so pervasive in organizations that it requires its own specific policy. In a recent survey, 80 percent of professional workers identified e-mail as their preferred means of corporate communications. Trends also show a dramatic increase in the adoption rate of instant messaging (IM) in the workplace. While e-mail and IM are terrific business communication tools, there are risks associated with using them.

For instance, a sent e-mail is stored on at least three or four different computers (see Figure B7.7). Simply deleting an e-mail from one computer does not delete it off the other computers. Companies can mitigate many of the risks of using electronic messaging systems by implementing and adhering to an e-mail privacy policy.[9]

One of the major problems with e-mail is the user's expectations of privacy. To a large extent, this exception is based on the false assumption that there exists e-mail privacy protection somehow analogous to that of U.S. first-class mail. This is simply not true. Generally, the organization that owns the e-mail system can operate the system as openly or as privately as it wishes. That means that if the organization wants to read everyone's e-mail, it can do so. If it chooses not to read any, that is allowable too. Hence, it is up to the organization to decide how much, if any, e-mail it is going to read. Then, when it decides, it must inform the users, so that they can consent to this level of intrusion. In other words, an *e-mail privacy policy* details the extent to which e-mail messages may be read by others.[10]

Organizations are urged to have some kind of e-mail privacy policy and to publish it no matter what the degree of intrusion. Figure B7.8 displays a few of the key stipulations generally contained in an e-mail privacy policy.

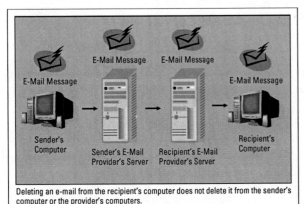

E-Mail Message
E-Mail Message   E-Mail Message
E-Mail Message

Sender's
Computer   Sender's E-Mail   Recipient's E-Mail   Recipient's
Provider's Server   Provider's Server   Computer

Deleting an e-mail from the recipient's computer does not delete it from the sender's computer or the provider's computers.

E-mail Privacy Policy Stipulations
1. The policy should be complementary to the ethical computer use policy.
2. It defines who legitimate e-mail users are.
3. It explains the backup procedure so users will know that at some point, even if a message is deleted from their computer, it will still be on the backup tapes.
4. It describes the legitimate grounds for reading someone's e-mail and the process required before such action can be taken.
5. It informs that the organization has no control of e-mail once it is transmitted outside the organization.
6. It explains what will happen if the user severs his or her connection with the organization.
7. It asks employees to be careful when making organizational files and documents available to others.

FIGURE B7.8

E-mail Privacy Policy
Stipulations

INTERNET USE POLICY

Similar to e-mail, the Internet has some unique aspects that make it a good candidate for its own policy. These include the large amounts of computing resources that Internet users can expend, thus making it essential that such use be legitimate. In addition, the Internet contains numerous materials that some might feel are offensive and, hence, some regulation might be required in this area. An *Internet use policy* contains general principles to guide the proper use of the Internet. Figure B7.9 displays a few important stipulations that might be included in an Internet use policy.

ANTI-SPAM POLICY

Chief technology officer (CTO) of the law firm Fenwick and West, Matt Kesner reduced incoming spam by 99 percent and found himself a corporate hero. Before the spam reduction, the law firm's partners (whose time is worth $350 to $600 an hour) found themselves spending hours each day sifting through 300 to 500 spam messages. The spam blocking engineered by Kesner traps between 5,000 and 7,000 messages a day.[11]

Spam is unsolicited e-mail. An *anti-spam policy* simply states that e-mail users will not send unsolicited e-mails (or spam). Spam plagues all levels of employees within an organization from receptionists to CEOs. Estimates indicate that spam accounts for 40 percent to 60 percent of most organizations' e-mail traffic. Ferris Research says spam costs U.S. businesses over $15 billion per year and Nucleus Research stated that companies forfeit $874 per employee annually in lost productivity from spam alone. Spam clogs e-mail systems and siphons IT resources away from legitimate business projects.[12]

Internet Use Policy Stipulations
1. The policy should describe available Internet services because not all Internet sites allow users to access all services.
2. The policy should define the organization's position on the purpose of Internet access and what restrictions, if any, are placed on that access.
3. The policy should complement the ethical computer use policy.
4. The policy should describe user responsibility for citing sources, properly handling offensive material, and protecting the organization's good name.
5. The policy should clearly state the ramifications if the policy is violated.

FIGURE B7.9

Internet Use Policy
Stipulations

FIGURE B7.10

Spam Prevention Tips

Spam Prevention Tips
■ **Disguise e-mail addresses posted in a public electronic place.** When posting an e-mail address in a public place, disguise the address through simple means such as replacing "jsmith@domain.com" with "jsmith at domain dot com." This prevents spam from recognizing the e-mail address.
■ **Opt-out of member directories that may place an e-mail address online.** Choose not to participate in any activities that place e-mail addresses online. If an e-mail address is placed online be sure it is disguised in some way.
■ **Use a filter.** Many ISPs and free e-mail services now provide spam filtering. While filters are not perfect, they can cut down tremendously on the amount of spam a user receives.

It is difficult to write anti-spam policies, laws, or software because there is no such thing as a universal litmus test for spam. One person's spam is another person's newsletter. End users have to be involved in deciding what spam is because what is unwanted can vary widely not just from one company to the next, but from one person to the next. What looks like spam to the rest of the world could be essential business communications for certain employees.

John Zarb, CIO of Libbey, a manufacturer of glassware, china, and flatware, tested Guenivere (a virus and subject-line filter) and SpamAssassin (an open source spam filter). He had to shut them off after 10 days because they were rejecting important legitimate e-mails. As Zarb quickly discovered, once an organization starts filtering e-mail, it runs the risk of blocking legitimate e-mails because they look like spam. Avoiding an unacceptable level of "false positives" requires a delicate balancing act. The IT team tweaked the spam filters and today the filters block about 70 percent of Libbey's spam. Zarb says the "false positive" rate is far lower but not zero. Figure B7.10 presents a few methods an organization can follow to prevent spam.[13]

Ethics in the Workplace

Concern is growing among employees that infractions of corporate policies—even accidental ones—will be a cause for disciplinary action. The Whitehouse.gov Internet site displays the U.S. president's official Web site and updates on bill signings and new policies. Whitehouse.com, however, leads to a trashy site that capitalizes on its famous name. A simple mistype from .gov to .com could potentially cost someone her or his job if the company has a termination policy for viewing illicit Web sites. Monitoring employees is one of the largest issues facing CIOs when they are developing information management policies.

The question of whether to monitor what employees do on company time with corporate resources has been largely decided by legal precedents that are already holding businesses financially responsible for their employees' actions. Increasingly, employee monitoring is not a choice; it is a risk-management obligation.

A recent survey of workplace monitoring and surveillance practices by the American Management Association (AMA) and the ePolicy Institute showed the degree to which companies are turning to monitoring:

■ 82 percent of the study's 1,627 respondents acknowledged conducting some form of electronic monitoring or physical surveillance.

■ 63 percent of the companies stated that they monitor Internet connections.

■ 47 percent acknowledged storing and reviewing employee e-mail messages.[14]

MONITORING TECHNOLOGIES

Many employees use their company's high-speed Internet access to shop, browse, and surf the Web. Fifty-nine percent of all Web purchases in the United States are made from the workplace, according to ComScore Networks. Vault.com determined that 47 percent of employees spend at least half an hour a day surfing the Web.[15]

<table>
<tr><td colspan="2" align="center">Employee Monitoring Effects</td></tr>
<tr><td>1.</td><td>Employee absenteeism is on the rise, almost doubling in 2004 to 21 percent. The lesson here might be that more employees are missing work to take care of personal business. Perhaps losing a few minutes here or there—or even a couple of hours—is cheaper than losing entire days.</td></tr>
<tr><td>2.</td><td>Studies indicate that electronic monitoring results in lower job satisfaction, in part because people begin to believe the quantity of their work is more important than the quality.</td></tr>
<tr><td>3.</td><td>Electronic monitoring also induces what psychologists call "psychological reactance": the tendency to rebel against constraints. If you tell your employees they cannot shop, they cannot use corporate networks for personal business, and they cannot make personal phone calls, then their desire to do all these things will likely increase.</td></tr>
</table>

FIGURE B7.11

Employee Monitoring Effects

This research indicates that managers should monitor what their employees are doing with their Web access. Most managers do not want their employees conducting personal business during working hours. For these reasons many organizations have increasingly taken the Big Brother approach to Web monitoring with software that tracks Internet usage and even allows the boss to read employees' e-mail. Figure B7.11 highlights a few reasons the effects of employee monitoring are worse than the lost productivity from employee Web surfing.

This is the thinking at SAS Institute, a private software company consistently ranked in the top 10 on many "Best Places to Work" surveys. SAS does not monitor its employees' Web usage. The company asks its employees to use company resources responsibly, but does not mind if they occasionally check sports scores or use the Web for shopping.

Many management gurus advocate that organizations whose corporate cultures are based on trust are more successful than those whose corporate cultures are based on distrust. Before an organization implements monitoring technology it should ask itself, "What does this say about how the organization feels about its employees?" If the organization really does not trust its employees, then perhaps it should find new ones. If an organization does trust its employees, then it might want to treat them accordingly. An organization that follows its employees' every keystroke is unwittingly undermining the relationships with its employees.[16]

Information technology monitoring is tracking people's activities by such measures as number of keystrokes, error rate, and number of transactions processed. Figure B7.12 displays different types of monitoring technologies currently available.

Employee Monitoring Policies

The best path for an organization planning to engage in employee monitoring is open communication surrounding the issue. A recent survey discovered that communication about monitoring issues is weak for most organizations. One in five companies did not even have an acceptable use policy and one in four companies did not have an Internet use policy.

Companies that did have policies usually tucked them into the rarely probed recesses of the employee handbook, and then the policies tended to be of the vague and legal jargon variety: "XYZ company reserves the right to monitor or review any information stored or transmitted on its equipment." Reserving the right to monitor is materially different from clearly stating that the company does monitor, listing what is tracked, describing what is looked for, and detailing the consequences for violations.

An organization must formulate the right monitoring policies and put them into practice. *Employee monitoring policies* explicitly state how, when, and where the company monitors its employees. CSOs that are explicit about what the company does in the way of monitoring and the reasons for it, along with actively educating

FIGURE B7.12

Monitoring Technologies

Common Monitoring Technologies	
Key logger, or key trapper, software	A program that, when installed on a computer, records every keystroke and mouse click.
Hardware key logger	A hardware device that captures keystrokes on their journey from the keyboard to the motherboard.
Cookie	A small file deposited on a hard drive by a Web site containing information about customers and their Web activities. Cookies allow Web sites to record the comings and goings of customers, usually without their knowledge or consent.
Adware	Software that generates ads that install themselves on a computer when a person downloads some other program from the Internet.
Spyware (sneakware or stealthware)	Software that comes hidden in free downloadable software and tracks online movements, mines the information stored on a computer, or uses a computer's CPU and storage for some task the user knows nothing about.
Web log	Consists of one line of information for every visitor to a Web site and is usually stored on a Web server.
Clickstream	Records information about a customer during a Web surfing session such as what Web sites were visited, how long the visit was, what ads were viewed, and what was purchased.

their employees about what unacceptable behavior looks like, will find that employees not only acclimate quite quickly to a policy, but also reduce the CSO's burden by policing themselves. Figure B7.13 displays several common stipulations an organization can follow when creating an employee monitoring policy.[17]

FIGURE B7.13

Employee Monitoring Policy Stipulations

Employee Monitoring Policy Stipulations
1. Be as specific as possible.
2. Always enforce the policy.
3. Enforce the policy in the same way for everyone.
4. Expressly communicate that the company reserves the right to monitor all employees.
5. Specifically state when monitoring will be performed.
6. Specifically state what will be monitored (e-mail, IM, Internet, network activity, etc.).
7. Describe the types of information that will be collected.
8. State the consequences for violating the policy.
9. State all provisions that allow for updates to the policy.
10. Specify the scope and manner of monitoring for any information system.
11. When appropriate, obtain a written receipt acknowledging that each party has received, read, and understood the monitoring policies.

★ PLUG-IN SUMMARY

Advances in technology have made ethics a concern for many organizations. Consider how easy it is for an employee to e-mail large amounts of confidential information, change electronic communications, or destroy massive amounts of important company information all within seconds. Electronic information about customers, partners, and employees has become one of corporate America's most valuable assets. However, the line between the proper and improper use of this asset is at best blurry. Should an employer be able to search employee files without employee consent? Should a company be able to sell customer information without informing the customer of its intent? What is a responsible approach to document deletion?

The law provides guidelines in many of these areas, but how a company chooses to act within the confines of the law is up to the judgment of its officers. Since CIOs are responsible for the technology that collects, maintains, and destroys corporate information, they sit smack in the middle of this potential ethical quagmire.

One way an organization can begin dealing with ethical issues is to create a corporate culture that encourages ethical considerations and discourages dubious information dealings. Not only is an ethical culture an excellent idea overall, but it also acts as a precaution, helping prevent customer problems from escalating into front-page news stories. The establishment of and adherence to well-defined rules and policies will help organizations create an ethical corporate culture. These policies include:

- Ethical computer use policy.
- Information privacy policy.
- Acceptable use policy.
- E-mail privacy policy.
- Internet use policy.
- Anti-spam policy.
- Employee monitoring policy.

★ KEY TERMS

Acceptable use policy
  (AUP), 390
Adware, 394
Anti-spam policy, 391
Clickstream, 394
Confidentiality, 384
Cookie, 394
Copyright, 384
Counterfeit software, 384
E-mail privacy policy, 390
Employee monitoring
  policy, 393
ePolicies, 384, 388

Ethical computer use
  policy, 388
Ethics, 384
Fair use doctrine, 384
Hardware key logger, 394
Information privacy policy, 389
Information technology
  monitoring, 393
Intellectual property, 384
Internet use policy, 391
Key logger or key trapper
  software, 394
Mail bomb, 390

Nonrepudiation, 390
Opt-in, 386
Pirated software, 384
Privacy, 384
Spam, 391
Spyware (sneakware or
  stealthware), 394
Web log, 394

★ CLOSING CASE ONE

Sarbanes-Oxley: Where Information Technology, Finance, and Ethics Meet

The Sarbanes-Oxley Act (SOX) of 2002 was enacted in response to the high-profile Enron and WorldCom financial scandals to protect shareholders and the general public from accounting errors and fraudulent practices by organizations. One primary component of the Sarbanes-Oxley Act is the definition of which records are to be stored and for how long. For this reason, the legislation not only affects financial departments, but also IT departments whose job it is to store electronic records. The Sarbanes-Oxley Act states that all business records, including electronic records and electronic messages, must be saved for "not less than five years." The consequences for noncompliance are fines, imprisonment, or both. The following are the three rules of Sarbanes-Oxley that affect the management of electronic records.

1. The first rule deals with destruction, alteration, or falsification of records and states that persons who knowingly alter, destroy, mutilate, conceal, or falsify documents shall be fined or imprisoned for not more than 20 years or both.

2. The second rule defines the retention period for records storage. Best practices indicate that corporations securely store all business records using the same guidelines set for public accountants, which state that organizations shall maintain all audit or review work-papers for a period of five years from the end of the fiscal period in which the audit or review was concluded.

3. The third rule specifies all business records and communications that need to be stored, including electronic communications. IT departments are facing the challenge of creating and maintaining a corporate records archive in a cost-effective fashion that satisfies the requirements put forth by the legislation.

Essentially, any public organization that uses IT as part of its financial business processes will find that it must put in place IT controls in order to be compliant with the Sarbanes-Oxley Act. The following are a few practices you can follow to begin to ensure organizational compliance with the Sarbanes-Oxley Act.

■ Overhaul or upgrade your financial systems in order to meet regulatory requirements for more accurate, detailed, and speedy filings.

■ Examine the control processes within your IT department and apply best practices to comply with the act's goals. For example, segregation of duties within the systems development staff is a widely recognized best practice that helps prevent errors and outright fraud. The people who code program changes should be different from the people who test them, and a separate team should be responsible for changes in production environments.

■ Homegrown financial systems are fraught with potential information-integrity issues. Although leading ERP systems offer audit-trail functionality, customizations of these systems often bypass those controls. You must work with internal and external auditors to ensure that customizations are not overriding controls.

■ Work with your CIO, CEO, CFO, and corporate attorneys to create a document-retention-and-destruction policy that addresses what types of electronic documents should be saved, and for how long.

Ultimately, Sarbanes-Oxley compliance will require a great deal of work among all of your departments. Compliance starts with running IT as a business and strengthening IT internal controls.[18]

Questions

1. Define the relationship between ethics and the Sarbanes-Oxley Act.
2. Why is records management an area of concern for the entire organization?
3. What are two policies an organization can implement to achieve Sarbanes-Oxley compliance? Be sure to elaborate on how these policies can achieve compliance.
4. Identify the biggest roadblock for organizations that are attempting to achieve Sarbanes-Oxley compliance.
5. What types of information systems might facilitate SOX compliance?
6. How will electronic monitoring affect the morale and performance of employees in the workplace?
7. What do you think an unethical accountant or manager at Enron thought were the rewards and responsibilities associated with his or her job?

✳ CLOSING CASE TWO

Invading Your Privacy

Can your employer invade your privacy through monitoring technologies? Numerous lawsuits have been filed by employees who believed their employer was wrong to invade their privacy with monitoring technologies. Below are a few cases highlighting lawsuits over employee privacy and employer rights to monitor.

Smyth versus Pillsbury Company

An employee was terminated for sending inappropriate and unprofessional messages over the company's e-mail system. The company had repeatedly assured its employees that e-mail was confidential, that it would not be intercepted, and that it would not be used as a basis for discipline or discharge. Michael Smyth retrieved, from his home computer, e-mail sent from his supervisor over Pillsbury's e-mail system. Smyth allegedly responded with several comments concerning the sales management staff, including a threat to "kill the backstabbing bastards" and a reference to an upcoming holiday party as "the Jim Jones Kool-aid affair." Pillsbury intercepted the e-mail and terminated Smyth, who then sued the company for wrongful discharge and invasion of privacy.

The court dismissed the case in 1996, finding that Smyth did not have a reasonable expectation of privacy in the contents of his e-mail messages, despite Pillsbury's assurances, because the messages had been voluntarily communicated over the company's computer system to a second person. The court went on to find that, even if some reasonable expectation of privacy existed, that expectation was outweighed by Pillsbury's legitimate interest in preventing inappropriate or unprofessional communications over its e-mail system.

Bourke versus Nissan Motor Corporation

While training new employees on the e-mail system, a message sent by Bonita Bourke was randomly selected and reviewed by the company. The message turned out to be a personal e-mail of a sexual nature. Once Bourke's e-mail was discovered, the company decided to review the e-mails of the rest of Bourke's workgroup. As a result of this investigation, several other personal e-mails were discovered. Nissan gave the employees who had sent the personal messages written warnings for violating the company's e-mail policy.

The disciplined employees sued Nissan for invasion of privacy. The employees argued that although they signed a form acknowledging the company's policy that company-owned hardware and software was restricted for company business use only, their expectation of privacy was reasonable because the company gave the plaintiffs passwords to access the computer system and told them to guard their passwords. However, a California court in 1993 held that this was not an objectively reasonable expectation of privacy because the plaintiffs knew that e-mail messages "were read from time to time by individuals other than the intended recipient."

McLaren versus Microsoft Corporation

The Texas Court of Appeals in 1999 dismissed an employee's claim that his employer's review and dissemination of e-mail stored in the employee's workplace personal computer constituted an invasion of privacy. The employee argued that he had a reasonable expectation of privacy because the e-mail was kept in a personal computer folder protected by a password. The court found this argument unconvincing because the e-mail was transmitted over his employer's network.

However, according to a news account of one case, a court held that an employer's use of a supervisor's password to review an employee's e-mail may have violated a Massachusetts state statute against interference with privacy. In that case, Burk Technology allowed employees to use the company's e-mail system to send personal messages, but prohibited "excessive chatting." To use the e-mail system, each employee used a password. The employer never informed employees that their messages would or could be monitored by supervisors or the company president. The president of the company reviewed the e-mails of two employees who had referred to him by various nicknames and discussed his extramarital affair. The two employees were fired by the company president, who claimed the terminations were for their excessive e-mail use and not because of the messages' content. The court denied the company's attempt to dismiss the suit and allowed the matter to be set for trial on the merits. The court focused on the fact that the employees were never informed that their e-mail could be monitored.

This case illustrates the importance of informing employees that their use of company equipment to send e-mail and to surf the Internet is subject to monitoring to prevent subsequent confusion, and a possible future defense, on the part of employees.[19]

Questions

1. Pick one of the above cases and create an argument on behalf of the employee.
2. Pick one of the above cases and create an argument against the employee.
3. Pick one of the above cases and create an argument on behalf of the employer's use of monitoring technologies.
4. Pick one of the above cases and create an argument against the employer's use of monitoring technologies.

★ MAKING BUSINESS DECISIONS

1. Information Privacy

A study by the Annenberg Public Policy Center at the University of Pennsylvania shows that 95 percent of people who use the Internet at home think they should have a legal right to know everything about the information that Web sites collect from them. Research also shows that 57 percent of home Internet users incorrectly believe that when a Web site has an information privacy policy it will not share personal information with other Web sites or companies. In fact, the research found that after showing the users how companies track, extract, and share Web site information to make money, 85 percent found the methods unacceptable, even for a highly valued site. Write a short paper arguing for or against an organization's right to use and distribute personal information gathered from its Web site.

2. Acting Ethically

Describe how you would react to the following scenarios:

- A senior marketing manager informs you that one of her employees is looking for another job and she wants you to give her access to look through her e-mail.

- A vice president of sales informs you that he has made a deal to provide customer information to a strategic partner and he wants you to burn all of the customer information onto a CD.

- You start monitoring one of your employees' e-mail and discover that he is having an affair with one of the other employees in the office.

- You install a video surveillance system in your office and discover that employees are taking office supplies home with them.

3. Spying on E-Mail

Technology advances now allow individuals to monitor computers that they do not even have physical access to. New types of software can capture an individual's incoming and outgoing e-mail and then immediately forward that e-mail to another person. For example, if you are at work and your child is home from school and she receives an e-mail from John at 3:00 p.m., at 3:01 p.m. you will receive a copy of that e-mail sent to your e-mail address. A few minutes later, if she replies to John's e-mail, within seconds you will again receive a copy of what she sent to John. Describe two scenarios (other than the above) for the use of this type of software: (1) where the use would be ethical, (2) where the use would be unethical.

4. Stealing Software

The issue of pirated software is one that the software industry fights on a daily basis. The major centers of software piracy are in places like Russia and China where salaries and disposable income are comparatively low. People in developing and economically depressed countries will fall behind the industrialized world technologically if they cannot afford access to new generations of software. Considering this, is it reasonable to blame someone for using pirated software when it could potentially cost him or her two months' salary to purchase a legal copy? Create an argument for or against the following statement: "Individuals who are economically less fortunate should be allowed access to software free of charge in order to ensure that they are provided with an equal technological advantage."

GLOSSARY

A

acceptable use policy (AUP) A policy that a user must agree to follow in order to be provided access to a network or to the Internet.

accounting Analyzes the transactional information of the business so the owners and investors can make sound economic decisions.

accounting and finance ERP component Manages accounting data and financial processes within the enterprise with functions such as general ledger, accounts payable, accounts receivable, budgeting, and asset management.

accounting department Provides quantitative information about the finances of the business including recording, measuring, and describing financial information.

adware Software that generates ads that install themselves on a computer when a person downloads some other program from the Internet.

agile methodology A form of XP, aims for customer satisfaction through early and continuous delivery of useful software components.

analysis phase Analyzing end-user business requirements and refining project goals into defined functions and operations of the intended system.

analytical CRM Supports back-office operations and strategic analysis and includes all systems that do not deal directly with the customers.

analytical information Encompasses all organizational information, and its primary purpose is to support the performing of managerial analysis tasks.

anti-spam policy States that e-mail users will not send unsolicited e-mails (or spam).

application architecture Determines how applications integrate and relate to each other.

application generation component Includes tools for creating visually appealing and easy-to-use applications.

application programming interface (API) A set of routines, protocols, and tools for building software applications. A good API makes it easier to develop a program by providing all the building blocks.

application service provider (ASP) A company that offers an organization access over the Internet to systems and related services that would otherwise have to be located in personal or organizational computers.

application software Used for specific information processing needs, including payroll, customer relationship management, project management, training, and many others.

arithmetic/logic unit (ALU) Performs all arithmetic operations (for example, addition and subtraction) and all logic operations (such as sorting and comparing numbers).

artificial intelligence (AI) Simulates human intelligence such as the ability to reason and learn.

As-Is process model Represent the current state of the operation that has been mapped, without any specific improvements or changes to existing processes.

asset Anything owned that has value or earning power.

associates program (affiliate program) Businesses can generate commissions or royalties from an Internet site.

association detection Reveals the degree to which variables are related and the nature and frequency of these relationships in the information.

attribute Characteristics or properties of an entity class.

authentication A method for confirming users' identities.

authorization The process of giving someone permission to do or have something.

automatic call distribution A phone switch routes inbound calls to available agents.

autonomic computing A self-managing computing model named after, and patterned on, the human body's autonomic nervous system.

availability Addresses when systems can be accessed by employees, customers, and partners.

B

backdoor program Viruses that open a way into the network for future attacks.

backup An exact copy of a system's information.

backward integration Takes information entered into a given system and sends it automatically to all upstream systems and processes.

balance sheet Gives an accounting picture of property owned by a company and of claims against the property on a specific date.

balanced scorecard A management system (not only a measurement system) that enables organizations to clarify their vision and strategy and translate them into action.

banner ad Small ad on one Web site that advertises the products and services of another business, usually another dot-com business.

benchmark Baseline values the system seeks to attain.

benchmarking The process of continuously measuring system results, comparing those results to optimal system performance (benchmark values), and identifying steps and procedures to improve system performance.

binary digit (bit) The smallest unit of information that a computer can process.

biometric The identification of a user based on a physical characteristic, such as a fingerprint, iris, face, voice, or handwriting.

Baltzan–Phillips–Haag:
Business Driven
Technology, Third Edition

Back Matter

Glossary

© The McGraw–Hill
Companies, 2009

299

black-hat hacker   Breaks into other people's computer systems and may just look around or steal and destroy information.

blog   Web site in which items are posted on a regular basis and displayed in reverse chronological order.

Bluetooth   An omnidirectional wireless technology that provides limited-range voice and data transmission over the unlicensed 2.4-GHz frequency band, allowing connections with a wide variety of fixed and portable devices that normally would have to be cabled together.

bookkeeping   The actual recording of the business's transactions, without any analysis of the information.

break-even point   The point at which revenues equal costs.

brick-and-mortar business   A business that operates in a physical store without an Internet presence.

bullwhip effect   Occurs when distorted product demand information passes from one entity to the next throughout the supply chain.

business-critical integrity constraint   Enforces business rules vital to an organization's success and often requires more insight and knowledge than relational integrity constraints.

business facing process   Invisible to the external customer but essential to the effective management of the business and includes goal setting, day-to-day planning, performance feedback, rewards, and resource allocation.

business intelligence   Refers to applications and technologies that are used to gather, provide access to, and analyze data and information to support decision-making efforts.

business process   A standardized set of activities that accomplish a specific task, such as processing a customer's order.

business process management (BPM)   Integrates all of an organization's business processes to make individual processes more efficient.

business process management tool   Used to create an application that is helpful in designing business process models and also helpful in simulating, optimizing, monitoring, and maintaining various processes that occur within an organization.

business process model   A graphic description of a process, showing the sequence of process tasks, which is developed for a specific purpose and from a selected viewpoint.

business process modeling (or **mapping**)   The activity of creating a detailed flow chart or process map of a work process showing its inputs, tasks, and activities, in a structured sequence.

business process outsourcing   The contracting of a specific business task, such as payroll, to a third-party service provider.

business process reengineering (BPR)   The analysis and redesign of workflow within and between enterprises.

business requirement   The detailed set of business requests that the system must meet in order to be successful.

business-to-business (B2B)   Applies to businesses buying from and selling to each other over the Internet.

business-to-business (B2B) marketplace   An Internet-based service that brings together many buyers and sellers.

business-to-consumer (B2C)   Applies to any business that sells its products or services to consumers over the Internet.

business wiki   Collaborative Web pages that allow users to edit documents, share ideas, or monitor the status of a project.

buyer power   High when buyers have many choices of whom to buy from and low when their choices are few.

byte   Group of eight bits represents one natural language character.

C

cache memory   A small unit of ultra-fast memory that is used to store recently accessed or frequently accessed data so that the CPU does not have to retrieve this data from slower memory circuits such as RAM.

call scripting system   Accesses organizational databases that track similar issues or questions and automatically generate the details for the CSR who can then relay them to the customer.

campaign management system   Guides users through marketing campaigns performing such tasks as campaign definition, planning, scheduling, segmentation, and success analysis.

capacity planning   Determines the future IT infrastructure requirements for new equipment and additional network capacity.

capital   Represents money whose purpose is to make more money, for example, the money used to buy a rental property or a business.

central processing unit (CPU) (or **microprocessor**)   The actual hardware that interprets and executes the program (software) instructions and coordinates how all the other hardware devices work together.

change control board (CCB)   Responsible for approving or rejecting all change requests.

change management   A set of techniques that aid in evolution, composition, and policy management of the design and implementation of a system.

change management system   Includes a collection of procedures to document a change request and define the steps necessary to consider the change based on the expected impact of the change.

chief information officer (CIO)   Responsible for (1) overseeing all uses of information technology and (2) ensuring the strategic alignment of IT with business goals and objectives.

chief knowledge officer (CKO)   Responsible for collecting, maintaining, and distributing the organization's knowledge.

chief privacy officer (CPO)   Responsible for ensuring the ethical and legal use of information within an organization.

chief security officer (CSO)   Responsible for ensuring the security of IT systems and developing strategies and IT safeguards against attacks from hackers and viruses.

chief technology officer (CTO)   Responsible for ensuring the throughput, speed, accuracy, availability, and reliability of an organization's information technology.

click-and-mortar business   A business that operates in a physical store and on the Internet.

clickstream   Records information about a customer during a Web surfing session such as what Web sites were visited, how long the visit was, what ads were viewed, and what was purchased.

clickstream data   Exact pattern of a consumer's navigation through a site.

click-through   A count of the number of people who visit one site and click on an advertisement that takes them to the site of the advertiser.

click-to-talk Buttons allow customers to click on a button and talk with a CSR via the Internet.

client Computer that is designed to request information from a server.

client/server network A model for applications in which the bulk of the back-end processing, such as performing a physical search of a database, takes place on a server, while the front-end processing, which involves communicating with the users, is handled by the clients.

cluster analysis A technique used to divide an information set into mutually exclusive groups such that the members of each group are as close together as possible to one another and the different groups are as far apart as possible.

coaxial cable Cable that can carry a wide range of frequencies with low signal loss.

cold site A separate facility that does not have any computer equipment, but is a place where employees can move after a disaster.

collaboration system An IT-based set of tools that supports the work of teams by facilitating the sharing and flow of information.

collaborative demand planning Helps organizations reduce their investment in inventory, while improving customer satisfaction through product availability.

collaborative engineering Allows an organization to reduce the cost and time required during the design process of a product.

commercial off-the-shelf (COTS) A software package or solution that is purchased to support one or more business functions and information systems.

communication device Equipment used to send information and receive it from one location to another.

competitive advantage A product or service that an organization's customers place a greater value on than similar offerings from a competitor.

complex instruction set computer (CISC) chip Type of CPU that can recognize as many as 100 or more instructions, enough to carry out most computations directly.

computer Electronic device operating under the control of instructions stored in its own memory that can accept, manipulate, and store data.

computer-aided software engineering (CASE) Software suites that automate systems analysis, design, and development.

computer simulation Complex systems, such as the U.S. economy, can be modeled by means of mathematical equations and different scenarios can be run against the model to determine "what if" analysis.

confidentiality The assurance that messages and information are available only to those who are authorized to view them.

consolidation Involves the aggregation of information and features simple roll-ups to complex groupings of interrelated information.

consumer-to-business (C2B) Applies to any consumer that sells a product or service to a business over the Internet.

consumer-to-consumer (C2C) Applies to sites primarily offering goods and services to assist consumers interacting with each other over the Internet.

contact center (call center) Customer service representatives (CSRs) answer customer inquiries and respond to problems through a number of different customer touch points.

contact management CRM system Maintains customer contact information and identifies prospective customers for future sales.

content filtering Occurs when organizations use software that filters content to prevent the transmission of unauthorized information.

content management system Provides tools to manage the creation, storage, editing, and publication of information in a collaborative environment.

content provider Companies that use the Internet to distribute copyrighted content, including news, music, games, books, movies, and many other types of information.

continuous process improvement model Attempts to understand and measure the current process, and make performance improvements accordingly.

control unit Interprets software instructions and literally tells the other hardware devices what to do, based on the software instructions.

cookie A small file deposited on a hard drive by a Web site containing information about customers and their Web activities.

copyright The legal protection afforded an expression of an idea, such as a song, video game, and some types of proprietary documents.

core competency An organization's key strength or business function that it does better than any of its competitors.

core competency strategy When an organization chooses to focus specifically on what it does best (its core competency) and forms partnerships and alliances with other specialist organizations to handle nonstrategic business processes.

core ERP component Traditional components included in most ERP systems and they primarily focus on internal operations.

corporation (also called **organization, enterprise,** or **business**) An artificially created legal entity that exists separate and apart from those individuals who created it and carry on its operations.

counterfeit software Software that is manufactured to look like the real thing and sold as such.

cracker A hacker with criminal intent.

critical path A path from the start to the finish that passes through all the tasks that are critical to completing the project in the shortest amount of time.

critical success factor (CSF) A factor that is critical to an organization's success.

CRM analysis technologies Help organizations segment their customers into categories such as best and worst customers.

CRM predicting technologies Help organizations make predictions regarding customer behavior such as which customers are at risk of leaving.

CRM reporting technologies Help organizations identify their customers across other applications.

cross-selling Selling additional products or services to a customer.

cube The common term for the representation of multidimensional information.

customer facing process Results in a product or service that is received by an organization's external customer.

customer metric Assesses the management of customer relationships by the organization.

customer relationship management (CRM) Involves managing all aspects of a customer's relationship with an organization to increase customer loyalty and retention and an organization's profitability.

cyberterrorist Seeks to cause harm to people or to destroy critical systems or information and use the Internet as a weapon of mass destruction.

cycle inventory The average amount of inventory held to satisfy customer demands between inventory deliveries.

D

data Raw facts that describe the characteristics of an event.

data administration component Provides tools for managing the overall database environment by providing facilities for backup, recovery, security, and performance.

database Maintains information about various types of objects (inventory), events (transactions), people (employees), and places (warehouses).

database-based workflow system Stores documents in a central location and automatically asks the team members to access the document when it is their turn to edit the document.

database management system (DBMS) Software through which users and application programs interact with a database.

data definition component Helps create and maintain the data dictionary and the structure of the database.

data dictionary A file that stores definitions of information types, identifies the primary and foreign keys, and maintains the relationships among the tables.

data-driven Web site An interactive Web site kept constantly updated and relevant to the needs of its customers through the use of a database.

data flow diagram (DFD) Illustrates the movement of information between external entities and the processes and data stores within the system.

data manipulation component Allows users to create, read, update, and delete information in a database.

data mart Contains a subset of data warehouse information.

data mining The process of analyzing data to extract information not offered by the raw data alone.

data-mining tool Uses a variety of techniques to find patterns and relationships in large volumes of information and infer rules from them that predict future behavior and guide decision making.

data model A formal way to express data relationships to a database management system (DBMS).

data warehouse A logical collection of information—gathered from many different operational databases—that supports business analysis activities and decision-making tasks.

decision support system (DSS) Models information to support managers and business professionals during the decision-making process.

demand planning software Generates demand forecasts using statistical tools and forecasting techniques.

denial-of-service attack (DoS) Floods a Web site with so many requests for service that it slows down or crashes the site.

dependency A logical relationship that exists between the project tasks, or between a project task and a milestone.

design phase Involves describing the desired features and operations of the system including screen layouts, business rules, process diagrams, pseudo code, and other documentation.

development phase Involves taking all of the detailed design documents from the design phase and transforming them into the actual system.

digital asset management system (DAM) Though similar to document management, DAM generally works with binary rather than text files, such as multimedia file types.

digital Darwinism Organizations that cannot adapt to the new demands placed on them for surviving in the information age are doomed to extinction.

digital dashboard Integrates information from multiple components and tailors the information to individual preferences.

digital divide When those with access to technology have great advantages over those without access to technology.

digital ink (or **electronic ink**) Technology that digitally represents handwriting in its natural form.

digital paper (or **electronic paper**) Any paper that is optimized for any type of digital printing.

digital wallet Both software and information—the software provides security for the transaction and the information includes payment and delivery information (for example, the credit card number and expiration date).

disaster recovery cost curve Charts (1) the cost to the organization of the unavailability of information and technology and (2) the cost to the organization of recovering from a disaster over time.

disaster recovery plan A detailed process for recovering information or an IT system in the event of a catastrophic disaster such as a fire or flood.

disruptive technology A new way of doing things that initially does not meet the needs of existing customers.

distributed denial-of-service attack (DDoS) Attacks from multiple computers that flood a Web site with so many requests for service that it slows down or crashes.

distribution management software Coordinates the process of transporting materials from a manufacturer to distribution centers to the final customer.

dividend A distribution of earnings to shareholders.

document management system (DMS) Supports the electronic capturing, storage, distribution, archival, and accessing of documents.

drill-down Enables users to get details, and details of details, of information.

E

e-business The conducting of business on the Internet, not only buying and selling, but also serving customers and collaborating with business partners.

e-business model   An approach to conducting electronic business on the Internet.

e-commerce   The buying and selling of goods and services over the Internet.

effectiveness IT metric   Measures the impact IT has on business processes and activities including customer satisfaction, conversion rates, and sell-through increases.

efficiency IT metric   Measures the performance of the IT system itself including throughput, speed, and availability.

e-government   Involves the use of strategies and technologies to transform government(s) by improving the delivery of services and enhancing the quality of interaction between the citizen-consumer within all branches of government.

electronic bill presentment and payment (EBPP)   System that sends bills over the Internet and provides an easy-to-use mechanism (such as clicking on a button) to pay the bill.

electronic catalog   Presents customers with information about goods and services offered for sale, bid, or auction on the Internet.

electronic check   Mechanism for sending a payment from a checking or savings account.

electronic data interchange (EDI)   A standard format for exchanging business data.

electronic marketplace (e-marketplace)   Interactive business communities providing a central market space where multiple buyers and suppliers can engage in e-business activities.

electronic tagging   A technique for identifying and tracking assets and individuals via technologies such as radio frequency identification and smart cards.

elevation of privilege   Process by which a user misleads a system into granting unauthorized rights, usually for the purpose of compromising or destroying the system.

e-logistics   Manages the transportation and storage of goods.

e-mail privacy policy   Details the extent to which e-mail messages may be read by others.

e-mall   Consists of a number of e-shops; it serves as a gateway through which a visitor can access other e-shops.

employee monitoring policy   States how, when, and where the company monitors its employees.

employee relationship management (ERM)   Provides employees with a subset of CRM applications available through a Web browser.

encryption   Scrambles information into an alternative form that requires a key or password to decrypt the information.

enterprise application integration (EAI) middleware   Represents a new approach to middleware by packaging together commonly used functionality, such as providing prebuilt links to popular enterprise applications, which reduces the time necessary to develop solutions that integrate applications from multiple vendors.

enterprise architect (EA)   Person grounded in technology, fluent in business, a patient diplomat, and provides the important bridge between IT and the business.

enterprise architecture   Includes the plans for how an organization will build, deploy, use, and share its data, processes, and IT assets.

enterprise resource planning (ERP)   Integrates all departments and functions throughout an organization into a single IT system (or integrated set of IT systems) so that employees can make decisions by viewing enterprisewide information on all business operations.

entity   In the relational database model, a person, place, thing, transaction, or event about which information is stored.

entity class   In the relational database model, a collection of similar entities.

entity-relationship diagram (ERD)   A technique for documenting the relationships between entities in a database environment.

entry barrier   A product or service feature that customers have come to expect from organizations in a particular industry and must be offered by an entering organization to compete and survive.

environmental scanning   The acquisition and analysis of events and trends in the environment external to an organization.

ePolicies   Policies and procedures that address the ethical use of computers and Internet usage in the business environment.

e-procurement   The B2B purchase and sale of supplies and services over the Internet.

e-shop (e-store or e-tailer)   A version of a retail store where customers can shop at any hour of the day without leaving their home or office.

ethernet   A physical and data layer technology for LAN networking.

ethical computer use policy   Contains general principles to guide computer user behavior.

ethics   Principles and standards that guide our behavior toward other people.

executive information system (EIS)   A specialized DSS that supports senior level executives within the organization.

expense   Refers to the costs incurred in operating and maintaining a business.

expert system   Computerized advisory programs that imitate the reasoning processes of experts in solving difficult problems.

explicit knowledge   Consists of anything that can be documented, archived, and codified, often with the help of IT.

extended ERP component   The extra components that meet the organizational needs not covered by the core components and primarily focus on external operations.

extraction, transformation, and loading (ETL)   A process that extracts information from internal and external databases, transforms the information using a common set of enterprise definitions, and loads the information into a data warehouse.

extranet   An intranet that is available to strategic allies (such as customers, suppliers, and partners).

extreme programming (XP) methodology   Breaks a project into tiny phases, and developers cannot continue on to the next phase until the first phase is complete.

F

failover   Backup operational mode in which the function of a computer component (such as a processor, server, network, or database) is assumed by secondary system components when the primary component becomes unavailable through either failure or scheduled down time.

fair use doctrine   In certain situations, it is legal to use copyrighted material.

fault tolerance   A computer system designed so that in the event a component fails, a backup component or procedure can immediately take its place with no loss of service.

feasibility study   Determines if the proposed solution is feasible and achievable from a financial, technical, and organizational standpoint.

feature creep   Occurs when developers add extra features that were not part of the initial requirements.

fiber optic (optical fiber)   The technology associated with the transmission of information as light impulses along a glass wire or fiber.

finance   Deals with the strategic financial issues associated with increasing the value of the business while observing applicable laws and social responsibilities.

financial accounting   Involves preparing financial reports that provide information about the business's performance to external parties such as investors, creditors, and tax authorities.

financial cybermediary   Internet-based company that facilitates payments over the Internet.

financial EDI (financial electronic data interchange)   Standard electronic process for B2B market purchase payments.

financial quarter   A three-month period (four quarters per year).

financial statement   Written records of the financial status of the business that allow interested parties to evaluate the profitability and solvency of the business.

firewall   Hardware and/or software that guards a private network by analyzing the information leaving and entering the network.

first-mover advantage   An organization can significantly impact its market share by being first to market with a competitive advantage.

Five Forces model   Helps determine the relative attractiveness of an industry.

flash memory   A special type of rewriteable read-only memory (ROM) that is compact and portable.

for profit corporations   Primarily focus on making money and all profits and losses are shared by the business owners.

forecast   Predictions made on the basis of time-series information.

foreign key   A primary key of one table that appears as an attribute in another table and acts to provide a logical relationship between the two tables.

forward integration   Takes information entered into a given system and sends it automatically to all downstream systems and processes.

fuzzy logic   A mathematical method of handling imprecise or subjective information.

G

Gantt chart   A simple bar chart that depicts project tasks against a calendar.

genetic algorithm   An artificial intelligence system that mimics the evolutionary, survival-of-the-fittest process to generate increasingly better solutions to a problem.

geographic information system (GIS)   Designed to work with information that can be shown on a map.

gigabyte (GB)   Roughly 1 billion bytes.

gigahertz (GHz)   The number of billions of CPU cycles per second.

global inventory management system   Provides the ability to locate, track, and predict the movement of every component or material anywhere upstream or downstream in the supply chain.

global positioning system (GPS)   A device that determines current latitude, longitude, speed, and direction of movement.

goal-seeking analysis   Finds the inputs necessary to achieve a goal such as a desired level of output.

graphical user interface (GUI)   The interface to an information system.

groupware   Software that supports team interaction and dynamics including calendaring, scheduling, and videoconferencing.

GUI screen design   The ability to model the information system screens for an entire system using icons, buttons, menus, and submenus.

H

hacker   People very knowledgeable about computers who use their knowledge to invade other people's computers.

hactivist   Person with philosophical and political reasons for breaking into systems who will often deface Web site as a protest.

hard drive   Secondary storage medium that uses several rigid disks coated with a magnetically sensitive material and housed together with the recording heads in a hermetically sealed mechanism.

hardware   Consists of the physical devices associated with a computer system.

hardware key logger   A hardware device that captures keystrokes on their journey from the keyboard to the motherboard.

help desk   A group of people who respond to internal system user questions.

hierarchical database model   Information is organized into a tree-like structure that allows repeating information using parent/child relationships, in such a way that it cannot have too many relationships.

high availability   Refers to a system or component that is continuously operational for a desirably long length of time.

historical analysis   Historical events are studied to anticipate the outcome of current developments.

hoaxes   Attack computer systems by transmitting a virus hoax, with a real virus attached.

hot site   A separate and fully equipped facility where the company can move immediately after a disaster and resume business.

human resource ERP component   Tracks employee information including payroll, benefits, compensation, and performance assessment, and assures compliance with the legal requirements of multiple jurisdictions and tax authorities.

human resources management (HRM)   Includes the policies, plans, and procedures for the effective management of employees (human resources).

hypertext transfer protocol (HTTP) The Internet standard that supports the exchange of information on the WWW.

I

identity theft The forging of someone's identity for the purpose of fraud.

implementation phase Involves placing the system into production so users can begin to perform actual business operations with the system.

income statement (also referred to as **earnings report, operating statement,** and **profit-and-loss (P&L) statement**) Reports operating results (revenues minus expenses) for a given time period ending at a specified date.

information Data converted into a meaningful and useful context.

information accuracy Extent to which a system generates the correct results when executing the same transaction numerous times.

information architecture Identifies where and how important information, like customer records, is maintained and secured.

information cleansing or scrubbing A process that weeds out and fixes or discards inconsistent, incorrect, or incomplete information.

information granularity Refers to the extent of detail within the information (fine and detailed or "coarse" and abstract information).

information integrity A measure of the quality of information.

information partnership Occurs when two or more organizations cooperate by integrating their IT systems, thereby providing customers with the best of what each can offer.

information privacy policy Contains general principles regarding information privacy.

information reach Refers to the number of people a business can communicate with, on a global basis.

information richness Refers to the depth and breadth of information transferred between customers and businesses.

information security A broad term encompassing the protection of information from accidental or intentional misuse by persons inside or outside an organization.

information security plan Details how an organization will implement the information security policies.

information security policy Identifies the rules required to maintain information security.

information technology (IT) The study, design, development, implementation, support or management of computer-based information systems, particularly software applications and computer hardware.

information technology monitoring Tracking people's activities by such measures as number of keystrokes, error rate, and number of transactions processed.

infrastructure architecture Includes the hardware, software, and telecommunications equipment that, when combined, provide the underlying foundation to support the organization's goals.

input device Equipment used to capture information and commands.

insider Legitimate users who purposely or accidentally misuse their access to the environment and cause some kind of business-affecting incident.

insourcing (in-house development) A common approach using the professional expertise within an organization to develop and maintain the organization's information technology systems.

instant messaging (IM or IMing) A type of communications service that enables someone to create a kind of private chat room with another individual in order to communicate in real-time over the Internet.

integration Allows separate systems to communicate directly with each other.

integrity constraint The rules that help ensure the quality of information.

intellectual property Intangible creative work that is embodied in physical form.

intelligent agent A special-purpose knowledge-based information system that accomplishes specific tasks on behalf of its users.

intelligent system Various commercial applications of artificial intelligence.

interactive voice response (IVR) Directs customers to use touch-tone phones or keywords to navigate or provide information.

interactivity Measures the visitor interactions with the target ad.

intermediary Agents, software, or businesses that bring buyers and sellers together that provide a trading infrastructure to enhance e-business.

Internet A global public network of computer networks that pass information from one to another using common computer protocols.

Internet service provider (ISP) A company that provides individuals and other companies access to the Internet along with additional related services, such as Web site building.

Internet use policy Contains general principles to guide the proper use of the Internet.

interoperability Capability of two or more computer systems to share data and resources, even though they are made by different manufacturers.

intranet An internalized portion of the Internet, protected from outside access, that allows an organization to provide access to information and application software to only its employees.

intrusion detection software (IDS) Searches out patterns in information and network traffic to indicate attacks and quickly responds to prevent any harm.

inventory management and control software Provides control and visibility to the status of individual items maintained in inventory.

IT infrastructure Includes the hardware, software, and telecommunications equipment that, when combined, provide the underlying foundation to support the organization's goals.

J

joint application development (JAD) A session where employees meet, sometimes for several days, to define or review the business requirements for the system.

Baltzan–Phillips–Haag:
Business Driven
Technology, Third Edition

Back Matter

Glossary

© The McGraw–Hill
Companies, 2009

305

K

key logger, or **key trapper, software**   A program that, when installed on a computer, records every keystroke and mouse click.

key performance indicator (KPI)   Measures that are tied to business drivers.

kiosk   Publicly accessible computer system that has been set up to allow interactive information browsing.

knowledge management (KM)   Involves capturing, classifying, evaluating, retrieving, and sharing information assets in a way that provides context for effective decisions and actions.

knowledge management system (KMS)   Supports the capturing, organization, and dissemination of knowledge (i.e., know-how) throughout an organization.

L

liability   An obligation to make financial payments.

limited liability   Means that the shareholders are not personally liable for the losses incurred by the corporation.

limited liability corporation (LLC)   A hybrid entity that has the legal protections of a corporation and the ability to be taxed (one time) as a partnership.

limited partnership   Much like a general partnership except for one important fundamental difference; the law protects the limited partner from being responsible for all of the partnership's losses.

list generator   Compiles customer information from a variety of sources and segments the information for different marketing campaigns.

local area network (LAN)   Computer network that uses cables or radio signals to link two or more computers within a geographically limited area, generally one building or a group of buildings.

logical view   Focuses on how users logically access information to meet their particular business needs.

logistics   The set of processes that plans for and controls the efficient and effective transportation and storage of supplies from suppliers to customers.

loss   Occurs when businesses sell products or services for less than they cost to produce.

loyalty program   Rewards customers based on the amount of business they do with a particular organization.

M

magnetic medium   Secondary storage medium that uses magnetic techniques to store and retrieve data on disks or tapes coated with magnetically sensitive materials.

magnetic tape   Older secondary storage medium that uses a strip of thin plastic coated with a magnetically sensitive recording medium.

mail bomb   Sends a massive amount of e-mail to a specific person or system resulting in filling up the recipient's disk space, which, in some cases, may be too much for the server to handle and may cause the server to stop functioning.

maintenance   The fixing or enhancing of an information system.

maintenance phase   Involves performing changes, corrections, additions, and upgrades to ensure the system continues to meet the business goals.

maintenance, repair, and operations (MRO) materials (also called **indirect materials**)   Materials necessary for running an organization but that do not relate to the company's primary business activities.

malicious code   Includes a variety of threats such as viruses, worms, and Trojan horses.

management information systems (MIS)   A general name for the business function and academic discipline covering the application of people, technologies, and procedures—collectively called information systems—to solve business problems.

managerial accounting   Involves analyzing business operations for internal decision making and does not have to follow any rules issued by standard-setting bodies such as GAAP.

market basket analysis   Analyzes such items as Web sites and checkout scanner information to detect customers' buying behavior and predict future behavior by identifying affinities among customers' choices of products and services.

marketing   The process associated with promoting the sale of goods or services.

marketing communication   Seeks to build product or service awareness and to educate potential consumers on the product or service.

marketing mix   Includes the variables that marketing managers can control in order to best satisfy customers in the target market.

market maker   Intermediaries that aggregate three services for market participants: (1) a place to trade, (2) rules to govern trading, and (3) an infrastructure to support trading.

market segmentation   The division of a market into similar groups of customers.

market share   Calculated by dividing the firm's sales by the total market sales for the entire industry.

mashup editor   WYSIWYGs (What You See Is What You Get) for mashups that provide a visual interface to build a mashup, often allowing the user to drag and drop data points into a Web application.

mass customization   Ability of an organization to give its customers the opportunity to tailor its products or services to the customers' specifications.

megabyte (MB or **M** or **Meg)**   Roughly 1 million bytes.

megahertz (MHz)   The number of millions of CPU cycles per second.

memory card   Contains high-capacity storage that holds data such as captured images, music, or text files.

memory stick   Provides nonvolatile memory for a range of portable devices including computers, digital cameras, MP3 players, and PDAs.

messaging-based workflow system   Sends work assignments through an e-mail system.

metropolitan area network (MAN)   A computer network that provides connectivity in a geographic area or region larger than that covered by a local area network, but smaller than the area covered by a wide area network.

microwave transmitter   Commonly used to transmit network signals over great distances.

middleware   Different types of software that sit in the middle of and provide connectivity between two or more software applications.

mobile commerce, or **m-commerce** The ability to purchase goods and services through a wireless Internet-enabled device.

model A simplified representation or abstraction of reality.

modeling The activity of drawing a graphical representation of a design.

multisourcing A combination of professional services, mission-critical support, remote management, and hosting services that are offered to customers in any combination needed.

multitasking Allows more than one piece of software to be used at a time.

N

nearshore outsourcing Contracting an outsourcing agreement with a company in a nearby country.

net income The amount of money remaining after paying taxes.

network A communications, data exchange, and resource-sharing system created by linking two or more computers and establishing standards, or protocols, so that they can work together.

network database model A flexible way of representing objects and their relationships.

network operating system (NOS) The operating system that runs a network, steering information between computers and managing security and users.

network topology Refers to the geometric arrangement of the actual physical organization of the computers (and other network devices) in a network.

network transmission media Various types of media used to carry the signal between computers.

neural network (an **artificial neural network**) A category of AI that attempts to emulate the way the human brain works.

nonrepudiation A contractual stipulation to ensure that e-business participants do not deny (repudiate) their online actions.

not for profit (or **nonprofit**) **corporation** Usually exists to accomplish some charitable, humanitarian, or educational purpose, and the profits and losses are not shared by the business owners.

O

offshore outsourcing Using organizations from developing countries to write code and develop systems.

online ad Box running across a Web page that is often used to contain advertisements.

online analytical processing (OLAP) The manipulation of information to create business intelligence in support of strategic decision making.

online broker Intermediaries between buyers and sellers of goods and services.

online service provider (OSP) Offers an extensive array of unique services such as its own version of a Web browser.

online training Runs over the Internet or off a CD-ROM.

online transaction processing (OLTP) The capturing of transaction and event information using technology to (1) process the information according to defined business rules, (2) store the information, and (3) update existing information to reflect the new information.

onshore outsourcing The process of engaging another company within the same country for services.

open system A broad term that describes nonproprietary IT hardware and software made available by the standards and procedures by which their products work, making it easier to integrate them.

operating system software Controls the application software and manages how the hardware devices work together.

operational CRM Supports traditional transactional processing for day-to-day front-office operations or systems that deal directly with the customers.

operations management (also called **production manage-ment**) Includes the methods, tasks, and techniques organizations use to produce goods and services.

opportunity management CRM system Targets sales opportunities by finding new customers or companies for future sales.

opt-in Indicates that a company will contact only the people who have agreed to receive promotions and marketing material via e-mail.

output device Equipment used to see, hear, or otherwise accept the results of information processing requests.

outsourcing An arrangement by which one organization provides a service or services for another organization that chooses not to perform them in-house.

owner's equity The portion of a company belonging to the owners.

P

packet-switching Occurs when the sending computer divides a message into a number of efficiently sized units called packets, each of which contains the address of the destination computer.

packet tampering Altering the contents of packets as they travel over the Internet or altering data on computer disks after penetrating a network.

partner relationship management (PRM) Focuses on keeping vendors satisfied by managing alliance partner and reseller relationships that provide customers with the optimal sales channel.

partnership Similar to sole proprietorships, except that this legal structure allows for more than one owner.

partnership agreement A legal agreement between two or more business partners that outlines core business issues.

peer-to-peer (P2P) network Any network without a central file server and in which all computers in the network have access to the public files located on all other workstations.

performance Measures how quickly a system performs a certain process or transaction.

personalization Occurs when a Web site can know enough about a person's likes and dislikes that it can fashion offers that are more likely to appeal to that person.

PERT (Program Evaluation and Review Technique) chart A graphical network model that depicts a project's tasks and the relationships between those tasks.

phishing Technique to gain personal information for the purpose of identity theft, usually by means of fraudulent e-mail.

physical view The physical storage of information on a storage device such as a hard disk.

pirated software The unauthorized use, duplication, distribution, or sale of copyrighted software.

planning phase Involves establishing a high-level plan of the intended project and determining project goals.

podcasting Distribution of audio or video files, such as radio programs or music videos, over the Internet to play on mobile devices and personal computers.

polymorphic virus and worm Change their form as they propagate.

pop-under ad Form of a pop-up ad that users do not see until they close the current Web browser screen.

pop-up ad Small Web page containing an advertisement that appears on the Web page outside the current Web site loaded in the Web browser.

portal A Web site that offers a broad array of resources and services, such as e-mail, online discussion groups, search engines, and online shopping malls.

predictive dialing Automatically dials outbound calls and when someone answers, the call is forwarded to an available agent.

primary key A field (or group of fields) that uniquely identifies a given entity in a table.

primary storage Computer's main memory, which consists of the random access memory (RAM), cache memory, and read-only memory (ROM) that is directly accessible to the CPU.

privacy The right to be left alone when you want to be, to have control over your own personal possessions, and not to be observed without your consent.

private exchange A B2B marketplace in which a single buyer posts its need and then opens the bidding to any supplier who would care to bid.

process modeling Involves graphically representing the processes that capture, manipulate, store, and distribute information between a system and its environment.

product life cycle Includes the four phases a product progresses through during its life cycle including introduction, growth, maturity, and decline.

production and materials management ERP component Handles the various aspects of production planning and execution such as demand forecasting, production scheduling, job cost accounting, and quality control.

profit Occurs when businesses sell products or services for more than they cost to produce.

project A temporary endeavor undertaken to create a unique product or service.

project deliverable Any measurable, tangible, verifiable outcome, result, or item that is produced to complete a project or part of a project.

project exclusion Products, services, or processes that are not specifically a part of the project.

project management The application of knowledge, skills, tools, and techniques to project activities in order to meet or exceed stakeholder needs and expectations from a project.

project management software Supports the long-term and day-to-day management and execution of the steps in a project.

project manager An individual who is an expert in project planning and management, defines and develops the project plan, and tracks the plan to ensure all key project milestones are completed on time.

project milestone Represents key dates when a certain group of activities must be performed.

project objective Quantifiable criteria that must be met for the project to be considered a success.

project plan A formal, approved document that manages and controls project execution.

project product A description of the characteristics the product or service has undertaken.

project risk An uncertain event or condition that, if it occurs, has a positive or negative effect on a project objective(s).

project scope Defines the work that must be completed to deliver a product with the specified features and functions.

protocol A standard that specifies the format of data as well as the rules to be followed during transmission.

prototype A smaller-scale representation or working model of the user's requirements or a proposed design for an information system.

public key encryption (PKE) Encryption system that uses two keys: a public key that everyone can have and a private key for only the recipient.

pull technology Organizations receive or request information.

pure-play (virtual) business A business that operates on the Internet only without a physical store.

push technology Organizations send information.

Q

query-by-example (QBE) tool Allows users to graphically design the answers to specific questions.

R

radio frequency identification (RFID) Technologies using active or passive tags in the form of chips or smart labels that can store unique identifiers and relay this information to electronic readers.

RadioPaper A dynamic high-resolution electronic display that combines a paper-like reading experience with the ability to access information anytime, anywhere.

random access memory (RAM) The computer's primary working memory, in which program instructions and data are stored so that they can be accessed directly by the CPU via the processor's high-speed external data bus.

rapid application development (RAD) (also called rapid prototyping) methodology Emphasizes extensive user involvement in the rapid and evolutionary construction of working prototypes of a system to accelerate the systems development process.

read-only memory (ROM) The portion of a computer's primary storage that does not lose its contents when one switches off the power.

real simple syndication (RSS) Family of Web feed formats used for Web syndication of programs and content.

real-time information Immediate, up-to-date information.

real-time system Provides real-time information in response to query requests.

recovery The ability to get a system up and running in the event of a system crash or failure and includes restoring the information backup.

reduced instruction set computer (RISC) chip Limits the number of instructions the CPU can execute to increase processing speed.

redundancy The duplication of information or storing the same information in multiple places.

reintermediation Using the Internet to reassemble buyers, sellers, and other partners in a traditional supply chain in new ways.

relational database model A type of database that stores information in the form of logically related two-dimensional tables.

relational integrity constraint The rules that enforce basic and fundamental information-based constraints.

reliability Ensures all systems are functioning correctly and providing accurate information.

report generator Allows users to define formats for reports along with what information they want to see in the report.

requirements definition document Contains the final set of business requirements, prioritized in order of business importance.

response time The time it takes to respond to user interactions such as a mouse click.

revenue Refers to the amount earned resulting from the delivery or manufacture of a product or from the rendering of a service.

reverse auction An auction format in which increasingly lower bids are solicited from organizations willing to supply the desired product or service at an increasingly lower price.

RFID tag Contains a microchip and an antenna, and typically works by transmitting a serial number via radio waves to an electronic reader, which confirms the identity of a person or object bearing the tag.

risk management The process of proactive and ongoing identification, analysis, and response to risk factors.

rivalry among existing competitors High when competition is fierce in a market and low when competition is more complacent.

router An intelligent connecting device that examines each packet of data it receives and then decides which way to send it onward toward its destination.

S

safety inventory Includes extra inventory held in the event demand exceeds supply.

sales The function of selling a good or service that focuses on increasing customer sales, which increases company revenues.

sales force automation (SFA) A system that automatically tracks all of the steps in the sales process.

sales management CRM system Automates each phase of the sales process, helping individual sales representatives coordinate and organize all of their accounts.

scalability Refers to how well a system can adapt to increased demands.

scope creep Occurs when the scope of the project increases.

script kiddies or **script bunnies** Find hacking code on the Internet and click-and-point their way into systems to cause damage or spread viruses.

search engine optimization (SEO) Set of methods aimed at improving the ranking of a Web site in search engine listings.

secondary storage Consists of equipment designed to store large volumes of data for long-term storage.

secure electronic transaction (SET) Transmission security method that ensures transactions are secure and legitimate.

secure socket layer (SSL) (1) Creates a secure and private connection between a client and server computer, (2) encrypts the information, and (3) sends the information over the Internet.

selling chain management Applies technology to the activities in the order life cycle from inquiry to sale.

semantic Web An evolving extension of the World Wide Web in which Web content can be expressed not only in natural language, but also in a format that can be read and used by software agents, thus permitting them to find, share, and integrate information more easily.

sensitivity analysis The study of the impact that changes in one (or more) parts of the model have on other parts of the model.

server Computer that is dedicated to providing information in response to external requests.

service level agreement (SLA) Defines the specific responsibilities of the service provider and sets the customer expectations.

service-oriented architecture (SOA) A collection of services that communicate with each other, for example, passing data from one service to another or coordinating an activity between one or more services.

shareholder Another term for business owners.

shopping bot Software that will search several retailer Web sites and provide a comparison of each retailer's offerings including price and availability.

sign-off The system users' actual signatures indicating they approve all of the business requirements.

slice-and-dice The ability to look at information from different perspectives.

smart card A device that is around the same size as a credit card, containing embedded technologies that can store information and small amounts of software to perform some limited processing.

sniffer A program or device that can monitor data traveling over a network.

social engineering Using one's social skills to trick people into revealing access credentials or other information valuable to the attacker.

social networking analysis (SNA) A process of mapping a group's contacts (whether personal or professional) to identify who knows whom and who works with whom.

software The set of instructions that the hardware executes to carry out specific tasks.

sole proprietorship A business form in which a single person is the sole owner and is personally responsible for all the profits and losses of the business.

solvency   Represents the ability of the business to pay its bills and service its debt.

source document   Describes the basic transaction data such as its date, purpose, and amount and includes cash receipts, canceled checks, invoices, customer refunds, employee time sheet, etc.

spam   Unsolicited e-mail.

spamdexing   Uses a variety of deceptive techniques in an attempt to manipulate search engine rankings, whereas legitimate search engine optimization focuses on building better sites and using honest methods of promotion.

spoofing   The forging of the return address on an e-mail so that the e-mail message appears to come from someone other than the actual sender.

spyware   Software that comes hidden in free downloadable software and tracks online movements, mines the information stored on a computer, or uses a computer's CPU and storage for some task the user knows nothing about.

statement of cash flow   Summarizes sources and uses of cash, indicates whether enough cash is available to carry on routine operations, and offers an analysis of all business transactions, reporting where the firm obtained its cash and how it chose to allocate the cash.

statement of owner's equity (also called the **statement of retained earnings** or **equity statement**)   Tracks and communicates changes in the shareholder's earnings.

structured collaboration (or **process collaboration**)   Involves shared participation in business processes, such as workflow, in which knowledge is hard coded as rules.

structured query language (SQL)   A standardized fourth-generation query language found in most DBMSs.

supplier power   High when buyers have few choices of whom to buy from and low when their choices are many.

supplier relationship management (SRM)   Focuses on keeping suppliers satisfied by evaluating and categorizing suppliers for different projects, which optimizes supplier selection.

supply chain   Consists of all parties involved, directly or indirectly, in the procurement of a product or raw material.

supply chain event management (SCEM)   Enables an organization to react more quickly to resolve supply chain issues.

supply chain execution (SCE) software   Automates the different steps and stages of the supply chain.

supply chain management (SCM)   Involves the management of information flows between and among stages in a supply chain to maximize total supply chain effectiveness and profitability.

supply chain planning (SCP) software   Uses advanced mathematical algorithms to improve the flow and efficiency of the supply chain while reducing inventory.

supply chain visibility   The ability to view all areas up and down the supply chain.

sustaining technology   Produces an improved product customers are eager to buy, such as a faster car or larger hard drive.

switching cost   The costs that can make customers reluctant to switch to another product or service.

system availability   Number of hours a system is available for users.

systems development life cycle (SDLC)   The overall process for developing information systems from planning and analysis through implementation and maintenance.

system software   Controls how the various technology tools work together along with the application software.

T

tacit knowledge   The knowledge contained in people's heads.

telecommunication system   Enables the transmission of data over public or private networks.

teleliving   Using information devices and the Internet to conduct all aspects of life seamlessly.

telematic   Blending computers and wireless telecommunications technologies with the goal of efficiently conveying information over vast networks to improve business operations.

terabyte (TB)   Roughly 1 trillion bytes.

test condition   The detailed steps the system must perform along with the expected results of each step.

testing phase   Involves bringing all the project pieces together into a special testing environment to test for errors, bugs, and interoperability and verify that the system meets all of the business requirements defined in the analysis phase.

threat of new entrants   High when it is easy for new competitors to enter a market and low when there are significant entry barriers to entering a market.

threat of substitute products or services   High when there are many alternatives to a product or service and low when there are few alternatives from which to choose.

throughput   The amount of information that can travel through a system at any point in time.

time-series information   Time-stamped information collected at a particular frequency.

To-Be process model   Shows the results of applying change improvement opportunities to the current (As-Is) process model.

token   Small electronic devices that change user passwords automatically.

transaction   Exchange or transfer of goods, services, or funds involving two or more people.

transaction processing system (TPS)   The basic business system that serves the operational level (analysts) in an organization.

transaction speed   Amount of time a system takes to perform a transaction.

transactional information   Encompasses all of the information contained within a single business process or unit of work, and its primary purpose is to support the performing of daily operational tasks.

Transmission Control Protocol/Internet Protocol (TCP/IP)   Provides the technical foundation for the public Internet as well as for large numbers of private networks.

transportation planning software   Tracks and analyzes the movement of materials and products to ensure the delivery of materials and finished goods at the right time, the right place, and the lowest cost.

trend analysis   A trend is examined to identify its nature, causes, speed of development, and potential impacts.

trend monitoring Trends viewed as particularly important in a specific community, industry, or sector are carefully monitored, watched, and reported to key decision makers.

trend projection When numerical data are available, a trend can be plotted to display changes through time and into the future.

Trojan-horse virus Hides inside other software, usually as an attachment or a downloadable file.

twisted-pair wiring A type of cable composed of four (or more) copper wires twisted around each other within a plastic sheath.

U

unstructured collaboration (or information collaboration) Includes document exchange, shared whiteboards, discussion forums, and e-mail.

up-selling Increasing the value of a sale.

user documentation Highlights how to use the system.

utility software Provides additional functionality to the operating system.

V

value-added network (VAN) A private network, provided by a third party, for exchanging information through a high-capacity connection.

value chain Views an organization as a series of processes, each of which adds value to the product or service for each customer.

videoconference A set of interactive telecommunication technologies that allow two or more locations to interact via two-way video and audio transmissions simultaneously.

view Allows users to see the contents of a database, make any required changes, perform simple sorting, and query the database to find the location of specific information.

viral marketing Technique that induces Web sites or users to pass on a marketing message to other Web sites or users, creating exponential growth in the message's visibility and effect.

virtual assistant A small program stored on a PC or portable device that monitors e-mails, faxes, messages, and phone calls.

virtualization Protected memory space created by the CPU allowing the computer to create virtual machines.

virtual private network (VPN) A way to use the public telecommunication infrastructure (e.g., Internet) to provide secure access to an organization's network.

virus Software written with malicious intent to cause annoyance or damage.

voice over IP (VoIP) Uses TCP/IP technology to transmit voice calls over long-distance telephone lines.

volatility Refers to RAM's complete loss of stored information if power is interrupted.

W

waterfall methodology A sequential, activity-based process in which each phase in the SDLC is performed sequentially from planning through implementation and maintenance.

Web 2.0 A set of economic, social, and technology trends that collectively form the basis for the next generation of the Internet—a more mature, distinctive medium characterized by user participation, openness, and network effects.

Web-based self-service system Allows customers to use the Web to find answers to their questions or solutions to their problems.

Web conference Blends audio, video, and document-sharing technologies to create virtual meeting rooms where people "gather" at a password-protected Web site.

Web content management system (WCM) Adds an additional layer to document and digital asset management that enables publishing content both to intranets and to public Web sites.

Web log Consists of one line of information for every visitor to a Web site and is usually stored on a Web server.

Web mashup A Web site or Web application that uses content from more than one source to create a completely new service.

Web service Contains a repertoire of Web-based data and procedural resources that use shared protocols and standards permitting different applications to share data and services.

Web traffic Includes a host of benchmarks such as the number of page views, the number of unique visitors, and the average time spent viewing a Web page.

what-if analysis Checks the impact of a change in an assumption on the proposed solution.

white-hat hacker Works at the request of the system owners to find system vulnerabilities and plug the holes.

wide area network (WAN) Computer network that provides data communication services for business in geographically dispersed areas (such as across a country or around the world).

wiki Web-based tools that make it easy for users to add, remove, and change online content.

wireless fidelity (wi-fi) A means of linking computers using infrared or radio signals.

wireless Internet service provider (WISP) An ISP that allows subscribers to connect to a server at designated hotspots or access points using a wireless connection.

wireless media Natural parts of the Earth's environment that can be used as physical paths to carry electrical signals.

wire media Transmission material manufactured so that signals will be confined to a narrow path and will behave predictably.

workflow Defines all the steps or business rules, from beginning to end, required for a business process.

workflow management system Facilitates the automation and management of business processes and controls the movement of work through the business process.

workshop training Set in a classroom-type environment and led by an instructor.

World Wide Web (WWW) A global hypertext system that uses the Internet as its transport mechanism.

worm A type of virus that spreads itself, not only from file to file, but also from computer to computer.